Eyewitness
SPACE

Hubble Space Telescope

High-energy particle tracks

Magellan Venus orbiter

Jupiter and its moon Io

Martian Volcano

The surface of Mars

Bust of Jupiter

Chandra X-ray satellite

Eyewitness
SPACE

DK

19th-century,
showing Uranu,
its four known sate.

19th-century printed
constellation card

Micrometer for use with
a telescope

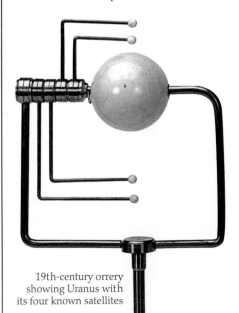

19th-century orrery
showing Uranus with
its four known satellites

DK

LONDON, NEW YORK,
MELBOURNE, MUNICH, and DELHI

Project Manager Nigel Duffield
Senior Editor Ros Walford
DTP Designer David McDonald
Production Controller Katherine Owers

The Eyewitness Guides were conceived by Dorling Kindersley Limited
and Editions Gallimard

Published in the United States by DK Publishing, Inc.,
375 Hudson Street, New York,
New York 10014.

Individual titles copyright ©:
Astronomy 1992, 2004, 2008;
Universe 2003, 2009;
Moon 2009;
Stars & Planets 2007.

Published in Great Britain by Dorling Kindersley Limited.

A catalog record for this book is available from
the Library of Congress.

ISBN 978-0-7566-5871-7

Color reproduction by Colourscan, Singapore
Printed and bound in China by L. Rex Printing Co. Ltd.

Discover more at
www.dk.com

Compass (19th century)

Drawing an ellipse

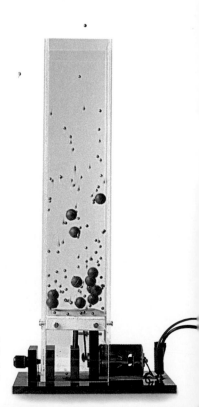

A demonstration to
show how different
elements behave in
the solar system

Contents

Apollo 11 mission patch

9
Astronomy
10
The study of the heavens
12
Ancient astronomy
14
Ordering the universe
16
The celestial sphere
18
The uses of astronomy
20
Astrology
22
The Copernican revolution
24
Intellectual giants
26
Optical principles
28
The optical telescope
30
Observatories
32
Astronomers
34
Spectroscopy
36
The radio telescope
38
Venturing into space
40
The solar system
42
The Sun
44
The Moon

46
Earth
48
Mercury
50
Venus
52
Mars
54
Jupiter
56
Saturn
58
Uranus
60
Neptune and beyond
62
Travelers in space
64
The birth and death of stars
66
Our galaxy and beyond
68
Did you know?
70
Cutting-edge astronomy
72
Find out more
74
Glossary

**77
Universe**
78
What is the universe?
80
How do we fit in?
82
How the universe works
84
In the beginning
86
Fate of the universe
88
Exploring the universe
90
Our corner of the universe
92
Our local star
94
Earth's Moon
96
Comparing the planets
98
Mercury and Venus
100
Home planet
102
Mars, the Red Planet
104
Jupiter, king of the planets

106
Saturn, the ringed wonder
108
New worlds
110
Asteroids, meteors, and meteorites
112
Icy wanderers
114
Distant suns
116
The variety of stars
118
Clusters and nebulae
120
Star birth
122
Star death
124
Pulsars and black holes
126
The Milky Way
128
Neighbors
130
Galaxies galore
132
Quasars and other active galaxies
134
A universe of life
136
Window on the universe
138
Discovery timeline
140
Find out more
142
Glossary

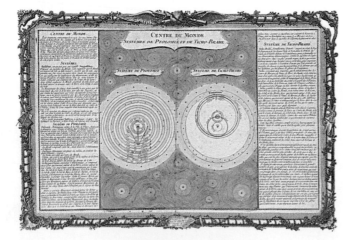

French astronomical print (19th century)

145
Moon
146
Moon, myth, imagination
148
Earth's partner
150
A waltz in space
152
The Moon's calendar
154
Eclipses
156
Tides
158
Birth of the Moon
160
The Moon takes shape
162
The Moon's surface
164
Craters
166
Moon rock
168
Other moons
170
The telescope era
172
From dream to reality
174
The space race
176
Destination Moon
178
Apollo spacecraft
180
Getting men on the Moon
182
Dressed for space
184
A giant leap

186
Exploring the Moon
188
Further Soviet exploration
190
Living in space
192
The new lunar invasion
194
Return to the Moon
196
This time to stay
198
A job on the Moon
200
Near side
202
Far side
204
Lunar timeline
206
Hall of fame
208
Find out more
210
Glossary
213
Stars & Planets Workbook
216
Stars and galaxies
217
The solar system
218
Planets

219
Planet Earth
220
The universe
221
Looking at space
222
Space travel
223
Living in space
224
The sky at night
225
Star distances
226
The life cycle of stars
227
The Milky Way
228
Stargazing
230
Our nearest star
231
Gravity in space
232
Orbiting the Sun
234
The inner planets
235
Our home planet
236
Moon-watching

237
Observing an eclipse
238
The red planet
239
Giant planets
240
Naming the planets
241
Asteroids, comets, and meteors
242
Expanding universe
243
Space shuttle
244
Astronauts
245
Living in space
246
Key dates of space exploration
248
Discovering the universe
249
Stars, galaxies,
and constellations
250
Planets and smaller space bodies
251
The Sun and solar system
252
Earth and the Moon
253
Astronauts and spacecraft
254
Activity answers
256
Quick quiz answers
257
Progress chart
258
Certificate
259
Index

Geological
map of the
Moon

ASTRONOMY

Eyewitness
Astronomy

Written by
KRISTEN LIPPINCOTT

The study of the heavens

THE WORD "ASTRONOMY" comes from a combination of two Greek words: *astron*, meaning "star" and *nemein*, meaning "to name." Even though the beginnings of astronomy go back thousands of years before the ancient Greeks began studying the stars, the science of astronomy h[as] always been based on the same principle of "naming the stars." Many of the names come directly from the Greeks, since they were the first astronomers to make a systematic catalog of all the stars they could see. A number of early civilizations remembered the relative positions of the stars by putting together groups that seemed to make patterns i[n] the night sky. One of these looked like a curling river, so it was called Eridanus, the Great River; another looked like a hunter with a bright belt and dagger and was called Orion, the Hunter (p.65). Stars are now named according to their placement inside the pattern and graded according to brightness. For example, the brightest star in the constellation Scorpius is called α Scorpii, because α is the first letter in the Greek alphabet. It is also called Antares, which means "the rival of Mars," because it shines bright red in the night sky and strongly resembles the blood-red planet Mars (pp.52–53).

WATCHING THE SKIES
The earliest astronomers were shepherds who watched the heavens for signs of the changing seasons. The clear nights would have given them the opportunity to recognize familiar patterns and movements of the brightest heavenly bodies.

STUDYING THE STARS
Almost every culture made a study of the stars. During the so-called "Dark Ages" in Europe, the science of astronomy was kept alive by the Arabic-speaking peoples. The Greek star catalogs were improved and updated by the great Arabic astronomers, such as al-Sufi (903–986).

An engraving of al-Sufi with a celestial globe

UNCHANGING SKY
In all but the largest cities, where the stars are shrouded by pollution or hidden by the glare of streetlights, the recurring display of the night sky is still captivating. The view of the stars from Earth has changed remarkably little during the past 10,000 years. The sky on any night in the 21st century is nearly the same as the one seen by people who lived thousands of years ago. The night sky for people of the early civilizations would have been more accessible because their lives were not as sheltered from the effects of nature as ours are. Despite the advances in the technology of astronomical observation, which include radio telescopes where the images appear on a computer screen, and telescopes launched into space to detect radiations that do not penetrate our atmosphere, there are still things the amateur astronomer can enjoy. Books and newspapers print star charts so that on a given night, in a specified geographical location, anyone looking upward into a clear sky can see the constellations for themselves.

FROM SUPERSTITION TO SCIENCE

The science of astronomy grew out of a belief in astrology (pp.20–21), the power of the planets and stars to affect life on Earth. Each planet was believed to have the personality and powers of one of the gods. Mars, the god of war, shown here, determined war, plague, famine, and violent death.

TRADITIONAL SYMBOLS

The heritage of the Greek science of the stars passed through many different civilizations. In each case, the figures of the constellations took on the personalities of the heroes of local legends. The Mediterranean animals of the zodiac were transformed by other cultures, such as the Persians and Indians, into more familiar creatures, like the ibex, Brahman bulls, or a crayfish. This page is from an 18th-century Arabic manuscript. It depicts the zodiacal signs of Gemini, Cancer, Aries, and Taurus. The signs are in the Arabic script, which is read from right to left.

Quetzalcoatl

AZTEC MYTHOLOGY

In the Americas, the mythology of the stars was stronger than it was in Europe and Asia. This Aztec calendar shows the god Quetzalcoatl, who combined the influences of the Sun and Venus. His worship included ritual human sacrifice.

Rays of light enter the objective lens

Two prisms fold up the light path

LOOKING AT STARS

Many of the sky's mysteries can be seen with a good pair of binoculars. This modern pair gives a better view of the heavens than Newton, Galileo, or other great astronomers could have seen with their best telescopes (pp.24–25).

Light passes to the eye

IMAGING SPACE

With large telescopes, such as the Hubble Space Telescope (HST), astronomers today can observe objects a billion times fainter than anything the ancients saw with the naked eye, including galaxies billions of light-years (p.64) away. The HST was put into Earth orbit by the Space Shuttle in 1990. Working above the atmosphere, it can make high-resolution observations in infrared and ultraviolet as well as visible light. Astronauts have repaired it several times. If repairs planned for 2008 are successful, HST should keep operating until about 2013.

Ancient astronomy

By watching the cyclic motion of the Sun, the Moon, and the stars, early observers soon realized that these repeating motions could be used to fashion the sky into a clock (to tell the passage of the hours of the day or night) and a calendar (to mark the progression of the seasons). Ancient monuments, such as Stonehenge in England and the pyramids of the Maya in Central America, offer evidence that the basic components of observational astronomy have been known for at least 6,000 years. With few exceptions, all civilizations have believed that the steady movements of the sky were the signal of some greater plan. The phenomenon of a solar eclipse (pp.42–43), for example, was believed by some ancient civilizations to be a dragon eating the Sun. A great noise would successfully frighten the dragon away.

DEFYING THE HEAVENS
The ancient poets warn that you should never venture out to sea until the constellation of the Pleiades rises with the Sun in early May. If superpower leaders Mikhail Gorbachev and George Bush Sr. had remembered their Greek poets, they would have known better than to try to meet on a boat in the Mediterranean in December 1989. Their summit was almost canceled because of bad weather.

PHASES OF THE MOON
The changing face of the Moon has always deeply affected people. A new moon was considered the best time to start an enterprise and a full moon was often feared as a time when spirits were free to roam. The word "lunatic" comes from the Latin name for the Moon, *luna*, because it was believed that the rays of the full moon caused insanity.

NAMING THE PLANETS
The spread of knowledge tends to follow the two routes of trade and war. As great empires expanded, they brought their gods, customs, and learning with them. The earliest civilizations believed that the stars and planets were ruled by the gods. The Babylonians, for example, named each planet after the god that had most in common with that planet's characteristics. The Greeks and the Romans adopted the Babylonian system, replacing the names with those of their own gods. All the planet names can be traced directly to the Babylonian planet-gods: Nergal has become Mars, and Marduk has become the god Jupiter.

The Roman god Jupiter

Station stone

Aubrey holes are round pits that were part of the earliest structure

THE WORLD'S OLDEST OBSERVATORY
The earliest observatory to have survived is the Chomsung Dae Observatory in Kyongju, Korea. A simple beehive structure, with a central opening in the roof, it resembles a number of prehistoric structures found all over the world. Many modern observatories (pp.30–31) still have a similar roof opening.

RECORDING THE SUN'S MOVEMENTS
Even though the precise significance of the standing stones at Stonehenge remains the subject of debate, it is clear from the arrangement of the stones that it was erected by prehistoric peoples specifically to record certain key celestial events, such as the summer and winter solstices and the spring and fall equinoxes. Although Stonehenge is the best known of the ancient megalithic monuments (those made of stone in prehistoric times), the sheer number of similar sites throughout the world underlines how many prehistoric peoples placed an enormous importance on recording the motions of the Sun and Moon.

BABYLONIAN RECORDS

The earliest astronomical records are in the form of clay tablets from ancient Mesopotamia and the great civilizations that flourished in the plains between the Tigris and Euphrates rivers for more than 2,000 years. The oldest surviving astronomical calculations are relatively late, dating from the 4th century BCE, but they are clearly based on generations of astronomical observations.

Back of a Persian astrolabe, 1707

Degree scale

Sight hole

Rotating alidade

Shadow square

Calendar scale

THE ASTROLABE

One of the problems faced by ancient astronomers was how to simplify the complex calculations needed to predict the positions of the planets and stars. One useful tool was the astrolabe, whose different engraved plates reproduce the sphere of the heavens in two dimensions. The alidade with its sight holes is used to measure the height of the Sun or the stars. By setting this against the calendar scale on the outside of the instrument, a number of different calculations can be made.

PLANNING THE HARVEST

For nearly all ancient cultures the primary importance of astronomy was as a signal of seasonal changes. The Egyptians knew that when the star Sirius rose ahead of the Sun, the annual flooding of the Nile was not far behind. Schedules for planting and harvesting were all set by the Sun, the Moon, and the stars.

Arabic manuscript from the 14th century showing an astrolabe being used

Heel stone marks the original approach to Stonehenge

Avenue

Sun

Slaughter stone formed a ceremonial doorway

Altar stone

Station stone

Barrow

Circular bank and ditch

Circle of sarsen stones with lintels

Ordering the universe

A GREAT DEAL OF OUR KNOWLEDGE about the ancient science of astronomy comes from the Alexandrian Greek philosopher Claudius Ptolemaeus (c. 100–178 CE), known as Ptolemy. He was an able scientist in his own right but, most importantly, he collected and clarified the work of all the great astronomers who had lived before him. He left two important sets of books. The *Almagest* was an astronomy textbook that provided an essential catalog of all the known stars, updating Hipparchus. In the *Tetrabiblos*, Ptolemy discussed astrology. Both sets of books were the undisputed authority on their respective subjects for 1,600 years. Fortunately, they were translated into Arabic, because with the collapse of the Roman Empire around the 4th century, much accumulated knowledge disappeared as libraries were destroyed and books burned.

STAR CATALOGER
Hipparchus (190–120 BCE) was one of the greatest of the Greek astronomers. He cataloged over 1,000 stars and developed the mathematical science of trigonometry. Here he is looking at the sky through a tube to help him isolate stars—the telescope was not yet invented (pp.26–27).

Julius Caesar

THE LEAP YEAR
One of the problems confronting the astronomer-priests of antiquity was the fact that the lunar year and the solar year (p.17) did not match up. By the middle of the 1st century BCE, the Roman calendar was so mixed up that Julius Caesar (100–44 BCE) ordered the Greek mathematician Sosigenes to develop a new system. He came up with the idea of a leap year every four years. This meant that the odd quarter day of the solar year was rationalized every four years.

Sirius, the Dog Star

FARNESE ATLAS
Very few images of the constellations have survived from antiquity. The main source for our knowledge is this 2nd-century Roman copy of an earlier Greek statue. The marble statue has the demigod Atlas holding the heavens on his shoulders. All of the 48 Ptolemaic constellations are clearly marked in low relief.

Navis, the Ship

Atlas

Europe
Red Sea

Facsimile (1908) of the Behaim terrestrial globe

Ocean

Africa

SPHERICAL EARTH
The concept of a spherical Earth can be traced back to Greece in the 6th century BCE. By Ptolemy's time, astronomers were accustomed to working with earthly (terrestrial) and starry (celestial) globes. The first terrestrial globe to be produced since antiquity, the 15th-century globe by Martin Behaim, shows an image of Earth that is half-based on myth. The Red Sea, for example, is colored red.

ARABIC SCHOOL OF ASTRONOMY
During the "Dark Ages" the great civilizations of Islam continued to develop the science of astronomy. Ulugh Beigh (c. 15th century) set up his observatory on this site in one of Asia's oldest cities—Samarkand, Uzbekistan. Here, measurements were made with the naked eye.

Geocentric universe

It is logical to make assumptions from what your senses tell you. From Earth it looks as if the heavens are circling over our heads. There is no reason to assume that Earth is moving at all. Ancient philosophers, naturally, believed that their Earth was stable and the center of the great cosmos. The planets were arranged in a series of layers, with the starry heavens—or the fixed stars, as they were called—forming a large crystalline casing.

Planet · Epicycle · Planet makes small circles during its orbit · Orbit · Earth

EARTH AT THE CENTER

The geocentric or Earth-centered universe is often referred to as the Ptolemaic universe by later scholars to indicate that this was how classical scientists, like the great Ptolemy, believed the universe was structured. He saw Earth as the center of the universe, with the Moon, the known planets, and the Sun moving around it. Aristarchus (c. 310–230 BCE) had already suggested that Earth travels around the Sun, but his theory was rejected because it did not fit in with the mathematical and philosophical beliefs of the time.

Engraving (1490) of the Ptolemaic universe

PROBLEMS WITH THE GEOCENTRIC UNIVERSE

The main problem with the model of an Earth-centered universe was that it did not help to explain the apparently irrational behavior of some of the planets, which sometimes appear to stand still or move backward against the background of the stars (p.23). Early civilizations assumed that these odd movements were signals from the gods, but the Greek philosophers spent centuries trying to develop rational explanations for what they saw. The most popular was the notion of epicycles. The planets moved in small circles (epicycles) on their orbits as they circled Earth.

TEACHING TOOL

Astronomers have always found it difficult to explain the three-dimensional motions of the heavens. Ptolemy used something like this armillary sphere to do his complex astronomical calculations and to pass these ideas on to his students.

Equinoctial colure passes through the poles and the equinoxes

Arctic circle

Solstitial colure passes through the poles and the solstices

Ecliptic

Celestial equator

Moon

Earth

Meridian ring

Horizon ring

Sun

Tropic of Cancer

French painted armillary sphere (1770)

Stand

The celestial sphere

THE POSITIONS OF ALL OBJECTS IN SPACE are measured according to specific celestial coordinates. The best way to understand the cartography, or mapping, of the sky is to recall how the ancient philosophers imagined the universe was shaped. They had no real evidence that Earth moves, so they concluded that it was stationary and that the stars and planets revolve around it. They could see the stars wheeling around a single point in the sky and assumed that this must be one end of the axis of a great celestial sphere. They called it a crystalline sphere, or the sphere of fixed stars, because none of the stars seemed to change their positions relative to each other. The celestial coordinates used today come from this old-fashioned concept of a celestial sphere. The starry (celestial) and earthly (terrestrial) spheres share the same coordinates, such as a north and south poles and an equator.

STAR TRAILS
A long photographic exposure of the sky taken from the northern hemisphere of Earth shows the way in which stars appear to go in circles around the Pole Star or Polaris. Polaris is a bright star that lies within 1° of the true celestial pole, which, in turn, is located directly above the North Pole of Earth. The rotation of Earth on its north-south axis is the reason why the stars appear to move across the sky. Those closer to the Poles appear to move less than those farther away.

Pole Star

Great Bear

Horizontal plane

Apex

Sight line   *Peep hole*

Peep hole

These two angles must add up to 90°

Degrees marked on arc

Angle read off where string crosses degree scale

Plumb bob

90°

MEASURING ALTITUDES
One of the earliest astronomical instruments is the quadrant. It is simply a quarter of a circle, whose curved edge has been divided into 90 degrees. Other similar instruments include the sextant, which is one-sixth of a circle. By sighting the object through the peep holes along one straight edge of the quadrant, the observer can measure the height, or altitude, of that object. The altitude is the height in degrees (°) of a star above the horizon; it is not a linear measurement. A string with a plumb bob falls from the apex of the quadrant so that it intersects the divided arc. Since the angle between the vertical of the plumb bob and the horizontal plane of the horizon is 90°, simple mathematics can be used to work out the angle of sphe altitude.

DOING THE MA
The apex of t quadrant is a 90° ang As the sum of angles of a triangle a up to 180°, this me that the sum of other two angles m add up to 90° t

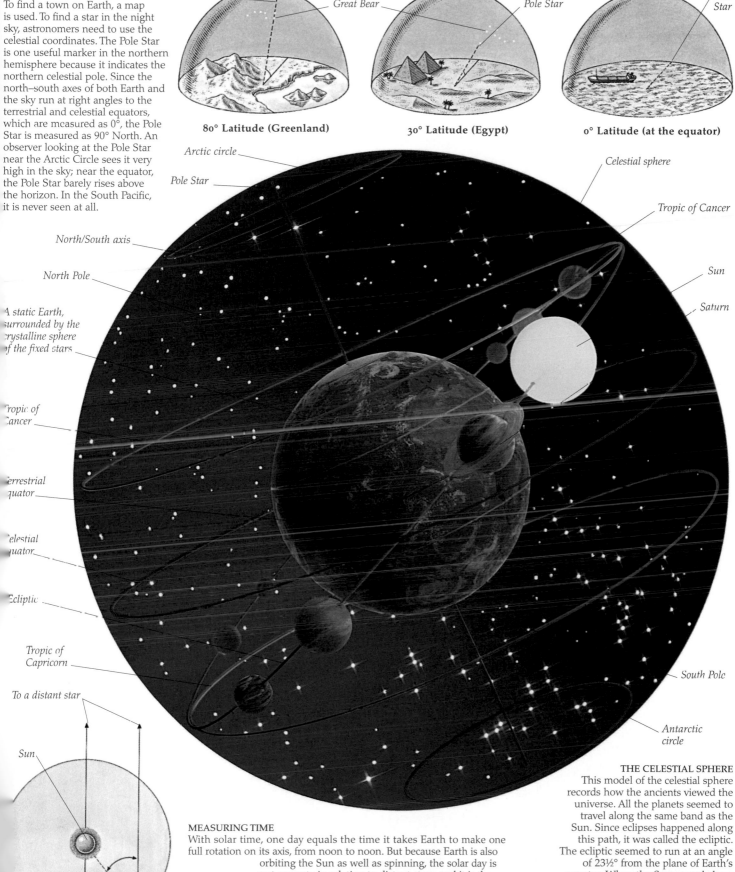

WHERE IS THE POLE STAR?

To find a town on Earth, a map is used. To find a star in the night sky, astronomers need to use the celestial coordinates. The Pole Star is one useful marker in the northern hemisphere because it indicates the northern celestial pole. Since the north–south axes of both Earth and the sky run at right angles to the terrestrial and celestial equators, which are measured as 0°, the Pole Star is measured as 90° North. An observer looking at the Pole Star near the Arctic Circle sees it very high in the sky; near the equator, the Pole Star barely rises above the horizon. In the South Pacific, it is never seen at all.

Pole Star — *Great Bear*

80° Latitude (Greenland)

Pole Star

30° Latitude (Egypt)

Pole Star

0° Latitude (at the equator)

Arctic circle

Pole Star

North/South axis

North Pole

A static Earth, surrounded by the crystalline sphere of the fixed stars

Tropic of Cancer

Terrestrial equator

Celestial equator

Ecliptic

Tropic of Capricorn

Celestial sphere

Tropic of Cancer

Sun

Saturn

South Pole

Antarctic circle

To a distant star

Sun

Second noon for sidereal time

Second noon for solar time

Noon first

MEASURING TIME

With solar time, one day equals the time it takes Earth to make one full rotation on its axis, from noon to noon. But because Earth is also orbiting the Sun as well as spinning, the solar day is not accurate in relation to distant stars, and it is the stars that concern astronomers. They measure time in relation to a distant star. This "day" is the time that passes between two successive "noons" of a star, noon being the moment when that star passes directly over the local meridian (p.31). This is called a sidereal day.

THE CELESTIAL SPHERE

This model of the celestial sphere records how the ancients viewed the universe. All the planets seemed to travel along the same band as the Sun. Since eclipses happened along this path, it was called the ecliptic. The ecliptic seemed to run at an angle of 23½° from the plane of Earth's equator. When the Sun passed along the ecliptic, it turned back as it passed through the signs of Cancer in the north and Capricorn in the south. These points where the Sun turned in its path were called tropics.

The uses of astronomy

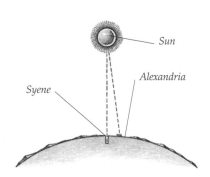

Sun

Alexandria

Syene

WITH ALL THE TOOLS OF MODERN TECHNOLOGY, it is sometimes hard to imagine how people performed simple functions such as telling the time or knowing where they were on Earth before the invention of clocks, maps, or navigational satellites. The only tools available were those provided by nature. The astronomical facts of the relatively regular interval of the day, the constancy of the movements of the fixed stars, and the assumption of certain theories, such as a spherical Earth, allowed people to measure their lives. By calculating the height of the Sun or certain stars, the ancient Greeks began to understand the shape and size of Earth. In this way, they were able to determine their latitude. By plotting coordinates against a globe, they could fix their position on Earth's surface. And by setting up carefully measured markers, or gnomons, they could begin to calculate the time of day.

MEASURING THE EARTH
About 230 BCE Eratosthenes (c. 270–190 BCE) estimated the size of Earth by using the Sun. He discovered that the Sun was directly above his head at Syene (present-day Aswan) in Upper Egypt at noon on the summer solstice. In Alexandria, directly north, the Sun was about 7° from its highest point (the zenith) at the summer solstice. Since Eratosthenes knew that the Earth was spherical (360° in circumference), the distance between the two towns should be 7/360ths of the Earth's circumference.

Latitude scale

Movable cursor

Sight hole

Sight hole

Hour scale

AN ANCIENT SUNDIAL
Very early on, people realized that they could keep time by the Sun. Simple sundials like this allowed the traveler or merchant to know the local time for several different towns during a journey. The altitude of the Sun was measured through the sight holes in the bow and stern of the "little ship." When the cursor on the ship's mast was set to the correct latitude, the plumb bob would fall on the proper time.

Zodiac scale

Plumb bob

HOW A SUNDIAL WORKS
As the Sun travels across the sky, the shadow it casts changes in direction and length. A sundial works by setting a gnomon, or "indicator," so that the shadow the Sun casts at noon falls due north–south along a meridian. (A meridian is an imaginary line running from pole to pole; another name for meridian is a line of longitude.) The hours can then be divided before and after the noon mark. The terms "a.m." and "p.m." for morning and afternoon come from the Latin words meaning before and after the Sun passes the north–south meridian (*ante meridiem* and *post meridiem*).

Su

Gnomon

Shadow cast by gnomon at noon

Towns with their latitudes

Qiblah

FINDING MECCA
Part of Islamic worship is regular prayers, in which the faithful face toward the holy city of Mecca. The qiblah (direction of Mecca) indicator is a sophisticated instrument, developed during the Middle Ages to find the direction of Mecca. It also uses the Sun to determine the time for beginning and ending prayers.

CROSSING THE SOUTH PACIFIC
It was thought that the early indigenous peoples of Polynesia were too "primitive" to have sailed the great distances between the north Pacific Ocean and New Zealand in the south. However, many tribes, including the Maoris, were capable of navigating thousands of miles using only the stars to guide them.

Rouen

Calais

Toulouse

Latitude marker

London

Latitude scale

Compass

CRUCIFORM SUNDIAL
Traveling Christian pilgrims often worried that any ornament might be considered a symbol of vanity. They solved this problem by incorporating religious symbolism into their sundials. This dial, shaped in the form of a cross, provided the means for telling the time in a number of English and French towns.

Magnetized ne

Degree scale

Compass

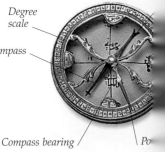

Compass bearing

Po

A CELESTIAL GLOBE

The celestial globe records the figures and stars of all the constellations against a grid of lines representing longitude and latitude. During the 17th and 18th centuries, all ships of the Dutch East India Company were given a matching pair of globes—terrestrial (p.14) and celestial. Calculations could be made by comparing the coordinates on the two different globes. In practice, however, most navigators seemed to use flat sea-charts to plot their journeys.

Argo, the Ship

Hydra, the water snake

Meridian ring

Centaurus, the Centaur

Celestial globe 1618

The Southern Cross

Southern Triangle

THE GREAT NAVIGATORS

Explorers of the 16th century had no idea what they would find when they set out to sea. Their heads were full of fables about mermaids and sea monsters. Even though this engraving of the Portuguese navigator Ferdinand Magellan (1480–1521) has many features that are clearly fantastical, it does show him using a pair of dividers to measure off an armillary sphere (p.15). Beside the ship, the sun god Apollo shines brightly; it was usually the Sun's position in the sky that helped a navigator find his latitude.

Sun

Shadow vane lined up with horizon vane

Holder

Sight vane

Navigator with his back to the Sun

Horizon vane

Scale in degrees

Horizon

Scale in degrees

USING A BACKSTAFF

The backstaff allowed a navigator to measure the height of the Sun without having to stare directly at it. The navigator held the instrument so that the shadow cast by the shadow vane fell directly on to the horizon vane. Moving the sight vane, the navigator lined it up so he could see the horizon through the sight vane and the horizon vane. By adding together the angles of the sight and shadow vanes, the navigator could calculate the altitude of the Sun, from which he could determine the precise latitude of his ship.

Two angles give the Sun's altitude

90° angle

Horizon

DOING THE MATHEMATICS

To work out latitude at sea, a navigator needs to find the altitude of the Sun at noon. He doesn't even need to know the time; as long as the Sun is at its highest point in the sky, the altitude can be measured with a backstaff or other instrument (p.15). Then, using nautical tables of celestial coordinates, he can find his latitude with a simple equation using the angle of altitude and the coordinates of the Sun in the celestial sphere (p.17).

Astrology

THE ASTROLOGER
In antiquity, the astrologers' main task was to predict the future. This woodcut, dating from 1490, shows two astrologers working with arrangements of the Sun, Moon, and planets to find the astrological effects on people's lives.

T HE WORD "ASTROLOGY" comes from the Greek *astron*, meaning "star," and the suffix "-logy," meaning "study of." Since Babylonian times, people staring at the night sky were convinced that the regular motions of the heavens were indications of some great cosmic purpose. Priests and philosophers believed that if they could map the stars and the movements of the stars, they could decode these messages and understand the patterns that had an effect on past and future events. What was originally observational astronomy—observing the stars and planets—gradually grew into the astrology that has today become a regular part of many people's lives. However, there is no evidence that the stars and planets have any effect on our personalities or our destinies. Astronomers now agree that astrology is superstition. Its original noble motives should not be forgotten, however. For most of the so-called "Dark Ages," when all pure science was in deep hibernation, it was astrology and the desire to know about the future that kept the science of astronomy alive.

RULERSHIP OVER ORGANS
Until the discoveries of modern medicine, people believed that the body was governed by four different types of essences called "humors." An imbalance in these humors would lead to illness. Each of the 12 signs of the zodiac (above) had special links with each of the humors and with parts of the human body. So, for example, for a headache due to moisture in the head (a cold), treatment would be with a drying agent—some plant ruled by the Sun or an "Earth-sign," like Virgo—when a new moon was well placed toward the sign of Aries, which ruled the head.

Dates in the month

Days in the week

Father Time

Back of calendar

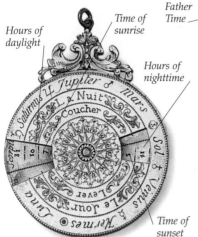

Hours of daylight

Time of sunrise

Hours of nighttime

Time of sunset

PERPETUAL CALENDAR
The names for the days of the week show traces of astrological belief—for example, Sunday is the Sun's day, and Monday is the Moon's day. This simple perpetual calendar, which has small planetary signs next to each day, shows the day of the week for any given date. The user can find the day by turning the inner dial to a given month or date and reading off the information.

LEO, THE LION
These 19th-century French constellation cards show each individual star marked with a hole through which light shines. Astrologically, each zodiac sign has its own properties and its own friendships and enemies within the zodiacal circle. Each sign is also ruled by a planet, which similarly has its own properties, friendships, and enemies. So, for example, a person born while the Sun is passing through Leo is supposed to be kingly, like a lion.

PLANETARY POSITIONS

One way in which planets are supposed to be in or out of harmony with one another depends on their relative positions in the heavens. When two planets are found within a few degrees of each other, they are said to be in conjunction. When planets are separated by exactly 180° in the zodiacal band, they are said to be in opposition.

Earth

Mars and Sun in opposition

Mars and Sun in conjunction

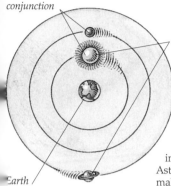

Saturn and Sun in opposition

Saturn and Sun in conjunction

Earth

BEING IN CONJUNCTION

The planets here are shown in a geocentric universe (pp.14–15) where Earth is at the center. Conjunctions can be good or bad, depending on whether the planets involved are mutually friendly or not. Astrologers believe that an opposition is malefic, or "evil-willing," because the planets are fighting against each other.

THE ZODIAC

Seen from Earth, the Sun, the Moon, and all the planets appear to travel along a narrow band called the ecliptic (p.17), which seems to pass through a number of constellations. Since Roman times, this series of constellations has been limited to 12 and is known as the zodiac, or "circle of animals." A person's horoscopic chart shows how the stars and planets were placed at the moment of birth. Astrologers believe that this pattern sets the boundaries for each individual's personality, career, strengths and weaknesses, illnesses, and love life.

Scorpio · *Sagittarius* · *Capricorn* · *Aquarius* · *Pisces* · *Aries* · *Taurus* · *Gemini* · *Cancer* · *Leo* · *Virgo* · *Libra*

SCORPIO, THE SCORPION

Most of the constellations are now known by the Latinized versions of their original Greek names. This card shows Scorpius, or Scorpio. This is the sign through which the Sun is traditionally said to pass between late October and late November. Astrologers believe that people born during this time of year are intuitive, yet secretive, like a scorpion scuttling under a rock.

CANCER, THE CRAB

Someone who is born while the Sun is transiting the constellation of Cancer is supposed to be a homebody, like a crab in its shell. These hand-painted cards are collectively known as *Urania's Mirror*—Urania is the name of the muse of astronomy (p.23). By holding the cards up to the light, it is possible to learn the shapes and relative brightnesses of the stars in each constellation.

The Copernican revolution

In 1543 NICOLAUS COPERNICUS published a book that changed the perception of the universe. In his *De revolutionibus orbium coelestium* ("Concerning the revolutions of the celestial orbs"), Copernicus argued that the Sun, and not Earth, is at the center of the universe. It was a heliocentric universe, *helios* being the Greek word for Sun. His reasoning was based on the logic of the time. He argued that a sphere moves in a circle that has no beginning and no end. Since the universe and all the heavenly bodies are spherical, their motions must be circular and uniform. In the Ptolemaic, Earth-centered system (pp.14–15), the paths of the planets are irregular. Copernicus assumed that uniform motions in the orbits of the planets appear irregular to us because Earth is not at the center of the universe. These discoveries were put forward by many different astronomers, but they ran against the teachings of both the Protestant and Catholic churches. In 1616 all books written by Copernicus and any others that put the Sun at the center of the universe were condemned by the Catholic Church.

NICOLAUS COPERNICUS
The Polish astronomer Nicolaus Copernicus (1473–1543) made few observations. Instead, he read the ancient philosophers and discovered that none of them had been able to agree about the structure of the universe.

— Sun

— Zodiac

COPERNICAN UNIVERSE
Copernicus based the order of his solar system on how long it took each planet to complete a full orbit. This early print shows Earth in orbit around the Sun with the zodiac beyond.

THE GREAT OBSERVER
In 1672, the Danish astronomer Tycho Brahe (1546–1601) discovered a bright new star in the constellation Cassiopeia. It was what astronomers today call a "supernova" (p.65). It was so bright that it was visible even during the day. This appearance challenged the inherited wisdom from the ancients, which claimed that the stars were eternal and unchanging. To study what this appearance might mean, a new observatory was set up near Copenhagen, Denmark. Brahe remeasured 788 stars of Ptolemy's great star catalog, thereby producing the first complete, modern stellar atlas.

Uranibourg, Tycho's observatory on the island of Hven

DRAWING AN ELLIPSE
An ellipse can be drawn by pushing two pins into a board and linking them with a loop of thread. When a pencil is placed within the loop and moved around the pins, keeping the loop tight, the shape it makes is an ellipse. The position of each pin is called a focus. In the solar system, the Sun is at one focus of the ellipse in a planetary orbit. The wider apart the pins are placed, the more eccentric the planetary orbit (pp.40–41).

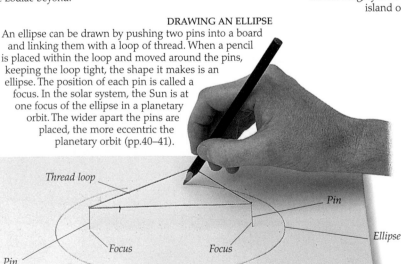

Thread loop

Pin

Pin

Focus   *Focus*

Ellipse

LAWS OF PLANETARY MOTION
Johannes Kepler (above right) added the results of his own observations to Tycho's improved planetary and stellar measurements. Kepler discovered that the orbits of the planets were not perfectly circular, as had been believed for 1,600 years. They were elliptical, with the Sun placed at one focus of the ellipse (left). While observing the orbit of Mars, Kepler discovered that there are variations in its speed. At certain points in its orbit, Mars seemed to be traveling faster than at other times. He soon realized that the Sun was regulating the orbiting speed of the planet. When it is closest to the Sun—its perihelion—the planet orbits most quickly; at its aphelion—farthest from the Sun—it slows down.

Perihelion

Plane

Sun

Aphelion

Pla

JOHANNES KEPLER (1571–1630)
It was due to the intervention of Tycho Brahe that the German mathematician Johannes Kepler landed the prestigious position of Imperial Mathematician in 1601. Tycho left all his papers to Kepler, who was a vigorous supporter of the Copernican heliocentric system. Kepler formulated three laws of planetary motion and urged Galileo (p.24) to publish his research in order to help prove the Copernican thesis.

Planet paths shown in a planetarium

Apparent path of Mars   *Line of sight*

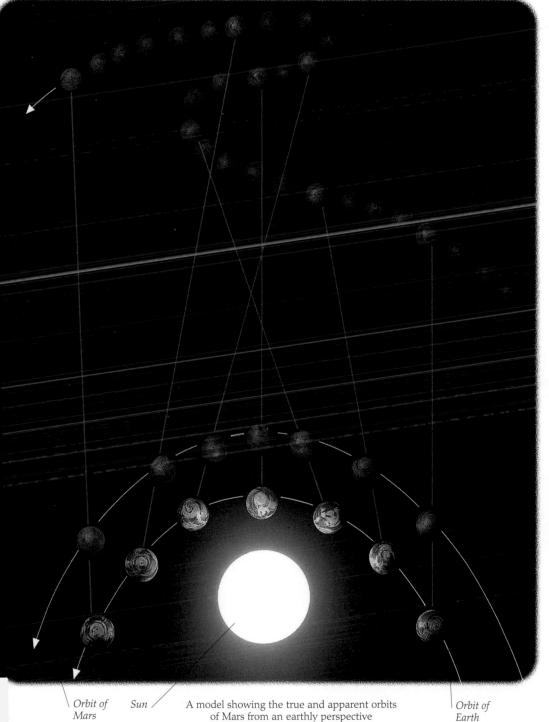

APPARENT PATHS
The irregular motion that disproved the geocentric universe was the retrograde motion of the planets. From an earthly perspective, some of the planets—particularly Mars—seem to double back on their orbits, making great loops in the night sky. (The light display above draws the apparent orbit of Mars.) Ptolemy proposed that retrograde motion could be explained by planets traveling on smaller orbits (p.15). Once astronomers realized that the Sun is the center of the solar system, the apparent path of Mars, for example, could be explained. But first it had to be understood that Earth had a greater orbiting speed than that of Mars, which appeared to slip behind. Even though the orbit of Mars seems to keep pace with Earth (below left), the apparent path is very different (above left).

WEIGHING UP THE THEORIES
This engraving from a 17th-century manuscript shows Urania, the muse of astronomy, comparing the different theoretical systems for the arrangement of the universe. Ptolemy's system is at her feet, and Kepler's is outweighed by Tycho's system on the right.

Orbit of *Sun*   A model showing the true and apparent orbits   *Orbit of*
Mars   of Mars from an earthly perspective   *Earth*

Intellectual giants

I**T TAKES BOTH LUCK AND COURAGE** to be a radical thinker. Galileo Galilei (1564–1642) had the misfortune of being brilliant at a time when new ideas were considered dangerous. His numerous discoveries, made with the help of the newly invented telescope, provided ample support for the Copernican heliocentric, or Sun-centered, universe (pp.22–23). Galileo's findings about the satellites of Jupiter (p.54) and the phases of Venus clearly showed that Earth could not be the center of all movement in the universe and that the heavenly bodies were not perfect in their behavior. For this Galileo was branded a heretic and sentenced to a form of life imprisonment. The great English physicist Isaac Newton (1642–1727), born the year Galileo died, had both luck and courage. He lived in an age enthusiastic for new ideas, especially those related to scientific discovery.

GALILEO'S TELESCOPE
Galileo never claimed to have invented the telescope. In *Il Saggiatore,* "The Archer," he commends the "simple spectacle-maker" who "found the instrument" by chance. When he heard of Lippershey's results (p.26), Galileo reinvented the instrument from the description of its effects. His first telescope magnified at eight times. Within a few days, however, he had constructed a telescope with 20x magnification. He went on to increase his magnification to 30x, having ground the lenses himself.

POPE URBAN VIII
Originally, the Catholic Church had welcomed Copernicus's work (pp.22– 3). However, by 1563 the Church was becoming increasingly strict and abandoned its previously lax attitude toward any deviation from established doctrine. Pope Urban VIII was one of the many caught in this swing. As a cardinal, he had been friendly with Galileo and often had Galileo's book, *Il Saggiatore,* read to him aloud at meals. In 1635, however, he authorized the Grand Inquisition to investigate Galileo.

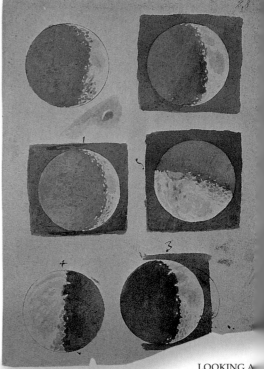

LOOKING A
THE MOON'S SURFAC
Through his telescope, Galileo measured the shadow on the Moon to show how the mountains there we: much taller than those on Earth. These ink sketche were published in his book *Sidereus nunciu* "Messenger of the Stars," in 161

RENAISSANCE MAN
In 1611, Galileo traveled to Rome to discuss his findings about the Sun and its position in the universe with the leaders of the Church. They accepted his discoveries, but not the theory that underpinned them— the Copernican, heliocentric universe (pp.22–23). Galileo was accused of heresy and, in 1635, condemned for disobedience and sentenced to house arrest until his death in 1642. He was pardoned in 1992.

PHASES OF VENUS
From his childhood days, Galileo was characterized as the sort of person who was unwilling to accept facts without evidence. In 1610, by applying the telescope to astronomy, he discovered the moons of Jupiter and the phases of Venus. He immediately understood that the phases of Venus are caused by the Sun shining on a planet that revolves around it. He knew that this was proof that Earth was not the center of the universe. He hid his findings in a Latin anagram, or word puzzle, as he did with many of the discoveries that he knew would be considered "dangerous" by the authorities.

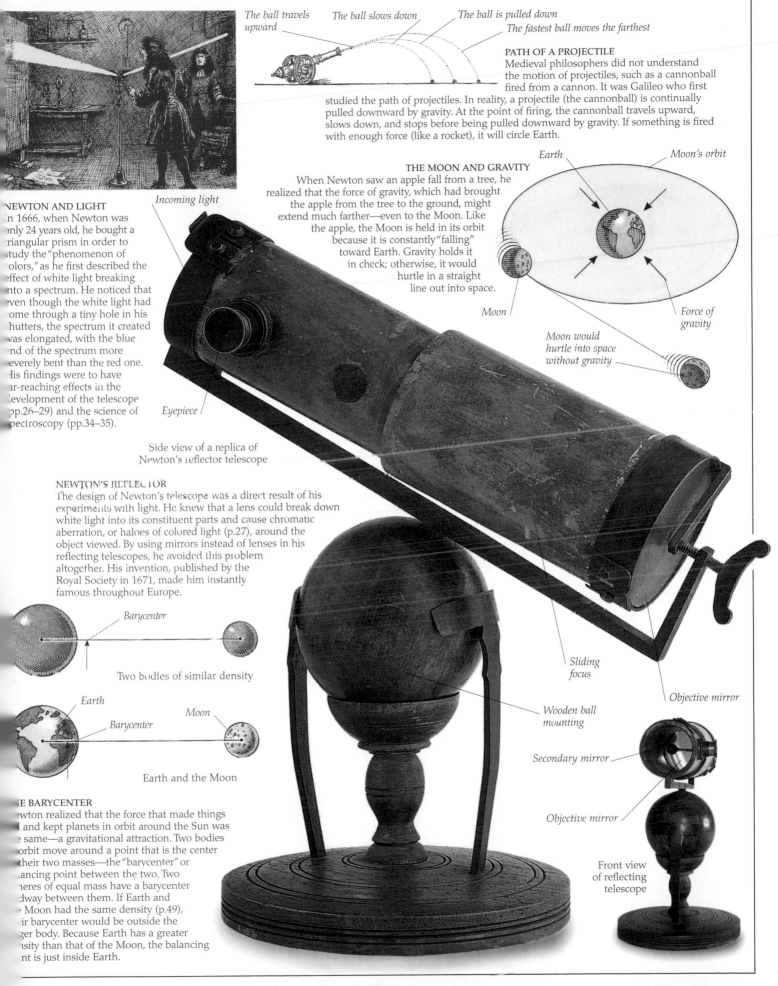

The ball travels upward · **The ball slows down** · **The ball is pulled down** · **The fastest ball moves the farthest**

PATH OF A PROJECTILE
Medieval philosophers did not understand the motion of projectiles, such as a cannonball fired from a cannon. It was Galileo who first studied the path of projectiles. In reality, a projectile (the cannonball) is continually pulled downward by gravity. At the point of firing, the cannonball travels upward, slows down, and stops before being pulled downward by gravity. If something is fired with enough force (like a rocket), it will circle Earth.

THE MOON AND GRAVITY
When Newton saw an apple fall from a tree, he realized that the force of gravity, which had brought the apple from the tree to the ground, might extend much farther—even to the Moon. Like the apple, the Moon is held in its orbit because it is constantly "falling" toward Earth. Gravity holds it in check; otherwise, it would hurtle in a straight line out into space.

Earth · *Moon's orbit* · *Moon* · *Force of gravity*

Moon would hurtle into space without gravity

NEWTON AND LIGHT
In 1666, when Newton was only 24 years old, he bought a triangular prism in order to study the "phenomenon of colors," as he first described the effect of white light breaking into a spectrum. He noticed that even though the white light had come through a tiny hole in his shutters, the spectrum it created was elongated, with the blue end of the spectrum more severely bent than the red one. His findings were to have far-reaching effects in the development of the telescope (pp.26–29) and the science of spectroscopy (pp.34–35).

Incoming light

Eyepiece

Side view of a replica of Newton's reflector telescope

NEWTON'S REFLECTOR
The design of Newton's telescope was a direct result of his experiments with light. He knew that a lens could break down white light into its constituent parts and cause chromatic aberration, or haloes of colored light (p.27), around the object viewed. By using mirrors instead of lenses in his reflecting telescopes, he avoided this problem altogether. His invention, published by the Royal Society in 1671, made him instantly famous throughout Europe.

Barycenter

Two bodies of similar density

Earth · *Barycenter* · *Moon*

Earth and the Moon

Sliding focus

Wooden ball mounting

Objective mirror

Secondary mirror

Objective mirror

Front view of reflecting telescope

THE BARYCENTER
Newton realized that the force that made things fall and kept planets in orbit around the Sun was the same—a gravitational attraction. Two bodies in orbit move around a point that is the center of their two masses—the "barycenter" or balancing point between the two. Two spheres of equal mass have a barycenter midway between them. If Earth and the Moon had the same density (p.49), their barycenter would be outside the larger body. Because Earth has a greater density than that of the Moon, the balancing point is just inside Earth.

Optical principles

PEOPLE HAVE BEEN AWARE of the magnifying properties of a curved piece of glass since at least 2,000 BCE. The Greek philosopher Aristophanes in the 5th century BCE had used a glass globe filled with water in order to magnify the fine print in his manuscripts. In the middle of the 13th century the English scientist Roger Bacon (1214–1292) proposed that the "lesser segment of a sphere of glass or crystal" will make small objects appear clearer and larger. For this suggestion, Bacon was branded by his colleagues a dangerous magician and imprisoned for ten years. Even though spectacles were invented in Italy some time between 1285 and 1300, superstitions were not overcome for another 250 years, when scientists discovered the combination of lenses that would lead to the invention of the telescope. There are two types of telescopes. The refractor telescope uses lenses to bend light; the reflector telescope uses mirrors to reflect the light back to the observer.

INVENTOR OF THE TELESCOPE
It is believed that the first real telescope was invented in 1608 in Holland by the spectacle-maker Hans Lippershey from Zeeland. According to the story, two of Lippershey's children were playing in his shop and noticed that by holding two lenses in a straight line they could magnify the weather vane on the local church. Lippershey placed the two lenses in a tube and claimed the invention of the telescope. In the mid-1550s an Englishman Leonard Digges had created a primitive instrument that, with a combination of mirrors and lenses, could reflect and enlarge objects viewed through it. There was controversy about whether this was a true scientific telescope or not. It was Galileo (p.24) who adapted the telescope to astronomy.

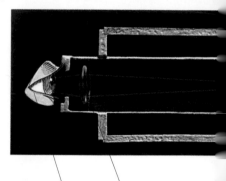

Viewer   *Convex eyepiece lens*

Light from laser

HOW REFRACTION WORKS
Light usually travels in a straight line, but it can be bent or "refracted" by passing it through substances of differing densities. This laser beam (here viewed from overhead) seems to bend as it is directed at a rectangular-shaped container of water because the light is passing through three different media—water, glass, and air.

Decorative ribbons might be attached here

Horn lens holder

Water

Convex lens

EARLY SPECTACLES (1750)
Most early spectacles like these had convex lenses. These helped people who were farsighted to focus on objects close to them. Later, spectacles were made with concave lenses for those who were nearsighted.

Path of light is bent again on reentering air

Light is bent

Reflected light beam   *Light from laser is bent back by a shiny surface*   *Incident light beam*

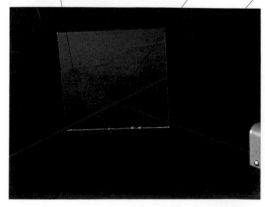

HOW REFLECTION WORKS
The word reflection comes from the Latin *reflectere*, meaning to "bend back." A shiny surface will bend back rays of light that strike it. The rays approaching the mirror are called incident rays and those leaving it are called outgoing, or reflected, rays. The angle at which the incident rays hit the mirror is the same as the angle of the reflected rays leaving it. What the eye sees are the light rays reflected in the mirror.

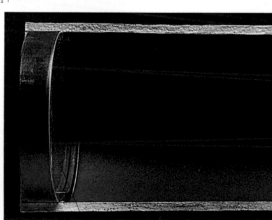

Large concave mirror

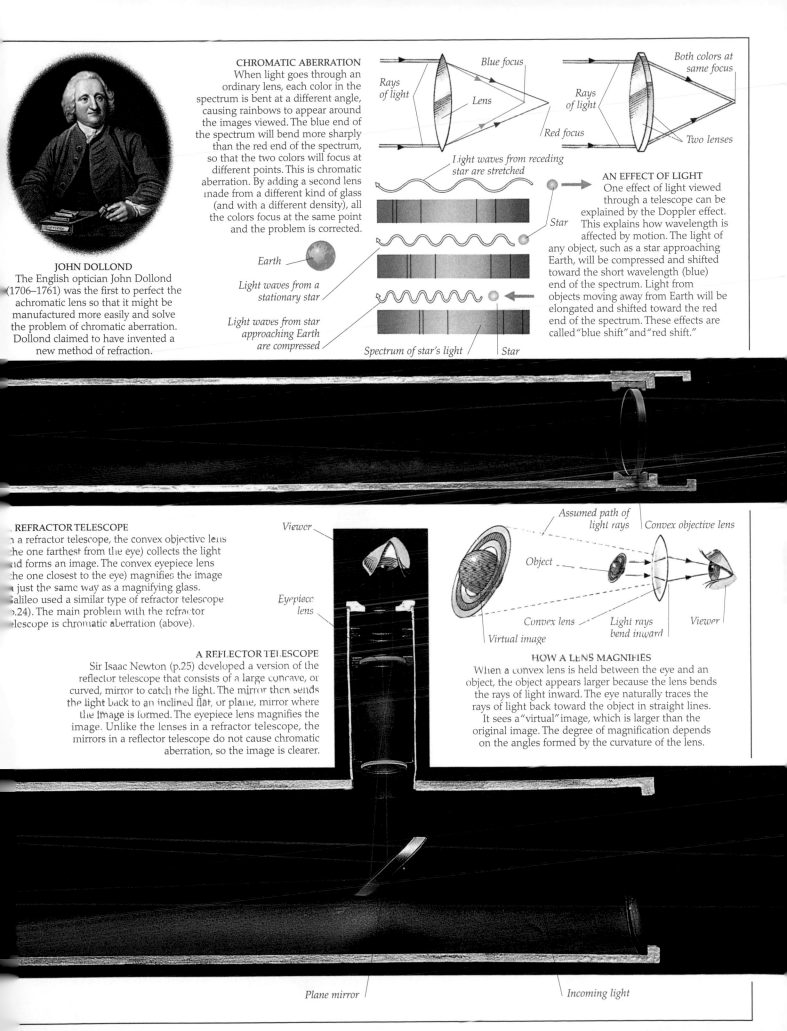

CHROMATIC ABERRATION

When light goes through an ordinary lens, each color in the spectrum is bent at a different angle, causing rainbows to appear around the images viewed. The blue end of the spectrum will bend more sharply than the red end of the spectrum, so that the two colors will focus at different points. This is chromatic aberration. By adding a second lens made from a different kind of glass (and with a different density), all the colors focus at the same point and the problem is corrected.

Blue focus

Rays of light

Lens

Red focus

Both colors at same focus

Rays of light

Two lenses

Light waves from receding star are stretched

Earth

Light waves from a stationary star

Light waves from star approaching Earth are compressed

Spectrum of star's light

Star

JOHN DOLLOND

The English optician John Dollond (1706–1761) was the first to perfect the achromatic lens so that it might be manufactured more easily and solve the problem of chromatic aberration. Dollond claimed to have invented a new method of refraction.

AN EFFECT OF LIGHT

One effect of light viewed through a telescope can be explained by the Doppler effect. This explains how wavelength is affected by motion. The light of any object, such as a star approaching Earth, will be compressed and shifted toward the short wavelength (blue) end of the spectrum. Light from objects moving away from Earth will be elongated and shifted toward the red end of the spectrum. These effects are called "blue shift" and "red shift."

REFRACTOR TELESCOPE

In a refractor telescope, the convex objective lens (the one farthest from the eye) collects the light and forms an image. The convex eyepiece lens (the one closest to the eye) magnifies the image in just the same way as a magnifying glass. Galileo used a similar type of refractor telescope (p.24). The main problem with the refractor telescope is chromatic aberration (above).

Viewer

Eyepiece lens

A REFLECTOR TELESCOPE

Sir Isaac Newton (p.25) developed a version of the reflector telescope that consists of a large concave, or curved, mirror to catch the light. The mirror then sends the light back to an inclined flat, or plane, mirror where the image is formed. The eyepiece lens magnifies the image. Unlike the lenses in a refractor telescope, the mirrors in a reflector telescope do not cause chromatic aberration, so the image is clearer.

Assumed path of light rays

Convex objective lens

Object

Convex lens

Light rays bend inward

Viewer

Virtual image

HOW A LENS MAGNIFIES

When a convex lens is held between the eye and an object, the object appears larger because the lens bends the rays of light inward. The eye naturally traces the rays of light back toward the object in straight lines. It sees a "virtual" image, which is larger than the original image. The degree of magnification depends on the angles formed by the curvature of the lens.

Plane mirror

Incoming light

The optical telescope

THE MORE LIGHT THAT REACHES THE EYEPIECE in a telescope, the brighter the image of the heavens will be. Astronomers made their lenses and mirrors bigger, they changed the focal length of the telescopes, and combined honeycombs of smaller mirrors to make a single, large reflective surface in order to capture the greatest amount of light and focus it onto a single point. During the 19th century, refractor telescopes (pp.26–27) were preferred and opticians devoted themselves to perfecting large lenses free of blemishes. In the 20th century there were advances in materials and mirror coatings. Large mirrors collect more light than small ones, but are also heavier. They may even sag under their own weight, distorting the image. One solution is segmented-mirror telescopes, where many smaller mirrors are mounted side by side. Another is "active optics," where mirrors move to compensate for any sagging.

CAMERAS ON TELESCOPES
Since the 19th century, astronomical photography has been an important tool for astronomers. By attaching a camera to a telescope that has been specially adapted with a motor that can be set to keep the telescope turning at the same speed as the rotation of Earth, the astronomer can take very long exposures of distant stars (p.16). Before the invention of photography, astronomers had to draw everything they saw. They had to be artists as well as scientists.

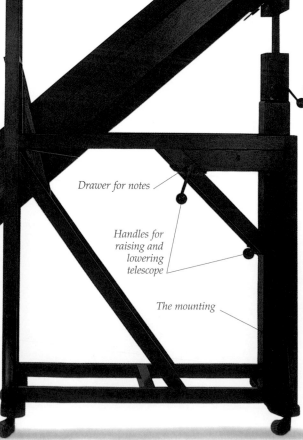

Eyepiece

Eyepiece mounting

Guide rails for raising telescope

Handle for adjusting angle of tube

Telescope tube

HERSCHEL'S TELESCOPE
First out of economic necessity and later as an indication of his perfectionism, the English astronomer William Herschel (1738–1822) always built his telescopes and hand-ground his own lenses and mirrors. The magnification of a telescope like his 6-in (15-cm) Newtonian reflector is about 200 times. This wooden telescope is the kind he would have used during his great survey of the sky, during which he discovered the planet Uranus (pp.58–59).

Main mirror located inside the tube

Drawer for notes

Handles for raising and lowering telescope

The mounting

Wheeled base

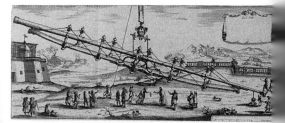

MORE MAGNIFICATION
Increasing the magnification of telescopes was one of the major challenges facing early astronomers. Since the technology to make large lenses was not sufficiently developed, the only answer was to make telescopes with a very long distance between the eyepiece lens and the objective lens. In some instances this led to telescopes of ridiculous proportions, as shown in this 18th-century engraving. These long focal length telescopes were impossible to use. The slightest vibration caused by someone walking past would make the telescope tremble so violently that observations were impossible.

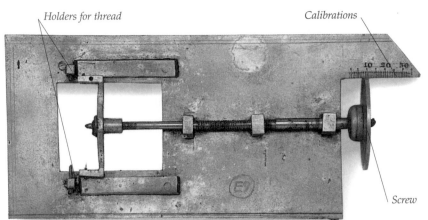

Holders for thread

Calibrations

10 20 50

Screw

MEASURING ACROSS VAST DISTANCES
The bigger the telescope, the larger its scale will be. This means that measurements become increasingly crude. A micrometer can be set to provide extremely fine gradations, a necessary element when measuring the distances between two stars in the sky that are a very long way away. This micrometer was made by William Herschel. To pinpoint the location of a star, a fine hair or piece of spiderweb was threaded between two holders that were adjusted by means of the finely turned screw on the side.

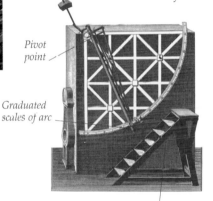

Pivot point

Graduated scales of arc

Ladder for an astronomer to reach the eyepiece

N EQUATORIAL MOUNT
elescopes have to be mounted in some way. The equatorial ount used to be the favored mount, and is still preferred y amateur astronomers. The telescope is lined up with arth's axis, using the Pole Star as a guide. In the southern emisphere, other stars near the sky's south pole are used. he telescope can swing around this axis, automatically llowing the tracks of stars in the sky as they circle around e Pole Star. The equatorial mount was used for this 28-in 1-cm) refractor, installed at Greenwich, England in 1893.

ASTRONOMICAL QUADRANT
Most early telescopes were mounted on astronomical quadrants (p.16), and to stabilize the telescope, the quadrant was usually mounted on a wall. These kinds of telescopes are called mural quadrants from the Latin word for "wall," *murus*. The telescope was hung on a single pivot-point, so that its eyepiece could be moved along the graduated scale of the arc of the quadrant (p.16). In this way, astronomers could accurately measure the altitude of the stars they were observing.

GEMINI TELESCOPE
There are two Gemini Telescopes, one in Hawaii (in the northern hemisphere) and one in Chile (in the southern hemisphere). Together they give optical and infrared coverage of the whole sky. Each Gemini Telescope has a single active mirror that is 26.6 ft (8.1 m) across. The mirrors have protective silver coatings that help prevent interference in the infrared spectrum.

GRINDING MIRRORS
The 16-ft (5-m) mirror of the famous Hale telescope on Mount Palomar in California was cast in 1934 from 35 tons of molten Pyrex. The grinding of the mirror to achieve the correct curved shape was interrupted by World War II. It was not completed until 1947. Mount Palomar was one of the first high-altitude observatories, built where the atmosphere is thinner and the effects of pollution are reduced.

A SEGMENTED-MIRROR TELESCOPE
Inside each of the twin Keck Telescopes on Hawaii, there is a primary six-sided mirror that is around 33 ft (10 m) wide. It is made up of 36 smaller hexagonal mirrors, which are 6 ft (1.8 m) across. Each small mirror is monitored by a computer and its position can be adjusted to correct any sagging. The two telescopes are also linked so that they can combine their signals for an even more accurate image.

Observatories

THE LEVIATHAN OF PARSONSTOWN
William Parsons (1800–1867), the third Earl of Rosse, was determined to build the largest reflecting telescope. At Parsonstown in Ireland he managed to cast a 72-in (182-cm) mirror, weighing nearly 4 tons and magnifying 800–1,000 times. When the "Leviathan" was built in 1845, it was used by Parsons to make significant discoveries concerning the structure of galaxies and nebulae (pp.64-67).

AN **OBSERVATORY IS A PLACE** where astronomers watch the heavens. The shapes of observatories have changed greatly over the ages (p.12). The earliest were quiet places set atop city walls or in towers. Height was important so that the astronomer could have a panoramic, 360° view of the horizon. The Babylonians and the Greeks certainly had rudimentary observatories, but the greatest of the early observatories were those in Islamic North Africa and the Middle East—Baghdad, Cairo, and Damascus. The great observatory at Baghdad had a huge 20-ft (6-m) quadrant and a 56-ft (17-m) stone sextant. It must have looked very much like the observatory at Jaipur—the only one of this type of observatory to remain relatively intact (below). As the great Islamic empires waned and science reawakened in western Europe, observatories took on a different shape. The oldest observatory still in use is the Observatoire de Paris, founded in 1667 (p.32). A less hospitable climate meant that open-air observatories were impractical. The astronomer and the instruments needed a roof over their heads. Initially, these roofs were constructed with sliding panels or doors that could be pulled back to open the building to the night sky. Since the 19th century, most large telescopes are covered with huge rotatable domes. The earliest domes were made of papier mâché, the only substance known to be sufficiently light and strong. Now most domes are made of aluminum.

BEIJING OBSERVATORY
The Great Observatory set on the walls of the Forbidden City in Beijing, China, was constructed with the help of Jesuit priests from Portugal in 1660 on the site of an older observatory. The instruments included two great armillary spheres (p.15), a huge celestial globe (p.14), a graduated azimuth horizon ring, and an astronomical quadrant and sextant (p.16). The shapes of these instruments were copied from woodcut illustrations in Tycho Brahe's *Mechanica* of 1598 (p.22).

JAIPUR, INDIA
Early observations were carried out by the naked eye from the top of monumental architectural structures. The observatory at Jaipur in Rajasthan, India, was built by Maharajah Jai Singh in 1726. The monuments include a massive sundial, the Samrat Yantra, and a gnomon inclined at 27°, showing the latitude of Jaipur and the height of the Pole Star (p.17). There is also a large astronomical sextant and a meridian chamber.

COMPUTER-DRIVEN TELESCOPE
Telescopes have become so big that astronomers are dwarfed by them. This 20-in (51-cm) solar coronagraph in the Crimean Astrophysical Observatory in the Ukraine is driven by computer-monitored engines. A coronagraph is a type of solar telescope that measures the outermost layers of the Sun's atmosphere (p.42).

What is a meridian?

Meridian lines are imaginary coordinates running from pole to pole that are used to measure distances east and west on Earth's surface and in the heavens. Meridian lines are also known as lines of longitude. The word meridian comes from the Latin word *meridies*, meaning "the midday," because the Sun crosses a local meridian at noon. Certain meridians became important because astronomers used them in observatories when they set up their telescopes for positional astronomy. This means that all their measurements of the sky and Earth were made relative to their local meridian. Until the end of the 19th century, there were a number of national meridians in observatories in Paris, Cadiz, and Naples.

Prime
Meridian

THE GREENWICH MERIDIAN
In 1884 there was an international conference in Washington, DC to establish a single Zero Meridian, or Prime Meridian, for the world. The meridian running through the Airy Transit Circle—a telescope mounted so that it rotated in a north–south plane—at the Royal Greenwich Observatory outside London was chosen. This choice was largely a matter of convenience. Most of the shipping charts and all of the American railroad system used Greenwich as their longitude zero at the time. South of Greenwich, the Prime Meridian crosses through France and Africa, and then runs across the Atlantic Ocean all the way to the South Pole.

CROSSING THE MERIDIAN
In 1850 the seventh Astronomer Royal of Great Britain, Sir George Biddle Airy (1801–1892), decided he wanted a new telescope. In building it, he moved the previous Prime Meridian for England 19 ft (5.75 m) to the east. The Greenwich Meridian is marked by a green laser beam projected into the sky and by an illuminated line that bisects Airy's Transit Circle at the Royal Observatory.

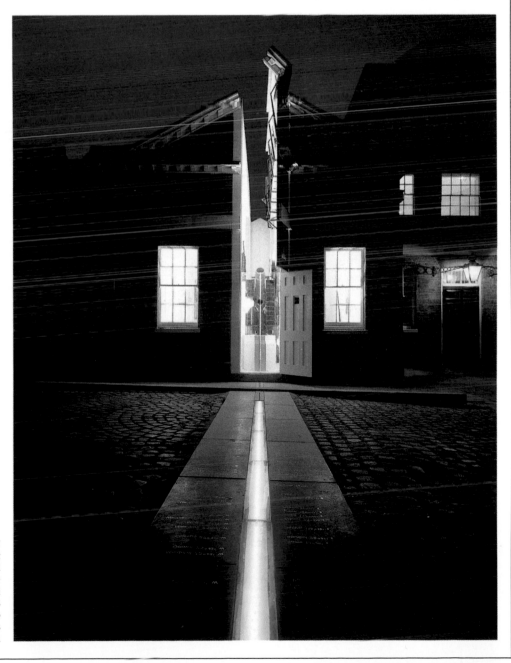

Astronomers

THE MAIN DIFFERENCE BETWEEN ASTRONOMERS and most other scientists is that astronomers can only conduct direct experiments in the solar system—by sending spacecraft. They cannot experiment on stars and galaxies. The key to most astronomy is careful and systematic observing. Astronomers must watch and wait for things to happen. Early astronomers could do little more than plot the positions of the heavenly bodies, follow their movements in the sky, and be alert for unexpected events, such as the arrival of a comet. From the 19th century, astronomers began to investigate the physics of the universe by analyzing light and other radiation from space. But the sorts of questions astrophysicists still try to answer today are very similar to the questions that puzzled the earliest Greek philosophers—what is the universe, how is it shaped, and how do I fit into it?

FASHIONABLE AMATEURS
By the 18th century the science of the stars became an acceptable pastime for the rich and sophisticated. The large number of small telescopes that survive from this period is evidence of how popular amateur astronomy had become.

THE NAUTICAL ALMANAC
First published in 1766, *The Nautical Almanac* provides a series of tables showing the distances between certain key stars and the Moon at three-hour intervals. Navigators can use the tables to help calculate their longitude at sea, when they are out of sight of land (p.31).

FIRST ASTRONOMER ROYAL
England appointed its first Astronomer Royal, John Flamsteed (1646–1719), in 1675. He lived and worked at the Royal Observatory, Greenwich, built by King Charles II of England in the same year.

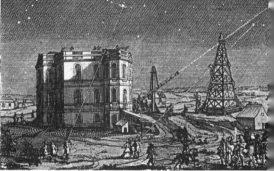

IN THE FAMILY
When the Observatoire de Paris was founded in 1667, the French King Louis XIV called a well-known Bolognese astronomer, Gian Domenico Cassini (1625–1712), to Paris to be the observatory's director. He was followed by three generations of Cassinis in the position: Jacques Cassini (1677–1756); César-François Cassini de Thury (1714–1784), who produced the first modern map of France; and Jean-Dominique Cassini (1748–1845). Most historians refer to this great succession of astronomers simply as Cassini I, Cassini II, Cassini III, and Cassini IV.

ASTRONOMY IN RUSSIA
The Russian astronomer Mikhail Lomonosov (1711–1765) was primarily interested in problems relating to the art of navigation and fixing latitude and longitude. During his observations of the 1761 transit of Venus (pp.50–51), he noticed that the planet seemed "smudgy," and suggested that Venus had a thick atmosphere, many times denser than that of Earth.

Peg marking α Cassiopeiae   *Peg marking α Aquarii*   *Rotating clock face*

Peg marking Antares

Peg marking α Hydrae

STAR CLOCK (1815)
One of the primary aspects of positional astronomy is measuring a star's position against a clock. This ingenious clock has the major stars inscribed on the surface of its rotating face. Placing pegs in the holes near the stars to be observed causes the clock to chime when the star is due to pass the local meridian.

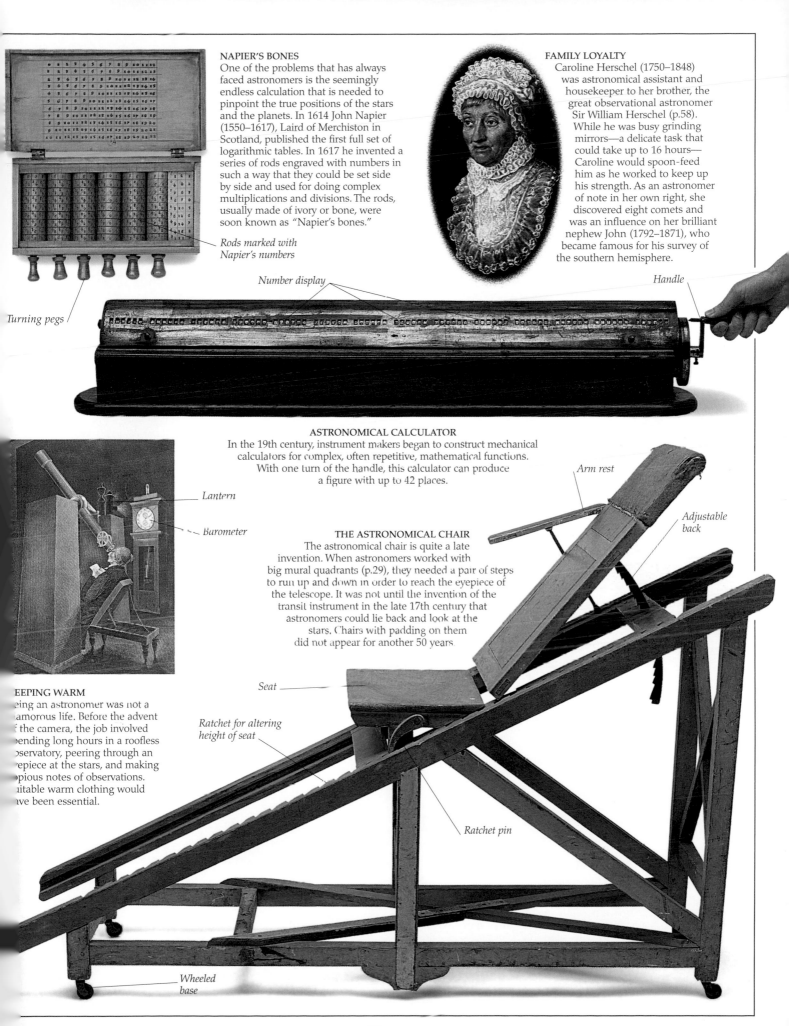

NAPIER'S BONES

One of the problems that has always faced astronomers is the seemingly endless calculation that is needed to pinpoint the true positions of the stars and the planets. In 1614 John Napier (1550–1617), Laird of Merchiston in Scotland, published the first full set of logarithmic tables. In 1617 he invented a series of rods engraved with numbers in such a way that they could be set side by side and used for doing complex multiplications and divisions. The rods, usually made of ivory or bone, were soon known as "Napier's bones."

Rods marked with Napier's numbers

Turning pegs

FAMILY LOYALTY

Caroline Herschel (1750–1848) was astronomical assistant and housekeeper to her brother, the great observational astronomer Sir William Herschel (p.58). While he was busy grinding mirrors—a delicate task that could take up to 16 hours— Caroline would spoon-feed him as he worked to keep up his strength. As an astronomer of note in her own right, she discovered eight comets and was an influence on her brilliant nephew John (1792–1871), who became famous for his survey of the southern hemisphere.

Number display

Handle

ASTRONOMICAL CALCULATOR

In the 19th century, instrument makers began to construct mechanical calculators for complex, often repetitive, mathematical functions. With one turn of the handle, this calculator can produce a figure with up to 42 places.

Lantern

Barometer

Arm rest

Adjustable back

THE ASTRONOMICAL CHAIR

The astronomical chair is quite a late invention. When astronomers worked with big mural quadrants (p.29), they needed a pair of steps to run up and down in order to reach the eyepiece of the telescope. It was not until the invention of the transit instrument in the late 17th century that astronomers could lie back and look at the stars. Chairs with padding on them did not appear for another 50 years.

Seat

Ratchet for altering height of seat

Ratchet pin

KEEPING WARM

Being an astronomer was not a glamorous life. Before the advent of the camera, the job involved spending long hours in a roofless observatory, peering through an eyepiece at the stars, and making copious notes of observations. Suitable warm clothing would have been essential.

Wheeled base

Spectroscopy

ASTRONOMERS HAVE BEEN ABLE to study the chemical composition of the stars and how hot they are for more than a century by means of spectroscopy. A spectroscope breaks down the "white" light coming from a celestial body into an extremely detailed spectrum. Working on Isaac Newton's discovery of the spectrum (p.25), a German optician, Josef Fraunhofer (1787–1826), examined the spectrum created by light coming from the Sun and noticed a number of dark lines crossing it. In 1859 another German, Gustav Kirchhoff (1824–1887), discovered the significance of Fraunhofer's lines. They are produced by chemicals in the cooler, upper layers of the Sun (or a star) absorbing light. Each chemical has its own pattern of lines, like a fingerprint. By looking at the spectrum of the Sun, astronomers have found all the elements that are known on the Earth in the Sun's atmosphere.

THE COLORS OF THE RAINBOW
A rainbow is formed by the Sun shining through raindrops. The light is refracted by droplets of water as if each one were a prism.

Prism splits the light into its colors

The spectrum

Infrared band

Red

Rays of white light

Sodium lamp

Violet

HERSCHEL DISCOVERS INFRARED
In 1800 Sir William Herschel (p.58) set up a number of experiments to test the relationship between heat and light. He repeated Newton's experiment of splitting white light into a spectrum (p.25) and, by masking all the colors but one, was able to measure the individual temperatures of each color in the spectrum. He discovered that the red end of the spectrum was hotter than the violet end, but was surprised to note that an area where he could see no color, next to the red end of the spectrum, was much hotter than the rest of the spectrum. He called this area infrared or "below the red."

The spectroscope would be mounted on a telescope here

Stand for photographic plate

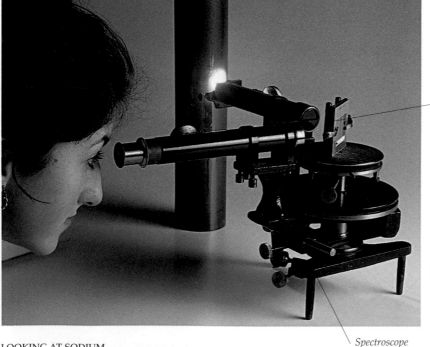

Diffraction grating

Solar spectrum showing absorption lines

Sodium

Emission spectrum of sodium

Sodium

Spectroscope

LOOKING AT SODIUM

Viewing a sodium flame through a spectroscope can help to explain how spectroscopy works in space. According to Gustav Kirchhoff's first law of spectral analysis, a hot dense gas at high pressure produces a continuous spectrum of all colors. His second law states that a hot rarefied gas at low pressure produces an emission line spectrum, characterized by bright spectral lines against a dark background. His third law states that when light from a hot dense gas passes through a cooler gas before it is viewed, it produces an absorption line spectrum—a bright spectrum riddled with a number of dark, fine lines.

WHAT IS IN THE SU[N]

When a sodium flame is viewed through a spectroscope (le[ft], the emission spectrum produces the characteristic bright yell[ow] lines (above). The section of the Sun's spectrum (top) show[s a] number of tiny "gaps" or dark lines. These are the Fraunho[fer] lines from which the chemical composition of the Sun [can] be determined. The two dark lines in the yellow part of [the] spectrum correspond to the sodium. As there is no sodi[um] in Earth's atmosphere, it must be coming from the S[un.]

KIRCHHOFF AND BUNSEN
Following the invention of
the clean-flame burner by the
German chemist Robert Bunsen
(1811–1899), it was possible to
study the effect of different
chemical vapors on the known
pattern of spectral lines. Together,
Gustav Kirchhoff and Bunsen
invented a new instrument
called the spectroscope to
measure these effects. Within
a few years, they had managed
to isolate the spectra for many
known substances, as well
as to discover a few
unknown elements.

*Continuous
spectrum*

ABSORBING COLOR
To prove his laws
of spectral analysis,
Kirchhoff used sodium
gas to show that when
white light is directed
through the gas, the
characteristic color
of the sodium is
absorbed and the spectrum shows black lines where the sodium should
have appeared. In the experiment shown above, a continuous spectrum (top)
is produced by shining white light through a lens. When a petri dish of the
chemical potassium permanganate in solution is placed between the lens
and the light, some of the color of the spectrum is absorbed.

*The spectrum
of potassium
permanganate*

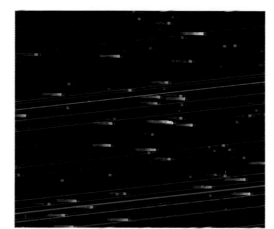

SPECTRUM OF THE STARS
By closely examining the spectral lines
in the light received from a distant star, the
astronomer can detect these "fingerprints" and
uncover the chemical composition of the object
being viewed. Furthermore, the heat of the
source can also be discovered by studying the
spectral lines. Temperature can be measured
by the intensities of individual lines in their
spectra. The width of the line provides
information about temperature, movement,
and presence of magnetic fields. With
magnification, each of these spectra
can be analyzed in more detail.

Eyepiece

Latticework frame

Prisms

Micrometer (p.29)

Eyepiece

NORMAN LOCKYER (1836–1920)
During the solar eclipse of 1868, a
number of astronomers picked up a
new spectral line in the upper surface of
the Sun, the chromosphere (p.43). The English
astronomer Lockyer realized that the line did not coincide with
any of the known elements. The newly discovered element was
named helium (Helios is Greek for the sun god). It was not until
1895, however, that helium was discovered on Earth.

THE SPECTROSCOPE
A spectroscope uses a series of
prisms or a diffraction grating—a device
that diffracts light through fine lines to form
a spectrum—to split light into its constituent
wavelengths (pp.36–37). Before the era of
photography, an astronomer would view the
spectrum produced with the eye, but now it is
mostly recorded with an electronic detector
called a CCD (p.41). This 19th-century spectroscope
uses a prism to split the light.

The radio telescope

W$_{\text{ITH THE DISCOVERY OF}}$ nonvisible light, such as infrared (p.34), and electromagnetic and X-ray radiation, scientists began to wonder if objects in space might emit invisible radiation as well. The first such radiation to be discovered (by accident) was radio waves—the longest wavelengths of the electromagnetic spectrum. To detect radio waves, astronomers constructed huge dishes in order to capture the long waves and "see" detail. Even so, early radio telescopes were never large enough, proportionally, to catch the fine features that optical telescopes could resolve. Today, by electronically combining the output from many radio telescopes, a dish the size of Earth can be synthesized, revealing details many times finer than optical telescopes. Astronomers routinely study all radiation from objects in space, often using detectors high above Earth's atmosphere (p.11).

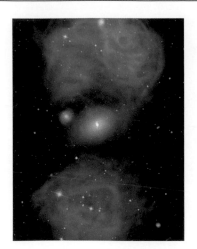

RADIO GALAXY
This image shows the radio emission from huge invisible clouds of very hot gas beamed out from a black hole in the center of a galaxy called NGC 1316. The maps of the radio clouds, shown in orange, were made by the Very Large Array (p.37).

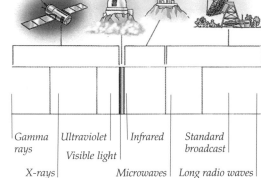

Space telescope　*Optical telescope*　*Infrared telescope*　*Radio telescope*

| Gamma rays | Ultraviolet | | Infrared | Standard broadcast |
| X-rays | | Visible light | Microwaves | Long radio waves |

ELECTROMAGNETIC SPECTRUM
The range of frequencies of electromagnetic radiation is known as the electromagnetic spectrum. Very low on the scale are radio waves, rising to infrared (p.34), visible light, ultraviolet, and X-rays, with gamma rays at the highest frequency end of the spectrum. The radiations that pass through Earth's atmosphere are light and radio waves, though infrared penetrates to the highest mountaintops. The remainder can only be detected by sending instruments into space (pp.38–39). All telescopes—radio, optical, and infrared—"see" different aspects of the sky, caused by the different physical processes going on.

EVIDENCE OF RADIO RADIATION
The first evidence of radio radiation coming from outer space was collected by the American scientist Karl Jansky (1905–1950) who, in 1931, using homemade equipment (above), investigated the static affecting short-wavelength radio-telephone communication. He deduced that this static must be coming from the center of our galaxy (pp.66–67).

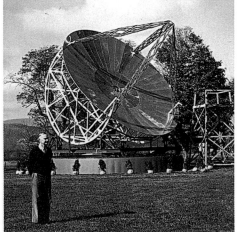

AMATEUR ASTRONOMER
On hearing about Jansky's discoveries, American amateur astronomer Grote Reber (1911–2002) built a large, movable radio receiver in his backyard in 1936. It had a parabolic surface to collect the radio waves. With this 29-ft (9-m) dish, he began to map the radio emissions coming from the Milky Way. For years Reber was the only radio astronomer in the world.

ARECIBO TELESCOPE
The mammoth Arecibo radio dish is built in a natural limestone concavity in the jungle south of Arecibo, Puerto Rico. The "dish," which is a huge web of steel mesh, measures 1,000 ft (305 m) across, providing a 20-acre (8-hectare) collecting surface. Although the dish is fixed, overhead antennae can be moved to different parts of the sky.

HOT SPOTS

Radio astronomers can create temperature maps of planets. This false-color map shows temperatures just below Mercury's surface. Because Mercury is so close to the Sun, the hottest area is on Mercury's equator, shown here as red. The blue areas are the coolest.

BERNARD LOVELL

The English astronomer Bernard Lovell (b. 1913) was a pioneer of radio astronomy. He developed a research station at Jodrell Bank, England, in 1945 using surplus army radar equipment. He is seen here in the control room of the 250-ft (76-m) diameter Mark 1 radio telescope (later renamed the Lovell Telescope in his honor). The telescope's giant dish was commissioned in 1957.

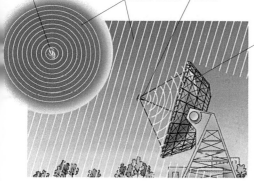

Galaxy

Radio waves *Focus*

Parabolic dish

HIGH-TECH TELESCOPE

Communications technology allows astronomers to work nearly anywhere in the world. All they need is a computer link. While optical telescopes are sited far from built-up areas (p.31), clear skies are not necessary for radio astronomy. This telescope is the world's largest, fully steerable, single-dish radio telescope; it is 330 ft (100 m) in diameter and is located near Bonn, Germany.

HOW A RADIO TELESCOPE WORKS

The parabolic dish of a radio telescope can be steered to pick up radio signals. It focuses them to a point from which they are sent to a receiver, a recorder, and then a data room at a control center. Computer equipment then converts intensities of the incoming radio waves into images that are recognizable to our eyes as objects from space (p.61).

Parabolic dish

A VERY LARGE ARRAY

Scientists soon realized that radio telescopes could be connected together to form very large receiving surfaces. For example, two dishes 60 miles (100 km) apart can be linked electronically so that their receiving area is the equivalent of a 60-mile- (100 km-) wide dish. One of the largest arrangements of telescopes is the Very Large Array (VLA) set up in the desert near Socorro, New Mexico. Twenty-seven parabolic dishes have been arranged in a huge "Y," covering more than 17 miles (27 km).

Mounting and support

Venturing into space

SINCE THE LAST APOLLO MISSION to the Moon in 1972, no human has traveled any farther into space than Earth orbit. But the exploration and exploitation of space have not stopped. Dozens of spacecraft carrying instruments and cameras have traveled far beyond the Moon to investigate planets and moons, asteroids and comets, the Sun and interplanetary space. Instead of competing, countries collaborate and share costs. Space science and technology bring huge benefits to our lives. TV services use orbiting communications satellites. Ships, aircraft, and road traffic navigate using satellite signals. Military satellites are used for surveillance. Weather forecasts use images from meteorological satellites and resources satellites gather detailed information about Earth's surface. And NASA is now planning to send more astronauts to the Moon by 2020. They will set up a lunar base for research and for testing the technologies needed to send humans to Mars.

LUNAR PROBES
The former USSR launched *Sputnik 1*, the first artificial satellite, into space in 1957. Between the late 1950s and 1976, several probes were sent to explore the surface of the Moon. *Luna 1* was the first successful lunar probe. It passed within 3,730 miles (6,000 km) of the Moon. *Luna 3* was the first probe to send back pictures to Earth of the far side of the Moon (pp.44–45). The first to achieve a soft landing was *Luna 9* in February 1966. *Luna 16* collected soil samples, bringing them back without any human involvement. The success of these missions forced people to take space exploration more seriously.

Luna 1

GETTING INTO SPACE
The American physicist Robert Goddard (1882–1945) launched the first liquid-fueled rocket in 1926. This fuel system overcame the major obstacle to launching an orbiting satellite, which was the weight of solid fuels. If a rocket is to reach a speed great enough to escape Earth's gravitational field, it needs a thrust greater than the weight it is carrying.

THE FIRST HUMAN IN SPACE
On April 12, 1961, the former USSR (now Russia) launched the 5-ton spaceship *Vostok 1*. It was flown by the cosmonaut Yuri Gagarin (1934–1968), who made a complete circuit of Earth at a height of 188 miles (303 km). He remained in space for 1 hour and 29 minutes before landing back safely in the USSR. He was hailed as a national hero and is seen here being lauded by the Premier of the USSR, Nikita Khrushchev.

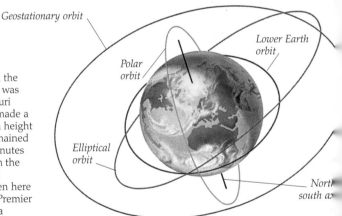

Geostationary orbit

Lower Earth orbit

Polar orbit

Elliptical orbit

North south a...

SATELLITE ORBI...
A satellite is sent into ... orbit that is most suitable for t... kind of work it has to do. Spa... telescopes such as Hubble (p.1... take the low orbits—375 mi... (600 km) above Earth's surfa... US spy and surveillance satelli... orbit on a north–south axis... get a view of the whole Ear... while those belonging to Rus... often follow elliptical orbits t... allow them to spend m... time over their own territo... Communications and weat... satellites are positioned above ... equator. They take exactly 24 ho... to complete an orbit, and theref... seem to hover above the same po... on Earth's surface—known ... geostationary or...

LUNAR LANDING
Between 1969 and 1972, six crewed lunar landings took place. The first astronaut to set foot on the Moon was Neil Armstrong (b. 1930) on July 21, 1969. Scientifically, one of the major reasons for Moon landings was to try to understand the origin of the Moon itself and to understand its history and evolution. This photograph shows American astronaut James Irwin with the *Apollo 15* Lunar Rover in 1971.

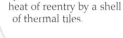

The Space Shuttle

The first flight of a Space Shuttle was in 1981. Since then, five Shuttles have made a total of over 120 flights into Earth orbit. Their tasks have included launching satellites, repairing the Hubble Space Telescope, and taking parts and crew to the International Space Station. Two of the Shuttles have been destroyed in accidents and the others will go out of service in 2010.

COOPERATION IN SPACE

The European Space Agency (ESA) is an organization through which 16 European countries collaborate on a joint space program. It provides the means for a group of smaller countries to participate in space exploration and share the benefits of space-age technology. ESA has its own rocket, called *Ariane*, which is launched from a spaceport in French Guiana. In 2003, this *Ariane 5* rocket launched the *SMART-1* spacecraft on a mission to orbit the Moon and to test a new spacecraft propulsion technology. In addition to the US and Russia, several other major countries have their own space agencies, including Japan and China.

THE SPACE SHUTTLE

The Shuttle is boosted into space by two huge, reusable, solid-fuel booster rockets. They are jettisoned and then fall back to Earth, slowed by parachutes, so they can be retrieved. The Shuttle returns to Earth and lands at about 215 mph (350 km/h). It is protected from the intense heat of reentry by a shell of thermal tiles.

UNDERWATER TRAINING

In space, astronauts experience weightlessness, or zero gravity. This is not an easy thing to simulate on Earth. The closest approximation is to train astronauts underwater to move and operate machinery. Even then the effect of resistance in water gives a false impression.

‸VING IN SPACE

‸nstruction of the International Space Station (ISS) began in ‸98 and continues until 2010. It is a joint project between the US, ‸rope, Russia, Canada, and Japan. The ten main modules and other ‸rts are being transported by the Space Shuttle or by an uncrewed ‸ssian space vehicle. The first crew arrived in 2000, and there ‸ve been at least two astronauts on board ever since. The ISS takes ‸ minutes to orbit Earth at an average height of 220 miles (354 km).

Felt protects parts where heat does not exceed 700°F (370°C)

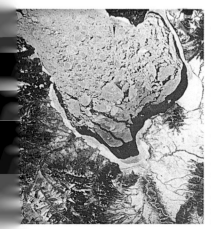

BENEFITS OF SATELLITES

Meteorological satellites can monitor the changing patterns of the weather and plot ocean currents, which play a major role in determining Earth's climate. Data gathered by monitoring such vast expanses as this Russian ice floe can be used to predict climate change. Resource satellites are used for geological and ecological research. For example, they map the distribution of plankton—a major part of the food chain—in ocean waters.

Solid-fuel rocket booster

Shuttle orbiter

The solar system

THE SOLAR SYSTEM is the group of planets, moons, and space debris orbiting around our Sun. It is held together by the gravitational pull of the Sun, which is nearly 1,000 times more massive than all the planets put together. The solar system was probably formed from a huge cloud of interstellar gas and dust that contracted under the force of its own gravity five billion years ago. The planets are divided into two groups. The four planets closest to the Sun are called "terrestrial," from the Latin word *terra*, meaning "land," because they are small and dense and have hard surfaces. The four outer planets are called "Jovian" because, like Jupiter, they are giant planets made largely of gas and liquid. Between Mars and Jupiter and beyond Neptune there are belts of very small bodies and dwarf planets called the asteroid belt and the Kuiper belt.

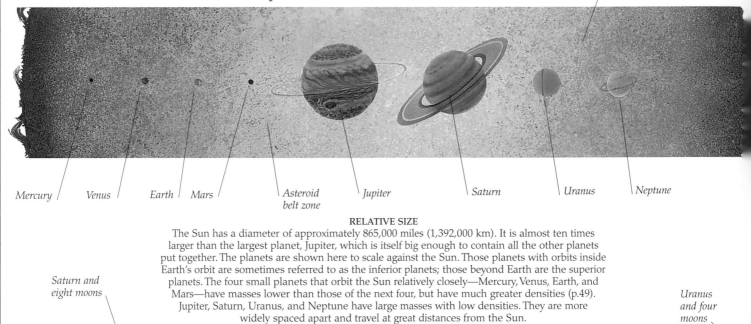

Sun

Mercury *Venus* *Earth* *Mars* *Asteroid belt zone* *Jupiter* *Saturn* *Uranus* *Neptune*

RELATIVE SIZE
The Sun has a diameter of approximately 865,000 miles (1,392,000 km). It is almost ten times larger than the largest planet, Jupiter, which is itself big enough to contain all the other planets put together. The planets are shown here to scale against the Sun. Those planets with orbits inside Earth's orbit are sometimes referred to as the inferior planets; those beyond Earth are the superior planets. The four small planets that orbit the Sun relatively closely—Mercury, Venus, Earth, and Mars—have masses lower than those of the next four, but have much greater densities (p.49). Jupiter, Saturn, Uranus, and Neptune have large masses with low densities. They are more widely spaced apart and travel at great distances from the Sun.

Saturn and eight moons

Neptune and one moon

Venus

Earth

Moon

Mercury

Mars and two Moons

Sun

Jupiter and nine moons

Uranus and four moons

Turning handle

Gearing mechanism

TEACHING ASTRONOMY
During the 19th century, the astronomy of the solar system was taught by mechanical instruments such as this orrery. The complex gearing of the machine is operated by a crank handle, which ensures that each planet completes its solar orbit relative to the other planets. The planets are roughly to a scale of 50,000 miles (80,500 km) to 1 in (3 cm), except for the Sun, which would need to be 17 in (43 in diameter for the model to be accurate.

CELESTIAL MECHANICS
The Frenchman Pierre Simon Laplace (1749–1827) was the first scientist to make an attempt to compute all the motions of the Moon and the planets by mathematical means. In his five-volume work, *Traité de méchanique céleste* (1799–1825), Laplace treated all motion in the solar system as a purely mathematical problem, using his work to support the theory of universal gravitation (p.25). His idea, for which he was severely criticized during the following century, was that the heavens were a great celestial machine, like a timepiece that, once set in motion, would go on forever.

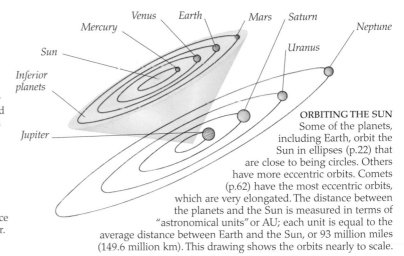

Mercury · Venus · Earth · Mars · Saturn · Neptune
Sun · Uranus
Inferior planets
Jupiter

ORBITING THE SUN
Some of the planets, including Earth, orbit the Sun in ellipses (p.22) that are close to being circles. Others have more eccentric orbits. Comets (p.62) have the most eccentric orbits, which are very elongated. The distance between the planets and the Sun is measured in terms of "astronomical units" or AU; each unit is equal to the average distance between Earth and the Sun, or 93 million miles (149.6 million km). This drawing shows the orbits nearly to scale.

Photographing the planets

One of the key tasks of space missions (pp.38–39) is to send back pictures of distant planets and moons. They do this using imaging devices very similar to those used in digital cameras. The heart of the system is a CCD, or charge-coupled device. This is a silicon chip with thousands of light-sensitive pixels, or picture elements. The amount of light falling on each pixel produces a different electrical signal. This is read by an onboard computer and converted into a stream of digital signals that can be radioed back to Earth, where they are reconstructed into the image by computer.

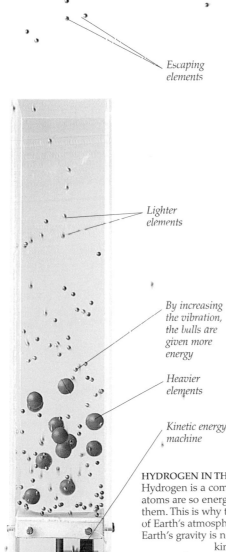

Escaping elements

Lighter elements

By increasing the vibration, the balls are given more energy

Heavier elements

Kinetic energy machine

Mariner 9 photographs of the surface of Mars

CREATING COLOR
The CCDs used in astronomy rarely produce color images directly, but use the most sensitive black-and-white chips. To get a color image, separate images are taken through color filters, and the results are combined in a computer to give a realistic color view.

HYDROGEN IN THE SOLAR SYSTEM
Hydrogen is a common element in the solar system. Hydrogen atoms are so energetic that lightweight planets cannot hang on to them. This is why the heavier nitrogen makes up such a high percentage of Earth's atmosphere (p.46). Lighter hydrogen has escaped because Earth's gravity is not strong enough to hold on to it. The red balls in this kinetic energy machine represent the heavier elements; the tiny silver balls represent the lighter elements, such as hydrogen. Our massive Sun is made up largely of hydrogen. Its great mass pulls the hydrogen inward and, at its core, hydrogen fuses into helium under the extreme heat and pressure. It is this reaction, like a giant hydrogen bomb, that makes the Sun shine. Hydrogen also makes up a large part of Jupiter, Saturn, Uranus, and Neptune (pp.54–61).

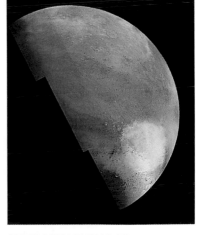

COLOR MOSAIC OF MARS
The detail in an individual CCD image of a planet is limited by the number of pixels on the chip. To get a high-quality image, several shots are taken of different parts of the planet, and then a mosaic is produced, like this one of Mars.

The Sun

Aʟᴍᴏsᴛ ᴇᴠᴇʀʏ ᴀɴᴄɪᴇɴᴛ ᴄᴜʟᴛᴜʀᴇ recognized the Sun as the giver of life and primary power behind events here on Earth. The Sun is the center of our solar system, our local star. It has no permanent features because it is gaseous—mainly incandescent hydrogen. The temperature of the Sun's visible yellow disk—the photosphere—is about 9,900°F (5,500°C). Over the photosphere, there are layers of hotter gas—the chromosphere and corona. The thin gas in the corona is at about a million degrees. By using spectroscopic analysis (pp.34–35), scientists know that the Sun, like most stars (pp.64–65), is made up mostly of hydrogen. In its core, the hydrogen nuclei are so compressed that they eventually fuse into helium. This is the same thing that happens in a hydrogen atomic bomb. Every minute, the Sun converts 240 million metric tons of mass into energy. Albert Einstein's famous formula, $E=mc^2$, shows how mass and energy are mutually interchangeable (p.67), helping scientists to understand the source of the Sun's energy.

VIEWING THE SUN
Even though the Sun is more than 93 million miles (149 million km) from Earth, its rays are still bright enough to damage the eyes permanently. The Sun should *never* be viewed directly and certainly not through a telescope or binoculars. Galileo went blind looking at the Sun. This astronomer is at the Kitt Peak National Observatory in Arizona. Two mirrors at the top of the solar telescope tower reflect the Sun's image down a tube to the mirror below. Inside the tube there is a vacuum. This prevents distortion that would be caused by the air in the tower.

THE DIPLEIDOSCOPE
Local noon occurs when the Sun crosses the local north–south meridian (p.31). In the 19th century a more accurate device than the gnomon (p.18) was sought to indicate when noon occurred. The dipleidoscope, invented in 1842, is an instrument with a hollow, right-angled prism, which has two silvered sides and one clear side. As the Sun passes directly overhead, the two reflected images are resolved into a single one. This shows when it is local noon.

CHANGING SEASONS
The seasons change because Earth rotates on a north–south axis (p.16) as it orbits the Sun. The axis is tilted at an angle of 23½°. When the South Pole is tilted toward the Sun, the southern hemisphere experiences summer and the northern hemisphere winter. The path of the Sun across the sky also changes because of this tilt. It is lower in winter, and the days are shorter, and higher in the summer when the days are longer. Countries close to the equator do not have such extremes of temperature or changes in the length of day.

Earth's axis

Southern hemisphere tilted toward the Sun

Summer in Australia

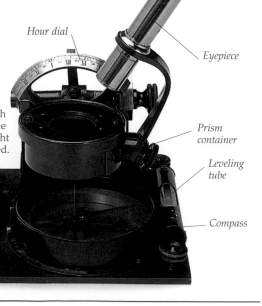

Hour dial

Eyepiece

Prism container

Leveling tube

Compass

Chromosphere

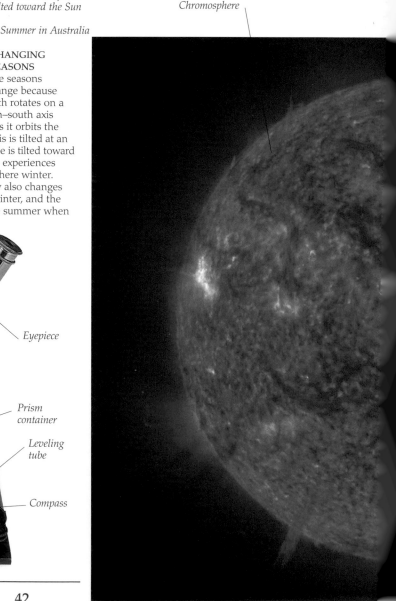

THE CORONA

The outermost layer of the Sun's atmosphere is called the corona. Even though it extends millions of miles into space, it cannot be seen during the day because of the brightness of the blue sky. During a total eclipse, the corona appears like a crown around the Moon. It is clearly seen in this picture of a total eclipse over Mexico in March 1970.

Corona

Sun

Moon   *Cast shadow*   *Earth*

SOLAR ECLIPSE

A solar eclipse happens when the Moon passes directly between Earth and the Sun, casting a shadow on the surface of Earth. From an earthly perspective, it looks as if the Moon has blocked out the light of the Sun. Total eclipses of the Sun are very rare in any given location, occurring roughly once every 360 years in the same place. However, several solar eclipses may occur each year.

Prominence

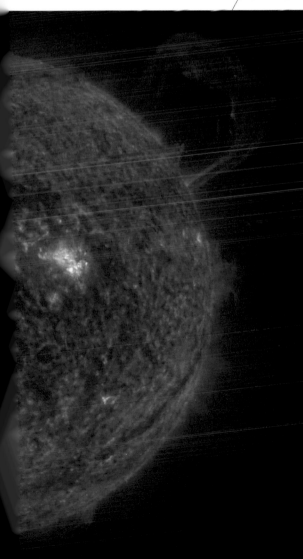

Sunspots

Sunspots are cooler areas on the Sun, where strong magnetic fields disturb the flow of heat from the core to the photosphere. Typical sunspots last about a week and are twice as big as Earth. They often form in pairs or groups. The number of sunspots appearing on the Sun rises and falls over an 11-year period. This is called the solar cycle. At sunspot maximum, the Sun also experiences large explosive eruptions called flares, which blast streams of particles into space.

PLOTTING THE SUNSPOTS

By observing the changing position of sunspots, we can see that the Sun is spinning. Unlike the planets, however, the whole mass of the Sun does not spin at the same rate because it is not solid. The Sun's equator takes 25 Earth days to make one complete rotation. The Sun's poles take nearly 30 days to accomplish the same task. These photographs are a record of the movements of a large spot group over 14 days in March/April 1947.

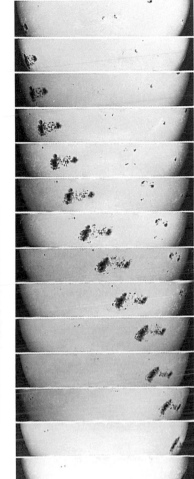

CORONAL LOOPS

Huge loops of very hot gas surge through the Sun's corona, guided by the magnetic field. These loops are about 30 times larger than Earth. This picture was taken from space in extreme ultraviolet light by NASA's TRACE satellite, launched in 1998 to study the Sun.

SOLAR PROMINENCE

Astronomers have learned much about the Sun from solar observatories operating in space, such as SOHO (the Solar and Heliospheric Observatory). This SOHO image of the Sun shows ultraviolet light from the chromosphere, a layer of hot gas above the yellow disk of the Sun we normally see. A huge prominence is erupting into the corona. Prominences like this usually last a few hours. They can fall back down or break off and cause gas to stream into space. Sometimes, the corona blasts huge clouds of gas into space. If one of these coronal mass ejections reaches Earth, it may cause a magnetic storm and trigger an aurora (northern or southern lights).

FACTS ABOUT THE SUN

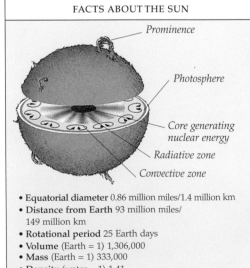

Prominence

Photosphere

Core generating nuclear energy

Radiative zone

Convective zone

- **Equatorial diameter** 0.86 million miles/1.4 million km
- **Distance from Earth** 93 million miles/ 149 million km
- **Rotational period** 25 Earth days
- **Volume** (Earth = 1) 1,306,000
- **Mass** (Earth = 1) 333,000
- **Density** (water = 1) 1.41
- **Temperature at surface** 9,900°F (5,500°C)

The Moon

EARLY MOON MAP
The same side of the Moon always faces toward Earth. Because the Moon's orbit is not circular and it travels at different speeds, we can see more than half of the Moon. This phenomenon, called libration, means that about 59 percent of the Moon's surface is visible from Earth. In 1647 Johannes Hevelius (1611–1687) published his lunar atlas *Selenographia* showing the Moon's librations.

THE MOON IS EARTH'S only satellite, about 239,000 miles (384,000 km) away. Next to the Sun it is the brightest object in our sky, more than 2,000 times as bright as Venus. Even without a telescope, we can see large areas on the Moon that are darker than the rest. Early observers imagined these might be seas, and they were given names such as the Sea of Tranquillity. We now know that there is neither liquid water nor an atmosphere on the Moon. The so-called "seas" are plains of volcanic rock where molten lava flowed into huge depressions caused by giant meteorites, then solidified. Volcanic activity on the moon ceased about two billion years ago.

Shadow is used to calculate the height of crater walls

COPERNICUS CRATER
The Moon's craters were formed between 3.5 and 4.5 billion years ago by the impact of countless meteorites. These impact craters are all named after famous astronomers and philosophers. Because the Moon has no atmosphere, there has been little erosion of its surface. This plaster model shows Copernicus crater, which is 56 miles (90 km) across and 11,000 ft (3,352 m) deep. Inside the crater there are mountains with peaks 8 miles (5 km) above the crater's floor.

Floor of the crater

Crater walls

Umbra or total shadow

Sun

Moon's orbit

Earth

Moon

Penumbra, or partial shadow

A LUNAR ECLIPSE
An eclipse happens when Earth passes directly between the Sun and the full Moon, so that Earth's shadow falls on the surface of the Moon. This obscures the Moon for the duration of the eclipse.

Lunar equator

Equatorial dial

Tide tables *Compass* *Latitude tables*

TIDE TABLES
The pull of the Moon's gravity (p.25), and to a lesser extent, the Sun's, causes the water of the seas on Earth to rise and fall. This effect is called a tide. When the Sun, the Moon, and Earth are all aligned at a new or full moon, the tidal "pull" is the greatest. These are called spring tides. When the Sun and the Moon are at right angles to each other, they produce smaller pulls called neap tides. This compendium (1569) contains plates with tables indicating the tides of some European cities. It was an essential instrument for sailors entering harbor.

PHASES OF THE MOON

The phases of the Moon are caused by the constantly changing series of angles formed by the Sun and the Moon as the Moon revolves around Earth. When the Moon and the Sun are on opposite sides of Earth, the Sun shines directly on the Moon's surface, resulting in a full moon. When the area of the lit surface increases, the Moon is said to be waxing; as it decreases, it is said to be waning.

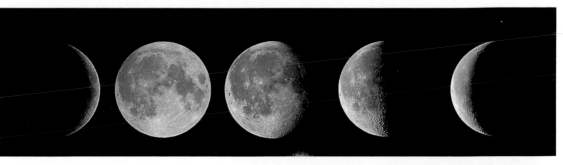

Waxing crescent moon at 4 days

Full moon at 14 days

Waning 19-day moon

Moon at 21 days

Moon at 24 days

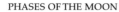

Gearing

Meridian circle

THE SURFACE OF THE MOON

The features on the far side of the Moon were a mystery until the late 1950s. This view of the terrain was taken by the *Apollo 11* lunar module in 1969. One of the primary purposes for exploring the Moon was to bring back samples of rock to study them and to discover their origins. The Moon is made up of similar but not identical material to that found on Earth. There is less iron on the Moon, but the major minerals are silicates as they are on Earth (p.47) –though they are slightly different in composition. This discovery supports the most popular theory of the Moon's origin. A small planet, about the size of Mars, is thought to have crashed into Earth about 4.5 billion years ago. The collision tore debris away from both bodies and the Moon formed from this material.

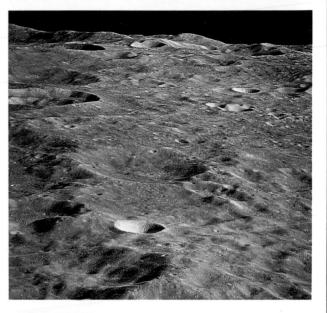

INVESTIGATING MOON ROCK

Rocks from the Moon have been investigated by geologists in the same way as they study Earth rocks. The rocks are ground down to thin slices and then looked at under a powerful microscope. The minerals, chiefly feldspar and olivine, which are abundant on Earth, are unweathered. This is exceptional for geologists because there are no Earth rocks that are totally unweathered.

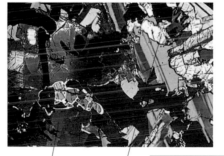

Cross-polarized light in the microscope gives colors

Watery clearness shows no weathering

Hour circle

Earth

A MOON GLOBE

Selenography is the study of the surface features of the Moon. This selenograph, created by the artist John Russell in 1797, is a Moon globe. Only a little more than half of the globe is filled with images because at that time the features on the far side of the Moon were unknown. Not until the Russians received the earliest transmissions from the *Luna 3* probe in October 1959 was it possible to see images of what was on the Moon's far side.

FACTS ABOUT THE MOON

Outer rocky crust

Partially molten region

Core (perhaps iron)

Dark rock mantle

- **Interval between two new moons** 29 days 12 hr 44 min
- **Temperature at surface** –245°F to 220°F (–155°C to 105°C)
- **Rotational period** 27.3 Earth days
- **Mean distance from Earth** 239,000 miles/384,000 km
- **Volume** (Earth = 1) 0.02
- **Mass** (Earth = 1) 0.012
- **Density** (water = 1) 3.34
- **Equatorial diameter** 2,160 miles/3,476 km

Earth

EARTH IS THE ONLY PLANET in the solar system that is capable of supporting advanced life. Its unique combination of liquid water, a rich oxygen- and nitrogen-based atmosphere, and dynamic weather patterns provide the basic elements for a diverse distribution of plant and animal life. Over millions of years, landforms and oceans have been constantly changing, mountains have been raised up and eroded away, and continental plates have drifted across Earth. The atmosphere acts like a blanket, evening out temperature extremes and keeping warmth in. Without this "greenhouse effect" (p.51), Earth would be about 60°F (33°C) cooler on average. Over the last few decades, scientists have measured a gradual increase in Earth's temperature. Glaciers and polar ice caps have begun to shrink. It is feared that human activity is causing this rapid change by increasing the amount of carbon dioxide and other "greenhouse gases" in the atmosphere.

EARTH AND THE MOON
The English astronomer James Bradley (1693–1762) noted that many stars appear to have irregularities in their paths. He deduced that this is due to the effect of observing from an Earth that wobbles on its axis, caused by the gravitational pull of the Moon (p.45).

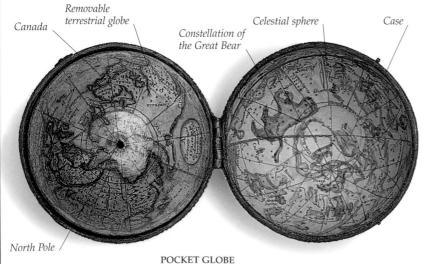

CONSTANT GEOGRAPHICAL CHANGE
Earth's crust is made up of a number of plates that are constantly moving because of currents that rise and fall from the molten iron core at the center of the planet. Where the plates collide, they can lift the rocky landscape upward to create mountain ranges that are then eroded into craggy shapes like the Andes in Patagonia. The tensions caused by these movements sometimes result in earthquakes and volcanic activity.

Sahara Desert

Water covers two-thirds of Earth's surface

Cloud layers

Canada

Removable terrestrial globe

Constellation of the Great Bear

Celestial sphere

Case

North Pole

POCKET GLOBE
A globe is a convenient tool for recording specific features of Earth's surface. This 19th-century pocket globe summarizes the face of the world from the geopolitical perspective where the continents are divided into nations and spheres of influence. On the inside of the case is a map of the celestial sphere (pp.16–17), with all the constellations marked out.

Collenia

FOSSILIZED ALGAE
Dead plants and creatures buried in sediment are slowly turned to rock, becoming fossils. This rock contains the fossilized remains of tiny algae that were one of the earliest life forms.

HUMAN DAMAGE
Many scientists wonder if humans, like the dinosaurs, might also become extinct. The dinosaur seems to have been a passive victim of the changing Earth, while humans are playing a key role in the destruction of their environment. In the year 2000 there were more than 6 billion people on Earth—all producing waste and pollution. In addition to global warming that may be occurring due to the greenhouse effect, chemicals are being released that deplete the ozone layer—a layer in the atmosphere that keeps out dangerous ultraviolet radiation.

EARLY LIFE ON EARTH
The first life on Earth was primitive plants that took carbon dioxide from the air and released oxygen during photosynthesis. Animals evolved when there was enough oxygen in the atmosphere to sustain them. Knowledge about evolving life forms comes in the form of fossils in the rocks (left). However, life forms survive only if environmental conditions on Earth are suitable for them. The dinosaurs, for example, though perfectly adapted to their age, became extinct about 65 million years ago.

Plant-eating *Edmontosaurus*

LIFE-GIVING ATMOSPHERE
Our atmosphere extends out for about 600 miles (1,000 km). It sustains life and protects us from the harmful effects of solar radiation. It has several layers, but the life-sustaining layer is the troposphere, up to 6 miles (10 km) above Earth's surface.

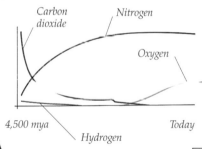

Carbon dioxide   Nitrogen

Oxygen

4,500 mya   Today

Hydrogen

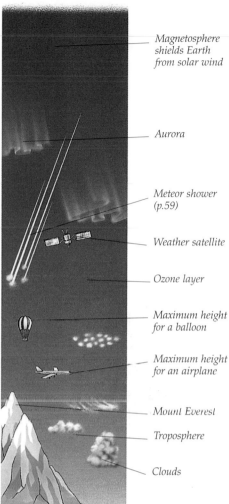

Magnetosphere shields Earth from solar wind

Aurora

Meteor shower (p.59)

Weather satellite

Ozone layer

Maximum height for a balloon

Maximum height for an airplane

Mount Everest

Troposphere

Clouds

EVOLUTION OF THE ATMOSPHERE
Since Earth was formed, the chemical makeup of the atmosphere has evolved. Carbon dioxide (CO_2) decreased significantly between 4,500 and 3,000 million years ago (mya). There was a comparable rise in nitrogen. The levels of oxygen began to rise at the same time, due to photosynthesis of primitive plants, which used up CO_2 and released oxygen.

THE SPHERICAL EARTH
As early as the 5th century BCE the Greek philosophers had proposed that Earth is spherical, and by the 3rd century BCE they had worked out a series of experiments to prove it. But it was not until the first satellites were launched in the late 1950s that humans saw what their planet looks like from space. The one feature that makes Earth unique is the great abundance of liquid water; more than two-thirds of the surface is covered with water. Water makes Earth a dynamic place. Erosion, tides, weather patterns, and plentiful forms of life are all tied to the presence of water. There is more water in the Sahara Desert in North Africa than there is on Venus (pp.50–51).

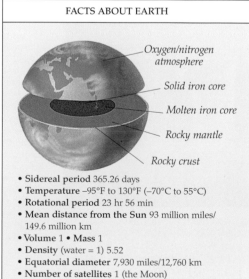

FACTS ABOUT EARTH

Oxygen/nitrogen atmosphere

Solid iron core

Molten iron core

Rocky mantle

Rocky crust

- **Sidereal period** 365.26 days
- **Temperature** –95°F to 130°F (–70°C to 55°C)
- **Rotational period** 23 hr 56 min
- **Mean distance from the Sun** 93 million miles/ 149.6 million km
- **Volume** 1 • **Mass** 1
- **Density** (water = 1) 5.52
- **Equatorial diameter** 7,930 miles/12,760 km
- **Number of satellites** 1 (the Moon)

Mercury

THE PLANET MERCURY IS NAMED after the Greco-Roman messenger of the gods, because it circles the Sun faster than the other planets, completing its circuit in 88 Earth days. Because it travels so close to the Sun, Mercury is often difficult to observe. Even though its reflected light makes it one of the brightest objects in the night sky, Mercury is never far enough from the Sun to be able to shine out brightly. It is only visible as a "morning" or "evening" star, hugging the horizon just before or after the Sun rises or sets. Like Venus, Mercury also has phases (p.24). Being so close to the Sun, temperatures during the day on Mercury are hot enough to melt many metals. At night they drop to −291°F (−180°C) making the temperature range the greatest of all the planets. The gravitational pull of the Sun has "stolen" any atmosphere that Mercury had to protect itself against these extremes.

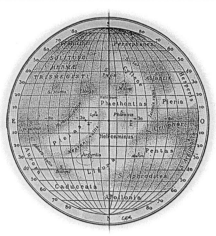

EARLY MERCURY MAP
Although many astronomers have tried to record the elusive face of Mercury, the most prolific observer was the French astronomer Eugène Antoniadi (1870–1944). His maps, drawn between 1924 and 1929, show a number of huge valleys and deserts. Close-up views by the *Mariner 10* space probe uncovered an altogether different picture (below).

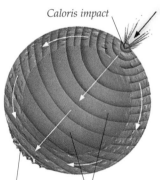

Caloris impact

SEISMIC WAVES
Some of Mercury's hills and mountains were created by the impact of a huge meteorite (p.63). The impact created a crater, known as Caloris Basin, where the meteorite struck the surface and sent out seismic, or shock, waves through the semi-molten core of the planet. These waves traveled through Mercury to the other side, where the crust buckled and mountain ranges were thrown up.

Mountain range *Seismic waves*

CRATERED TERRAIN
The surface of Mercury closely resembles our crater-covered Moon (p.44). Mercury's craters were also formed by the impact of meteorites, and the lack of atmosphere has kept the landscape unchanged. Around the edges of the craters, a series of concentric ridges record how the surface was pushed outward by the force of the impact.

MESSENGER TO MERCURY
In 2004, NASA launched the *Messenger* spacecraft to explore Mercury. After flying past Mercury three times, it will go into orbit around the planet in 2011. It is the first mission to Mercury since *Mariner 10* in 1974–75.

SURFACE OF MERCURY
This image is a mosaic of photographs taken during *Mariner 10*'s journey past Mercury in 1974. Mercury seems to have shrunk a great deal after it was formed. This has caused a series of winding ridges, called scarps, that are unique to the planet. The entire surface is heavily cratered. The space probe *Mariner 10* also discovered that Mercury has a magnetic field about 1 percent the strength of Earth's magnetic field.

LOOKING AT VOLUME

These blocks—wood, aluminum, and iron—all have the same volume, that is they occupy the same amount of space. Despite being the same size, however, these materials do not have the same mass and density, nor do they weigh the same. This is also true of the planets. For example, Mercury, though small, has a higher density than that of some of the larger planets.

Wood   Aluminum   Iron

Measuring planets

Whereas we can weigh and measure objects on Earth, we have to assess the space a planet occupies (volume), how much matter it contains (mass), and its density by looking at its behavior, by analyzing its gravitational pull on nearby objects, and by using data gained by space probes (pp.38–39). Density is the mass for every unit of volume of an object (mass divided by the volume).

Wood

Iron

MEASURING MASS

Mass is how much matter an object contains. A beam balance can be used to find the mass of a material. Here a piece of wood and a piece of iron of identical proportions and volume are placed on the balance. The iron has the greater mass. By dividing the mass (measured in grams) of the wood and the iron by their volume (measured in cubic centimeters), their relative densities can be calculated.

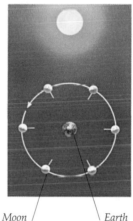

Saturn

Mercury

COMPARING DENSITY

Mercury has great mass for its size. Even though it is only slightly larger than Earth's Moon, its mass is four times that of the Moon. This means its density must be nearly as high as Earth's, most likely due to a very high quantity of iron. Astronomers believe that Mercury must have a massive iron core that takes up nearly three-fourths of its radius to achieve such great mass—a fact backed up by *Mariner 10*'s evidence of a magnetic field. When the densities of Mercury and Saturn, the huge gas giant (pp.56–57), are compared, Saturn would float and Mercury, whose density is seven times as great, would sink.

ORBITAL PERIOD

The tidal force of Earth has locked its Moon into rotating so that one side of the Moon always faces Earth (p.44). This means the rotational period of the Moon equals its monthly period of revolution around Earth. Since the orbit of Mercury is elongated, like an oval, it is locked into a rotational period where the planet spins 1½ times during each orbit of the Sun. This means that its year (how long it takes to orbit the Sun) is 88 Earth days, while its day (the time it takes to rotate—sunrise to sunrise) is 58.6 Earth days.

Moon   *Earth*   *Mercury*

Crater

Mosaic of separate photographs

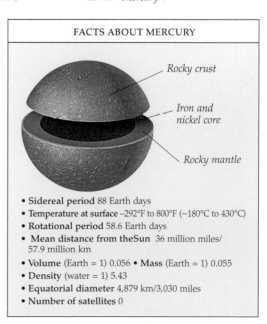

FACTS ABOUT MERCURY

Rocky crust

Iron and nickel core

Rocky mantle

- **Sidereal period** 88 Earth days
- **Temperature at surface** −292°F to 800°F (−180°C to 430°C)
- **Rotational period** 58.6 Earth days
- **Mean distance from theSun** 36 million miles/ 57.9 million km
- **Volume** (Earth = 1) 0.056 • **Mass** (Earth = 1) 0.055
- **Density** (water = 1) 5.43
- **Equatorial diameter** 4,879 km/3,030 miles
- **Number of satellites** 0

Venus

PEOPLE OFTEN MISTAKE VENUS for a star. After the Moon, it is the brightest object in our night sky. Because it is so close in size to Earth, until the 20th century astronomers assumed that it might be in some ways like Earth. The probes sent to investigate have shown that this is not so. The dense cloudy atmosphere of Venus hides its surface from even the most powerful telescope. Only radar can penetrate to map the planet's features. Until it became possible to determine the surface features—largely flat, volcanic plains—scientists could not tell how long the Venusian day was. The atmosphere would be deadly to humans. It is made up of a mixture of carbon dioxide and sulfuric acid that causes an extreme "greenhouse effect," in which heat is trapped by the atmosphere. The ancients, however, saw only a beautifully bright planet, and so they named it after their goddess of love. Nearly all the features mapped on the surface of Venus have been named after women, such as Pavlova, Sappho, and Phoebe.

VENUS IN THE NIGHT SKY
This photograph was taken from Earth. It shows the crescent Moon with Venus in the upper left of the sky. Shining like a lantern at twilight, Venus looks so attractive that astronomers were inspired to believe it must be a beautiful planet.

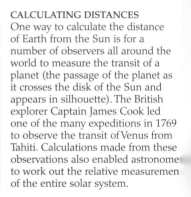

CALCULATING DISTANCES
One way to calculate the distance of Earth from the Sun is for a number of observers all around the world to measure the transit of a planet (the passage of the planet as it crosses the disk of the Sun and appears in silhouette). The British explorer Captain James Cook led one of the many expeditions in 1769 to observe the transit of Venus from Tahiti. Calculations made from these observations also enabled astronomer to work out the relative measuremen of the entire solar system.

FACTS ABOUT VENUS

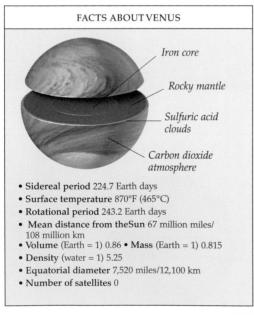

- Iron core
- Rocky mantle
- Sulfuric acid clouds
- Carbon dioxide atmosphere

- **Sidereal period** 224.7 Earth days
- **Surface temperature** 870°F (465°C)
- **Rotational period** 243.2 Earth days
- **Mean distance from theSun** 67 million miles/ 108 million km
- **Volume** (Earth = 1) 0.86 • **Mass** (Earth = 1) 0.815
- **Density** (water = 1) 5.25
- **Equatorial diameter** 7,520 miles/12,100 km
- **Number of satellites** 0

Blue-filtered color

Dense clouds

LOOKING AT VENUS
In 1978 the United States launched the *Pioneer* Orbiter, designed to map the surface of Venus by using radar to penetrate its densely clouded atmosphere. It was followed in 1989 by *Magellan*, which circled Venus every 3 hours and 9 minutes and had a 12-ft (3.7-m) radar dish that beamed radar images back to Earth for analysis. Computers were used to build up pictures of the surface—mainly volcanic plains. This view from space does not show the true color of the planet; a blue filter has been used to emphasize the cloud layers. Another Venus mapper is the large radio telescope near Arecibo in Puerto Rico (p.36).

PUZZLING SURFACE

Even with the best telescope, Venus looks almost blank. This led the Russian astronomer Mikhail Lomonosov (p.32) to propose that the Venusian surface is densely covered with clouds. As recently as 1955, the British astronomer Fred Hoyle (1915–2001) argued that the clouds are actually drops of oil and that Venus has oceans of oil. In fact, the clouds are droplets of weak sulfuric acid, and the planet has a hot, dry volcanic surface.

ASSEMBLING VENERA PROBES

During the 1960s and 1970s the former USSR sent a number of probes called *Venera* to investigate the surface of Venus. They were surprised when three of the probes stopped functioning as soon as they entered the Venusian atmosphere. Later *Venera* probes showed the reason why—the atmospheric pressure on the planet was 90 times that of Earth, the atmosphere itself was highly acidic, and the temperature was 900°F (465°C).

Carbon dioxide atmosphere lets heat radiation in but not out

Sunlight reflected

Sulfuric acid layer

Color balance

Feet of probe

GREENHOUSE EFFECT

The great amount of carbon dioxide in Venus's atmosphere means that, while solar energy can penetrate, heat cannot escape. This has led to a runaway "greenhouse effect." Temperatures on the surface easily reach 870°F (465°C), even though the thick cloud layers keep out as much as 80 percent of the Sun's rays

Hot surface

Infrared radiation

Sif Mons volcano

LANDING ON VENUS

This image was sent back by *Venera 13* when it landed on Venus in 1982. Part of the space probe can be seen at bottom left and the color balance, or scale, is in the lower middle of the picture. The landscape appears barren, made up of volcanic rocks. There was plenty of light for photography, but the spacecraft succumbed to the ovenlike conditions after only an hour.

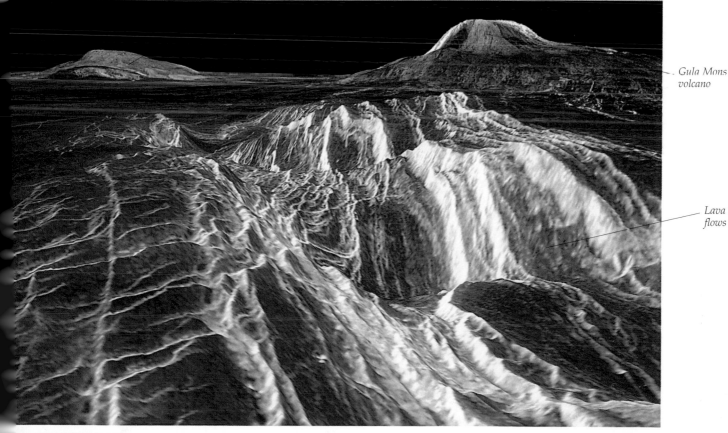

Gula Mons volcano

Lava flows

THREE-DIMENSIONAL VIEW

radar image of the Western Eistla Region, sent by *Magellan*, shows the volcanic flows (see here as the bright features) that cover the landscape and blanket the nal Venusian features. Most of the landscape is covered by shallow craters. The lated colors are based on those recorded by the Soviet *Venera* probes.

Mars

MARS APPEARS PALE ORANGE IN THE NIGHT SKY. The Babylonians, Greeks, and Romans all named it after their gods of war. In reality, Mars is a small planet—only half the size of Earth—but there are similarities. Mars, like Earth, has a 24-hour day, polar caps, and an atmosphere. Not surprisingly, Mars has always been the most popular candidate as a site for possible extraterrestrial life. Many scientists believe that some form of life—or at least evidence of past life—may remain within the planet, but no life could survive on the surface. The atmosphere is too thin to block out deadly ultraviolet rays. Mars is also farther from the Sun than Earth, making it much colder.

Arabia region

MARTIAN MARKINGS
In 1659 the Dutch scientist Christiaan Huygens (1629–1695) drew the first map of Mars, showing a V-shaped mark on the surface that reappeared in the same place every 24 hours. This was Syrtis Major. He concluded, correctly, that its regular appearance indicated the length of the Martian day. The American astronomer, Percival Lowell (1855–1916), made a beautiful series of drawings of the Martian "canals" (above) described by Schiaparelli (see below). Closer inspections showed that these canals were optical illusions caused by the eye's connecting unrelated spots.

CANALS ON MARS
The Italian astronomer Giovanni Schiaparelli (1835–1910) made a close study of the surface of Mars. In 1877 he noticed a series of dark lines that seemed to form some sort of network. Schiaparelli called them *canali*, translated as "channels" or "canals." This optical illusion seems to be the origin of the myth that Mars is occupied by a sophisticated race of hydraulic engineers. It was Eugène Antoniadi (p.48) who made the first accurate map of Mars.

Ice cap

Water ice

Cliff

AROUND THE PLANET MARS
The Martian atmosphere is much thinner than that of Earth and is composed mostly of carbon dioxide. There is enough water vapor for occasional mist, fog, and clouds to form. *Mariner 9*, the first spacecraft to orbit Mars, revealed a series of winding valleys in the Chryse region that could be dried-up river beds. Mars also has large volcanoes. One of them—Olympus Mons—is the largest in the solar system. There are also deserts, canyons, and polar ice caps.

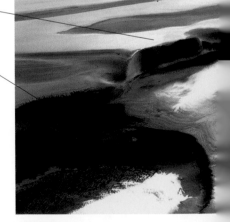

POLAR ICE
The polar regions of Mars are covered by a thin layer of ice, which is a mixture of frozen water and solid carbon dioxide. This image of the north polar ice cap, taken by ESA's *Mars Express* spacecraft, shows layers of water ice, dune fields and cliffs almost 1 mile (2 km) high. The polar caps are not constant, but grow and recede with the Martian seasons.

Computer-processed view of Mars from *Viking* orbiters (1980)

Robotic arm

SAMPLING ROCK
In 1997, *Pathfinder* landed on Mars with a 25-in- (63-cm-) long robot rover called *Sojourner*. The rover carried special instruments to analyze the composition of Martian rocks.

TESTING FOR LIFE
The two *Viking* probes in the 1970s carried out simple experiments on Martian soil. They found no signs of life.

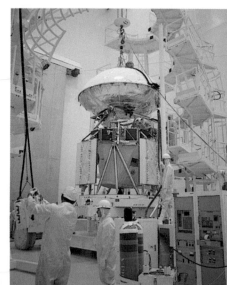

Assembling the *Viking* lander

GLOBAL SURVEYOR
Mars Global Surveyor returned thousands of high-resolution images of Mars between 1999 and 2006. It also studied the planet's weather and chemical makeup.

DESERT LANDSCAPE
Mars resembles a desert. Winds whip up the red dust and it becomes suspended in the atmosphere, giving the sky a reddish hue. To make sure that the *Viking* images could be reproduced in their proper colors, the spacecraft carried a series of color patches (p.51). Its photographs of these were corrected until the patches were in their known colors, so the scientists could be confident that the landscape colors were also shown correctly.

MARTIAN MOONS
Mars has two small moons, Phobos (right) and Deimos, 17 and 10 miles (28 and 16 km) in diameter. Since the orbit of Deimos is only 14,580 miles (23,460 km) from the center of Mars, it will probably be pulled down to the surface with a crash in about 50 million years.

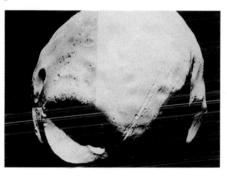

GULLIES ON MARS
Images sent back by *Mars Global Surveyor* show these intriguing marks. They are gullies on the wall of a meteor impact crater. It is possible that they formed when the permafrost beneath the surface melted, allowing groundwater up to the surface. They provided evidence for the existence of water on Mars. The ripples at the bottom of the picture are sand dunes.

FACTS ABOUT MARS

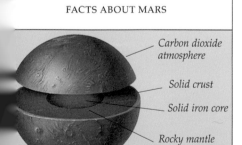

- *Carbon dioxide atmosphere*
- *Solid crust*
- *Solid iron core*
- *Rocky mantle*

- **Sidereal period** 687 Earth days
- **Surface temperature** –184°F to 77°F (–120°C to 25°C)
- **Rotational period** 24 hr 37 min
- **Mean distance from the Sun** 141 million miles/ 230 million km
- **Volume** (Earth = 1) 0.15
- **Mass** (Earth = 1) 0.11
- **Density** (water = 1) 3.95
- **Equatorial diameter** 4,220 miles/6,790 km
- **Number of satellites** 2

Jupiter

THIS HUGE, BRIGHT PLANET is the largest world in our solar
system; four of its moons are the size of planets. It is different
in structure from the solid inner planets. Apart from a small
rocky core, Jupiter is mainly hydrogen and helium. Below the
cloudy atmosphere, the pressure is so great that these are liquid
rather than gas. Deep down, the liquid hydrogen behaves like
a metal. As a result, Jupiter has a strong magnetic field and
fierce radiation belts. Jupiter emits more heat radiation than it
receives from the Sun, because it continues shrinking at a rate
of a fraction of an inch per year. Had Jupiter been only 13 times
more massive, this contraction would have made the center
hot enough for nuclear fusion reactions (p.42) to begin, though
not to be sustained for as long as in a star.
It would have become a brown dwarf—
a body between a planet and a
star. The *Galileo* spacecraft, which
orbited Jupiter from 1995–2003,
transmitted some amazing
photographs of Jupiter
and its moons.

JUPITER'S RINGS
The US *Pioneer* missions were sent past Jupiter in
the early 1970s, *Pioneer 10* sending back the first
pictures. In 1977 the US sent two *Voyager* probes to
explore Jupiter's cloud tops and five of its moons.
Voyager 1 uncovered a faint ring—like Saturn's
rings (p.57)—circling the planet. The thin yellow
ring (approximately 18 miles thick/30 km) can be
seen at the top of the photograph.

SEEING THE RED SPOT
In 1660 the English scientist, Robert
Hooke (1635–1702), reported seeing
"a spot in the largest of the three belts
of Jupiter." Gian Cassini (p.32) saw the
spot at the same time, but subsequent
astronomers were unable to find it. The
Great Red Spot was observed again in
1878 by the American astronomer
Edward Barnard (1857–1923).

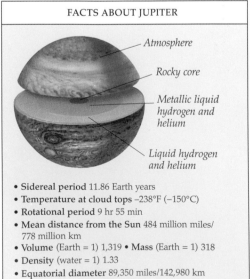

Storm system

Equatorial belt

Great Red Spot

North polar region

North temperate belt

North tropical
zone

Equatorial
zone

South
tropical
zone

South
temperate
belt

South polar region

FACTS ABOUT JUPITER

Atmosphere

Rocky core

Metallic liquid
hydrogen and
helium

Liquid hydrogen
and helium

- **Sidereal period** 11.86 Earth years
- **Temperature at cloud tops** –238°F (–150°C)
- **Rotational period** 9 hr 55 min
- **Mean distance from the Sun** 484 million miles/
  778 million km
- **Volume** (Earth = 1) 1,319 • **Mass** (Earth = 1) 318
- **Density** (water = 1) 1.33
- **Equatorial diameter** 89,350 miles/142,980 km
- **Number of satellites** at least 63

JUPITER'S CLOUDS
The cloud tops of Jupiter seem to be divided into a series of bands that are
different colors. The light bands are called zones, and the dark bands belts. The
north tropical zone (equivalent to our northern temperate zone) is the brightest, its
whiteness indicating high-level ammonia clouds. The equatorial belt, surrounding
Jupiter's equator, always seems in turmoil, with the atmosphere constantly whipped
up by violent winds. Across the planet are a number of white or red ovals. These are
huge cloud systems. The brown and orange bands indicate the presence of organic
molecules including ethane.

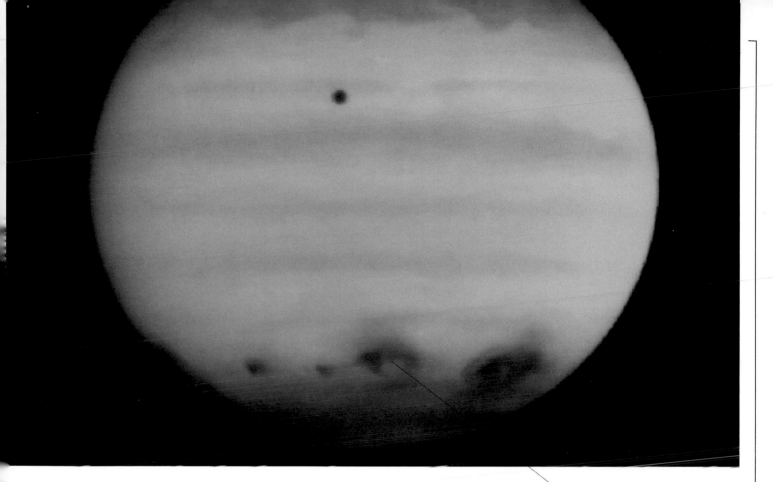

A MOMENTOUS IMPACT

In July 1994, fragments of the comet Shoemaker-Levy 9 crashed into Jupiter's southern hemisphere at speeds of around 130,500 mph (210,000 km/h). The comet had been discovered in 1993 by astronomers Carolyn and Eugene Shoemaker and David Levy, who also predicted its path. It was the first time in history that astronomers had been able to predict a collision between two bodies in the solar system and then observe the event. Over 20 pieces of the comet hit Jupiter, some of them sending up 1,865-mile- (3,000-km-) high fireballs and plumes.

Jupiter's moons

In 1610, Galileo (p.24) made the first systematic study of the four largest moons of Jupiter. Since they seemed to change their positions relative to the planet every night, he concluded, correctly, that these objects must be revolving around Jupiter. This insight provided more ammunition for the dismantling of the geocentric theory (p.15), which placed Earth at the center of the universe. In 1892 another small moon was discovered circling close to the cloud tops of the planet. To date, a total of 63 moons have been discovered.

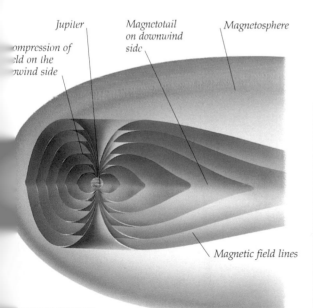

Jupiter

Magnetotail on downwind side

Magnetosphere

Compression of field on the windward side

Magnetic field lines

ERUPTION ON IO

Io is the Moon that is closest to Jupiter. It is one of the "Galilean" moons, named after Galileo, who discovered them. The others are Callisto, Europa, and Ganymede. The erupting plume of a massive volcano can be seen here on the horizon, throwing sulfuric materials 185 miles (300 km) out into space. The photograph was taken by *Voyager* from a distance of 310,700 miles (500,000 km) and has been specially colored using filters.

CALLISTO

Callisto is the second-largest of Jupiter's moons, and the most heavily cratered, not unlike our Moon, except that the craters are made of ice. The bright areas are the ice craters formed by impacts of objects from space.

SPINNING JUPITER

Jupiter spins so quickly that a day is only 9 hours and 55 minutes long and its equator bulges outward. Another effect of the rapid rotation is that the spinning of Jupiter's metallic hydrogen core generates a huge magnetic field around the planet. This magnetosphere is pushed back by the solar wind and its tail spreads out over a vast distance, away from the Sun.

Saturn

THE GIANT PLANET SATURN, with its flat rings, is probably the most widely recognized astronomical image. For the classical world, Saturn was the most distant known planet. They named it after the original father of all the gods. Early astronomers noted its 29-year orbit and assumed that it moves sluggishly. Composed mostly of hydrogen, its atmosphere and structure are similar to Jupiter's, but its density is much lower. Saturn is so light that it could float on water (p.49). Like Jupiter, Saturn rotates at great speed causing its equator to bulge outward. Saturn also has an appreciable magnetic field. Winds in its upper atmosphere can travel at 1,100 mph (1,800 km/h) but major storms are rare. White spots tend to develop during Saturn's northern-hemisphere summer, which happens every 30 years or so, the last being in 1990.

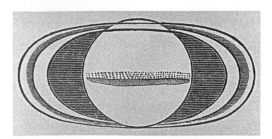

17TH-CENTURY VIEW
In 1675 the Bolognese director of the Paris Observatory, Gian Domenico Cassini (p.32), discovered that, despite appearances, Saturn did not have a single, solid ring. He could see two rings, with a dark gap in between. His drawing, made in 1676, shows the gap, which was called the Cassini division in his honor.

SATURN AND THE RINGS
Though Saturn's rings look solid from Earth, astronomers have known since the 19th century that they cannot be. In fact, they consist of countless individual particles, made of ice and dust, ranging in size from specks to hundreds of yards. The rings are only about 100 ft (30 m) thick, but their total width is more than 169,000 miles (272,000 km).

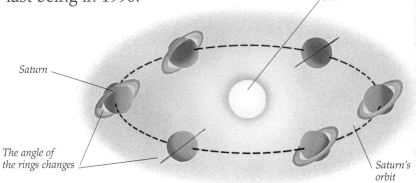

Sun

Saturn

The angle of the rings changes

Saturn's orbit

CHANGING VIEW
Saturn's axis is tilted. Because the rings lie around its equator, they incline as the planet tilts. This means that the rings change dramatically in appearance, depending on what time during Saturn's year they are being observed (Saturn's year is equal to 29.4 Earth years). The angle of the rings appears to change according to how Saturn and Earth are placed in their respective orbits.

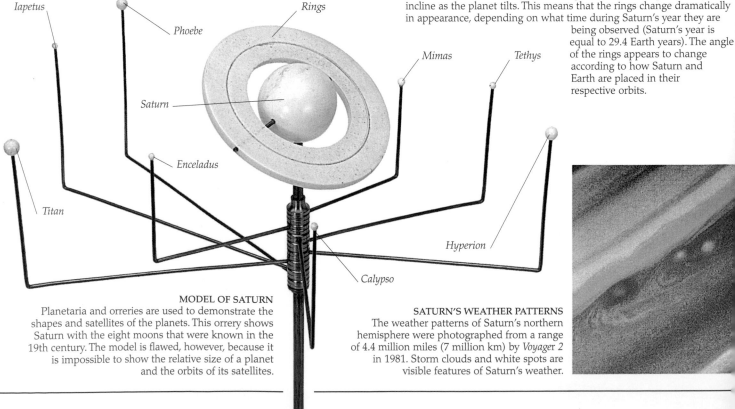

Iapetus

Phoebe

Rings

Mimas

Tethys

Saturn

Enceladus

Titan

Hyperion

Calypso

MODEL OF SATURN
Planetaria and orreries are used to demonstrate the shapes and satellites of the planets. This orrery shows Saturn with the eight moons that were known in the 19th century. The model is flawed, however, because it is impossible to show the relative size of a planet and the orbits of its satellites.

SATURN'S WEATHER PATTERNS
The weather patterns of Saturn's northern hemisphere were photographed from a range of 4.4 million miles (7 million km) by *Voyager 2* in 1981. Storm clouds and white spots are visible features of Saturn's weather.

Ring A

Cassini Division

Shadow cast by rings

Ring B

Cloud bands

CLOSE-UP DETAIL
In this image of Saturn, the colors are exaggerated to show more clearly the cloud bands encircling the planet. We can also see that the rings are made up of many separate ringlets. The principal rings, called A and B, are easily visible from Earth with a small telescope. Saturn also has five fainter rings. As Saturn orbits the sun, we see the ring system from different angles. Sometimes the rings look open, as in this image. Every 15 years, the rings are presented to us edge-on and they virtually disappear from view. The most detailed images of Saturn have been returned by the Cassini-Huygens mission, which was launched in 1997 and arrived in 2004. The Huygens probe was released, and landed on Titan, Saturn's largest moon, which is hidden by opaque haze. Using radar, the orbiting Cassini spacecraft has discovered that Titan has lakes of liquid methane.

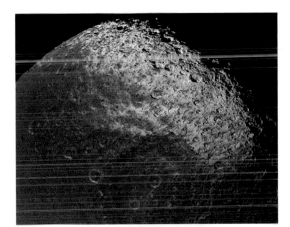

TWO-TONE MOON
Iapetus is Saturn's third-largest moon, with a diameter of 892 miles (1,436 km). It is made mostly of ice. One of its strangest features is that one half of the surface is very much darker that the other. The dark area is coated with material as black as tar, which seems to have fallen on it. This picture was taken by the Cassini spacecraft. Cassini revealed a range of mountains up to 12 miles (20 km) high extending for about 800 miles (1,300 km).

FACTS ABOUT SATURN

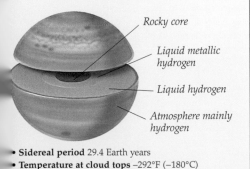

Rocky core

Liquid metallic hydrogen

Liquid hydrogen

Atmosphere mainly hydrogen

- **Sidereal period** 29.4 Earth years
- **Temperature at cloud tops** −292°F (−180°C)
- **Rotational period** 10 hr 40 min
- **Mean distance from the Sun** 886 million miles/ 1.43 billion km
- **Volume** (Earth = 1) 744 • **Mass** (Earth = 1) 95.18
- **Density** (water = 1) 0.69
- **Equatorial diameter** 74,900 miles/120,535 km
- **Number of satellites** 60

SEEING THE RINGS
When Galileo first discovered Saturn's rings in 1610, he misinterpreted what he saw. He thought Saturn was a triple planet. It was not until 1655 that the rings were successfully identified and described by the Dutch scientist and astronomer Christiaan Huygens (1629–1695), using a powerful telescope that he built himself.

TIGER STRIPES
Saturn's moon Enceladus is about 310 miles (500 km) across. This false-color image of its icy surface from the Cassini spacecraft reveals a series of parallel fissures (in blue), which astronomers nicknamed "tiger stripes." Other images have shown plumes of icy droplets jetting out of these fissures from liquid water below the frozen crust. Large areas of the surface have no craters, or very few. This means that it has greatly altered since Enceladus first formed.

Uranus

URANUS WAS THE FIRST PLANET to be discovered since the use of the telescope. It was discovered by accident, when William Herschel, observing from Bath, England, set about remeasuring all the major stars with his 6-in (15-cm) reflector telescope (p.28). In 1781 he noticed an unusually bright object in the zodiacal constellation of Gemini. At first he assumed it was a nebula (pp.64–65) and then a comet (pp.62–63), but it moved in a peculiar way. The name of Uranus was suggested by the German astronomer Johann Bode, who proposed that the planet be named after the father of Saturn, in line with established classical traditions. Bode is also famous as the creator of Bode's law—a mathematical formula that predicted roughly where planets should lie.

WILLIAM HERSCHEL (1738–1822)
William Herschel was so impressed by a treatise on optics, which described the construction of telescopes, that he wanted to buy his own telescope. He found them too expensive, so in 1773 he decided to start building his own. From that moment on, astronomy became Herschel's passion.

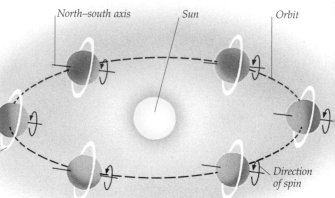

North–south axis   Sun   Orbit

Ring   Direction of spin

ECCENTRIC TILT
Uranus spins on an axis that is tilted at an angle of nearly 98° from the plane of its orbit. This means that, compared with all the other planets in the solar system, Uranus is spinning on its side. During its 84-year orbit of the Sun, the north pole of Uranus will have 42 years of continuous, sunny summer, while the south pole has the same length of sunless winter, before they swap seasons. This odd tilt may be the result of a catastrophic collision during the formation of the solar system.

Ariel   Umbriel

Uranus

Titania

Oberon

19TH-CENTURY MODEL
Because of the odd angle of Uranus's rotational axis, all its known satellites also revolve at right angles to this axis, around Uranus's equator. This fact is demonstrated by an early model, which shows the planet and four of its moons tilted at 98°. This orrery (p.40) dates from the 19th century when only four of the 27 moons had been discovered.

VIEW FROM SPACE
Uranus is a giant planet, four times larger than Earth. The Hubble Space Telescope took these contrasting views in 2004. On the left, Uranus is seen in natural color. It looks blue because of absorption by methane in the atmosphere. The image on the right is false color, which shows bright clouds and hazy bands parallel to the equator.

AIRBORNE OBSERVATION OF URANUS
The covering of one celestial body by another is known as occultation. A team of scientists observed the occultation of a star by Uranus in 1977 from NASA's Kuiper Airborne Observatory over the Indian Ocean. This was when the faint rings of Uranus were observed for the first time.

LITERARY MOONS
All the satellites of Uranus are named after sprites and spirits drawn from English literature. The American astronomer Gerard P. Kuiper (1905–1973) discovered Miranda in 1948. (Miranda and Ariel are characters from William Shakespeare's *The Tempest*.) It has a landscape unlike any other in the solar system. Miranda seems to be composed of a jumble of large blocks. Scientists have suggested that these were caused by some huge impact during which Miranda was literally blown apart. The pieces drifted back together through gravitational attraction, forming this strange mixture of rock and ice.

URANUS RING SYSTEM
While watching the occultation of Uranus in 1977, astronomers noticed that the faint star "blinked on and off" several times at the beginning and end of the occultation. They concluded that Uranus must have a series of faint rings that caused the star to "blink" by blocking off its light as it passed behind them. The *Voyager 2* flyby in 1986 uncovered two more rings. The rings of Uranus are thin and dark, made up of particles only about a yard (1 m) across. The broad bands of dust between each ring suggest that the rings are slowly eroding.

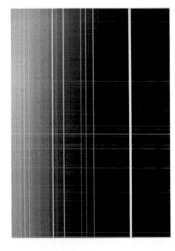

THE MOON TITANIA
William Herschel discovered Uranus's two largest moons in 1789, naming them Oberon and Titania, the fairy king and queen in William Shakespeare's *A Midsummer Night's Dream*. The English astronomer William Lassell (1799-1880) discovered Ariel and Umbriel in 1851. Miranda was discovered in 1948. Since then, a further 22 moons have been found.

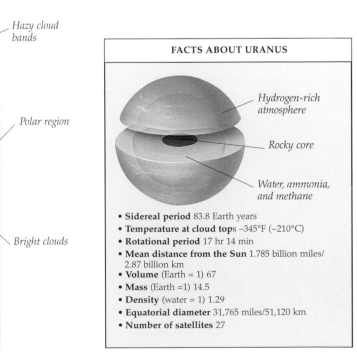

Hazy cloud bands

Polar region

Bright clouds

Hydrogen-rich atmosphere

Rocky core

Water, ammonia, and methane

FACTS ABOUT URANUS

- **Sidereal period** 83.8 Earth years
- **Temperature at cloud top**s −345°F (−210°C)
- **Rotational period** 17 hr 14 min
- **Mean distance from the Sun** 1.785 billion miles/ 2.87 billion km
- **Volume** (Earth = 1) 67
- **Mass** (Earth =1) 14.5
- **Density** (water = 1) 1.29
- **Equatorial diameter** 31,765 miles/51,120 km
- **Number of satellites** 27

Neptune and beyond

URBAIN LE VERRIER (1811–1877)
Le Verrier was a teacher of chemistry and astronomy at the *Ecole Polytechnique*. Having calculated the position of Neptune, Le Verrier relied on others to do the actual "looking" for the planet for him.

NEPTUNE WAS DISCOVERED AS THE RESULT of calculations. By the early 19th century, astronomers realized that Uranus was not following its expected orbit. The gravitational pull of an unknown planet beyond Uranus seemed the most likely explanation. In 1845, the English mathematician John Couch Adams (1819–1892) announced that he had calculated the probable position of a planet beyond Neptune, but his findings were ignored. In June 1846, the Frenchman Urbain Le Verrier did the same. This time, observers took notice. Johann Galle (1812–1910) of the Berlin Observatory found Neptune on September 23, 1846. Astronomers continued to speculate about another planet beyond Neptune. Pluto was eventually discovered in 1930 and was considered to be the ninth major planet until 2006. Between 1992 and 2006, hundreds of small icy bodies had been found beyond Neptune, in what is called the Kuiper belt. They include Eris, which is larger than Pluto. In 2006, astronomers decided to class both Pluto and Eris as dwarf planets.

NEPTUNE'S RINGS
Neptune, like all the giant planets, has a series of rings encircling it. The rings were discovered when the planet passed in front of a star. Results of an occultation (p.59) in July 1984 showed the typical "blinking on and off," indicating that Neptune's rings were blocking out the light of the distant star. There seem to be two main rings, with two faint inner rings. The inner ring is less than 9 miles (15 km) wide. The rings were confirmed by *Voyager 2* in 1989.

FACTS ABOUT NEPTUNE

Atmosphere of hydrogen

Small rocky core

Water, ammonia, and methane

- **Sidereal period** 163.7 Earth years
- **Temperature at cloud tops** –346°F (–210°C)
- **Rotational period** 16 hr 7 min
- **Mean distance from theSun** 2.795 billion miles/ 4.495 biliion km
- **Volume** (Earth = 1) 57 • **Mass** (Earth = 1) 17.14
- **Density** (water = 1) 1.64
- **Equatorial diameter** 30,775 miles/49,530 km
- **Number of satellites** 13

Great Dark Spot

Small clouds

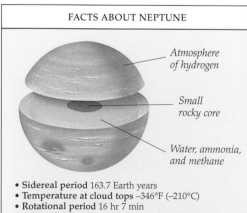

Small clouds

Great Dark Spot

South polar region

NEPTUNE'S VANISHING GREAT DARK SPOT
In 1989 *Voyager* photographed a great storm system in Neptune's southern hemisphere. The storm, actually a hole in Neptune's upper cloud layer, was about the size of Earth. Smaller clouds at the edges of the hole in this sequence—taken over a four-day period—suggested that the storm rotated counterclockwise. However, in the photographs taken of Neptune by the Hubble Space Telescope in 1995, the storm had disappeared.

Discovering Pluto

Pluto was discovered in 1930 as the result of a systematic search by an American astronomer, Clyde Tombaugh (1906–1997), working at the Lowell Observatory in Arizona. Its orbit was found to be unusual, being much more elongated than the orbits of the previously known planets. Pluto is sometimes closer to the Sun than Neptune. Gradually, astronomers realized that Pluto was much smaller than they originally thought. It has only one-fifth the mass of our Moon. The first spacecraft ever to be sent to Pluto, *New Horizons*, was launched in 2006 and will fly by Pluto in 2015.

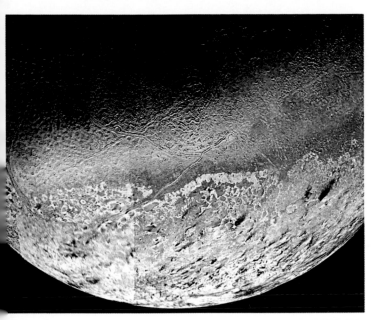

THE DISCOVERY OF TRITON

The moon Triton was discovered in 1846. It interests scientists for several reasons. It has a retrograde orbit around Neptune—that is, the moon moves in the opposite direction in which the planet rotates. It is also the coldest object in the solar system, with a temperature of –391°F (–235°C). Triton is a fascinating world. It has a pinkish surface, probably made of methane ice, which has repeatedly melted and refrozen. It has active volcanoes that spew nitrogen gas and darkened methane ice high into the thin atmosphere.

THE KUIPER BELT

In 1951, the Dutch-American astronomer Gerard Kuiper (1905–1973) predicted the existence of a whole belt of small icy worlds beyond Neptune, of which Pluto would be just the first. The next one was not found until 1992, but since then, hundreds have been identified, including Eris in 2005. Some of the smaller ones transform into comets (p.62) when they stray closer to the Sun. This artist's impression is based on what is known about Eris, which has a small moon called Dysnomia.

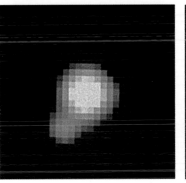

PLUTO AND CHARON

The distance between Pluto and its moon, Charon, is only 12,240 miles (19,700 km). Charon was discovered in 1978 by a study of images of Pluto that looked suspiciously elongated. The clear image on the right was taken by the Hubble telescope (p.11), which allows better resolution than anything photographed from Earth (left).

Sea-blue atmosphere

Ocean of water and gas

Smaller dark spot

CLOSE-UP OF NEPTUNE

This picture was taken by *Voyager* 2 in 1989 after its 12-year voyage through the solar system. It was 3.8 million miles (6 million km) away. *Voyager* went on to photograph the largest moon, Triton, and to reveal a further six moons orbiting the planet. Neptune has a beautiful, sea-blue atmosphere, composed mainly of hydrogen and a little helium and methane. This covers a huge internal ocean of warm water and gases—appropriate for a planet named after the god of the sea. (Many French astronomers had wanted the new planet to be named "Le Verrier," in honor of its discoverer.) *Voyager* 2 discovered several storm systems on Neptune, as well as beautiful white clouds high in the atmosphere.

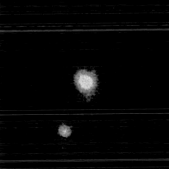

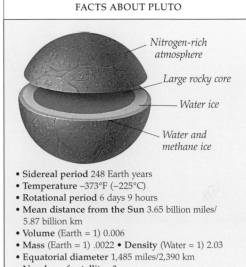

FACTS ABOUT PLUTO

Nitrogen-rich atmosphere

Large rocky core

Water ice

Water and methane ice

- **Sidereal period** 248 Earth years
- **Temperature** –373°F (–225°C)
- **Rotational period** 6 days 9 hours
- **Mean distance from the Sun** 3.65 billion miles/ 5.87 billion km
- **Volume** (Earth = 1) 0.006
- **Mass** (Earth = 1) .0022 • **Density** (Water = 1) 2.03
- **Equatorial diameter** 1,485 miles/2,390 km
- **Number of satellites** 3

Travelers in space

Not all matter in the solar system has been brought together to form the Sun and the planets. Clumps of rock and ice travel through space, often in highly elliptical orbits that carry them toward the Sun from the far reaches of the solar system. Comets are icy planetary bodies that take their name from the Greek description of them as *aster kometes*, or "long-haired stars." Asteroids are mainly bits of rock that have never managed to come together as planets. However, Ceres, the largest by far at 585 miles (940 km) across, is like a little planet and since 2006 has been classed as a dwarf planet. A meteor is a piece of space rock—usually a small piece of a comet—that enters Earth's atmosphere. As it falls, it begins to burn up and produces spectacular fireworks. A meteor that survives long enough to hit the ground—usually a stray fragment from the asteroid belt—is called a meteorite.

PREDICTING COMETS
Going through astronomical records in 1705, Edmond Halley (1656–1743) noticed that three similar descriptions of a comet had been recorded at intervals of 76 years. Halley used Newton's recently developed theories of gravity and planetary motion (p.25) to deduce that these three comets might be the same one returning to Earth at regular intervals, because it was traveling through the solar system in an elliptical orbit (p.17). He predicted that the comet would appear again in 1758, but he did not live to see the return of the comet that bears his name.

Comet's orbit

Sun

Comet's tail

Nucleus

COMET'S TAIL
Comets generally have elongated orbits. They can be seen by the light they reflect. As they get closer to the Sun's heat, their surface starts to evaporate and a huge tail of dust and gas is given off. This tail always points away from the Sun because the dust and gas particles are pushed by solar wind and radiation pressure.

Erratic asteroid

Sun

Jupiter

Asteroid belt

Mars

POSITION OF THE ASTEROID BELT
Since the Sicilian monk Guiseppe Piazzi discovered the first asteroid in January 1801, nearly 200,000 asteroids have been confirmed and numbered. Most of them travel in a belt between Mars and Jupiter, but Jupiter's great gravitational influence has caused some asteroids to swing out into erratic orbits.

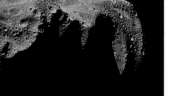

KIRKWOOD GAPS
Measuring the distances of the known asteroids from the Sun in 1866, the American astronomer David Kirkwood (1814–1895) noticed that they tended to travel in loosely formed bands and that there were large, peculiar gaps between these bands. The gaps, which are now known as Kirkwood gaps, are due to recurring "bumps" from Jupiter's gravitational field. Asteroids can be catapulted into the inner solar system by Jupiter's gravity.

Numbers of asteroids

Distance from Sun in astronomical units

CLOSE-UP OF AN ASTEROID
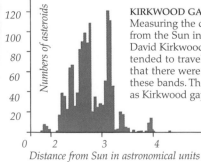
This photograph of the asteroid Ida was taken by the *Galileo* spacecraft in 1993 as the space probe traveled to Jupiter. The cratered surface probably resulted from collisions with smaller asteroids. Ida is 32 miles (52 km) long.

HALLEY'S COMET FROM GIOTTO

When Halley's comet returned in 1986, the space probe *Giotto* was sent out to intercept and study it. The probe flew within 600 miles (960 km) of the comet, took samples of the vapor in its tail, and discovered that its nucleus was a jagged lump of dirt and ice measuring 10 x 5 miles (16 x 8 km).

Dust tail

Plasma (gas) tail

Meteorites

was not until 1803 that the scientific community accepted at meteorites did, indeed, fall from space. Over 95 percent of l the meteorites recovered are stone meteorites. Meteorites e divided into three types with names that describe the mix elements found within each specimen. Stony meteorites look e stones but usually have a fused crust caused by intense eating as the meteorite passes through Earth's mosphere. Iron meteorites contain nickel-iron crystals, d stony iron meteorites are part stone, part iron.

MOLTEN DROPLET

Tektites are small, round, glassy objects that are usually the size of marbles. They are most often found on Earth in great numbers, all together. When a blazing meteorite hits a sandstone region, the heat temporarily melts some of the minerals in Earth's soil. These molten droplets harden to form tektites.

Tektite

METEORITE IN AUSTRALIA

This meteorite (left) fell near the Murchison River, Western Australia, in 1969. It contains significant amounts of carbon and water. The carbon comes from chemical reactions and not from once-living organisms like those carbon compounds found on Earth, such as coal.

Geminids are seen in mid-December

Perseids occur in mid-August

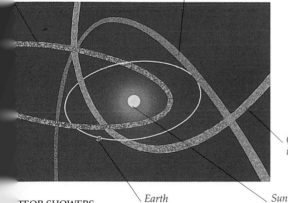

Quadrantids are seen in early January

Earth

Sun

Murchison meteorite

TEOR SHOWERS

en Earth's orbit cuts through a stream of meteors, the eoritic material seems to radiate out from one point he sky, creating a meteor shower. The showers are given es, such as "Geminids," derived from the constellations he sky from which they seem to be coming.

ICY CRATER

The Earth bears many scars from large meteorites, but the effects of erosion and vegetation cover up some of the spectacular craters. This space view shows an ice-covered crater near Quebec, Canada. It is now a 41-mile- (66-km-) wide reservoir used for hydroelectric power.

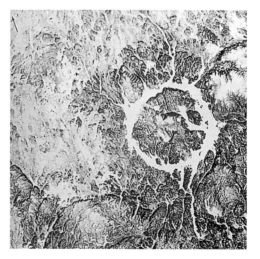

The birth and death of stars

APART FROM THE SUN, the closest star to Earth is Proxima Centauri, which is 4.2 light-years or 25 million million miles (40 million million km) away. A light-year is the distance that light or other electromagnetic radiation (p.36) travels in a year. Stars are luminous, gaseous bodies that generate energy by means of nuclear fusion in their cores (pp.42–43). As a star ages, it uses up its fuel. The core shrinks under its own weight while the nuclear "burning" continues. The shrinkage heats up the core, making the outer layers of the star expand and cool. The star becomes a "red giant." As the remains of the star's atmosphere escape, they leave the core exposed as a "white dwarf." The more massive stars will continue to fuse all their lighter elements until they reach iron. When a star tries to fuse iron, there is a massive explosion and the star becomes a "supernova." After the explosion, the star's core may survive as a pulsar or a "black hole" (p.66).

HENRIETTA LEAVITT (1868–1921)
In 1912 the American astronomer Henrietta Leavitt was studying Cepheid variable stars. These are a large group of bright yellow giant and supergiant stars named after their prototype in the constellation of Cepheus. Variable stars are stars that do not have fixed brightness. Leavitt discovered that the brighter stars had longer periods of light variation. This variation can be used to determine stellar distances beyond 100 light-years.

Distant stars

Star in January

Star in July

Parallax shift

Nearby star

Parallax angle

Sun

Earth in July

Earth in January

CALCULATING DISTANCE
As Earth orbits the Sun, stars that are closer to Earth will seem to shift their location in relation to the background of more distant stars. This effect is called parallax and it is used to calculate a star's distance from Earth. The shift is measured in terms of its angle across the sky. This method is only accurate for stars within a few hundred light years of Earth. To show the effect, the illustration is not to scale.

Venus

Pole star

Faintest star visible to the naked eye

Faintest star visible by optical telescope

−4

0

1

Zodiac scale

Month scale

Pole Star

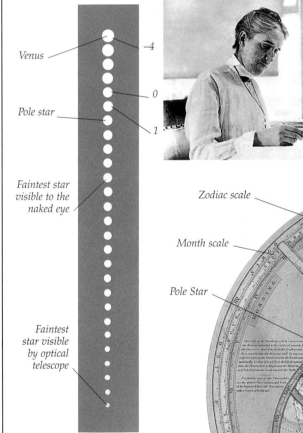

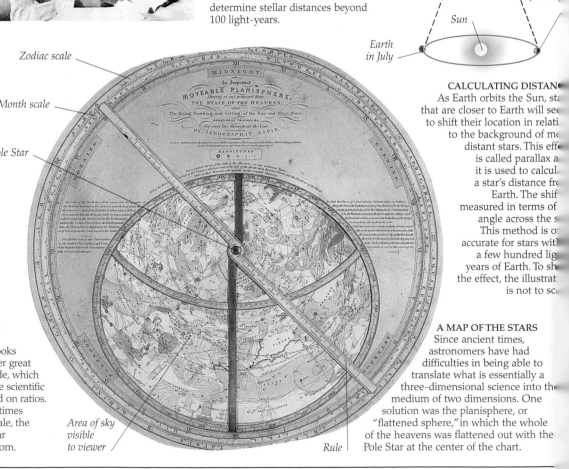

STAR MAGNITUDES
A star is measured in terms of its brightness and its temperature. There is a difference between the apparent magnitude of a star—how bright it looks from Earth, where we are looking over great distances—and its absolute magnitude, which is a measure of its real brightness. The scientific scale for apparent magnitude is based on ratios. Magnitude 1 is defined as being 100 times brighter than Magnitude 5. In this scale, the punched holes show the brightest star at the top and the faintest at the bottom.

Area of sky visible to viewer

Rule

A MAP OF THE STARS
Since ancient times, astronomers have had difficulties in being able to translate what is essentially a three-dimensional science into the medium of two dimensions. One solution was the planisphere, or "flattened sphere," in which the whole of the heavens was flattened out with the Pole Star at the center of the chart.

STUDYING THE STARS

The British astronomer Williams Huggins (1824–1910) was one of the first to use spectroscopy for astronomical purposes (pp.34–35). He was also the first astronomer to connect the Doppler effect (which relates to how sound travels) with stellar red shift (p.27). In 1868 he noticed that the spectrum of the bright star Sirius has a slight shift toward the red end of the spectrum. Although his measurement proved spurious, he correctly deduced that this effect is due to that star's traveling away from Earth.

BETELGEUSE

Betelgeuse is a variable star that is 17,000 times brighter than the Sun. It lies on the shoulder of Orion the Hunter, 400 light-years from Earth. Astronomers believe that it will "die" in a supernova explosion (above right).

NOVAE AND SUPERNOVAE

Novae and supernovae are stars that suddenly become much brighter, then gradually fade. Novae are close double stars in which material dumped onto a white dwarf from its partner detonates a nuclear explosion. Supernovae are even brighter and more violent explosions. One type is triggered like a nova but the nuclear explosion destroys the white dwarf. A supernova also occurs when the core of a massive dying star collapses. The core may survive as a neutron star or black hole. The gas blown off forms an expanding shell called a supernova remnant. These pictures show supernova 1987A before (right) and after (left) it exploded.

Outline of Orion, the Hunter

Bellatrix

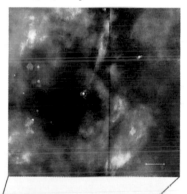

THE STELLAR NURSERY

The material in a nebula—a stellar nursery made up of gases and dust—collapses under gravity and eventually creates a cluster of young stars. Each star develops a powerful wind, which clears the area to reveal the star surrounded by a swirling disk of dust and gas. This may form a system of planets or blow away into space.

Rigel

THE CONSTELLATION ORION

A constellation is a group of stars that appear to be close to each other in the sky but that are usually spread out in three-dimensional space. Orion's stars include the bright Betelgeuse and Rigel.

ORION NEBULA M42

Stars have a definite life cycle that begins in a mass of gas that turns into stars. This "nebula" glows with color because of the cluster of hot, young stars within it. This is part of the Great Nebula in Orion.

Our galaxy and beyond

T**HE FIRST STARS WERE FORMED** a few hundred million years after the universe was born. Clumps containing a few million brilliant young stars merged to form galaxies. A typical galaxy contains about 100 billion stars and is around 100,000 light-years in diameter. Edwin Hubble was the first astronomer to study these distant star systems systematically. While observing the Andromeda galaxy in 1923, he was able to measure the brightness of some of the stars in it, although his first estimate of their distance was incorrect. After studying the different red shifts of the galaxies (p.27), Hubble proposed that the galaxies are moving away from our galaxy at speeds proportional to their distances from us. His law shows that the universe is expanding.

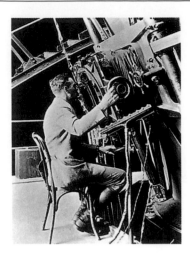

EDWIN HUBBLE (1889–1953)
In 1923 the American astronomer Edwin Hubble studied the outer regions of what appeared to be a nebula (p.65) in the constellation of Andromeda. With the high-powered 100-in (254-cm) telescope at Mount Wilson, he was able to see that the "nebulous" part of the body was composed of stars, some of which were bright, variable stars called Cepheids (pp.64–65). Hubble realized that for these intrinsically bright stars to appear so dim, they must be extremely far away from Earth. His research helped astronomers to begin to understand the immense size of the universe.

THE MILKY WAY
From Earth, the Milky Way appears particularly dense in the constellation of Sagittarius because this is the direction of the galaxy's center. Although optical telescopes cannot penetrate the galactic center because there is too much interstellar dust in the way, radio and infrared telescopes can.

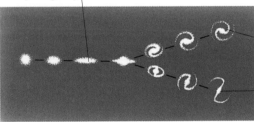

Elliptical galaxy

Spiral galaxy

Barred spiral galaxy

CLASSIFYING GALAXIES
Hubble devised a classification of galaxies according to shape. Elliptical galaxies were subdivided by how flat they appeared. He classified spiral and barred spiral galaxies (where the arms spring from a central bar) according to the tightness of their arms.

The Milky Way photographed from Chile with a wide-angle lens

Observatory building

WHIRLPOOL GALAXY
The Whirlpool Galaxy is a typical spiral galaxy, approximately 25 million light-years away. It can be found in the faint constellation Canes Venatici, at the end of the tail of the constellation of Ursa Major, or the Great Bear. It was one of the nebulae drawn by the third Earl of Rosse (p.30) in the 19th century.

THE SHAPE OF OUR GALAXY

The Milky Way, seen edge-on (top), has an oval central bulge surrounded by a very thin disk containing the spiral arms. It is approximately 100,000 light-years in diameter and about 15,000 light-years thick at its center. Our Sun is located about 30,000 light-years away from the center. The Milky Way looks like a band in our skies because we see it from "inside"—its disk is all around us. Viewed from above (bottom), it is a typical spiral galaxy with the Sun situated on one of the arms, known as the Orion arm.

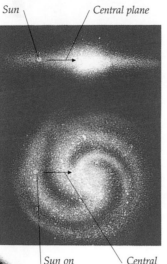

Sun   Central plane

Sun on Orion's arm   Central plane

Horizon

ANDROMEDA GALAXY

The Andromeda galaxy is a spiral galaxy, shaped like our Milky Way, but it has nearly half as much mass again. It is the most distant object that is visible to the unaided eye. It has two small elliptical companion galaxies.

What is cosmology?

Cosmology is the name given to the branch of astronomy that studies the origin and evolution of the universe. It is an ancient study, but in the 20th century the theory of relativity, advances in particle physics and theoretical physics, and the discoveries about the expanding universe gave cosmology a more scientific basis and approach.

ALBERT EINSTEIN (1879–1955)

In proposing that mass is a form of energy, the great German-American scientist Albert Einstein redefined the laws of physics dominant since Newton's time (p.25). The fact that gravitation could affect the shape of space and the passage of time meant that scientists were finally provided with the tools to understand the birth and death of the stars, especially the phenomenon of the black hole.

Massive star

Black hole   X-rays

BLACK HOLES

A supernova (p.65) can leave behind a black hole —an object so dense and so collapsed that even light cannot escape from it. Although black holes can be detected when gas spirals into them, because the gases emit massive quantities of X-rays as they are heated, they are otherwise very hard to find. Sometimes they act as "gravitational lenses," distorting background starlight.

Did you know?

AMAZING FACTS

The International Space Station

The *Pioneer 10* spacecraft, which was launched in 1972, is still transmitting signals back to Earth, although NASA stopped monitoring them in 1997. Now more than 7 billion miles (11 billion km) away, *Pioneer 10* should reach the stars in the constellation of Taurus in about two million years.

Apollo (US) and *Luna 17* and *21* (Russia) have brought back samples of rocks from the surface of the Moon. Some of these rocks are up to 4.5 billion years old—older than any rocks found on Earth.

The Large Magellanic Cloud is a galaxy that orbits the Milky Way. It contains a dazzling star cluster known as NGC 1818, which contains over 20,000 stars, some of which are only about a million years old.

In 2000, scientists identified the longest comet tail ever. Comet Hyakutake's core was about 5 miles (8 km) across—but its tail measured over 350 million miles (570 million km) long.

When Pluto was discovered in 1930, it was given its name as a result of a suggestion made by 11-year-old English schoolgirl Venetia Burney.

Designed to carry out invaluable research, work on the International Space Station (ISS) started in 1998. Due for completion in 2010, it is being built entirely in orbit, involving spacewalks by astronauts and the use of space robotics.

Since 1995, astronomers have discovered hundreds of planetary systems around ordinary stars. The star 55 Cancri, which is similar to the Sun and 41 light-years away, has a family of at least five planets similar to the giant planets of the solar system.

Some galaxies are "cannibals"—they consume other galaxies. Hubble has taken pictures of the Centaurus A galaxy. At its center is a black hole that is feeding on a neighboring galaxy.

Jupiter's moon Europa has an ocean of liquid water or slush under its icy crust. Parts of the surface look as if great rafts of ice have broken up and moved around.

Wolf-Rayet stars are among the hottest, most massive stars known and one of the rarest types. At least 25 times bigger than the Sun, and with temperatures up to 180,000°F (100,000°C), they are close to exploding as phenomenally powerful supernovae.

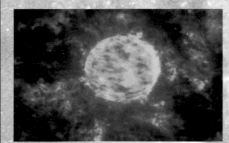

A Wolf-Rayet star in its final hours

The world's largest optical telescopes are the Keck Telescopes in Hawaii. Each one is the height of an eight-story building.

The twin Keck Telescopes on Mauna Kea, Hawaii

A color-enhanced view of Europa's surface

The four telescopes that make up the Very Large Telescope

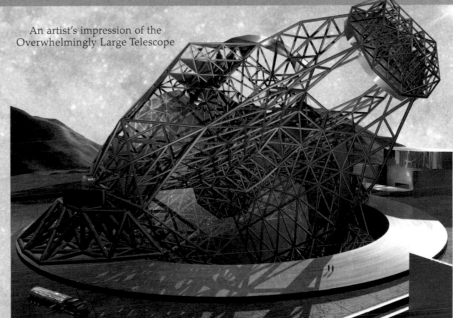

An artist's impression of the Overwhelmingly Large Telescope

Q Which are the world's most powerful telescopes?

A The performance of a telescope depends on the total area of its mirrors, and its ability to distinguish detail. The most powerful combine two or more mirrors. The twin Keck Telescopes (p.68) have mirrors 33 ft (10 m) across, each made of 36 hexagonal segments, and can work together. The Large Binocular Telescope in Arizona has two 27.6-ft (8.4-m) mirrors. Together they work like an 38.7-ft (11.8-m) mirror. The Very Large Telescope in Chile (above) consists of four 27-ft (8.2-m) telescopes that can observe together or separately.

Q How far can astronomers see?

A The most distant galaxies so far detected are about 13 billion light-years away. This means that they were formed only a few hundred million years after the Big Bang.

Q How big will telescopes be in the future?

A The Overwhelmingly Large Telescope (OWL) may be built in the Atacama Desert, Chile, and be operational around 2017. Its main mirror, made up of hexagonal segments, would be over 330 ft (100 m) across. OWL's designers hope to make use of both active and adaptive optics to achieve the best possible resolution. Active optics adjust the mirror segments so they work as a single sheet of glass. Adaptive optics work by shining a powerful laser into the sky, then adjusting the mirrors to keep the laser sharply in focus. This lets the telescope correct for distortions caused by the atmosphere.

Q Is Hubble the only space telescope?

A Launched in 1990, the Hubble Space Telescope (HST) was the first major observatory in space and is the most famous, but many others have operated in orbit around Earth or the Sun. They are usually designed to last for several years and to make particular kinds of observations. Some of the most important are NASA's four "Great Observatories," of which HST is one. The others are the Compton Gamma-Ray Observatory, which operated between 1991 and 2000, the Chandra X-Ray Observatory, launched in 1999, and the Spitzer Space Telescope. Spitzer is an infrared telescope launched in 2003. The successor to HST will be the James Webb Space Telescope, due for launch in about 2013.

Q How does space technology help us find our way on Earth?

A As well as helping us map the universe, satellites are also improving our ability to navigate on Earth. The Global Positioning System (GPS) is a collection of 27 satellites that are orbiting Earth— 24 in operation and three backups. Their orbits have been worked out so that at any time there are at least four of them visible from any point on the planet. The satellites constantly broadcast signals that indicate their position. These signals can be picked up by devices called GPS receivers. A receiver compares the information from the satellites in its line of sight. From this, it can work out its own latitude, longitude, and altitude—and so pinpoint its position on the globe. GPS technology has some amazing applications. It is already being used in cars. By linking a GPS receiver to a computer that stores data such as street maps, an in-car system can plot the best route to a particular location.

GPS car navigation system

Record Breakers

☾ USING A TELESCOPE
The first astronomers to study the night sky through a telescope were Thomas Harriott (1560–1621) and Galileo Galilei (1564–1642).

☾ LARGEST INFRARED TELESCOPE
The mirror of the Hobby-Eberly Telescope (HET) on Mount Fowlkes in Texas is 36 ft (11 m) across.

☾ PLANET WITH THE MOST MOONS
Jupiter's moons numbered at least 63 at the last count—but astronomers are still finding new ones.

☾ HIGHEST VOLCANO
At 86,600 ft (26,400 m) high, Olympus Mons on Mars is the highest volcano in our solar system.

☾ NEAREST NEBULA
The closest nebula to Earth is the Merope Nebula, 380 light-years away.

Cutting-edge astronomy

FINDING OUT HOW THE UNIVERSE was born and has evolved is a great challenge for astronomers. In 1964 the universe was found to be full of radiation, predominantly microwaves. This is called the cosmic microwave background (CMB) and is a relic from the "Big Bang" when the universe began. It gives a glimpse of the universe as it was when just a few hundred thousand years old. Since the Big Bang, the universe has been expanding, and this expansion has been speeding up for the last five billion years, driven by a mysterious force—"dark energy."

Back-to-back dishes scan deep space

Solar array shields telescope from Sun's heat

Instrument cylinder houses the equipment

SOUTH POLE INTERFEROMETER
The Degree Angular Scale Interferometer (DASI) spent several years measuring in fine detail how the cosmic microwave background radiation varies across the sky. It was sited at the Amundsen-Scott research station at the South Pole. The freezing temperatures there keep the atmosphere nearly free of water vapor, which is important for detecting microwaves.

MICROWAVE ANISOTROPY PROBE
The Wilkinson Microwave Anisotropy Probe (WMAP) was launched by NASA in 2001 on a mission of about six years to survey the cosmic microwave background radiation with unprecedented accuracy. It was put in an orbit around the Sun, on the opposite side of the Earth from the Sun, and four times farther away than the Moon. From this vantage point it could view the whole sky without interference.

BOOMERANG TELESCOPE
In 1998, a microwave telescope nicknamed Boomerang flew over Antarctica for ten days at an altitude of 121,000 ft (37,000 m). The picture it sent back of around three percent of the sky showed regular patterns in the CMB. They appear to be shock waves traveling through the young universe—perhaps even echoes of the Big Bang.

The telescope waits to be lifted into the upper atmosphere

Giant weather balloon filled with helium to float at very high altitudes

QUASAR HOME GALAXY
Quasars are so bright, the galaxies surrounding them are overwhelmed by their light and are almost invisible in normal images. The Hubble Space Telescope used a specially equipped camera to block the glare from the quasar 3C 273 and make this image (left) of the much fainter galaxy surrounding it.

Black disk in camera blocks glare from quasar

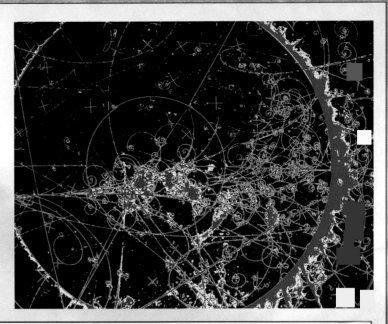

NEUTRINOS
This bubble chamber shows the pattern left by a subatomic particle called a neutrino after a high-speed collision. Huge numbers of neutrinos reach Earth from space, but they are very difficult to detect. Studying them helps to understand nuclear processes in stars.

BIG BANG

BIG BANG
The CMB map is a strong piece of evidence for the Big Bang theory. If the universe was once extremely hot and dense, and then cooled and expanded, a point should be reached when radiation would separate from matter. The trace this would leave behind matches the CMB.

CMB MAP
This map of the sky is laid out like any map of a globe—it shows the view in all directions from Earth. The most exciting thing for astronomers is that it is not perfectly uniform, but has patterns that give us clues about the forces at work in the universe around 13 billion years ago.

Dark areas are cooler by a tiny percentage

Hot spots show where galaxies will form

Cosmic microwave background as seen by the WMAP probe

STEPHEN HAWKING
Cosmologist Stephen Hawking worked with Roger Penrose to show how Einstein's theories about space and time support the Big Bang idea. Hawking used similar calculations to predict that black holes should be found to emit radiation.

Find out more

IF YOU WANT TO KNOW MORE about astronomy, just look at the sky! Binoculars or telescopes help, but there are around 2,500 stars that are visible to the naked eye. Invest in a pocket-sized guide to the constellations, so that you can identify what you observe. You can find tips on what to look for on a particular night at astronomy Web sites, on special television programs, and even in some newspapers. You can also fuel your star-gazing hobby by visiting science museums, which have lots of displays on space science of the past and the future.

Without tent light, stars would appear even brighter and clearer

ASTRONOMY ON TV
Television programs are a good introduction to the night sky. *The Sky at Night* is the world's longest-running astronomy program. In 1959, its presenter, Patrick Moore, showed audiences the first pictures of the far side of the Moon.

TV astronomer Patrick Moore

VISITING A PLANETARIUM
At a planetarium, stunning footage of the cosmos from world-class telescopes is projected onto a domed screen above your head. The planetarium shown below is in Brittany, France.

VIEWING THE NIGHT SK
Anyone can be a stargazer. Using standard pair of binoculars, th amateur astronomer has a gre view of the Milky Way. The sta above the tent are in t constellation Sagittariu

A seamless screen makes viewers feel like they are really viewing the sky

The alien stars of *Mars Attacks!* (1996)

ALIEN LIFE?
Perhaps one day astronomers will find definite proof of alien life. In the meantime, there are plenty of movies about other life forms. Of course they are pure fiction, and "real" aliens would probably look nothing like the movie versions, but they are still great fun to watch!

WHITE NOISE
You can see traces of the cosmic microwave background just by turning on your television. When it is tuned between channels, the "snow" you see is partly microwave radiation from space.

WAITING FOR AN ECLIPSE

Eclipses are amazing events, but be sure to protect your eyes from the Sun's dangerous rays if you are lucky enough to see one. In any year, there can be up to seven solar or lunar eclipses. Although solar eclipses are more common, they seem rarer because they are only ever visible in a narrow area.

THE GIBBOUS MOON

The Moon is the ideal starting point for the amateur astronomer. Over a month you can observe each of its phases. This Moon, superimposed onto a photograph of Vancouver, Canada, is gibbous—that is, more than half full.

Places to visit

ADLER PLANETARIUM AND ASTRONOMY MUSEUM, CHICAGO, ILLINOIS
www.adlerplanetarium.org
• Virtual-reality experiences of the Universe
• Historical astronomical instruments

HAYDEN PLANETARIUM, AMERICAN MUSEUM OF NATURAL HISTORY, NEW YORK CITY
www.haydenplanetarium.org
• Exhibits and lectures that bring astrophysics to life

MUSEUM OF SCIENCE PLANETARIUM, BOSTON
www.mos.org/exhibits_shows/planetarium
• Shows about real and imagined space exploration

SPACE CENTER HOUSTON, HOUSTON, TEXAS
www.spacecenter.org
• A lifesize space shuttle to explore
• Real spacesuits, including John Young's ejection suit

KENNEDY SPACE AND ROCKET CENTER, CAPE CANAVERAL, FLORIDA
www.kennedyspacecenter.com
• Hands-on exhibits demonstrating what it is like to explore space
• Rockets and hardware used in space

NATIONAL MARITIME MUSEUM AND ROYAL OBSERVATORY, GREENWICH, UK
www.rog.nmm.ac.uk
• Over two million objects, including a vast collection of astronomical instruments

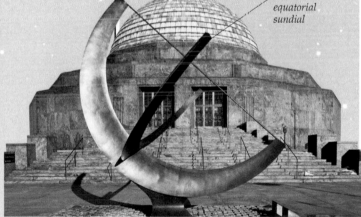

Bronze equatorial sundial

ADLER PLANETARIUM AND ASTRONOMY MUSEUM

Most science museums have galleries dedicated to astronomy, but there are also specialty museums. Chicago's Adler Astronomy Museum has multimedia exhibits and an impressive array of antique telescopes.

USEFUL WEB SITES

• An excellent introduction from NASA for amateur astronomers:
http://spacekids.hq.nasa.gov
• Up-to-the-minute tips on what to look for in the night sky
www.jb.man.ac.uk/public/nightsky.html
• The Web site of the Planetary Society, an international group that aims to involve the world's public in space exploration
www.planetary.org
• A different astronomical picture to look at every day
http://antwrp.gsfc.nasa.gov/apod/astropix.html

Glossary

Aurora borealis

APHELION The point in a planet's orbit where it is farthest from the Sun.

ASTEROID A chunk of planet material in the solar system.

ASTROLOGY The prediction of human characteristics or activities according to the motions of the stars and planets.

ASTRONOMICAL UNIT (AU) The average distance between Earth and the Sun—93 million miles (150 million km).

ASTRONOMY The scientific study of the stars, planets, and universe as a whole.

ASTROPHYSICIST Someone who studies the way stars work.

ATMOSPHERE The layer of gases held around a planet by its gravity. Earth's atmosphere stretches 600 miles (1,000 km) into space.

ATOM Smallest part of an element, made up of subatomic particles, such as protons, electrons, and neutrons.

Charge-coupled device (CCD)

AURORA Colorful glow seen in the sky near the poles, when electrically-charged particles hit gases in the atmosphere.

AXIS Imaginary line through the center of a planet or star, around which it rotates.

BIG BANG Huge explosion that created the universe around 13,000 million years ago.

BLACK HOLE A collapsed object with such powerful gravity that nothing can escape it.

CHARGE-COUPLED DEVICE (CCD) Light-sensitive electronic device used for recording images in modern telescopes.

COMET An object of ice and rock. When it nears the Sun, it has a glowing head of gas with tails of dust and gas.

CONCAVE Curving inward.

CONSTELLATION The pattern that a group of stars seems to make in the sky.

CONVEX Curving outward.

CORONA The Sun's hot upper atmosphere.

CORONAGRAPH A telescope used to observe the edge (corona) of the Sun.

COSMIC BACKGROUND RADIATION (CBR) A faint radio signal left over from the Big Bang.

COSMOS The universe.

DOPPLER EFFECT The change in a wave frequency when a source is moving toward or away from an observer.

ECLIPSE When one celestial body casts a shadow on another. In a lunar eclipse, Earth's shadow falls on the Moon. In a solar eclipse, the Moon casts a shadow on Earth.

ECLIPTIC Imaginary line around the sky along which the Sun appears to move.

ELECTROMAGNETIC RADIATION Waves of energy that travel through space at the speed of light.

ELECTROMAGNETIC SPECTRUM The complete range of electromagnetic radiation.

EQUINOX Twice-yearly occasion when day and night are of equal length, falling on about March 21 and September 23.

FOCAL LENGTH The distance between a lens or mirror and the point where the light rays it collects are brought into focus.

FOSSIL The naturally preserved remains of animals or plants, or evidence of them.

FREQUENCY The number of waves of electromagnetic radiation that pass a point every second.

GALAXY A body made up of millions of stars, gas, and dust, held together by gravity.

A communications satellite in geostationary orbit

GAMMA RAY Electromagnetic radiation with a very short wavelength.

GEOLOGIST Someone who studies rocks.

GEOSTATIONARY ORBIT An orbit 22,295 miles (35,880 km) above the equator, in which a satellite takes as long to orbit Earth as Earth takes to spin on its axis.

GRAVITY Force of attraction between any objects with mass, such as the pull between Earth and the Moon.

INFRARED Type of electromagnetic radiation also known as heat radiation.

LATITUDE Position to the north or south of the equator, in degrees.

LIBRATION A wobble in the Moon's rotation that allows observers to see slightly more than half its surface.

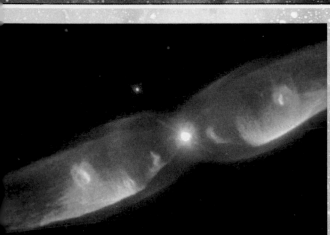

M2–9 planetary nebula

NEUTRON STAR A collapsed star left over after a supernova.

NOVA A white dwarf star that suddenly flares up and shines about 1,000 times brighter than before, after receiving material from a companion star.

NUCLEAR FUSION When the nuclei (centers) of atoms combine to create energy.

OBSERVATORY A place where astronomers study space.

SIDEREAL TIME Time measured by the stars rather than by the Sun.

SOLAR SYSTEM Everything held by the Sun's gravity, including planets and comets.

SOLSTICE Twice-yearly occasion when the Sun is farthest from the Equator, falling on about June 21 and December 21.

SPECTROSCOPY The study of the spectrum of a body that emits radiation.

STAR A hot, massive, shining ball of gas that makes energy by nuclear fusion.

SUBATOMIC PARTICLE Particle smaller than an atom—for example, a proton, neutron, or electron.

SUNSPOT A cool dark spot on the Sun's surface, created by the Sun's magnetic field.

SUPERNOVA An enormous explosion, created when a supergiant star runs out of fuel, or when a white dwarf explodes.

TIDE The regular rise and fall of the sea caused by the gravitational pull of the Sun and the Moon on Earth.

LIGHT-YEAR The distance light travels in a year—around 5.9 million million miles (9.5 million million km).

LONGITUDE Position to the east or west of the Greenwich Meridian, in degrees.

MASS A measure of the amount of matter in an object and how it is affected by gravity.

MATTER Anything that has mass and occupies space.

MERIDIAN An imaginary line linking the poles. The one at Greenwich marks 0 degrees.

METEOR The streak of light seen when comet dust burns up as it enters Earth's atmosphere.

METEORITE A fragment of space rock that has fallen onto a planet or moon.

METEOROLOGICAL To do with weather.

MICROWAVE The type of radio wave that has the shortest radio wavelengths.

NEBULA A cloud of dust and gas in space.

NEUTRINO A subatomic particle produced by nuclear fusion in stars or the Big Bang.

OCCULTATION When one heavenly body passes in front of another, hiding it from view.

OORT CLOUD Huge spherical comet cloud, about 1.6 light-years wide, that surrounds the Sun and planets.

ORBIT The path of one object around another more massive object in space.

PARALLAX Shift in a nearby object's position against a more distant background when seen from two separate points, used to measure the distance of nearby stars.

PAYLOAD Cargo carried by a space vehicle or an artificial satellite.

PERIHELION The point in an object's orbit where it is closest to the Sun.

PHASE Size of the illuminated part of a planet or moon seen from Earth.

PHOTOSPHERE A star's visible surface, from which its light shines.

PLANET Large globe of rock, liquid, or gas that orbits a star.

PRISM A transparent block used to change the direction of a beam of light.

PROMINENCE A huge arc of gas in the Sun's lower corona.

PULSAR A spinning neutron star.

QUASAR A distant active galaxy releasing lots of energy from a central small area.

RADIO TELESCOPE Telescope that detects radio waves from objects in space.

REFLECTOR TELESCOPE Telescope that gathers light with a concave mirror.

REFRACTOR TELESCOPE Telescope that gathers light with a combination of lenses.

SATELLITE Any object held in orbit around another object by its gravity, including moons and artificial satellites.

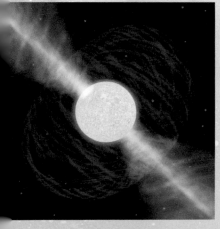

Pulsar with magnetic field shown in purple

The Sun, through a filter, shows prominences as dark streaks

ULTRAVIOLET Electromagnetic radiation with a shorter wavelength than visible light.

VACUUM A perfectly empty—or very nearly empty—space.

WAVELENGTH Distance between the peaks or troughs in waves of radiation.

X-RAY Electromagnetic radiation with a very short wavelength.

ZODIAC The 12 constellations through which the Sun, Moon, and planets appear to move.

Acknowledgments

Dorling Kindersley would like to thank:
Maria Blyzinsky for her invaluable assistance in helping with the objects at the Royal Observatory, Greenwich; Peter Robinson & Artemi Kyriacou for modeling; Peter Griffiths for making the models; Jack Challoner for advice; Frances Halpin for assistance with the laboratory experiments; Paul Lamb, Helen Diplock, & Neville Graham for helping with the design of the book; Anthony Wilson for reading the text; Harris City Technology College & The Royal Russell School for the loan of laboratory equipment; the Colour Company & the Roger Morris Partnership for retouching work; lenses supplied by Carl Lingard Telescopes; Jane Parker for the index; Stewart J. Wild for proof-reading; Christine Heilman for Americanization.

Illustrations Janos Marffy, Nick Hall, John Woodcock and Eugene Fleury

Photography Colin Keates, Harry Taylor, Christi Graham, Chas Howson, James Stevenson and Dave King.

Picture credits
t=top b=bottom c=center l=left r=right

American Institute of Physics: Emilio Segrè Visual Archives/Bell Telephone Laboratories 36cl; Research Corporation 36bl; Shapley Collection 64cl; **Ancient Art and Architecture Collection:** 13tl, 13cr, 24tl; **Anglo-Australian Telescope Board:** D. Malin 65tr; **Archive für Kunst und Geschichte, Berlin:** 23tl; National Maritime Museum 50c; **Associated Press:** 12tl; **The Bridgeman Art Library:** 32tl Lambeth Palace Library, London 21tr; **Ben Bussey:** 8bl; **The Observatories of the Carnegie Institution of Washington:** 43cr; Jean-Loup Charmet: 64tl; Bruce Coleman Ltd: 47c; © **CERN Geneva:** 2tr; **Corbis:** Bettmann 3tl; Roger Ressmeyer 1; Russeil Christophe/Kipa 73tl; Sandy Felsenthal 73r; Hulton-Deitsch Collection 72tl; **DK Images:** Rough Guides/Tim Draper 260-261b; **ESA:** 52bl; CNES/Arianespace 39tl; **ET Archive:** 13tr; **European Southern Observatory:** 69tr; **Mary Evans Picture Library:** 10tl, 18bl, 22cb, 46tl, 65tcl; **Galaxy Picture Library:** Boomerang Team 70b; JPL 68bl; MSSS 53tr, 53br; Margaret Penston 71br; Robin Scagell 72bc; STScI 71tl; University of Chicago 70cl; Richard Wainscoat 31tl, 68br; **Gemini Observatory:** Neelon Crawford/Polar Fine Arts/US National Science Foundation 29cl; **Ronald Grant Archive:** 72cl; **Robert Harding:** R. Frerck 36bc; C. Rennie l4br; **Hulton Deutsch:** 24c; **Henry E. Huntington Library and Art Gallery** 66tl; **Images Colour Library** 11tl, 11tr, 11c, 20tl, 20cl, 22cl; **Image Select** 23br, 25tc, 27tl, 30cl, 32cr; **JPL** 41cr, 53c, 53cr, 54tr, 55crb, 56cl, 56br, 59cr, 60cl, 67tr; **Lowell Observatory** 52tr; **Magnum:** E. Lessing 23tr; **NASA:** 2cl, 3c, 3tr, 7tr, 12cl, 39cr, 39cl, 39bl, 45cr, 48bl, 48cl, 50br, 51b, 60–61bc, 61tl, 259b; Dana Berry/Sky Works Digital 68c; ESA and Erich Karkoschka (University of Arizona) 57t; Hubble Space Telescope Comet Team 55t; JPL/Space Science Institute 38bc, 43tc, 53tl, 54br, 55bc, 57br, 57c, 55c, 59cr, 60cb, 65cr; LMSAL 43c; Project Apollo Archive 145; WMAP Science Team 70tr; **National Geophysical Data Centre:** NOAA 2cra, 2crb, 31cl; **National Maritime Museum Picture Library:** 10cl, l4cr, 19tl, 19tr, 29tl, 31br, 33tr, 58tl; **National Radio Astronomy Observatory:** AUI/ J M Uson 36tl; **Novosti (London):** 32br, 39cl, 51tr; **Planétarium de Brétagne:** 72-73; **Popperfoto:** 51bl; 71crb; **Rex Features Ltd:** 38clb; **Scala/Biblioteca Nationale:** 24cr; **Science Photo Library:** 22tl, 29bc, 35tl, 35bl, 52c, 57bc, 60tl, 61cr; Dr. J. Burgess 30tl; Chris Butler 74-75 bckgrd, 75br; Cern 71tr; Jean-Loup Charmet 15tl, 41tl;J-C Cuillandre/Canada-France-Hawaii telescope 72-73 bckgrd; F. Espenak 50tr; European Space Agency 39tl, 46-47bc; Mark Garlick 61cra; GE Astrospace 74cr; Jodrell Bank 37tr; Mehau Kulyk 71c, Dr. M J. Ledlow 37tl; Chris Madeley 74tl; F. D. Miller 35c; NASA 11crb, 24bc, 24bcr, 24br, 38cr, 45crb, 48-49bc, 53c, 61cr, 62bl, 63br, 68t, 70-71 bckgrd, 71bc; NOAO 65cl, 75cr; NASA/ESA/STSCI/E. KARKOSCHKA, U.ARIZONA 58–59b; Novosti 51cr; David Nunuk 29br, 69tl, 73tc; David Parker 74bl; Physics Dept. Imperial College 34crb, 34br; P. Plailly 42cl; Philippe Psaila 69br; Dr. M. Read 34tl; Royal Observatory, Edinburgh 63tr; J. Sandford 45t, 65bl; Space Telescope Science Institute/NASA 68-69 bckgrd, 75tl; Starlight/R. Ressemeyer 16tl, 31tr, 37cr, 59tl, 66-67c; U.S. Geological Survey 41br, 52l; Frank Zullo 72tr; **SOHO (ESA & NASA):** 42–43b; **Tony Stone Images:** 46cl; **Roger Viollet/Boyes** 42tl; Zefa UK:10-11bc, 12bl, 37b, 65br, 66bl; G. Heil 30bc.

With the exception of the items listed above, the object from the British Museum on page 12c, from the Science Museum on pages 25, 26 cl, and from the Natural History Museum on page 47tl, the objects on pages 4, 15b, 16, 18c, 18bc, 18r, 19tl, 19b, 20bl, 20br, 21bl, 21b, 24bl, 28bc, 29tr, 32cl, 32c, 32bl, 33tl, 33c, 33b, 35b, 40b, 42b, 44cl, 44bl, 44/8b, 46bl, 56bl, 58, 62tr, 64b, are all in the collection of the Roy Observatory, Greenwich.

WALL CHART: Corbis: Roger Ressmeyer crb; **DK Images:** Courtesy of The Science Museum, London tl; **iStockPhoto.com:** ca, **NASA:** br, cl, fbl; Johnson Space Center cb, Project Apollo Archives bl, cr, cra

DIVIDERS: Corbis: (moon divider). **HubbleSite:** Hubble Heritage / AURA / STScI / NASA (astronomy divider).

JACKET IMAGES: Front: DK Images: London Planetarium ftr (venus), tc (jupiter), (uranus); NASA tc (saturn), tl (neptune). **NASA.** Back: **DK Images:** NASA cl (moon), fbl, t (badges); NASA / Bob Gathany fcl; National Maritime Museum, London ca; The Science Museum, London br.

All other images © Dorling Kindersley. For further information, see:
www.dkimages.com

UNIVERSE

UNIVERSE

Eyewitness
Universe

Written by
ROBIN KERROD

What is the universe?

THE UNIVERSE IS EVERYTHING THAT EXISTS—today, in the past, and in the future. It is the immensity of space, populated by innumerable galaxies of stars and permeated with light and other radiation. When we look up into the blackness of the night sky, we are peering deep into the fathomless depths of the universe. Although the stars we see are all trillions of miles away, they are actually close neighbors, because the universe is unimaginably vast. Humans have been fascinated with the starry heavens from the earliest times and have been studying them systematically for at least 5,000 years. But although astronomy is probably the oldest science, it has changed continually throughout its history.

SPACESHIP EARTH
The *Apollo 8* astronauts were the first people to see our planet floating alone in the universe, as they headed for the Moon in 1968. Other astronauts had remained too close to Earth to see the planet whole. It is Spaceship Earth, a beautiful, cloud-flecked azure world, which is the only place we know where there is life. Profoundly important to us Earthlings, no doubt, but completely insignificant in the universe as a whole.

"The history of astronomy is a history of receding horizons."

EDWIN HUBBLE
Discoverer of galaxies beyond our own

ANCIENT ASTRONOMERS
Ancient Britons were familiar with the regular movements of the Sun, Moon, and stars. In around 2600 BCE they completed Stonehenge. In its circles of huge megaliths and smaller standing stones, there were alignments that marked critical positions of the Sun and Moon during the year. Many other ancient monuments around the world also have astronomical alignments.

Sun orbits Earth

Earth at center of Ptolemaic universe

ASTROLOGY
The priests of ancient Babylon looked to the skies for good and bad signs that they thought might affect the people and matters of state. The idea that what happened in the heavens could affect human lives formed the basis of astrology, a belief that held sway for thousands of years and still has its followers even today.

Babylonian astrological tablet

PTOLEMY'S UNIVERSE
The last of the great classical astronomers, an Alexandrian Greek named Ptolemy, summed up the ancient concept of the universe in about 150 CE. The Ptolemaic universe had Earth at its center, with the Sun, Moon, and planets circling around it, within a sphere of fixed stars.

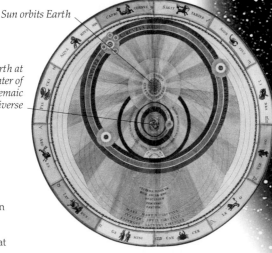

WORLD IN MOTION

Johannes Kepler
(1571–1630)

In 1543, astronomy was revolutionised when Nicolaus Copernicus put forward the idea of a Sun-centered universe. In the Copernican system, Earth and the other planets traveled around the Sun in circular orbits, but astronomers couldn't match the observed motions of the planets with this idea. Then German Johannes Kepler discovered why—the planets travel around the Sun, not in circles, but in ellipses. This discovery formed Kepler's first law of planetary motion.

Neptune   Saturn   Earth   Sun   Mars   Jupiter   Uranus

CELESTIAL CLOCKWORK

Kepler's laws of planetary motion explained precisely how the planets move. He likened what he called the "celestial machine" to clockwork and came close to fathoming the underlying cause, believing that the Sun must assert a magnetic force on the planets. In 1687, Isaac Newton finally explained why the planets orbit as they do, showing that gravity, not magnetism, is the fundamental force that holds the universe together.

Hand-wound mechanism

Mechanical model (orrery) of the solar system

STARS AND GALAXIES

Early astronomers visualized the stars as points on the inside of a great celestial sphere that enveloped Earth. By the late 1700s, astronomers were beginning to work out what our galaxy was really like. By plotting the distribution of stars, William Herschel proved that our galaxy was lens-shaped (it is, in fact, a bulging spiral). The existence of galaxies beyond our own was not proved until 1923, when Edwin Hubble discovered that the Andromeda "nebula" lay far beyond our home star system.

The Andromeda
Galaxy, M31

Andromeda is a spiral galaxy like our own

Stars in our own galaxy

EVERYTHING'S RELATIVE

Early last century, a young German physicist named Albert Einstein transformed the way in which we look at space and the universe. He introduced his theories of relativity—the special theory in 1905 and the general theory 10 years later. One of the ideas presented in these theories is that nothing can move faster than the speed of light and that energy and mass are equivalent and can be converted into each other. Also, three-dimensional space and time are not separate entities, but are interrelated.

A field of galaxies whose light has taken up to 10 billion years to reach us

How do we fit in?

To us earthlings, our planet is the most important thing there is, and not very long ago, people thought our planet was the center of the universe. Nothing could be farther from the truth—in the universe as a whole, Earth is not the least bit special. It is an insignificant speck of rock circling a very ordinary star in an ordinary galaxy in one tiny corner of space. Exactly how big the universe is, no one really knows, but astronomers are now detecting objects so far away that their light has been traveling toward us for about 13 billion years. This puts them at a distance of some 76 sextillion miles (123 sextillion kilometers)—a distance beyond our comprehension.

Medieval world map

SMALL COSMOS
In medieval times, before the great voyages of discovery and exploration that began in the 15th century, people assumed that Earth was the whole universe. Many supported the idea of a flat Earth—go too far and you would fall over the edge.

SCALE OF THE UNIVERSE
Our insignificance in the universe as a whole is graphically portrayed in this sequence of images, from life at the human scale to the immeasurable immensity of intergalactic space. One way to help understand the scale of the universe is to consider how long it would take to travel from place to place, at the speed of light, 186,000 miles per second (300,000 km/s). Astronomers frequently use the light-year (5.9 trillion miles or 9.5 trillion km) as a measure of cosmic distances.

From space, Earth looks blue due to the vast expanses of surface water. White clouds surround the planet.

The Oort Cloud of icy, cometlike bodies forms an outer boundary around the whole solar system. It would take over a year and a half to reach the outer edge of the Oort Cloud at the speed of light.

Runners in a marathon cross a crowded bridge.

A satellite in orbit, hundreds of miles above Earth, looks down on the city.

OUR VIEW OF THE UNIVERSE
We look out at the universe from inside a layer of stars that forms the disk of our galaxy. We see the greatest density of stars when we look along the plane of this disk—in this direction the galaxy extends for tens of thousands of light-years. In the night sky, we see this dense band as the Milky Way. To either side of the Milky Way, we are looking through the disk, but this time perpendicular to its plane and see far fewer stars. By combining satellite images of the sky in all directions, we can capture an overall picture of what the universe looks like from inside our galaxy (left).

In the solar system, Earth lies three planets out from the Sun. It would take more than eight minutes to travel to the Sun at the speed of light.

While it would take only a few hundred thousand years to reach our closest galactic neighbors at light speed, most galaxies would require journey times of millions of years. The farthest ones would take billions of years to reach.

...o reach the next nearest star would take over four years at the speed of light. Crossing the galaxy from edge to edge would take 100,000 years.

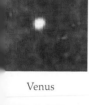

Venus

Earth

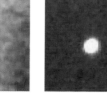

Jupiter

Saturn

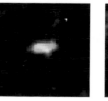

Uranus

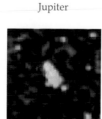

Neptune

FAMILY PORTRAIT
Since the beginning of the Space Age, knowledge about our neighbors in space, the planets, has mushroomed. On a remarkable 12-year voyage of discovery, the *Voyager* probes visited all four giant planets—Jupiter, Saturn, Uranus, and Neptune. In 1990, *Voyager 1* looked back on its way out of the solar system and snapped a family portrait of six of the planets. They appear as little more than tiny specks lost in the vastness of space.

THE LOCAL UNIVERSE
Through the most powerful telescopes, astronomers can see galaxies in every direction they look. The picture above shows a plot of the positions of around two million galaxies in one region of space. Careful study shows that the galaxies are arranged in clusters and superclusters, which themselves form interconnecting sheets and ribbons around vast empty spaces, or voids—the large-scale structure of the cosmos.

How the universe works

THE UNIVERSE IS MADE UP of scattered islands of matter in a vast ocean of empty space. Energy travels through the universe in the form of light and other radiation. Fundamental forces and laws dictate what matter is like and how it behaves. The strongest of the four fundamental forces (the strong force) binds particles together in the nucleus of atoms. The weak and electromagnetic forces also act within the atom. Electromagnetism binds electrons to the nucleus; it also creates the phenomena of electricity and magnetism. Gravity is the weakest of the fundamental forces, but operates over the greatest distances to hold the universe together.

Water droplet

Water molecule consists of one oxygen and two hydrogen atoms

Inside atom, electrons orbit a tiny nucleus

Protons have a positive electric charge

Electrons have a negative electric charge

Neutrons have no charge

Nucleus

Protons and neutrons are made up of even tinier particles called quarks

INSIDE ATOMS
The atoms that make up matter are not indivisible, as Democritus and Dalton thought. They are made up in turn of tinier, subatomic particles. The three main particles are protons, neutrons, and electrons. The protons and neutrons are found in the center, or nucleus, of an atom, while the electrons circle in orbits around the nucleus.

ELEMENTS AND ATOMS
Greek philosopher Empedocles (around 490–430 BCE) believed matter was made up of four ingredients, or elements—fire, air, water, and earth. His fellow philosopher Democritus (around 460–370 BCE) thought instead that matter was made of tiny, indivisible parts he called atoms. His ideas were forgotten until English chemist John Dalton (1766–1844) laid the foundations of modern atomic theory in 1808. Matter is made of different chemical elements; each is unique because it is made up of different atoms.

Empedocles

Peak

Trough

Trough

Wavelength

Radio waves
(wavelengths 1 mm or more)

A FAMILY OF WAVES
The radiation that carries energy through the universe takes the form of electric and magnetic disturbances that we call electromagnetic waves. There are many kinds of radiation, differing in wavelength—the distance between one peak or trough of the wave and the next. Visible light is radiation that our eyes can detect. It has wavelengths between 390 and 700 nanometers (nm) that we see as colors from violet to red (one nanometer is a billionth of a meter). There are invisible wavelengths shorter than violet light and longer than red. Gamma rays have wavelengths of fractions of a nanometer, while radio waves can be miles long.

Particle tracks at the European nuclear research center in Geneva

Similar poles of magnets repel each other

Iron filings reveal invisible lines of magnetic field

PROBING THE ATOM
Physicists use incredibly powerful machines called particle accelerators, or "atom smashers," to investigate the structure of atoms. These machines accelerate beams of subatomic particles and smash them into atoms or other particle beams. The force of collision generates showers of subatomic particles, which leave trails of tiny bubbles in detectors called bubble chambers.

MAGNETISM
Magnetism is the force that makes magnets attract iron filings. The Earth has magnetism, too. When suspended, a magnet will align itself north-south, in the direction of our planet's magnetic field. Earth's magnetism extends far out into space, creating a bubblelike region called the magnetosphere. Other planets have powerful magnetic fields; so do the Sun and the stars.

GRAVITY

English scientist Isaac Newton (1642–1727) established the basic law of gravity: that every body attracts every other body because of its mass. The more massive a body, the greater its gravitational attraction. With nearly 100 times the mass of Earth, Saturn has enormous gravity. Its pull keeps rings of particles circling around its equator and at least 60 moons in orbit around it. In turn, Saturn is held in the grip of the Sun's gravity, like all the planets. The Sun's gravity reaches out trillions of miles into space.

Saturn, its rings, and three of its satellites photographed by the Hubble Space Telescope

> *"The most incomprehensible thing about the world is that it is comprehensible."*
>
> **ALBERT EINSTEIN**

| Infrared (700 nm to 1 mm) | Ultraviolet (10 nm to 390 nm) | X rays (0.001 nm to 10 nm) | Gamma rays (up to 0.001 nm) |

Visible light
(390 nm to 700 nm)

Europe's infrared observatory ISO

ISO view of Rho Ophiuchi star-forming region

THE HIDDEN UNIVERSE

With our eyes, we see the universe as it appears in visible light. But the universe gives out radiation at invisible wavelengths as well, from gamma rays to radio waves. We can study radio waves from the heavens with ground-based radio telescopes. Other invisible radiations can only be studied from space, using satellites. If we could see at other wavelengths, the universe would appear quite different.

ENERGY AND LIGHT

When you heat up an iron poker in a fire, its color changes, from gray to dull red, to bright red, and to yellow-white. As the temperature rises, the iron gives out shorter wavelengths (colors) of light. It is the same in space—the coolest red stars have a temperature of less than 5,500°F (3,000°C), while the hottest blue-white stars have temperatures more than 10 times greater. Even hotter, higher-energy objects emit mostly ultraviolet and X-ray radiation.

In the beginning

WE HAVE A GOOD IDEA of what the universe is like today and what makes it tick. But where did it come from? How old is it? How has it evolved? What will happen to it in the future? The branch of astronomy that studies and attempts to answer these questions is known as cosmology. Cosmologists think they know when and how the universe began and has evolved, although they are not so certain about how it might end (p. 86). They believe that an explosive event called the Big Bang, around 13.75 billion years ago, created the universe and started it expanding. Amazingly, cosmologists have figured out the history of the universe since it was one-ten-million-trillion-trillion-trillionth of a second old. It was at this time that the known laws of physics and the fundamental forces of nature came into being.

WHAT CAME BEFORE?
Nothing existed before the Big Bang—no matter, no space, no radiation, no laws of physics, no time. The birth of a baby marks the start of its independent life, in the same way that the Big Bang marks the start of time for the universe. But the baby was formed from its parents, whereas all the material of the universe was created in the Big Bang.

HOW THE UNIVERSE EVOLVED
The most drastic changes in the universe occurred in the first three minutes after the Big Bang. During this time, the temperature of the universe fell from countless trillion trillions of degrees to about a billion degrees. This dramatic cooling allowed the conversion of energy into subatomic particles, such as electrons, and hydrogen and helium nuclei. But it took a further 300,000 years before these particles combined to form atoms of hydrogen and helium, which would later seed the first galaxies.

ABBÉ GEORGES LEMAÎTRE
Around 1930, Georges Lemaître (1894–1966), a Belgian priest turned cosmologist, suggested the universe was created in a single moment when a "primeval atom" exploded. Matter was scattered into space and eventually condensed into stars and galaxies. Lemaître's ideas laid the foundation for the Big Bang theory.

Big Bang creates the universe, which is infinitely small, infinitely hot, and full of energy

Energy from the Big Bang creates particles of matter and antimatter, which annihilate one another

As the universe cools, combinations of particles become stable

A fraction of a second into its life, the universe expands to an enormous size in an event called inflation

As the universe cools down, quarks become the dominant type of matter

Quarks collide to form protons and neutrons, the particles found in atomic nuclei

Lightweight electrons and positron particles form

Matter too dense for light to travel freely

Light waves bounce off particles before traveling far, just as in a fog

Temperature drops through 5,500°F (3,000°C) and electrons are soaked up into atoms

Most electrons and positrons collide and annihilate each other

Universe expanding from Big Bang

Temperature is steadily dropping

BECOMING TRANSPARENT
Until the universe was about 300,000 years old, it was full of particles and opaque. Then electrons began combining with atomic nuclei to form the first atoms, an event called decoupling. The fog of particles suddenly cleared, and radiation was able to travel long distances for the first time. The universe became transparent.

Matter condenses to form galaxies and clusters

Photons now travel freely in largely empty space

Photons from the time of decoupling are the earliest we can hope to dete...

Penzias and Wilson with their radio horn antenna

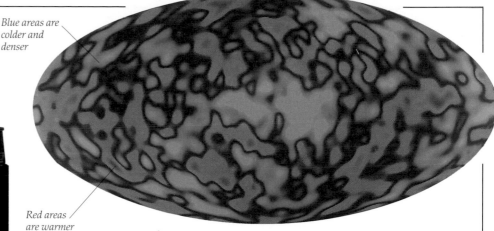

Blue areas are colder and denser

Red areas are warmer and emptier

ECHOES OF THE BIG BANG

If the Big Bang really happened, physicists calculate that by now the temperature of the whole universe would have fallen to about 5.5°F (3°C) above absolute zero, -459°F (-273°C). In 1965, US physicists Arno Penzias and Robert Wilson picked up weak radio signals coming from all parts of the sky. They were equivalent to a cosmic background temperature of around -454°F (-270°C), providing convincing evidence for the Big Bang.

RIPPLES IN THE COSMOS

For the galaxies we see today to have formed, the universe must be "lumpy"—even at the earliest times, matter must have clumped together in certain areas. The COBE (Cosmic Background Explorer) satellite made the first accurate map of the radiation left over from the Big Bang (above). It shows slight variations in the background temperature that are believed to reflect the lumpiness in the early universe.

BOOMERANG

The joint US/European BOOMERANG project flew microwave instruments into the stratosphere around Antarctica in balloons. In 1998 and again in 2003, the balloons rode the winds that circle the South Pole. With their detectors cooled to a fraction of a degree above absolute zero, BOOMERANG mapped the microwave background with great precision.

A relatively small number of electrons survive

Protons and neutrons combine to form atomic nuclei

Electrons still unattached

Electrons combine with nuclei to form atoms

The universe as it is today, full of galaxies, stars, and planets, and still expanding

Universe still opaque. Pressure of radiation stops most matter from clumping together.

Universe becomes transparent

Matter starts to condense

Fate of the universe

THE BIG BANG CREATED THE UNIVERSE and started it growing, and it has been expanding ever since. But what will happen in the future—what is the ultimate fate of the cosmos? Will the universe expand forever, or will it one day stop expanding and endure a long, protracted cold death? Or, perhaps it will be ripped apart, or even shrink until it is squashed together in a reverse Big Bang. The answer depends on the density of the universe's matter and energy, and on the effect of dark energy. This unknown gravity-opposing force constitutes about 73 percent of the universe compared to atom-based matter such as stars and galaxies which makes up just four percent.

EINSTEIN'S MISTAKE?
In 1917, when Albert Einstein (1879–1955) set out to describe the universe mathematically, he included a "cosmological constant"— an outward force to prevent the universe from collapsing. At the time he did not know that the cosmos is in fact expanding. His "mistaken" idea has recently been revived with the concept of dark energy.

THE EXPANDING UNIVERSE
In 1917, US astronomer Vesto Slipher found that most galaxies he studied were rushing away from us (see below). The universe seemed to be expanding. Using the Hooker telescope (above) at Mount Wilson Observatory, Edwin Hubble discovered that the rate of expansion depends on distance. The more distant a galaxy, the faster it is traveling.

Earth

Star moving away from Earth

Spectral lines formed by elements in star shift to the red

RED SHIFTS
When an ambulance speeds past us, we hear the pitch of its siren drop. The wavelength of sound waves reaching us is stretched as the source moves away and each wave takes longer to reach us. Similarly, light waves from a receding galaxy are stretched to longer (redder) wavelengths. The color change is hard to detect, but the shift is easily measured in changes to the dark "spectral lines."

UNIVERSAL EXPANSION
From Earth, we find that galaxies are rushing away from us in every direction. They are not just rushing away from us, but also from one another. You can imagine the expansion by thinking of the universe as being like a balloon, with the galaxies scattered on the surface. With each extra blow into the balloon, the universe expands, and the galaxies move farther apart.

Galaxies were closer together in the early universe

Big Bang—origin of the universe's expansion

Distance between galaxies is increasing

Present-day universe

Universe a few billion years ago

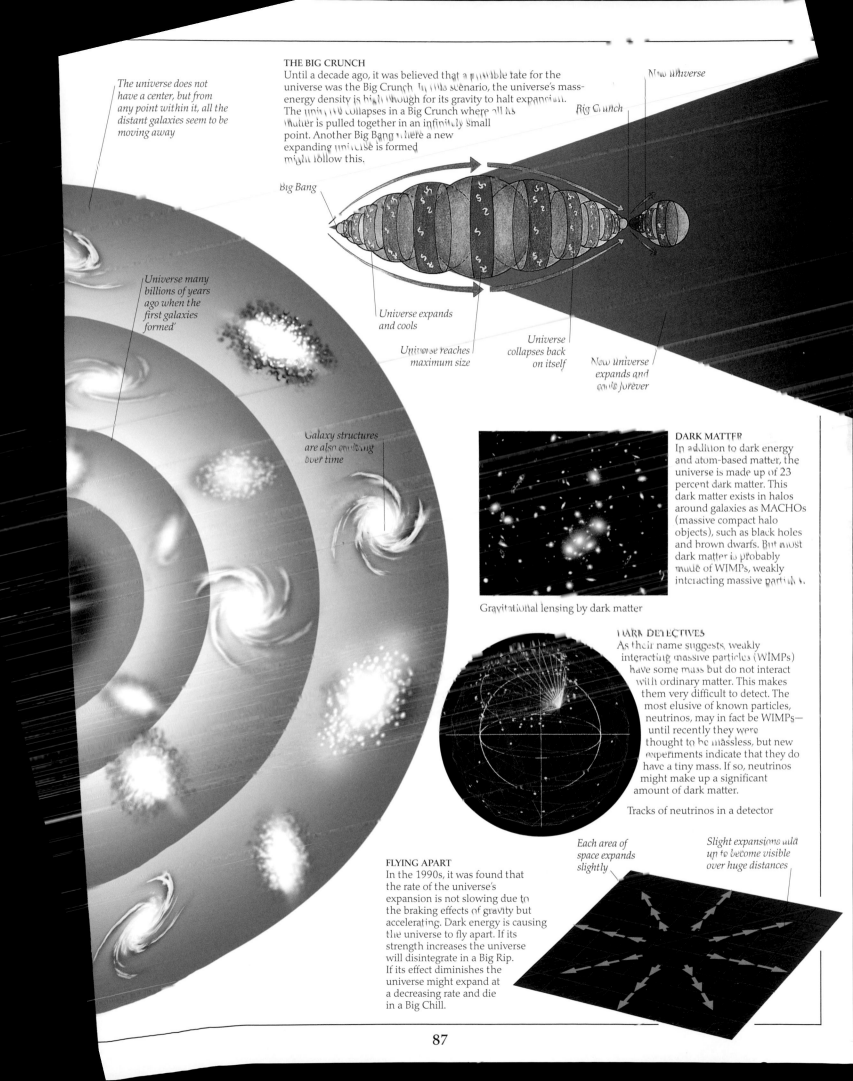

THE BIG CRUNCH

Until a decade ago, it was believed that a possible fate for the universe was the Big Crunch. In this scenario, the universe's mass-energy density is high enough for its gravity to halt expansion. The universe collapses in a Big Crunch where all its matter is pulled together in an infinitely small point. Another Big Bang where a new expanding universe is formed might follow this.

New universe

Big Crunch

Big Bang

The universe does not have a center, but from any point within it, all the distant galaxies seem to be moving away

Universe many billions of years ago when the first galaxies formed

Universe expands and cools

Universe reaches maximum size

Universe collapses back on itself

New universe expands and cools forever

Galaxy structures are also evolving over time

DARK MATTER

In addition to dark energy and atom-based matter, the universe is made up of 23 percent dark matter. This dark matter exists in halos around galaxies as MACHOs (massive compact halo objects), such as black holes and brown dwarfs. But most dark matter is probably made of WIMPs, weakly interacting massive particles.

Gravitational lensing by dark matter

DARK DETECTIVES

As their name suggests, weakly interacting massive particles (WIMPs) have some mass but do not interact with ordinary matter. This makes them very difficult to detect. The most elusive of known particles, neutrinos, may in fact be WIMPs—until recently they were thought to be massless, but new experiments indicate that they do have a tiny mass. If so, neutrinos might make up a significant amount of dark matter.

Tracks of neutrinos in a detector

FLYING APART

In the 1990s, it was found that the rate of the universe's expansion is not slowing due to the braking effects of gravity but accelerating. Dark energy is causing the universe to fly apart. If its strength increases the universe will disintegrate in a Big Rip. If its effect diminishes the universe might expand at a decreasing rate and die in a Big Chill.

Each area of space expands slightly

Slight expansions add up to become visible over huge distances

Exploring the universe

ASTRONOMERS HAVE SPENT more than five millennia gazing at the heavens, studying the stars and constellations, following the Moon through its phases, watching the planets wander through the zodiac, seeing comets come and go, and witnessing eclipses. A giant leap in astronomy came when Galileo first turned a telescope on the heavens in 1609. Since then, ever larger telescopes have revealed ever more secrets of a universe vaster than anyone can imagine. Other kinds of telescopes have been built to study the invisible radiations stars and galaxies give out. Radio waves can be studied from the ground, but other rays have to be studied from space because Earth's atmosphere absorbs them as they pass through it.

LOOKING WITH LENSES
Some of the lens-type telescopes, or refractors, used by early astronomers reached an amazing size. They used small light-gathering lenses with a long "focal length" to achieve greater magnification. Christiaan Huygens' giant "aerial telescope" (above) was 210 ft (64 m) long.

Eyepiece

Incoming light rays

Aperture allows light to reach primary mirror

Magnetometer detects Earth's magnetic field

Light rays reflected inward

Primary mirror

Secondary mirror bounces light to eyepiece

Mounting allows accurate pointing of telescope—this is a "Dobsonian" mount

NEWTONIAN REFLECTOR
Most astronomical telescopes use mirrors to gather and focus light. Some still follow Isaac Newton's original design of 1671. A large curved primary mirror gathers and focuses the light, reflecting it back along the telescope tube onto a secondary plane (flat) mirror. This mirror in turn reflects the light into an eyepiece mounted near the front of the tube. In most professional telescopes, the eyepiece is replaced by cameras or other instruments.

THE HUBBLE SPACE TELESCOPE
The Hubble Space Telescope (HST) is a reflector with a 8-ft (2.4-m) diameter mirror. It circles Earth every 90 minutes in an orbit about 380 miles (610 km) high. It made a disastrous debut in 1990, when its primary mirror was found to be flawed. But its vision was corrected, and the satellite is now sending back some of the most spectacular images ever taken in space. High above the atmosphere, it views the universe with perfect clarity, not only at visible wavelengths but in the ultraviolet and infrared as well.

Solar arrays produce 3,000 watts of electricity

Comet Wild 2

GOING THERE
Space probes have been winging their way to explore the Moon, planets, and other bodies in the solar system since 1959. Some fly by their targets; some go into orbit around them; and others land. *Stardust* flew by Comet Wild 2 on January 2, 2004, and captured comet dust which it returned to Earth just over two years later.

Stardust probe

Domes of the Keck Telescopes, Mauna Kea, Hawaii

TWIN KECKS
The two Keck telescopes in Hawaii are among the most powerful in the world. They have light-gathering mirrors measuring 33 ft (10 m) across. These mirrors are made not in one piece, but from 36 separate segments. Each is individually supported and computer controlled so that it always forms, with the others, a perfect mirror shape. When the two telescopes are linked, they can create an effective mirror 280 ft (85 m) in diameter.

RADIO ASTRONOMY

The first radio signals from space were detected in 1931 by Bell Telephone engineer Karl Jansky. Because radio waves are so much longer than light waves, radio astronomers must use huge dishes to form a detailed image. Many radio astronomy observatories use sets of dishes in unison to form effective collecting areas miles across. The Very Large Array radio telescope near Socorro in New Mexico uses 27 dishes in various configurations. An even greater receiving area is produced by linking radio telescopes in different countries.

Telescopes of the Very Large Array

Sunshade prevents strong light from damaging instruments

Handrail for astronauts

High-gain antenna

Telescope tube is covered in insulating foil to prevent expansion and contraction as external temperature changes

HST is powered by two 22-ft (6.6-m) solar panels. Batteries store power for the dark periods of Hubble's orbit

Housing for computers and other equipment

Position of primary mirror

Instrument segment houses cameras and spectrometers

Access panels allow individual instruments to be replaced and upgraded

High-gain antenna for communications with Earth. Pictures are sent back like TV signals

Integral

HIGH-ENERGY TELESCOPES

[Tel]escopes like *Integral* are needed to detect high-[en]ergy radiation from the most violent regions of the [un]iverse—around quasars, supernovae, and black [ho]les. Integral detects gamma rays; other telescopes [su]ch as XMM-Newton detect X-rays.

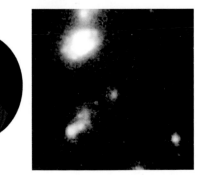

RECORD BREAKER

With its formidable resolution, the HST has been able to spot objects as far away as 13 billion light-years. Their light has taken so long to reach us that we are seeing them as they were when the universe was in its infancy.

HST image of a supernova 10 billion light-years away

Our corner of the universe

THE COPERNICAN SYSTEM
In 1543, Polish astronomer and priest Nicolaus Copernicus (1473–1543) put our corner of the universe in order, suggesting that the Sun and not Earth was at the center of our planetary system. The idea contradicted the teachings of the Church, but was eventually proved by Galileo.

ANCIENT ASTRONOMERS BELIEVED that Earth had to be the center of the universe. Didn't the Sun, the Moon, and all the other heavenly bodies and the stars revolve around it? Of course today we know they don't—the Sun is really the center of our little corner of the universe, and the Earth and planets circle around that body. They are part of the Sun's family, or solar system. The Sun is different from all other bodies in the solar system because it is a star, and it is the only body that produces light of its own. We see all the other objects by the sunlight they reflect. Eight planets, including Earth, are the most important members of the solar system, along with three dwarf planets and over one hundred and fifty moons. The billions of minor members include rocky lumps called asteroids and icy bodies called comets.

PLANETS
A planet is a world massive enough to pull itself into a roughly spherical shape that orbits the Sun in a neighborhood cleared of other objects. Our planet Earth is the third from the Sun, and its position provides perfect conditions for life.

MOONS
All the planets except Mercury and Venus have satellites, or moons, circling around them. The four giant outer planets have more than 150 moons between them. This is Saturn's moon Mimas.

Mercury

Neptune takes 164.8 years to orbit the Sun

Mars takes 1.9 years to orbit the Sun

Mars

Pluto

Pluto takes 248 years to orbit the Sun once; it was classed as a planet from its discovery in 1930 until 2006

Jupiter takes 11.9 years to orbit the Sun

Jupiter

Asteroid Belt contains the dwarf planet Ceres and billions of asteroids

Uranus

Saturn takes 29.5 years to orbit the Sun

DWARF PLANETS IN KUIPER BELT
Beyond Neptune is the Kuiper Belt of rock-and-ice objects. The largest are the dwarf planets Eris (above) and Pluto. Dwarf planets are a class of almost round bodies orbiting the Sun, introduced in 2006. Since 2008 they are also known as plutoids—dwarf planets in the Kuiper Belt.

Uranus takes 84 years to orbit the Sun

HOW IT ALL BEGAN

Five billion years ago there was nothing in our corner of space but a huge billowing cloud of gas and dust, which had remained unchanged for millions of years. Then something disturbed it, and it began to collapse and spin under gravity. Over time, a thick disk of matter formed, which had a denser region at the center. This central mass became progressively denser and hotter and evolved into our Sun. Once the Sun had formed, the surrounding disk thinned out and formed into separate planets.

Gas and dust collapse into disk

Central regions heat up

Sun ignites and blows away much of surrounding gas cloud

Planets formed as at first tiny and then increasingly large particles came together

Asteroid Ida

ASTEROIDS

Sometimes called minor planets, the asteroids are lumps of rock and sometimes metal left over from the formation of the solar system. They are found mainly in the space between the orbits of Mars and Jupiter, in a region known as the Asteroid Belt. However, some asteroids stray outside the Asteroid Belt and may come uncomfortably close to Earth. The space probe *Galileo* photographed asteroid Ida on its way to Jupiter in 1995—it is about 35 miles (55 km) long.

All eight planets follow orbits close to the plane of the Sun's equator, which is called the plane of the ecliptic

Near Earth Asteroids orbit close to our planet

Sun

Venus

Earth

Some asteroids, called Trojans, share Jupiter's orbit

> "We shall prove Earth to be a wandering body... and not the sink of all dull refuse of the universe."
>
> **GALILEO**

Neptune

Saturn

MAP OF THE SOLAR SYSTEM

The planets orbit the Sun at different distances, from about [58] million miles (58 million km) for innermost Mercury, to [ab]out 2.8 billion miles (4.5 billion km) for the outermost planet [Ne]ptune. The planets don't move in perfect circles but in [el]liptical (oval) orbits, trapped by the pull of the Sun's [gra]vity. They travel in much the same plane.

COMETS

Comets are icy bodies that form a vast sphere called the Oort Cloud, which surrounds the planetary part of the solar system. Occasionally one leaves the cloud and travels in toward the Sun. The heat turns its snow and ice to gas and the comet becomes big and bright enough to be seen.

Our local star

THE STAR WE CALL THE SUN dominates our corner of space. With a diameter of about 870,000 miles (1,400,000 km), it is more than a hundred times wider than Earth. Because of its huge mass, it has powerful gravity and attracts a vast collection of objects both large (such as Earth and the other planets) and small (such as comets). These bodies form the Sun's family, or solar system. Like other stars, the Sun is a great ball of incandescent gas, or rather, gases. The two main ones are hydrogen and helium, but there are small amounts of more than 70 other chemical elements as well. To us on Earth, 93 million miles (150 million kilometers) away, the Sun is all-important. It provides the light and warmth needed to make our planet suitable for life.

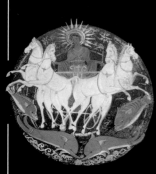

SUN LEGENDS
The Sun was worshiped as a god from the earliest times. In ancient Egypt, the falcon-headed Sun god Re was the most powerful deity. In early Greek mythology, the Sun god Helios carried the Sun across the heavens every day in a horse-drawn flying chariot.

Visible surface of the Sun is called the photosphere

Prominences are fountains of hot gas that loop above the surface

The Sun's visible surface is made up of fine "granulations"

Photosphere's temperature is around 9,900°F (5,500°C)

The Sun has powerful magnetism, which gives rise to sunspots, prominences, and huge outbursts called flares. Magnetism and activity vary regularly over a period of about 11 years. This is called the solar, or sunspot cycle. Over this period, activity on the Sun goes from minimum to maximum and back again, as shown in this series of X-ray images.

Corona extends millions of miles into space

X-rays from hot magnetized gas

Sun emits most X-rays at maximum

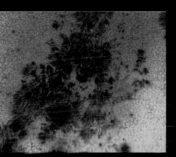

Moon blots out Sun's surface during total eclipse

SUNSPOTS

Sunspots are dark patches on the Sun's surface, about 2,700°F (1,500°C) cooler than the surrounding surface. They vary from short-lived "pores" less than 600 miles (1,000 km) across to huge features a hundred times bigger that persist for months,

Convective zone

Radiative zone

Photosphere at about 9,900°F (5,500°C)

THE CORONA

An extensive atmosphere of gases surrounds the Sun, gradually thinning until it merges into space. We can see the nearly white outer atmosphere, or corona ("crown"), only during a total eclipse, when the Sun's brilliant surface is blotted out. Temperatures in the corona can hit 4 million°F (3 million°C).

INSIDE THE SUN

The Sun is a great ball of glowing gas that is hottest and most dense at the center, or core. There, in a kind of nuclear furnace, fusion reactions produce the energy that keeps the Sun shining. Energy takes over a million years to transfer from the core to the surface— first by radiation, then by convection, or currents of rising gas.

Core, temperature about 27 million°F (15 million°C)

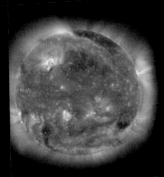

HIGH-ENERGY SUN

The Sun radiates not only light and heat, but also ultraviolet rays and X-rays. These forms of radiation pack great energy and pose a danger to life on Earth. Fortunately, our planet's atmosphere prevents most of the ultraviolet and all the X-rays from reaching the ground.

Subatomic particles released

Radiation emitted

Excess energy emitted

Proton (hydrogen nucleus)

Two protons fuse, one changing into neutron

Another proton joins

Two identical groups fuse, ejecting spare protons to form helium

THE SOLAR FURNACE

Within the Sun's core, energy is produced by nuclear fusion reactions. In fusion, four hydrogen atom nuclei (centers) join together or fuse to form the nucleus of a helium atom—a process that can only happen at tremendous temperatures and pressures. In the process, a tiny amount of excess mass is lost, transformed directly into a vast amount of energy.

The nuclear fusion process

Earth's Moon

THE MOON IS EARTH'S CLOSEST companion in space, its only natural satellite. On average, it lies 239,000 miles (384,000 km) away. It has no light of its own, but shines by reflected sunlight. As the Moon circles the Earth every month, it appears to change shape, from slim crescent to full circle, and back again every 29.5 days. We call these changing shapes the phases of the Moon, and they mark one of the great rhythms of nature. With a diameter of 2,160 miles (3,476 km), the Moon is a rocky world like Earth, but has no atmosphere, water, or life. Astronomers think that the Moon was formed from the debris flung into space in a collision between Earth and a Mars-sized body about 4.5 billion years ago.

Bright crater surrounded by rays

Craters formed when meteorites crashed into the Moon

New Moon

Crescent

First quarter

Waxing gibbous

Full Moon

Waning gibbous

Last quarter

Decrecent

The dark part of the crescent Moon sometimes dimly reflects light from Earth

Actor Lon Chaney Jr. in The *Wolf Man* (1941)

LUNAR LEGENDS
The Greeks and Romans worshiped the Moon as the goddess Artemis or Diana. Ancient people thought the Moon had magic powers, and that staying too long in the light of the full Moon could make them insane. Our word lunatic comes from *luna*, the Latin word for the Moon. People also believed the full Moon could turn some people into werewolves who preyed on humans and ate human flesh.

THE CHANGING FACE
The changing phases of the Moon happen as the Sun lights up different amounts of the side that faces Earth. At new Moon we can't see the Moon at all because the Sun is lighting up only the far side. As the Moon moves farther around in its orbit, more and more of its face gets lit up until all of it is illuminated at full Moon. Then the sunlit side moves on and the Moon's phase decreases, until it disappears completely.

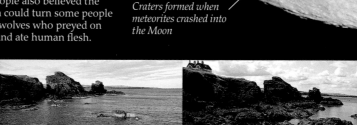

LUNAR GRAVITY
The Moon's gravity is only about one-sixth of Earth's, so it has been unable to hang onto any gases to make an atmosphere. The lack of atmosphere means the temperature varies widely from day (around 230°F, 110°C) to night (around -290°F, -180°C). Weak though it is, the Moon's gravity still affects Earth. It tugs at the oceans to create tides. The water bulges to form a high tide directly beneath the Moon and also forms a bulge on the opposite side of Earth. On either side of high tide is a low tide where water has been drawn away. There are two highs and two lows roughly every day.

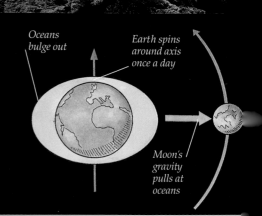

Oceans bulge out

Earth spins around axis once a day

Moon's gravity pulls at oceans

THE FACE OF THE MOON

The Moon always presents the same face toward Earth. This happens because it spins once on its axis in exactly the same time as it circles once around Earth—27.3 days. This motion is called captured rotation and other large moons do it. The dark regions we see on the Moon's face are vast dusty plains. Early astronomers thought they might be seas and called them *maria*, which is Latin for seas. The brighter regions are much older highlands, which are heavily cratered and are thought to be part of the Moon's original crust.

Aitken Basin is the largest crater in the solar system

The Moon's south polar region

WALKING ON THE MOON

On July 20, 1969, *Apollo 11* astronauts Neil Armstrong and Buzz Aldrin planted the first human footprints on the Moon. They were the first of 12 US astronauts who explored "seas" and highland areas, set up scientific stations, and brought back samples of soil and rock. They found that lunar soil, called regolith, is somewhat like plowed-up soil on Earth—it has been crushed by constant bombardment from space. The majority of the rocks are volcanic, often like Earth rocks called basalts.

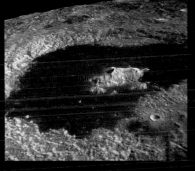

THE FAR SIDE

No one had seen the far side of the Moon until orbiting probes mapped it in the 1960s. It is much more rugged and heavily cratered than the nearside and has no large "seas." One of its most prominent features is the 115-mile (185-km) crater Tsiolkovsky.

THE HIDDEN POLES

We never see the Moon's poles from Earth, but space probes have inspected them. They show that some polar craters and basins are in perpetual darkness and could contain hidden deposits of ice. If proven, these ice deposits could provide water for future human explorers.

Dark maria (seas) are plains of solidified lava'

Lunar highlands

Seen from the Moon, Earth goes through phases

Lunar surface many miles below

EARTHRISE

The *Apollo* astronauts took stunning photographs of the Moon on the surface and also from orbit. None are more dramatic than the shots showing Earth rising over the Moon's horizon. They show the huge contrast between our colorful, living world and its drab, dead satellite.

Comparing the planets

GOING OUT FROM THE SUN, the eight planets are
Mercury, Venus, Earth, Mars, Jupiter, Saturn, Uranus,
and Neptune. They are all different from one another,
but divide mainly into two kinds, depending on their
composition. The four small inner planets are made up
mainly of rock, and the four giant outer ones are made
up mainly of gas. All the planets have two motions in
space: the period in which a planet spins on its axis
is its rotation period, sometimes thought of as
its "day," and the time it takes to make one
orbit of the Sun is its "year."

THE PLANETS TO SCALE
The planets vary widely in size. Jupiter is truly
gigantic, containing more matter than all the other
planets put together. It could swallow more than
1,300 bodies the size of the Earth and over 25,000
worlds the size of Mercury. Yet the cores at the
centers of the giant planets are much smaller—
around the size of Earth. At the other extreme,
Mercury is tiny—Jupiter and Saturn each have
a moon bigger than Mercury.

MERCURY
Diameter: 3,032 miles/
4,880 km
Distance from Sun:
36 million miles/
58 million km
Rotation period: 58.7 days
Time to orbit Sun: 88 days
No. of moons: 0

EARTH
Diameter: 7,926 miles/12,756 km
Distance from Sun:
93 million miles/
149.6 million km
Rotation period: 23.93 hours
Time to orbit Sun: 365.25 days
No. of moons: 1

VENUS
Diameter: 7,521 miles/
12,104 km
Distance from Sun:
67 million miles/108 million km
Rotation period: 243 days
Time to orbit Sun: 224.7 days
No. of moons: 0

MARS
Diameter: 4,222 miles/
6,794 km
Distance from Sun:
142 million miles/
228 million km
Rotation period: 24.6 hours
Time to orbit Sun: 687 days
No. of moons: 2

*Most gas giants have
turbulent atmospheres
powered by an internal
energy source*

JUPITER
Diameter: 88,846 miles/142,984 km
Distance from Sun: 484 million miles/
778 million km
Rotation period: 9.93 hours
Time to orbit Sun: 11.9 years
No. of moons: 63

ORBITS TO SCALE
The diagram across the bottom of this page
shows the distances of the planets from the
Sun to scale. The four inner planets lie
relatively close together, while the four outer
planets lie very far apart. The solar system
consists mainly of empty space.

*An extensive system of rings surrounds
Saturn's equator, spanning a distance of
over 250,000 miles (400,000 km) out
from the edge of the planet. All four gas
giants have ring systems, but Saturn's
rings are by far the most impressive.*

Mercury
Earth
Venus
Mars
Jupiter
Saturn

IN THE ECLIPTIC
The planets circle the Sun close to a flat plane called the plane of the ecliptic. In Earth's skies, the ecliptic is the path the Sun appears to take through the heavens during a year. From Earth, the planets appear to travel close to this plane, through the constellations of the zodiac. Dust around the ecliptic causes a faint glow in the night sky called the zodiacal light.

The five naked-eye planets aligned along the ecliptic

SATURN
Diameter: 74,900 miles/120,536 km
Distance from Sun:
887 million miles/1,429 million km
Rotation period: 10.66 hours
Time to orbit Sun: 29.5 years
No. of moons: 60

As shown by the tilt of Saturn's rings, planets do not orbit the Sun bolt upright—most are tilted over to some extent

URANUS
Diameter: 31,770 miles
/51,118 km
Distance from Sun:
1.79 billion miles/
2,875 million km
Rotation period: 17.24 hours
Time to orbit Sun: 84 years
No. of moons: 27

NEPTUNE
Diameter: 30,780 miles/49,532 km
Distance from Sun: 2.8 billion miles
/4,505 million km
Rotation period: 16.11 hours
Time to or bit Sun: 164.8 years
No. of moons: 13

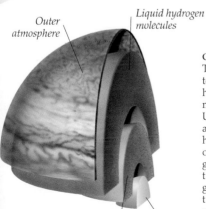

Outer atmosphere

Liquid hydrogen molecules

Structure of Jupiter

Liquid atomic hydrogen

Core

GAS GIANTS
The four planets from Jupiter to Neptune are gas giants. They have a deep atmosphere of mainly hydrogen and helium. Underneath the atmosphere is a planet-wide ocean of liquid hydrogen in Jupiter and Saturn, or of slushy ices in the smaller giants. Only at the center is there a small core of rock. The gas giants have two other things in common: they have many moons circling around them, and they have systems of rings.

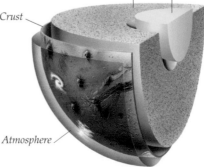

Crust

Mantle

Core

Atmosphere

Structure of Mars

ROCKY PLANETS
The four inner planets, from Mercury to Mars, have a similar, rocky structure. They are known as the terrestrial or Earthlike planets. They have a thin, hard outer layer, or crust, which overlays another thicker layer called the mantle. In the center is a core of metal, mainly iron. All the planets except Mercury have an atmosphere.

Uranus

Neptune

Mercury and Venus

TWO ROCKY PLANETS, Mercury and Venus, orbit closer to the Sun than Earth. We see them shining in the night sky like bright stars. Venus is by far the brightest, shining prominently for much of the year as the evening star. Mercury lies so close to the Sun that it is only visible briefly at certain times of year, just before sunrise or just after sunset. Both planets are much hotter than Earth—surface temperatures on Mercury can rise as high as 840°F (450°C), and on Venus up to 55°F (30°C) higher. But the two planets are very different. Mercury is less than half as big across as Venus, is almost completely covered in craters, and has no appreciable atmosphere. Venus has a very dense atmosphere, full of clouds, which stops us seeing the surface underneath.

Crust

Mantle

Core

INSIDE MERCURY
Mercury is a small planet, with a diameter of 3,032 miles (4,880 km). It is rocky like Earth and has a similar layered structure. Underneath a hard outer layer, or crust, it has a rocky mantle, then a core of iron. The core is unusually large, extending three-quarters of the way to the surface.

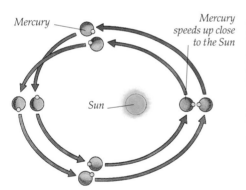

Mercury

Mercury speeds up close to the Sun

Sun

SPEEDY ORBIT
Mercury is the fastest-moving planet, orbiting the Sun in just 88 days. But it rotates very slowly, just once in roughly 59 days. As a result, Mercury rotates three times every two orbits (shown by the dot in the diagram) and there is an interval of 176 Earth days between one sunrise and the next. Temperatures vary from 840°F (450°C) in daytime to -290°F (-180°C) at night.

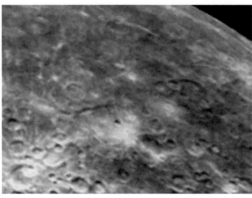

Clouds of sulfuric acid

THE CRATERED SURFACE
Mercury was heavily bombarded with meteorites billions of years ago, resulting in the heavily cratered, Moonlike landscape we see today. There are some smoother plains here and there, but nothing like the Moon's seas. The biggest feature is the huge Caloris Basin, an impact crater about 800 miles (1,300 km) across.

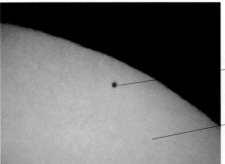

Mercury

Sun's surface

TRANSITS
Mercury and Venus circle the Sun inside Earth's orbit and can sometimes pass in front of the Sun as seen from Earth. We call these crossings transits. They are rare because Earth, the planets, and the Sun only very occasionally line up precisely in space. Transits of Venus are rarest, coming in pairs every century or so.

COOK'S TOUR
In 1768, Britain's Royal Society appointed James Cook to command the first scientific expedition to the Pacific Ocean. One of the expedition's prime goals was to record the transit of Venus from Tahiti on June 3, 1769, which could be used to measure the distance from Earth to the Sun. After making these measurements, Cook sailed his ship *Endeavour* to New Zealand and Australia, where in 1770 he landed at Botany Bay. He claimed the land for Britain and named it New South Wales.

Earth's deadly twin

Venus and Earth are almost identical in size but are very different worlds. At 7,521 miles (12,104 km) across, Venus is the smaller of the two. Its very high temperature and crushing atmosphere make it a most hostile planet, and its clouds are made up of droplets of sulfuric acid. If you went to Venus, you would simultaneously be burned, crushed, and roasted to death—and suffocated, too, because the atmosphere is nearly all carbon dioxide.

Solar panels

Surface of Venus below the clouds

Radar antenna

Magellan radar map of volcanoes on Venus

VOLCANIC WORLD
Venus's surface has been shaped by volcanoes and some are possibly still active. Wave upon wave of lava flows can be seen where the volcanoes have erupted. Other geological activity has also created strange structures—circular coronae and spidery networks called arachnoids. Volcanic eruptions have also wiped out most traces of impact craters on Venus.

Magellan Venus probe

THROUGH THE CLOUDS
We can't actually see the surface of Venus because of the clouds, but we can use radar to image the surface, because radio waves can penetrate the cloud cover. Orbiting space probes like *Magellan* (1990–1994) have now mapped virtually all of Venus, revealing a mostly low-lying planet with just a few highland regions. The largest are two continentlike outcrops, Ishtar Terra in the north and Aphrodite Terra near the equator.

GODDESS OF LOVE
Venus is named after the Roman goddess of love and beauty; the Greeks called her Aphrodite. This female theme is reflected in the names given to Venus's features. The continent Ishtar Terra is named after the Babylonian goddess of love. There is a crater called Cleopatra, a plain called Guinevere, and a deep valley (chasma) called Diana.

Venus de Milo in the Louvre, Paris

Atmosphere is transparent beneath the clouds

19th-century artist's impression

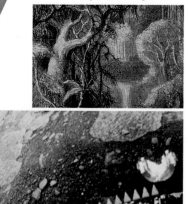

THE SURFACE OF VENUS
Early last century, people had no idea what Venus was like. Some imagined it to be a steamy tropical world of luxuriant vegetation, similar to Earth hundreds of millions of years ago. The first close-up pictures of the surface by Russian *Venera* probes in 1975 revealed the reality. Venus is baked, barren, and devoid of any life, luxuriant or otherwise.

1982 *Venera* photograph of Venus's surface

Home planet

WITH A DIAMETER of 7,926 miles (12,756 km) at the equator, Earth is Venus's near twin in size, but the similarity ends there. At an average distance of 93 million miles (150 million km) from the Sun, Earth is not a hellish place like Venus, but a comfortable world that is a haven for all kinds of life. It is a rocky planet like the other three inner planets of the solar system, but is the only one whose surface is not solid—instead, it is broken up into a number of sections, called plates. The plates move slowly over the surface, causing the continents to drift and the oceans to widen.

Temperate regions between poles and equator experience a moderate, changing climate

Earth's oceans are on average over 2.5 miles (4 km) deep

PLATE TECTONICS
The study of Earth's shifting crust is known as plate tectonics. At plate boundaries, colliding plates may destroy rocks and create volcanoes. Here, at the San Andreas fault in California, plates grind past each other and cause earthquakes.

INSIDE EARTH
Earth has a layered structure, a bit like an onion. It has an outer layer, or crust, of hard rock. This is very thin, averaging about 25 miles (40 km) on the continents but only about 6 miles (10 km) under the oceans. The crust overlays a heavier rocky mantle, the top part of which is relatively soft and can flow. Deeper down lies a huge iron core. The outer core is liquid, while the inner core is solid. Currents and eddies in the liquid outer core are believed to give rise to Earth's magnetism.

OCEANS AND ATMOSPHERE
Oceans cover more than 70 percent of Earth's surface. The evaporation of ocean water into the atmosphere plays a crucial role in the planet's climate. This never-ending exchange of moisture between the surface and atmosphere dictates weather patterns around the globe. Most of Earth's weather takes place in the troposphere, the lowest layer of atmosphere, up to about 10 miles (16 km) high.

Earth seen from orbit

Crust of silicate
minerals floats
on molten
interior

Ice caps cover North
and South poles

Arid desert regions lie
close to the equator

Earth bulges at the
equator—its diameter
here is 13 miles (21 km)
more than at the poles

Antarctica

Death Valley, California

CLIMATE EXTREMES

Antarctica experiences the coldest
temperatures on Earth, with a low of
-128.6°F (-89.2°C) recorded at Vostok
Station in 1983. Death Valley in California
is one of the world's hottest places, where
temperatures regularly nudge 122°F
(50°C) in summer.

Inner core of
solid iron

Outer core of
molten iron
and nickel

Core may contain
a small dense
"kernel" at its
very center

THE MAGNETIC SHIELD

Earth's magnetism extends into
space, creating a bubblelike
cocoon around our planet
called the magnetosphere.
It acts as a shield against
deadly radiation and
particles streaming out
from the Sun. However,
particles trapped in the
magnetosphere are often
shaken out over the poles.
As they interact with the
upper atmosphere, they
create the beautiful light
displays we call the aurorae, or
northern and southern lights.

Aurorae photographed
from the Space Shuttle

Outer mantle

Inner mantle
richer in iron than
outer mantle

Although shown upright, Earth's poles are
in fact tilted 23.5° from vertical. As Earth
orbits the Sun, one pole and then the other
gets more sunlight, creating the seasons.

LIFE IN ABUNDANCE

With comfortable
temperatures, liquid water,
and oxygen in the
atmosphere, Earth can
support an amazing variety
of life. This can vary from
primitive microscopic
organisms like viruses and
bacteria to towering redwood
trees and a multitude of
flowering plants; from
creepy-crawly creatures like
slugs and spiders to warm-
blooded birds and intelligent
mammals, like ourselves.

Life thriving on and
around a coral reef

Mars, the Red Planet

THE REDDISH HUE OF MARS makes it a distinctive member of our solar system. Mars was named after the Roman god of war. With a diameter of 4,222 miles (6,794 km), Mars is about half the size of Earth, but it is like our planet in several respects. Its day is only about half an hour longer than our own. It also has seasons, an atmosphere, and ice caps at the poles. But in other ways, Mars is very different. Its atmosphere is very thin and contains mainly carbon dioxide. The surface is barren and the average temperature is below freezing. Conditions now are not suitable for life, but recent findings support the theory that Mars was once a warmer, wetter place.

Northern half of Mars is mostly low-lying plains

Valles Marineris canyon system is 4 miles (6 km) deep in places

Southern hemisphere is dominated by Moonlike, cratered highlands

A WET WORLD?
We have known for years that Mars has water ice in its polar caps, but recent observations by the Mars Odyssey spacecraft suggest that ice is present in the soil as well, particularly in southern polar regions. On this map the icy regions are colored deep blue. In these areas, as much as 50 percent of the top 3 ft (1 m) of soil could be water ice.

EXPLORING THE SURFACE

The surface of Mars has been more extensively explored than that of any planet other than Earth. Craft such as *Mars Express* (since 2003) have photographed its landscape from orbit and landing probes such as the two *Vikings* (1976) and *Mars Pathfinder* (1997) have taken close-up pictures of its surface. These pictures show rust-colored rocks strewn across a sandy surface. *Mars Pathfinder* released the *Sojourner* rover that explored an ancient floodplain. Twin rovers *Spirit* and *Opportunity* have been exploring the surface since January 2004. Each is a robot geologist using its cameras and tools to locate signs of past water activity on Mars.

Phobos

Deimos

DOGS OF WAR

Mars has two moons, Phobos and Deimos (meaning Fear and Terror). Both are tiny—Phobos measures about 16 miles (26 km) across; Deimos, just 10 miles (16 km). Astronomers think they are asteroids that Mars captured long ago. They are dark and rich in carbon, like many asteroids.

Rockstrewn landscape of Ares Vallis region

Sojourner rover

ON TOP OF THE WORLD

Olympus Mons (Mount Olympus) is the largest of four big volcanoes near Mars's equator. It rises some 15 miles (24 km) above its surroundings—nearly three times higher than Mount Everest. Measuring 370 miles (600 km) across its base, it has a summit caldera (crater) 56 miles (90 km) wide. It probably last erupted about 25 million years ago.

MARTIAN WEATHER

Although Mars has only a slight atmosphere, strong winds often blow across the surface, reaching speeds as high as 200 mph (300 kph). They whip up fine particles from the surface to create dust storms that can sometimes shroud the whole planet.

Deadly heat ray

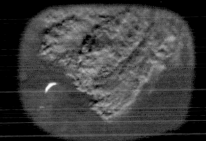

Martian war machine

THE MARTIANS ARE COMING

Thoughts of a desperate Martian race, fighting to survive in an increasingly hostile climate, stimulated the imaginations of many people, including English author H. G. Wells. In 1898, he published a groundbreaking science fiction novel entitled *The War of the Worlds*. It featured a Martian invasion of Earth, with terrifying, invincible war machines and weapons. A masterly radio adaptation of the invasion by Orson Welles, presented as though it were a news report, created a minor panic in the United States in 1938.

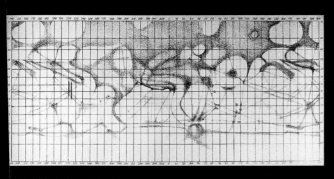

THE CANALS OF MARS

Italian astronomer Giovanni Schiaparelli first reported seeing *canali* (channels) on Mars in 1877. This led other astronomers to suppose that there was a dying Martian race digging canals to irrigate parched farmland. Prominent among them was Percival Lowell, who produced maps of the canal systems.

1907 illustration from
The War of the Worlds

Jupiter, king of the planets

Jupiter is 88,846 miles (142,984 km) in diameter

MORE MASSIVE THAN ALL THE OTHER PLANETS put together, Jupiter is the largest member of the solar system after the Sun. The planet is one of the gas giants, with an atmosphere of hydrogen and helium above a vast ocean of liquid hydrogen. Its colorful face is crossed by dark and pale bands, called belts and zones. These are clouds that have been drawn out by the planet's rapid rotation—Jupiter spins around once in less than 10 hours. This high-speed spin also causes the planet to bulge noticeably around its equator. At least 63 moons circle the planet, but only the four so-called Galilean moons are large. Jupiter also has a ring system around it, but it is small and much too faint to be seen from Earth.

RULER OF THE GODS
Jupiter is an appropriate name for the king of the planets, because Jupiter was the king of the gods in Roman mythology. The ancient Greeks called him Zeus, and told stories of his many amorous conquests. All Jupiter's moons except one (Amalthea) are named after Zeus's lovers and descendants.

Antenna sends data back to Earth and receives instructions

Heat from nuclear fuel powers the spacecraft

Science instruments

GALILEO TO JUPITER
The US space probe *Galileo* went into orbit around Jupiter in 1995 after a five-year journey through space, using gravity boosts from Venus and Earth. *Galileo* confirmed that the top layer of Jupiter's clouds consists of ammonia ice; it detected winds in the atmosphere speeding at 400 mph (650 kph); and data collected from Europa suggest the moon may have a liquid ocean beneath its surface ice.

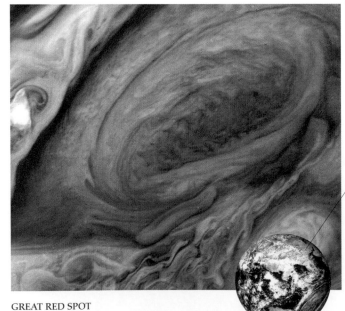

Earth to same scale

GREAT RED SPOT
Jupiter's Great Red Spot has been seen for more than 300 years. It seems to be a super-hurricane, with winds swirling around counterclockwise at high speeds. The Spot towers 5 miles (8 km) above the surrounding cloud tops as the swirling currents rise. It changes in size, but averages about 25,000 miles (40,000 km) across. Its vivid red color is probably due to the presence of phosphorus or perhaps carbon compounds.

TARGET JUPITER
In July 1994, the 20 or so fragments of Comet Shoemaker-Levy 9 smashed into Jupiter after the giant planet had disrupted the comet's orbit. The impacts created huge fireballs in the atmosphere up to 2,500 miles (4,000 km) across. The "scars" persisted for weeks.

The plume (bottom) and the developing scar made by the impact of a comet fragment

Sulfur-covered surface

IO
The most colorful moon in the solar system, Io is covered with flows of sulfur from many volcanoes. Volcanic eruptions send plumes of sulfur dioxide gas shooting 150 miles (250 km) above the surface. With a diameter of 2,264 miles (3,643 km), Io is about the same size as the Moon.

Volcanic eruption on Io

Europa's surface reflects light well

EUROPA
Europa, diameter 1,945 miles (3,130 km), has a relatively smooth icy surface. A network of grooves and ridges crisscrosses the surface, showing where the icy crust has cracked. Some astronomers think that a liquid ocean could lie beneath the ice and might be a haven for life. Both Europa and Io are heated up by the gravitational tug of Jupiter.

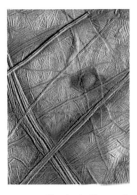

Cracks in Europa's surface ice

Light areas seem to show where ice has welled up from inside Ganymede

GANYMEDE
Ganymede, diameter 3,273 miles (5,268 km), is not only Jupiter's biggest moon, but also the biggest in the whole solar system. It is bigger even than the planet Mercury. Ganymede has an old icy surface, with dark areas and paler grooved regions. Craters are widespread, with recent ones showing up white, where fresh ice has been exposed. Astronomers believe that Ganymede probably has a core of molten iron, like Earth.

Dark regions of older surface

CALLISTO
Callisto orbits farther out than Ganymede and is a little smaller (diameter 2,986 miles/4,806 km). It looks quite different, being almost completely covered with craters. Its crust is thought to be very ancient, dating back billions of years. From variations detected in the moon's magnetism, astronomers think that there might be a salty ocean underneath its icy crust.

rk surface

Bright craters reveal fresh ice below surface

GALILEO'S MOONS
Italian astronomer Galileo Galilei was among the first to observe the heavens through a telescope (above) in 1609. He saw mountains on the Moon, sunspots, and Venus's phases. He also saw the four biggest moons of Jupiter, which are now known as the Galilean moons.

Saturn, the ringed wonder

SATURN IS EVERYONE'S FAVORITE PLANET because of the glorious system of shining rings that girdles its equator. Three other planets have rings—Jupiter, Uranus, and Neptune—but they are no rival to Saturn's. In the solar system, Saturn is the sixth planet from the Sun, orbiting at an average distance of about 888 million miles (1.4 billion km). The second largest planet after Jupiter, it measures 74,900 miles (120,536 km) across at the equator. Saturn is made up mainly of hydrogen and helium around a rocky core, like Jupiter, but is even less dense. Indeed, Saturn is so light that it would float in water. In appearance, the planet's surface is a pale imitation of Jupiter's, with faint bands of clouds drawn out by its rapid rotation.

F ring

THE RING CYCLE
Saturn's axis is tilted in space at an angle of nearly 27 degrees. Because of this, we see the ring system at various angles during the planet's journey around the Sun. Twice during the near-30-year orbit, the rings lie edge-on to Earth, and almost disappear from view.

B ring

Shadow cast by Saturn across rings

INSIDE THE RINGS
Pictures taken by the *Voyager* probes show that Saturn's rings are made up of thousands of narrow ringlets. The ringlets are formed from chunks of matter whizzing around in orbit at high speed. These chunks are made of dirty water ice and vary widely in size from particles the size of sand grains to lumps as big as boulders.

RING WORLD
Through telescopes, astronomers can make out three rings around Saturn—working inward these are the A, B, and C rings. The broadest and brightest ring is the B ring, while the faintest is the C ring (also called the Crepe ring). The B ring is separated from the A ring by the Cassini Division, and there is a smaller gap, called the Encke Division, near the edge of the A ring. The space probes *Pioneer 11* and *Voyagers 1* and *2* discovered several other rings—a very faint D ring extends from the C ring nearly down to Saturn's cloud tops, and F, G, and E rings lie beyond the A ring. Overall, the ring system extends out from the planet about three and a half times Saturn's diameter.

Shadow of rings on planet

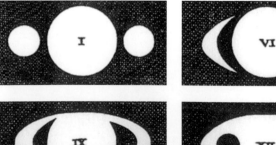

MYSTERY PLANET
Early astronomers were puzzled by Saturn's strange appearance. In his book *Systema Saturnium* (1659), Dutch astronomer Christiaan Huygens showed drawings of Saturn by astronomers from Galileo (I) onward and examined various explanations of its unusual appearance. Huygens concluded that the planet was, in fact, surrounded by a thin, flat ring.

GIOVANNI CASSINI
Late 17th-century astronomers believed that Saturn's rings must be solid or liquid. But doubts emerged in 1675, when Italian astronomer Giovanni Domenico Cassini (1625–1712) discovered a dark line in Saturn's ring. This proved to be a gap between two rings, and became known as the Cassini Division. Cassini realized then that the rings couldn't be solid, but their true structure was not resolved until the 19th century.

Saturn's rapid rotation makes it bulge out at the equator

STORM WORLD
The bands in Saturn's atmosphere are streams of gases coursing around the planet at high speeds and in opposite directions. At the boundary between streams, the atmosphere gets churned up and furious storms break out. This false-color picture highlights three such regions.

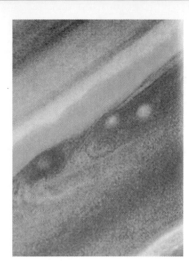

B ring

Cassini division

SNOW WHITE
With a diameter of about 300 miles (500 km), Enceladus is the sixth largest of Saturn's 60 moons and by far the brightest. Parts of its icy surface are cratered and crisscrossed with grooves, but much of it is very smooth and is geologically much younger.

D ring

C ring

Inner A ring

Encke division

Outer A ring

Thick orange clouds block our view of Titan's surface

PLANET-SIZED TITAN
Saturn's largest moon, Titan, is huge. With a diameter of 3,200 miles (5,150 km), it is bigger than Mercury and second only to Ganymede among the solar system's moons. It is also unique because it is covered with a thick atmosphere that we can only see through at long wavelengths such as infrared waves.

Infrared map of Titan's surface

UNDER THE CLOUDS
Titan's atmosphere is mainly hydrogen, with traces of other gases, including methane. In 2005, the *Huygens* space probe descended through the atmosphere to Titan's surface. It recorded river- and channel-like features, and in July 2006 lakes of liquid methane were imaged by the *Cassini* probe (upper right) as it passed overhead.

New worlds

FOR CENTURIES, NO ONE seriously thought there might be planets too faint to see with the naked eye, lying in the darkness beyond Saturn. But in March 1781, musician-turned-astronomer William Herschel discovered one. Later named Uranus, this seventh planet proved to orbit the Sun at a distance of 1,79 billion miles (2,88 billion km), twice as far away as Saturn. At a stroke, Herschel's discovery had doubled the size of the known solar system! Oddities in Uranus's orbit suggested that another planet's gravity might be at work. This planet, Neptune, was eventually discovered by Johann Galle. Much later, in 1930, Clyde Tombaugh discovered Pluto, which was thought of as a ninth planet until 2006.

A WORLD ON EDGE
Uranus is the third largest planet with a diameter of about 31,770 miles (51,118 km). It is a near-twin of Neptune both in size and in composition—both have deep atmospheres with warm oceans beneath. But they differ in one important respect. Neptune spins around in space more or less upright as it orbits the Sun, but Uranus has its axis tilted right over, so it is nearly spinning on its side.

Almost featureless atmosphere

Methane colors the atmosphere blue-green

DEEP-SPACE EXPLORER
Most of our detailed knowledge about the twin planets Uranus and Neptune has come from the *Voyager 2* probe. Launched in 1977, it spent 12 years visiting the four gas-giant planets. After Jupiter and Saturn, it sped past Uranus in 1986 and Neptune three years later. By the time it reached Neptune, *Voyager 2* had journeyed for 4.4 billion miles (7 billion km)—and it was still working perfectly.

Cameras

Science instruments

Dish antenna

Magnetometer boom

Miranda

Tracklike surfaces

Cracked crust

Temperature at cloud tops -345°F (-210°C)

Hydrogen and helium are the main gases in the atmosphere

CRAZED MOONS
Uranus has at least 27 moons. Made up of rock and ice, they are all distinctly different. Ariel has deep cracks running across its surface. Miranda has all kinds of different surface features mixed together. Some astronomers think this moon once broke apart, then came together again.

Ariel

*Dark spots are lower in
atmosphere than bright,
high-speed "scooters"*

BLUE PLANET

Neptune lies 1 billion miles (1.6 billion km) beyond
Uranus. It is slightly smaller than its inner neighbor,
with a diameter of 30,780 miles (49,532 km) and
has a fainter ring system. The atmosphere is flecked
with bright clouds and sometimes with dark oval
storm regions, and is bluer than Uranus because
it contains more methane. *Voyager 2* recorded
a huge storm there in 1989. For Neptune to
have so much atmospheric activity, it must
have some kind of internal heating. This heat
also keeps Neptune's cloud tops at the same
temperature as Uranus's, even though
it is very much farther from the Sun.

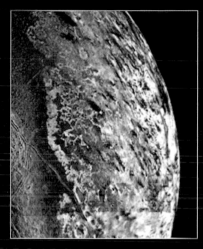

*Temperature at
cloud tops
-345°F (-210°C)*

FINDING NEPTUNE

Johann Galle first
observed Neptune
in 1846 after French
mathematician Urbain
Leverrier (1811–1877)
had calculated where
it should be found.
John Couch Adams
(1819–1892) of
England had made
similar calculations a
year earlier, but no one
had acted upon them.

TRITON'S GEYSERS

Triton is by far the largest of Neptune's
thirteen moons, 1,680 miles (2,710 km)
across. It is a deep-frozen world, similar
to Pluto, and both are probably large
members of a swarm of icy bodies that
orbits beyond Neptune. Triton's surface
is covered with frozen nitrogen and
methane and, amazingly, has geysers
erupting on it. The geysers don't spurt
out steam and water, of course, but
nitrogen gas and dust.

REPUBLIQUE FRANÇAISE
POSTES
12F
1811 LE VERRIER 1877

*Uranus has a total
of 11 rings around
its equator*

*Ring particles
average about
3 ft (1 m) across*

*Charon
circles around
Pluto every 6
days 9 hours*

ICY OUTCASTS

Pluto has been classed as a dwarf
planet since 2006. It is smaller than
Earth's moon, measuring only 1,413 miles
(2,274 km) across. It has three moons of its
own—Charon which is half its size and tiny Nix and
Hydra. Pluto is made up of rock and ice, with frozen
nitrogen and methane covering its surface. For 20 years
of Pluto's 248-year orbit it travels closer to the Sun than
Neptune. Pluto was last inside Neptune's orbit in 1999.

*Outer ring
is brightest*

*Pluto lies on average
3,670 miles
(5,900 million km)
from the Sun*

Asteroids, meteors, and meteorites

THE SOLAR SYSTEM has many members besides planets, dwarf planets, and moons. The largest are the rocky lumps we call asteroids, orbiting relatively close to the Sun. Swarms of smaller icy bodies lurk much farther away, at the edge of the solar system. Some occasionally travel in toward the Sun, where they warm up, release clouds of gas and dust, and become visible as comets (p. 112). Asteroids often collide and chip pieces off one another, and comets leave trails of dust in their wake. Asteroid and comet particles, called meteoroids, exist in interplanetary space. When they cross Earth's orbit and enter its atmosphere, most burn up in the atmosphere as shooting stars, also termed meteors. Those that survive the journey through the atmosphere and reach the ground are called meteorites.

Asteroid Ida

THE ASTEROID BELT
About 200,000 individual asteroids have been identified but there are billions altogether. Most of them circle the Sun in a broad band roughly midway between the orbits of Mars and Jupiter. We call this band the Asteroid Belt. The center of the belt lies roughly 250 million miles (400 million km) from the Sun. Some asteroids, however, stray outside the belt, following orbits that can take them inside Earth's orbit or out beyond Saturn's.

ASTEROID VARIETY
Even the largest asteroid, Ceres, is only about 580 miles (930 km) across, which makes it less than one-third the size of the Moon. The next largest, Pallas and Vesta, are only about half the size of Ceres. But most asteroids are very much smaller—Ida, for example, is about 35 miles (56 km) long; Gaspra only about 11 miles (18 km). These were the first asteroids photographed, by the *Galileo* spacecraft on its way to Jupiter. Gaspra is made up mostly of silicate rocks, like many asteroids. Ida's structure is more of a mystery. Other asteroids are mainly metal, or a mixture of rock and metal.

THE CELESTIAL POLICE
In 1800, Hungarian baron Franz von Zach organized a search party of German astronomers to look for a planet in the apparent "gap" in the solar system between Mars and Jupiter. They became known as the Celestial Police. But they were upstaged by Italian astronomer Giuseppe Piazzi, who spotted a new "planet" in the gap on January 1, 1801. Named Ceres, it was the first asteroid and in 2006 was also classed as a dwarf planet.

Giuseppe Piazzi
(1746–1826)

Sample of nickel-iron meteorite

ASTEROID MINING
The metallic asteroids are rich in iron, as well as nickel and other metals that are comparatively rare on Earth. Metals in asteroids exist in pure form, not in ores a[s] on Earth, and this makes them much easier to extra[ct]. So when supplies of these ra[re] metals start to run out, we migh[t] send astronauts or robotic mining machines into space to mine the asteroids and send their materials bac[k] to Earth. Near-Earth asteroids—the on[es] that come closest to our planet—wou[ld] be the first targets.

Eros

NEAR-Shoemaker spacecraft

NEAR EROS
In February 2001, the probe *NEAR-Shoemaker* performed a remarkable feat. It landed on the asteroid Eros, a rocky lump only about 20 miles (33 km) long. *NEAR* (the Near-Earth Asteroid Rendezvous) had already orbited the asteroid for a year.

SHOWERS OF METEORS
The short-lived streaks of light we see in the night sky are meteors. They are produced by meteoroid particles usually little bigger than sand grains. As they move through the atmosphere the particles cause the gas atoms in the atmosphere to glow. On average, up to about 10 meteors can be seen in the night sky every hour. But during meteor showers and storms, thousands may be seen.

The 1833 Leonid meteor storm over Niagara Falls

Ida's deeply gouged surface probably formed as it broke up from a larger asteroid millions of years ago

Meteorites stand out in a rockless landscape

NASA's NOMAD robot is designed to hunt for meteorites in hostile regions

Gaspra has fewer craters than Ida—it probably also formed in a breakup

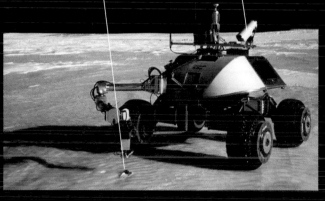

LOOKING FOR METEORITES
The southern continent of Antarctica has provided rich pickings for hunters of meteorites—meteoroid lumps that have survived passage through the atmosphere. A combination of ice movements and harsh winds causes meteorites scattered over a wide area to accumulate in certain places.

Crater rim is filled with a lake now used as a reservoir

Crater floor may hide huge nickel deposits

Asteroid Gaspra

Manicouagan crater, Quebec

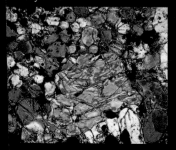

Micrograph showing crystals in a stony meteorite.

INSIDE METEORITES
Most of the meteorites that have been recovered are made up of stony material. But all the biggest ones are made up of metal, mainly iron and nickel. The giant Hoba West meteorite found in Namibia weighs at least 60 tons. Some meteorites are rich in carbon compounds, which form the building blocks of life.

METEOR CRATERS
From time to time, really big meteorites smash into Earth's surface and gouge out large pits, or craters. 200 million years ago, a big meteorite created this crater in Canada, which has since filled with ice. The best-preserved crater is Meteor Crater in the arid Arizona desert, formed around 50,000 years ago. It measures about 4,150 ft (1,265 m) across and 575 ft (175 m) deep.

Icy wanderers

IN THE OUTER REACHES of the solar system, there are great clouds of icy debris, relics of the time the solar system was born. Each of these chunks is the city-sized nucleus of a comet; a dirty-snowball that remains invisible unless it travels in toward the Sun and is heated up. It then develops a large head and tails and is big enough and close enough to be seen. At their brightest, comets can rival the brightest planets, and can develop tails that stretch for millions of miles. Comets seem suddenly to appear out of nowhere. In the past, people believed they were signs of ill-omen, and brought famine, disease, death, and destruction.

HAPPY RETURNS
In his famous painting *Adoration of the Magi*, the Florentine painter Giotto (1267–1337) included a comet as the Star of Bethlehem, based on one he had seen in 1301. Giotto's comet was in fact one of the regular appearances of Halley's Comet, whose orbit brings it close to the Sun once every 76 years. The comet has been spotted on every return since 240 BCE.

Gas plume bursts out of surface

HEART OF A COMET
In March 1986, the space probe *Giotto* took spectacular close-up pictures of Halley's Comet. They showed bright jets of gas spurting out of the central nucleus. Shaped a bit like a potato, it measures about 10 miles (16 km) long and about half as big across. The surface is rough, covered with what look like hills and craters. It is also very dark. Analysis of the gases coming off showed them to be 80 percent water vapor. There were also traces of carbon-based organic compounds, and some astronomers think that comets might distribute these building blocks of life around the galaxy.

Dark surface absorbs heat from sunlight

Straight gas tail streams away, driven by solar wind

Dark dust coats nucleus

Gas tail glows as solar wind strikes gas from comet

Nucleus is too small to be seen inside comet's glowing coma

FRAGILE SNOWBALLS
Like snowballs, comets are not firmly held together and often break up. Early in July 1992, a comet passed very close to Jupiter and was ripped apart by the giant planet's gravity. The following spring, the fragments were spotted by comet-watchers Carolyn and Gene Shoemaker and David Levy. It soon became evident that this fragmented comet, called Shoemaker-Levy 9, was going to collide with Jupiter, which it did in July 1994.

COMET OF THE CENTURY
In spring 1997, Earth's sky was dominated by one of the brightest comets of the 20th century. It had been discovered by US astronomers Alan Hale and Thomas Bopp two years earlier. Comet Hale-Bopp outshone all but the brightest stars and hung in the night sky for weeks. It had two well-developed tails streaming away from the bright head, or coma. There was a curved, yellowish dust tail and a straighter blue gas, or ion tail. Hale-Bopp's nucleus is estimated to be 20–30 miles (30–40 km) across.

Orbit of Saturn

COMET ORBITS

Comets travel in orbits around the Sun just like the planets. But they do not usually orbit in the same plane—they may journey in toward the Sun from any direction. For much of the time, they remain in deep freeze. Only when they get inside Saturn's orbit do they begin to warm up and start to glow. As they get closer to the Sun, their tails start to form, always pointing away from the Sun.

Tail follows comet as it approaches Sun

Tail leads comet as it recedes from Sun

Orbit of Uranus

Short-period comet from Kuiper Belt orbits in a few decades

Orbit of Neptune

Long-period comet from Oort Cloud orbits in centuries or more

EDMOND HALLEY

English astronomer Edmond Halley (1656–1742) was the first to discover that some comets are regular visitors to Earth's skies. He observed a comet in 1682, and after checking the orbits of previous comets, he deduced that it was the same one that had appeared in 1531 and 1607. He predicted that it would return again in 1758. When the comet reappeared as forecast, it was named after him—usually, a comet is named after the person who first discovers it.

Edm. Halley A.P.R.

Dust tail curves, affected by Sun's gravity

Dust tail is simply comet dust reflecting sunlight

COMET RESERVOIRS

Comets journey in toward the Sun from the outer reaches of the solar system, where there are great reservoirs of icy bodies. Many come from the Kuiper Belt, a region stretching for 2 billion miles (3 billion km) or more beyond the orbit of Neptune. Others arrive from much farther afield—from the Oort Cloud, a spherical shell containing trillions of comets. The Cloud extends out to 9.4 trillion miles (15 trillion km) from the Sun.

THE TUNGUSKA EVENT

On the last day of June 1908, a terrifying explosion occurred in Siberia near the Stony Tunguska River. It generated a dazzling fireball and shock waves reminiscent of a thermonuclear blast. In an instant, 60,000 trees lay flattened and charred. No one knows for sure what caused the event, but astronomers think it was probably part of a comet nucleus impacting the atmosphere at high speed and exploding 4 miles (6 km) above the ground.

Distant suns

Every clear night, if you were very patient, you could probably count as many as 2,500 stars in the sky. Through binoculars or a small telescope, you could see millions more. They always appear as tiny, faint pinpricks of light, but if you traveled trillions of miles to look at them close up, you would find that they are huge, bright bodies like the Sun. Even the closest star (Proxima Centauri) lies so far away that its light takes over four years to reach us—we say that it lies over four light-years away. Astronomers often use the light-year— the distance light travels in a year—as a unit to measure distances to stars. They also use a unit called the parsec, which equals about 3.3 light-years.

A UNIVERSE OF STARS
In the dense star clouds of the Milky Way, stars appear crammed together in their millions. There are many different kinds of stars, with different brightness, color, size, and mass. Altogether in our own great galaxy—a "star island" in space—there are as many as 500 billion stars. And there are billions more galaxies like it in the universe.

Stars of the Sagittarius Star Cloud

Star Cloud lies 25,000 light-years from Earth, toward the center of the Milky Way

Gamma Cassiopeiae (615 light-years)

Epsilon Cassiopeiae (440 light-years)

Alpha Cassiopeiae (240 light-years)

Beta Cassiopeiae (54 light-years)

True distances to Cassiopeia's stars (not to scale)

Star pattern in the constellation Cassiopeia

STARS AND CONSTELLATIONS
Some of the bright stars form patterns in the sky that we can recognize. We call them the constellations. Ancient astronomers named them after figures that featured in their myths and legends. The stars in the constellations look as if they are the same distance from Earth, but actually are far apart. They appear together only because they happen to lie in the same direction in space. This also means that stars that seem to have the same brightness may, in fact, be very different.

Delta Cassiopeiae (100 light-years)

Betelgeuse (magnitude 0.8)

Rigel and Betelgeuse appear roughly the same brightness, but Rigel is really twice as far away and five times more luminous than Betelgeuse.

HOW FAR AWAY?
The distance to a few hundred of the nearest stars can be measured directly by the parallax method. Parallax is the effect that makes a nearby object appear to move against a more distant background when you look at it first with one eye, then the other. Astronomers view a nearby star first from one side of Earth's orbit, then from the other. They measure the amount a star appears to move against the background of more distant stars. From these parallax shifts they can work out the star's distance.

Closer star B has larger parallax shift than more distant star A

Distant stars

Parallax shift against distant background stars

Line of sight to star B

Line of sight to star A

Earth's position in January

Earth's position in July

Sun

Rigel (magnitude 0.1)

STAR BRIGHTNESS
The stars in the constellations differ widely in brightness, as here in Orion. We measure brightness on a scale of magnitude introduced by the Greek astronomer Hipparchus over 2,000 years ago. He graded the brightest stars we can see as first-magnitude stars, and the dimmest ones as sixth-magnitude. Today, we extend the scale to negative magnitudes for very bright stars, and beyond 6 for stars too faint for the eye to detect.

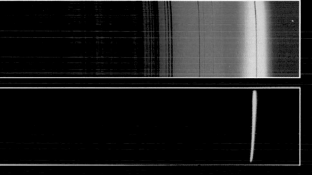

More massive star pulls material off its neighbor

Stars of Algol are very close together

Artist's impression of Algol star system

BINARY STARS

Most stars travel through space with one or more companions. Two-star, or binary, systems are common. Each star orbits around an imaginary point, called the barycenter, that marks the center of mass of the system. The two components in a binary system may orbit very close together and appear as a single star to the eye, but they can often be seen separately in a telescope. When they are really close together, they can be separated only by studying their spectrum.

Sodium absorption and emission lines

THE SPECTRAL LINES

The dark lines in a star's spectrum are produced when certain wavelengths are removed from starlight by elements in the star's atmosphere. Sodium, for example, removes wavelengths in the yellow region of the spectrum (top picture). It is the same wavelength that sodium itself would emit if it were heated (lower picture).

Sagittarius region is rich in old red and yellow stars

SPECTROSCOPY

The white light we receive from the stars (and the Sun) is actually made up of a mixture of different colors, or wavelengths. Using an instrument called a spectroscope, we can split starlight into its separate colors to form a rainbowlike spectrum. Dark lines cross the spectrum at intervals. By studying these spectral lines, astronomers can tell all kinds of things about a star, such as its composition, temperature, color, true brightness, and even how fast it is moving.

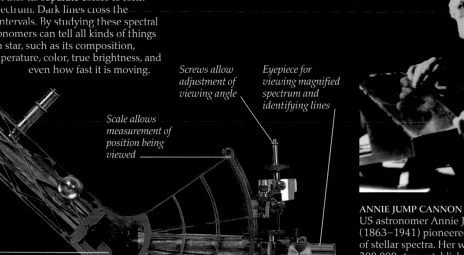

Spectroscope attaches to end of a telescope here

Screws allow adjustment of viewing angle

Eyepiece for viewing magnified spectrum and identifying lines

Scale allows measurement of position being viewed

An antique spectroscope

Prism or grating splits light into a spectrum

ANNIE JUMP CANNON

US astronomer Annie Jump Cannon (1863–1941) pioneered the classification of stellar spectra. Her work on some 300,000 stars established that stars of different colors contain different chemicals, and led to the division of the stars into different spectral types.

The variety of stars

STUDYING THE SPECTRA of stars tells us all kinds of things about them—their composition, color, temperature, speed of travel, and size. Other techniques allow astronomers to measure the distance to stars and their mass. Stars turn out to vary enormously. There are dwarfs with only a hundredth the diameter of the Sun and supergiants hundreds of times the Sun's size. The lightest stars have around one-tenth of the Sun's mass, the heaviest around 50 solar masses. The least luminous are a million times fainter than the Sun, while the most luminous are a million times brighter. But there do seem to be some rules—red stars are either very faint or very luminous, while the bluer a star, the more luminous it is.

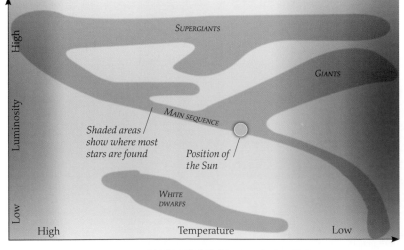

SUPERGIANTS
The biggest stars of all, hundreds of millions of miles across, relatively cool but amazingly luminous

STARS LARGE AND SMALL
A range of typical stars is shown across this page. The most luminous are at the top, the hottest on the left, and the coolest on the right. The true size differences are far greater than those shown, but some patterns are obvious—stars get bigger as luminosity increases, and the most luminous are either bright blue or orange-red. A star's color is governed by its surface temperature—the amount of energy pumping out of each square meter of its surface. This means that if two stars have the same luminosity but one is cool and red while the other is hot and blue, then the red one must be far bigger than the blue one.

BLUE STARS
Tens of times bigger than the Sun, and tens of thousands of times more luminous, with a surface temperature up to 90,000°F (50,000°C)

WHITE DWARFS
Tiny hot stars only about the size of Earth

Line of main sequence

THE HERTZSPRUNG-RUSSELL DIAGRAM AND STELLAR EVOLUTION
The Hertzsprung-Russell (HR) diagram is a way of looking at relationships between the luminosity (amount of light produced) of stars and their color and temperature. The majority of stars lie along a diagonal strip from faint red to bright blue called the main sequence—this must be where most stars spend most of their lives. Stars spend much of their lives close to one point on the main sequence—they only move off it toward the end of their lives, as they grow bigger and more luminous.

Shaded areas show where most stars are found

Position of the Sun

SUPERGIANTS

GIANTS

MAIN SEQUENCE

WHITE DWARFS

Luminosity — High / Low

Temperature — High / Low

FIRST DWARF
Stars similar to the Sun end their lives as white dwarfs, which gradually fade away. The faint companion of Sirius, called Sirius B (left), was the first white dwarf discovered, by US astronomer Alvan Clark in 1862. It proved to be exceptionally hot and very dense.

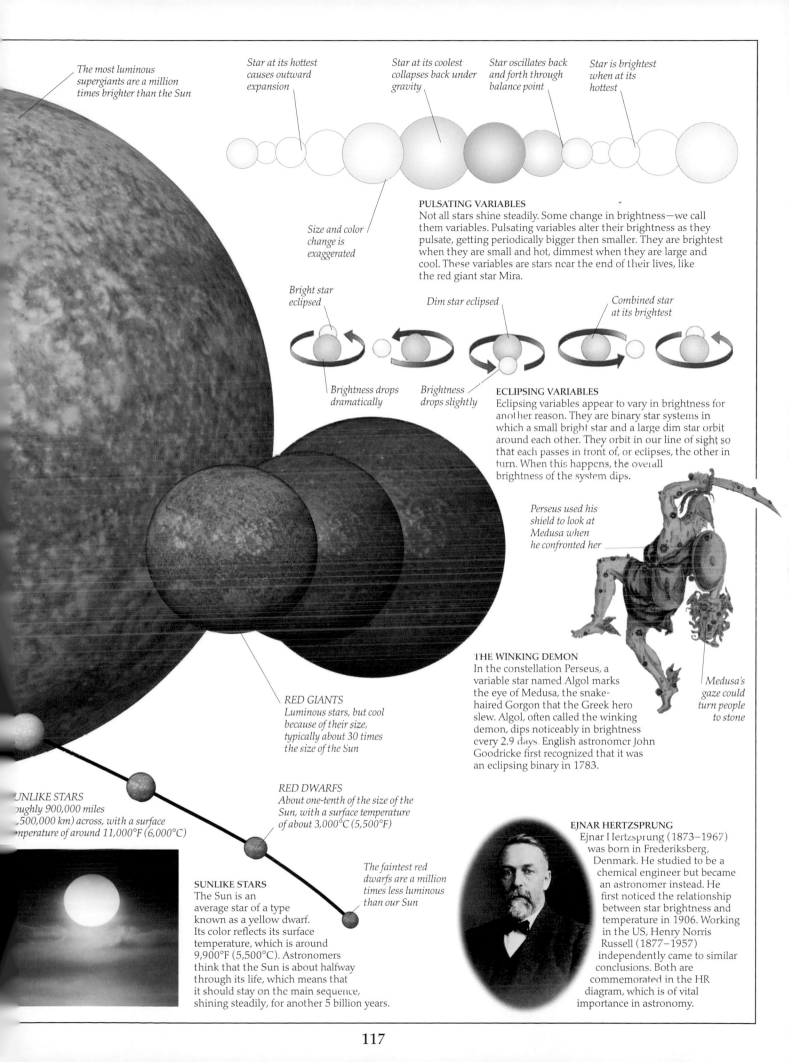

The most luminous supergiants are a million times brighter than the Sun

Star at its hottest causes outward expansion

Star at its coolest collapses back under gravity

Star oscillates back and forth through balance point

Star is brightest when at its hottest

Size and color change is exaggerated

PULSATING VARIABLES

Not all stars shine steadily. Some change in brightness—we call them variables. Pulsating variables alter their brightness as they pulsate, getting periodically bigger then smaller. They are brightest when they are small and hot, dimmest when they are large and cool. These variables are stars near the end of their lives, like the red giant star Mira.

Bright star eclipsed

Dim star eclipsed

Combined star at its brightest

Brightness drops dramatically

Brightness drops slightly

ECLIPSING VARIABLES

Eclipsing variables appear to vary in brightness for another reason. They are binary star systems in which a small bright star and a large dim star orbit around each other. They orbit in our line of sight so that each passes in front of, or eclipses, the other in turn. When this happens, the overall brightness of the system dips.

Perseus used his shield to look at Medusa when he confronted her

Medusa's gaze could turn people to stone

THE WINKING DEMON

In the constellation Perseus, a variable star named Algol marks the eye of Medusa, the snake-haired Gorgon that the Greek hero slew. Algol, often called the winking demon, dips noticeably in brightness every 2.9 days. English astronomer John Goodricke first recognized that it was an eclipsing binary in 1783.

RED GIANTS
Luminous stars, but cool because of their size, typically about 30 times the size of the Sun

SUNLIKE STARS
oughly 900,000 miles ,500,000 km) across, with a surface mperature of around 11,000°F (6,000°C)

RED DWARFS
About one-tenth of the size of the Sun, with a surface temperature of about 3,000°C (5,500°F)

The faintest red dwarfs are a million times less luminous than our Sun

SUNLIKE STARS

The Sun is an average star of a type known as a yellow dwarf. Its color reflects its surface temperature, which is around 9,900°F (5,500°C). Astronomers think that the Sun is about halfway through its life, which means that it should stay on the main sequence, shining steadily, for another 5 billion years.

EJNAR HERTZSPRUNG

Ejnar Hertzsprung (1873–1967) was born in Frederiksberg, Denmark. He studied to be a chemical engineer but became an astronomer instead. He first noticed the relationship between star brightness and temperature in 1906. Working in the US, Henry Norris Russell (1877–1957) independently came to similar conclusions. Both are commemorated in the HR diagram, which is of vital importance in astronomy.

Clusters and nebulae

In MANY PARTS OF THE HEAVENS there are fuzzy patches that look as if they might be comets. Through a telescope, some turn out to be close groupings of stars, known as clusters—in general, stars are born in groups rather than alone. Open clusters are relatively loose collections of a few hundred stars. Globular clusters are dense groupings of many thousands of stars. Other fuzzy patches turn out to be cloudlike regions of glowing gas. We call these nebulae, from the Latin word for clouds. They are the visible part of the interstellar medium, the stuff that occupies the space between the stars. The darker, denser parts of nebulae are where stars are born.

Alcyone

OPEN CLUSTERS

The best-known of all open clusters is the Pleiades, in the constellation Taurus. It is also called the Seven Sisters because keen-sighted people can make out its seven brightest stars with the naked eye, and sometimes the sisters' parents, Atlas and Pleione. In total, the Pleiades contains more than 100 stars, all of them hot, blue and young— probably less than 80 million years old. Most open clusters contain similar kinds of stars.

Pleione

Atlas

The spectacular globular cluster Omega Centauri

GLOBES OF STARS

Globular clusters are made up of hundreds of thousands of stars packed together in a ball. They contain mostly ancient stars, typically about 10 billion years old. While open clusters are found among the stars in the disk of our galaxy, globular clusters lie in the center and in a spherical halo above and below the disk. They follow their own orbits around the central bulge.

Merope

Between the stars

The interstellar medium is made up mainly of hydrogen gas and specks of dust. It also contains traces of many other compounds, including water, alcohol, hydrogen sulfide, and ammonia. Altogether, the interstellar medium accounts for a one-tenth of the mass of our galaxy. It can become visible as both bright and dark nebulae.

Asterope

Taygeta

Maia

Celaeno

Electra

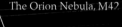

DARK NEBULAE
Some clouds of gas and dust are lit up, while others remain dark. We see dark nebulae only when they blot out the light from stars or glowing gas in the background. The aptly named Horsehead Nebula (above) is a well-known dark nebula in Orion. Another, in far southern skies, is the Coal Sack in Crux, the Southern Cross. Dark nebulae are generally cold, around -436°F (-260°C), and made up mainly of hydrogen molecules. Such molecular clouds give birth to stars.

The Orion Nebula, M42

BRIGHT NEBULAE
Many interstellar gas clouds are lit up by stars, creating some of the most beautiful sights in the heavens. Sometimes the clouds just reflect the light from nearby stars, and we see them as reflection nebulae. Sometimes radiation from stars embedded within the clouds gives extra energy to the gas molecules, causing them to emit radiation. Then we see the clouds as emission nebulae. The famous Orion Nebula (above) is primarily an emission nebula.

M42's position in Orion

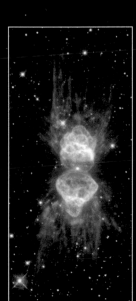

STELLAR REMNANTS
Stars are born from nebulae, and give rise to nebulae when they die. Stars like the Sun first swell up to become red giants, then shrink into tiny white dwarfs. As they do so, they puff off layers of gas, which become planetary nebulae. Some of these nebulae are circular and look a little like the disks of planets; others, like the Ant Nebula, consist of luminous jets.

Reflection nebula surrounding young stars

MESSIER'S CATALOG
French astronomer Charles Messier (1730–1817) was nicknamed the "ferret of comets" for his skill in searching for new comets. He discovered 15 in all. He also compiled a catalog in which he listed 104 star clusters and nebulae that might be mistaken for comets. The objects in the catalog are still often identified by their Messier (M) numbers.

Star birth

Sᴛᴀʀs ᴀʀᴇ ʙᴏʀɴ in the vast, dark fogs of gas and dust that occupy interstellar space. Called giant molecular clouds, they are very cold (around -436°F, -260°C) and consist mainly of hydrogen gas. In places within these clouds, gravity pulls the gas molecules together to make denser clumps. Within these clumps there are even denser regions, called cores, and it is from cores that individual stars are born. Gravity makes a core collapse in on itself, greatly compressing the material at the center. As the collapse continues, the central region becomes more and more compressed and gets hotter and hotter. Now called a protostar, it begins to glow. When its temperature reaches around 18 million°F (10 million°C), its nuclear furnace fires up, and it begins to shine brightly as a new star.

Central core heats up

Matter spirals in

IN A WHIRL
The molecular clouds that spawn stars move around slowly in space. When cores of matter collapse during star formation, they start to rotate—the smaller they become, the faster they spin. The collapsing matter, with the glowing protostar inside, forms into a disk as a result of the rotation.

STELLAR NURSERIES
Stars are being born in vast numbers in giant molecular clouds all around the heavens. M16, the Eagle Nebula in Serpens, is one of these stellar nurseries. The Hubble Space Telescope has taken dramatic pictures of dark columns nicknamed "the pillars of creation," where star formation is taking place. This picture of the top of one pillar shows fingerlike blobs of gas called EGGs, or evaporating gaseous globules where material is collapsing to form stars.

Collapsing gas clouds

EGG

Stars are hidden within gas

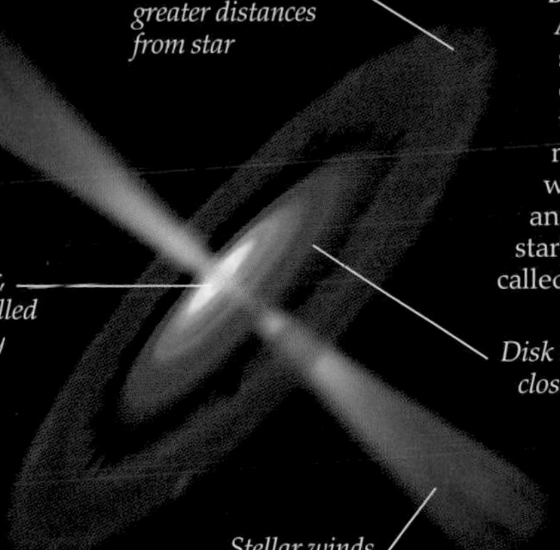

Birth Pangs area

Disk more stable at greater distances from star

BIRTH PANGS
A newborn star is surrounded by a swirling disk of matter with may be three times its mass, but not for long. Powerful stellar winds gather up the matter and force it away from the star's poles as twin jets. This is called bipolar outflow.

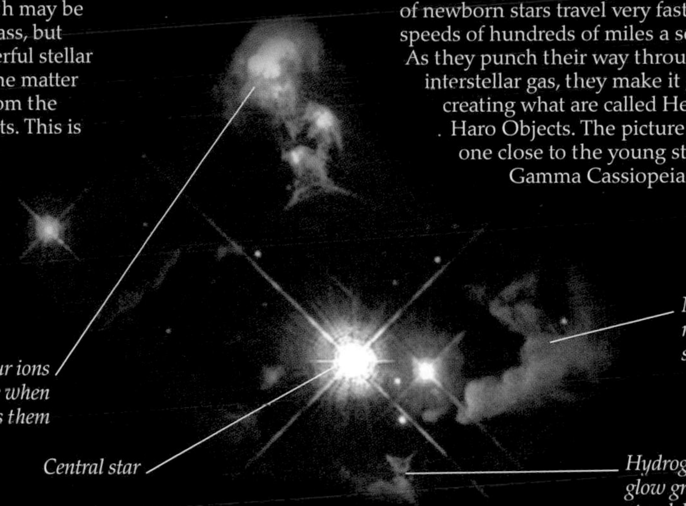

Close to star, matter is pulled in by gravity

Disk heats up close to star

Stellar winds blow material out in jets

JET EFFECTS
The two jets that emerge from the poles of newborn stars travel very fast—at speeds of hundreds of miles a second. As they punch their way through interstellar gas, they make it glow, creating what are called Herbig-Haro Objects. The picture shows one close to the young star Gamma Cassiopeiae.

Nearby gas reflecting starlight

Sulfur ions glow blue when jet hits them

Central star

Hydrogen atoms glow green when struck by jet

Worlds beyond

Newborn stars blow most of the matter surrounding them into space, but usually a disk of material remains. It is from such disks that planetary systems form. Astronomers first began discovering planets around ordinary stars in 1995. Today, we know of more than 300 of these extrasolar planets, or exoplanets.

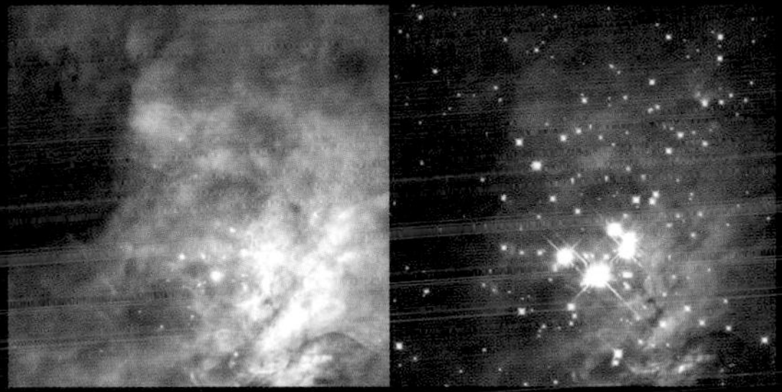

Star blacked out

Disk seen edge-on to Earth

THE HIDDEN MILLIONS
The Orion Nebula is one of the closest star-forming regions. In visible light (above left), glowing gas in the nebula hides most of the young stars. But viewed in the infrared (above right), a wealth of stars becomes visible, many of them red and brown dwarfs. Red dwarfs are small, cool stars. Brown dwarfs are the stars that never made it. They have a low mass and couldn't reach a high enough temperature for nuclear fusion to begin.

Disk of gas and dust

Star moves toward us

Planet

Barycenter

Star

Star moves away

PLANETS IN FORMATION
Space probes like *IRAS* (Infrared Astronomy Satellite) began detecting disks of material around other stars in the 1980s. One is Beta Pictoris, which is pictured above. Another is the bright star Vega in Lyra. Planets could form in these systems within a few million years.

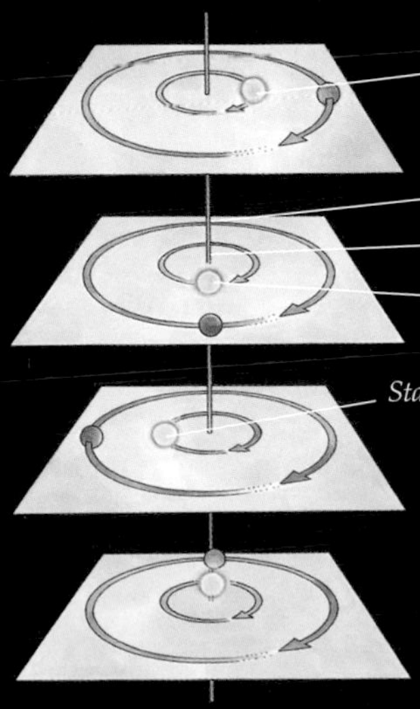

LOOKING FOR PLANETS
The planets around other stars are much too faint to be seen directly. Astronomers have to find them indirectly, by observing the effect they have on their star. Planet and star both orbit around a shared center of gravity or barycenter, usually deep within the star but not quite at the center. During an orbit, the star appears from Earth to move repeatedly toward and away from us. We can detect this motion by examining the shift in the lines in the star's spectrum (p. 114).

GIANTS LIKE JUPITER
Astronomers detected the first extrasolar planets in 1991, orbiting a dead star called a pulsar. Four years later, a planet was found around the Sunlike 51 Pegasi. It has half the mass of Jupiter and orbits only about 6 million miles (10 million km) from its star. Most exoplanets detected so far are heavier than Jupiter, and orbit close to their stars.

Star death

STARS BURST INTO LIFE when they begin fusing hydrogen into helium in nuclear reactions in their cores. They spend most of their lives shining steadily until they use up their hydrogen fuel—then they start to die. First they pass through a phase when they brighten and swell to enormous size as red giants and supergiants. The way a star ultimately dies depends on its mass. Low-mass stars puff off their outer layers and then fade away. High-mass stars die in a spectacular explosion called a supernova.

FATES OF STARS

A star that is burning hydrogen in its core changes its color and brightness very little. How long the star can keep burning hydrogen depends on its mass. Stars like the Sun burn their fuel slowly and so can shine steadily for up to 10 billion years.

RED GIANT

When a star has used up the hydrogen in its core, fusion moves out to a thin shell around the center. This produces so much heat that the star's atmosphere balloons outward. As it expands, its surface cools and its light reddens—it has become a red giant. Meanwhile, the inner core of helium collapses, until it is hot and dense enough for new nuclear reactions to begin. These turn helium into heavier elements and give the star a new lease of life—for about 2 billion years.

SUPERGIANT

In stars with more than eight times the Sun's mass, the core gets so hot that carbon and oxygen, produced by helium fusion, can themselves fuse into heavier elements. The star balloons out to become a supergiant, many times larger than a normal red giant.

PLANETARY NEBULA

When all the helium in the core of a solar-mass red giant runs out, the core collapses again, releasing energy that blows the outer layers of the star into space. Radiation from the hot core makes the ejected gas light up, forming a ring-shaped planetary nebula.

LIVE FAST, DIE YOUNG

Stars more massive than the Sun have hotter, denser cores. This allows them to burn their hydrogen fuel in a much more efficient way, but also shortens their lifespans dramatically—the heaviest are stable for just a few million years.

New fusion reactions produce sodium, magnesium, silicon, sulfur, and other elements

Heaviest element produced is iron

Core not shown to scale

Core develops "onion layers"

WHITE DWARF

Within a planetary nebula, the star's core continues collapsing until the electrons in its atoms are forced up against the central nuclei. It is now about the same size as Earth, and a matchbox of its material would weigh as much as an elephant. This incredibly dense, hot star is called a white dwarf. It is very difficult to see because of its tiny size.

White dwarf pulls material off companion

Companion star swells into red giant

Gas builds up on white dwarf's surface

Gas ignites and burns off in a blast of fusion

Companion is caught in blast

NOVAE

When a white dwarf forms in a close binary star system, it may attract gas from the other star. Over time, gas builds up on the white dwarf's surface until it is hot and dense enough to trigger nuclear fusion. A gigantic explosion takes place that makes the star flare up and become a nova, an apparently new star.

SUPERNOVA

Iron builds up rapidly in a supergiant's core—it cannot be burned by nuclear reactions in the same way as lighter elements. When the core runs out of other fuel, it cannot support itself and suddenly collapses. So much energy is released that the star blasts itself apart in a supernova explosion that can briefly outshine an entire galaxy. The explosion scatters heavy elements across space, providing material for later generations of stars and planets.

Neutron star

SUPERNOVAE IN HISTORY

Tycho Brahe saw a supernova in 1572 (shown above), which caused him to realize that the heavens were not unchanging. But the most famous historical supernova is probably the one Chinese astronomers saw in 1054: today its remains form the Crab Nebula in the constellation Taurus.

END STATES

What survives after a supernova depends on the mass of the collapsing core. If the core has less than about three solar masses, it will shrink to an incredibly dense neutron star. If the core has a greater mass, it will end up as a black hole and vanish forever from the visible universe (p. 124).

Black hole

SUPERNOVA 1987A

On February 23, 1987, astronomers spotted a bright supernova (left) in the Large Magellanic Cloud, one of the closest galaxies to our own. It flared up over 85 days to become easily visible to the naked eye. The star that exploded was a blue giant called Sanduleak -69°202 (far left), with about 20 times the mass of the Sun.

Pulsars and black holes

When a massive star dies in a supernova (p. 122), only the core is left behind, collapsed under its own enormous gravity. The force as the core collapses is so great that atoms are broken down. Negatively charged electrons are forced into the central nucleus of each atom, combining with positively charged protons to turn all the matter into tightly packed neutrons that have no electric charge. The collapsed core becomes a city-sized neutron star, spinning furiously as it emits pulses of radiation. When we detect the pulses from a neutron star, we call it a pulsar. Collapsing cores with more than three solar masses suffer a different fate. The force of collapse is so great that even neutrons get crushed. Eventually, the core is so dense that not even light can escape its gravity—it has become that most mysterious of bodies, a black hole.

THE CRAB PULSAR
In the year 1054, Chinese astronomers recorded seeing a star in the constellation Taurus bright enough to be visible in daylight. We now know that it was a supernova explosion, which created the famous Crab Nebula. Buried inside the nebula is the collapsed core, which we detect as a pulsar.

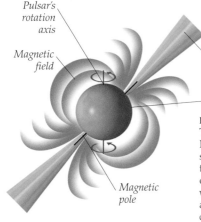

Pulsar's rotation axis

Magnetic field

Inner ring one light-year across

Jets from magnetic poles

Neutron star

Magnetic pole

NEUTRON STARS
Neutron stars are tiny bodies that spin around rapidly. The fastest one known spins 1,122 times a second. They are highly magnetic, so their magnetic field sweeps around rapidly as well. This generates radio waves, which are emitted as beams from the magnetic poles. When the beams sweep past Earth, we see them as pulsing signals, a bit like the flashes from a lighthouse.

INSIDE THE CRAB
The pulsar in the Crab Nebula has been closely studied. It spins around 30 times a second and pours out energy not only as radio waves but also as visible light and X-rays. This picture combines an X-ray image from the Chandra X-ray Observatory satellite (in blue) with a visible light photo.

Jet from pulsar poles

Pulsar jet billows into clouds as it contacts interstellar gas

Material blown out from equator reaches half the speed of light

Neutron star

SUPERDENSE MATTER
A neutron star is typically only around 12 miles (20 km) across. Yet it contains the mass of up to three Suns. This makes it incredibly dense. Just a pinhead of neutron-star matter would weigh twice as much as the world's heaviest supertanker. It is unlike any kind of matter found on Earth.

PULSAR DISCOVERY
Working at Cambridge University in 1967, astronomy research student Jocelyn Bell Burnell (born 1943) was testing new equipment to study fluctuating radio sources. On August 6, she picked up signals pulsating every 1.337 seconds. It was the first pulsar to be found, now called PSR 1919+21.

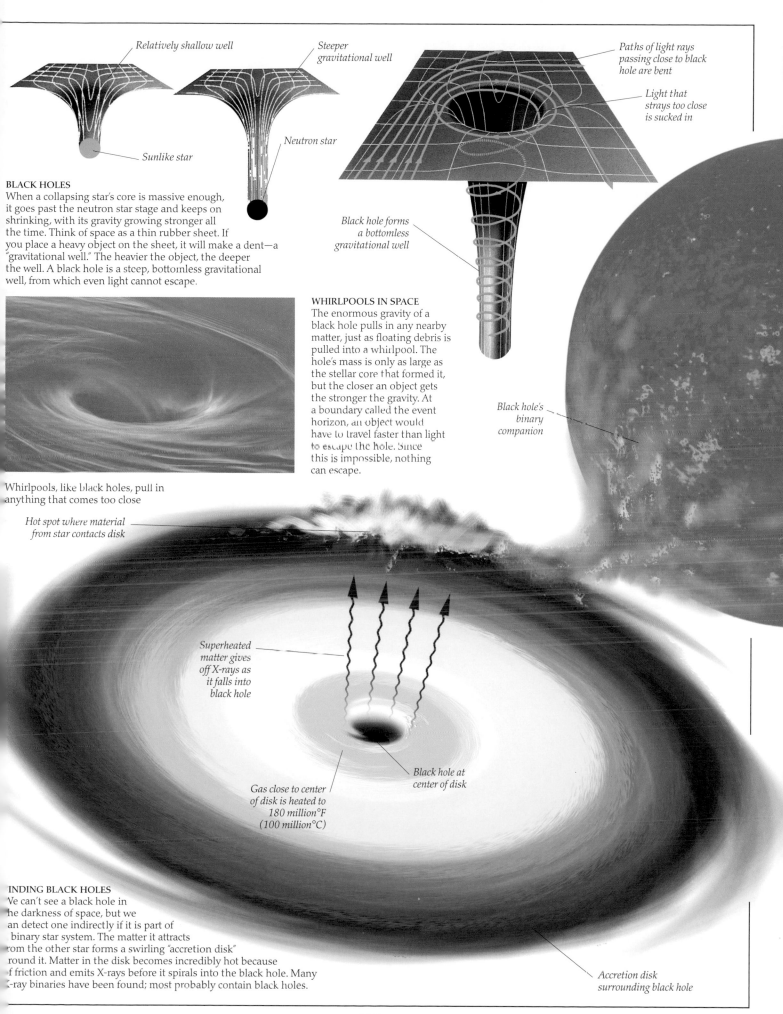

Relatively shallow well

Steeper gravitational well

Paths of light rays passing close to black hole are bent

Light that strays too close is sucked in

Sunlike star

Neutron star

BLACK HOLES

When a collapsing star's core is massive enough, it goes past the neutron star stage and keeps on shrinking, with its gravity growing stronger all the time. Think of space as a thin rubber sheet. If you place a heavy object on the sheet, it will make a dent—a "gravitational well." The heavier the object, the deeper the well. A black hole is a steep, bottomless gravitational well, from which even light cannot escape.

Black hole forms a bottomless gravitational well

WHIRLPOOLS IN SPACE

The enormous gravity of a black hole pulls in any nearby matter, just as floating debris is pulled into a whirlpool. The hole's mass is only as large as the stellar core that formed it, but the closer an object gets the stronger the gravity. At a boundary called the event horizon, an object would have to travel faster than light to escape the hole. Since this is impossible, nothing can escape.

Black hole's binary companion

Whirlpools, like black holes, pull in anything that comes too close

Hot spot where material from star contacts disk

Superheated matter gives off X-rays as it falls into black hole

Black hole at center of disk

Gas close to center of disk is heated to 180 million°F (100 million°C)

FINDING BLACK HOLES

We can't see a black hole in the darkness of space, but we can detect one indirectly if it is part of a binary star system. The matter it attracts from the other star forms a swirling "accretion disk" around it. Matter in the disk becomes incredibly hot because of friction and emits X-rays before it spirals into the black hole. Many X-ray binaries have been found; most probably contain black holes.

Accretion disk surrounding black hole

The Milky Way

ON A CLEAR, DARK NIGHT, a faint, hazy band of light arches across the heavens, running through many of the best-known constellations. We call it the Milky Way. What we are seeing is a kind of "slice" through the star system, or galaxy, to which the Sun and all the other stars in the sky belong. It passes through Cygnus, Perseus, and Cassiopeia in the northern hemisphere, and Centaurus, Crux, and Sagittarius in the southern hemisphere. When you look at the Milky Way through binoculars or a telescope, you can see that it is made up of countless stars, seemingly packed close together. We also call our star system the Milky Way Galaxy, or just the galaxy. It has a spiral shape, with star-studded "arms" curving out from a dense bulge of stars in the middle.

MILKY WAY MYTHS
In the mythology of the Aztecs of Mexico, the Milky Way was identified with Mixcoatl, the cloud-serpent god. In ancient Egypt and India, it was seen as the celestial mirror of rivers like the Nile and Ganges. The Greeks believed it was a stream of milk from the breast of the goddess Hera, wife of Zeus the ruler of the gods.

Star-forming molecular clouds

ANATOMY OF THE GALAXY
Our galaxy is a vast system of around 500 billion stars. It measures 100,000 light-years across, but for the most part is only about 2,000 light-years thick. The spiral arms around the central bulge form the disk of the galaxy. There are two major arms, the Sagittarius and the Perseus, named from the constellations where they appear brightest. Between the two lies the Orion, or Local Arm, on which the Sun lies, 26,000 light-years from the galactic center.

Milky Way star clouds in Scorpius and Sagittarius

Orion arm

THE BACKBONE OF NIGHT
The Milky Way is best seen on clear, Moonless nights away from urban light pollution. Its brightest areas are most visible between June and September. The dark patches, or rifts, in the Milky Way are not starless regions, but areas in which dense dust clouds block the light from the stars behind them.

Location of our solar system

Central bulge of
old red stars

*Spiral arms are rich
in young blue and
white stars*

Perseus arm

Outer arm

IN A SPIN
The Milky Way Galaxy spins around in space. If it didn't,
it would soon collapse in on itself. Shifts in the spectra
of stars scattered throughout the galaxy reveal
that it is rotating. The stars on one side show
a shift in spectral lines toward the blue,
indicating that they are moving toward
us. The stars on the other side show
a red shift, showing that they are
moving away. The same pattern
shows up in other galaxies.

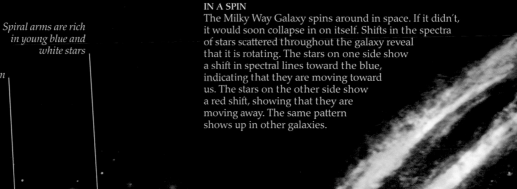

*Blue shift on
edge moving
toward us*

*Red shift on edge
moving away*

Red and blue shifts in
Andromeda Galaxy

Sagittarius A*

Molecular ring

Radio lobe

HEART OF THE MILKY WAY
Radio and infrared studies have probed the gas- and
dust-filled heart of the Milky Way Galaxy. At the very
center is an intense radio source, Sagittarius A*, which is
believed to be a massive black hole. Farther out are rings
of magnetised gas (the radio lobe) and giant molecular
clouds (the molecular ring). The molecular ring lies about
500 light-years from the center.

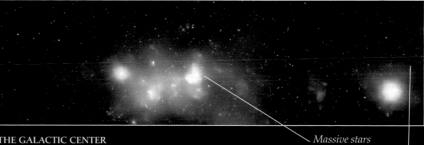

THE GALACTIC CENTER
This Chandra X-ray Observatory image shows the gas clouds
and central cluster of stars in the very heart of the Milky Way
Galaxy. The cluster contains nearly three million stars, many
of them massive and very hot. It surrounds the Sagittarius A*
black hole, which appears to have the mass of more than two
million Suns. The black hole is dormant at present, but could
become active if enough gas exists to feed it.

*Massive stars
close to central
black hole*

*Glowing gas
heated to
18 million°F
(10 million°C)*

Sagittarius arm

*A typical spiral
arm star orbits the
center of the galaxy
every 250 million
or so years*

Neighbors

IN FAR SOUTHERN SKIES, two misty patches can be seen in the constellations Tucana and Dorado. They are called the Large and Small Magellanic Clouds. They are not, as was once thought, clouds or nebulae in our own galaxy—instead, they are separate star systems, neighboring galaxies. The Large Magellanic Cloud lies just 160,000 light-years away, a mere stone's throw in space. It is small compared with our Galaxy and is irregular in shape, as is the Small Magellanic Cloud. The Magellanic Clouds and a number of smaller dwarf elliptical galaxies are not just neighbors of the Milky Way; they also come under its gravitational influence. In turn, the Milky Way and its satellites are bound by gravity into the Local Group, a family of galaxies some 3 million light-years across.

MAGELLAN'S CLOUDS
The Magellanic Clouds are named after Portuguese navigator Ferdinand Magellan (1480–1521). He commanded the first expedition to voyage around the world, which set out in 1519. He was one of the first Europeans to see the clouds and probably used them to navigate.

Small Magellanic Cloud

Large Magellanic Cloud

THE LOCAL GROUP
The Milky Way and its satellite galaxies form part of a much larger collection of galaxies called the Local Group. This group also includes two more spiral galaxies in the constellations Andromeda and Triangulum. All the other galaxies are elliptical or irregular galaxies, and are very much smaller. In all there are more than 40 galaxies in the Local Group, bound loosely together by gravity. In turn, the group forms part of a much larger cluster of galaxies.

SATELLITE GALAXIES
The Large Magellanic Cloud is 30,000 light-years across, less than one-third the size of the Milky Way. It contains much the same mix of stars and gas as our own galaxy, but has no features like a central bulge or spiral arms. It does have a broad band of relatively old stars, and also vast star-forming regions, such as the Tarantula Nebula. This nebula is one of the biggest and brightest known, lit up by a cluster of young, hot, massive stars. The Small Magellanic Cloud is only a quarter as massive as the Large Cloud and lies slightly farther away, 190,000 light-years from Earth.

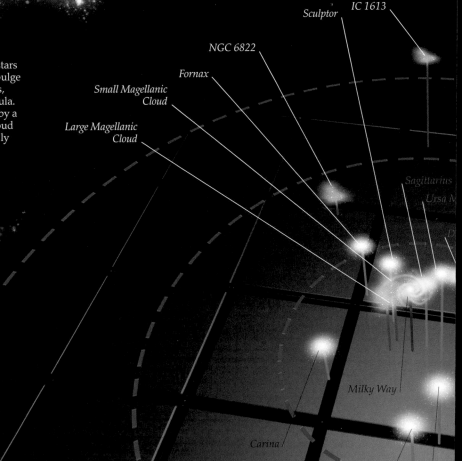

IC 1613

Sculptor

NGC 6822

Fornax

Small Magellanic Cloud

Large Magellanic Cloud

Sagittarius

Ursa M

Milky Way Galaxy

Milky Way

Carina

Sagittarius Dwarf Elliptical

Leo I   Leo II

OUR CANNIBAL GALAXY
There are small galaxies even closer to us than the Large Magellanic Cloud. The Sagittarius Dwarf Elliptical lies 80,000 light-years away, hidden behind the dense gas clouds in the center of our galaxy and only discovered in 1994. It is surprising that this dwarf galaxy has not been pulled apart by the Milky Way as it orbits it. Large amounts of invisible dark matter are believed to be keeping the galaxy together.

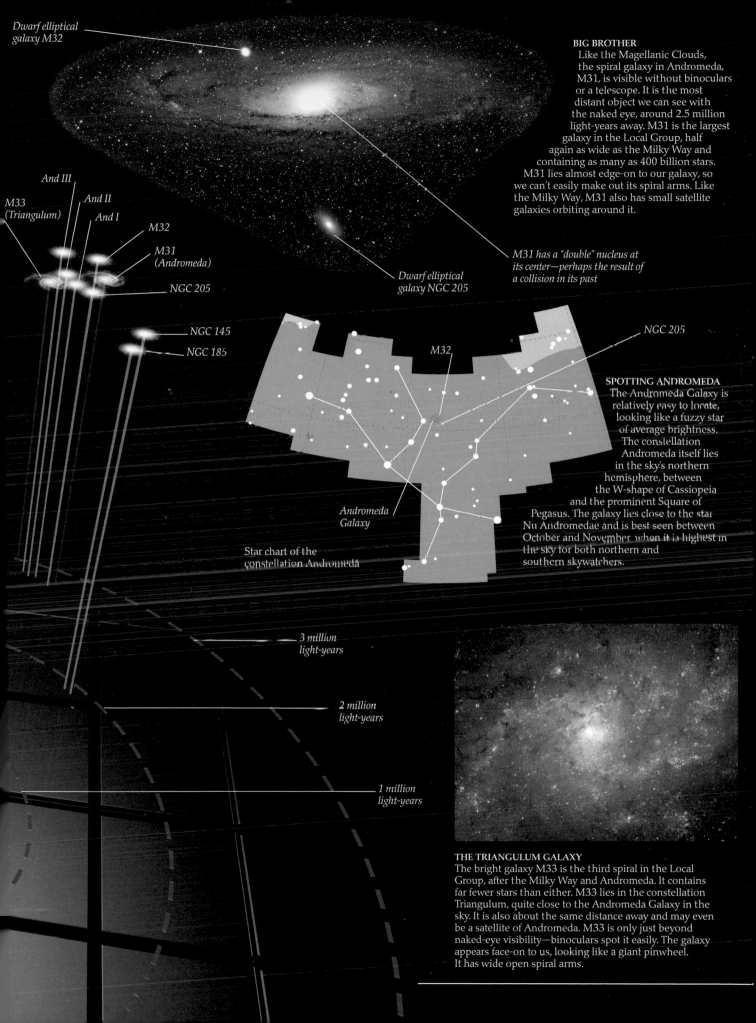

Dwarf elliptical galaxy M32

And III

And II

And I

M33 (Triangulum)

M32

M31 (Andromeda)

NGC 205

NGC 145

NGC 185

Dwarf elliptical galaxy NGC 205

M31 has a "double" nucleus at its center—perhaps the result of a collision in its past

NGC 205

M32

BIG BROTHER

Like the Magellanic Clouds, the spiral galaxy in Andromeda, M31, is visible without binoculars or a telescope. It is the most distant object we can see with the naked eye, around 2.5 million light-years away. M31 is the largest galaxy in the Local Group, half again as wide as the Milky Way and containing as many as 400 billion stars. M31 lies almost edge-on to our galaxy, so we can't easily make out its spiral arms. Like the Milky Way, M31 also has small satellite galaxies orbiting around it.

SPOTTING ANDROMEDA

The Andromeda Galaxy is relatively easy to locate, looking like a fuzzy star of average brightness. The constellation Andromeda itself lies in the sky's northern hemisphere, between the W-shape of Cassiopeia and the prominent Square of Pegasus. The galaxy lies close to the star Nu Andromedae and is best seen between October and November when it is highest in the sky for both northern and southern skywatchers.

Andromeda Galaxy

Star chart of the constellation Andromeda

3 million light-years

2 million light-years

1 million light-years

THE TRIANGULUM GALAXY

The bright galaxy M33 is the third spiral in the Local Group, after the Milky Way and Andromeda. It contains far fewer stars than either. M33 lies in the constellation Triangulum, quite close to the Andromeda Galaxy in the sky. It is also about the same distance away and may even be a satellite of Andromeda. M33 is only just beyond naked-eye visibility—binoculars spot it easily. The galaxy appears face-on to us, looking like a giant pinwheel. It has wide open spiral arms.

Galaxies galore

THE MILKY WAY AND THE OTHER GALAXIES that make up the Local Group occupy only a tiny region of space, a few million light-years across. Scattered throughout the rest of space, across tens of billions of light-years, are tens of billions of other galaxies. Many are spiral in shape, like the Milky Way and the Andromeda Galaxy. Many are oval, or elliptical, and others have no regular shape at all. Some galaxies are dwarfs, with maybe less than a million stars, but others are giants with hundreds of billions. Occasionally, galaxies create spectacular celestial fireworks as they crash into one another. Astronomers don't know exactly when galaxies started to form, but it was probably less than 2 billion years after the universe itself was born.

COLLIDING GALAXIES
Typically, adjacent galaxies are 10 galaxy diameters apart. From time to time they crash into one another. Usually, it is not the individual stars that collide but the vast gas clouds inside the galaxies. The crashing together of the clouds triggers off bouts of furious star formation, known as starbursts.

Stars are flung out of both galaxies during collision

Elliptical galaxies classified E0–E9 in order of increasing ellipticity

Spiral galaxy NGC 2207

Elliptical galaxies (E)

Barred spiral galaxies (SB)

Spiral galaxies (S)

Spirals and barred spirals classified Sa–Sc and SBa–SBc, depending on the structure of their arms

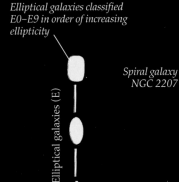

Colliding galaxies
NGC 2207 and IC 2163

HUBBLE'S TUNING FORK
Galaxy pioneer Edwin Hubble devised the method astronomers use to classify galaxies. He divided up regular galaxies into ellipticals (E), spirals (S), and barred spirals (SB), according to their shape, in his so-called tuning-fork diagram.

Starburst region—a vast stellar nursery

IRREGULAR GALAXIES
Galaxies with no particular shape are classed as irregulars. They are rich in gas and dust, and have many young stars with plenty of star-forming regions. The Magellanic Clouds are irregulars, as is M82 in Ursa Major (left). M82 is crossed by prominent dark dust lanes and is undergoing a massive burst of star formation.

CLUSTERS AND SUPERCLUSTERS

All galaxies interact with one another. Gravity binds them loosely together into small groups, like the Local Group, or often into much bigger clusters. The nearest big group is the Virgo Cluster, which spans a region of space about 10 million light-years across and contains more than 2,000 galaxies. In turn, the Milky Way and the Virgo Cluster form part of a much bigger supercluster. Strings of superclusters make up the large-scale structure of the universe.

Galaxy cluster Abell 2218

Stars orbit at many different angles

Elliptical galaxies contain old yellow stars

ELLIPTICAL GALAXIES

Elliptical, or ball-shaped, galaxies include the smallest and largest galaxies. The biggest may be up to a million light-years across. Giant ellipticals like M87 (right) are found in the heart of galaxy clusters. Ellipticals vary in shape from spherical to flattened oval. They are made up mainly of old stars and lack the gas to support much star formation.

Collision compresses gas clouds and triggers bursts of star formation

Jet emerging from galaxy core

Spiral galaxy IC 2163

Larger galaxy's gravity distorts smaller galaxy

Silhouetted dust lane in NGC 2207

LENTICULAR GALAXIES

Some galaxies seem to be a cross between spiral and elliptical galaxies. They are termed lenticular, or lens-shaped. Lenticular galaxies appear to be spirals without the spiral arms. They have a central bulge of old stars like spirals, and there are some young stars in the narrow surrounding disk, but they have no vast star-forming regions.

Lenticular galaxy NGC 2787

HOW FAR?

Astronomers can measure the distance to some galaxies by using Cepheid variables. The period over which Cepheid stars vary in brightness relates directly to their true brightness. From their true brightness and their apparent brightness in the sky, their distance can easily be calculated. Edwin Hubble (left) was first to use this method, calculating the distance to the Andromeda Galaxy in 1923.

Quasars and other active galaxies

MOST GALAXIES GIVE OUT THE ENERGY of hundreds of billions of stars shining together, but some give out much more. We call these active galaxies, and they include radio galaxies, quasars, blazars, and Seyfert galaxies. Quasars are perhaps the most intriguing of active galaxies. Their name is short for "quasi-stellar radio source," because they look like faint stars and give off radio waves. But quasars have enormous red shifts, and so must lie billions of light-years away, far beyond the stars. Powerful telescopes reveal that they are in fact galaxies with very bright centers. To be visible at such distances, quasars must be hundreds of times brighter than normal galaxies, but rapid changes in their brightness mean that most of their light must be generated in a region little larger than our system system. Today, astronomers think that quasars and other active galaxies get their energy from massive black holes at their centers.

LOOKING AT QUASARS
A former assistant to Edwin Hubble, US astronomer Allan Sandage (born 1926) helped discover quasars. In 1960, he linked radio source 3C48 with a faint starlike object but could not explain its spectrum. It was three years before 3C48 was identified as a quasar with a large red shift.

RADIO GALAXIES
NGC 5128 in the constellation Centaurus is an elliptical galaxy cut in two by a dark band of obscuring dust. It houses a powerful radio source called Centaurus A, and is the nearest active galaxy to us, just 15 million light-years away. This picture combines optical, X-ray (blue) and radio (red and green) views of the central region. A halo of X-ray-emitting gas surrounds the galaxy and a jet shoots out from its center, billowing out into huge radio-emitting lobes.

Camera

Polished metal mirror assembly used to reflect and focus X-rays

Solar panels

STUDYING ACTIVE GALAXIES
Violent activity in the heart of active galaxies produces copious amounts of high-energy radiation such as X-rays and gamma rays. Satellites such as the Chandra X-ray Observatory (above) and the Compton Gamma Ray Observatory are used to study high-energy rays from space, because these rays are blocked by the atmosphere.

Faint spiral arms 36,000 light-years across

Ring of intense starbirth around core

Bright core powered by black hole

Seyfert galaxy NGC 7742

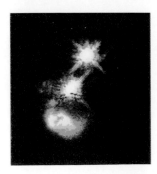

DISTANT QUASARS
The Hubble Space Telescope has spotted this quasar in the constellation Sculptor, emitting radiation as visible light. The quasar's powerful energy emission is fueled by a collision between two galaxies—the remains of one spiral ring lie just below the quasar itself. The quasar lies 3 billion light-years away—a much closer star shines just above it.

SEYFERT GALAXIES
Some spiral galaxies have particularly bright centers and are classed as Seyfert galaxies after US astronomer Carl Seyfert, who first noticed them in 1943. They are now thought to be closer and less powerful versions of quasars. About one in 10 large spiral galaxies appear to be Seyferts, and our own Milky Way may become one in time.

Intergalactic gas emits radio waves as jet slams into it

Jets billow out to form a lobe as they meet intergalactic gas

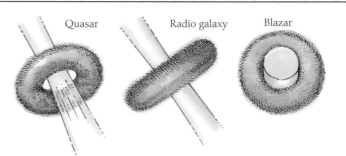

Quasar   Radio galaxy   Blazar

Quasar jets can travel at almost the speed of light

SAME ENGINE, DIFFERENT VIEWS
Astronomers believe that the various kinds of active galaxy are views of the same basic black-hole-driven "engine" from different angles. For example, quasars and Seyferts are views of the brilliant accretion disk. Radio galaxies show a side-on view, with the disk completely hidden from view, while blazars appear when we are looking right down the jet into the core.

Accretion disk is fueled by gas clouds and stars

Material in disk is heated up by friction and gravity, emitting brilliant light and X-rays

UNDERSTANDING ACTIVE GALAXIES
The "engine" that powers every active galaxy has a distinctive structure. In the heart of the galaxy is a huge torus (ring) of gas, dust, and stars. A black hole lies in the center of the ring, surrounded by a spiraling disk of gas and dust that feeds into the black hole. The disk is searing hot and emits radiation and subatomic particles. These get caught up in powerful magnetic fields and ejected along the rotation axis as high-energy jets.

Flattened accretion disk of material spiraling onto black hole

Supermassive black holes are produced by collapsing gas clouds in the center of galaxies

Central black hole weighs millions or billions of solar masses

Black hole's intense magnetic field drives jets of particles and radiation out from poles

SUPERMASSIVE BLACK HOLES
This image reveals a giant black hole blowing bubbles of gas. Powerful jets are creating a glowing shell where they meet surrounding gas. It now seems most galaxies may have supermassive black holes at their cores.

Stars straying too close to black hole are torn to pieces

Dense ring of gas and dust surrounds central engine

Radio lobes are much farther away in reality

A universe of life

OUR PLANET TEEMS WITH LIFE in extraordinary variety, but we know of no other place in the solar system or even in the universe where life exists. Surely there must be other life "out there." There are billions of stars like the Sun in our galaxy alone, and some of them must have planets capable of supporting life. And on some of these worlds, intelligent life should arise, capable of communicating across space. Since the 1960s, various projects have been set up to search for extraterrestrial intelligence (SETI) using radio telescopes. It seems likely that aliens would use radio waves of some sort to communicate, just as we do.

Crab on a black smoker

EXTREMES OF LIFE
Scientists used to think that life could only arise in mild conditions like those on Earth's surface, but recent discoveries of creatures in extreme environments have changed their minds. Creatures even thrive on the deep-sea floor around black smokers—volcanic vents spewing out sulfur-laden water at 660°F (350°C).

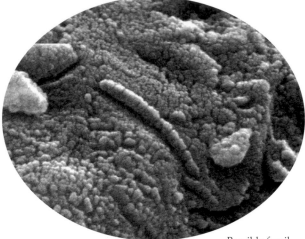
Possible fossil bacteria in Martian meteorite

LIFE IN THE SOLAR SYSTEM?
Mars has long been considered as a place where life of some sort might exist, either now or in the past. The planet is inhospitable to life now, but it probably had a more suitable climate long ago. If life gained a foothold at that time, it could have left fossils in the Martian soil. In 1996, NASA scientists thought they had found traces of ancient life in a meteorite from Mars but others are unconvinced.

HARBINGERS OF LIFE
Many carbon-based, organic molecules have been found in the gas clouds that exist between the stars. There are even simple amino acids, which are essential building blocks for life. This suggests that life might be common in the universe. It could be spread through solar systems by the most primitive of celestial bodies—the comets.

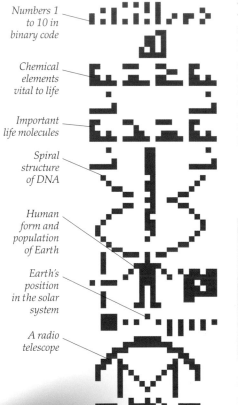

Numbers 1 to 10 in binary code

Chemical elements vital to life

Important life molecules

Spiral structure of DNA

Human form and population of Earth

Earth's position in the solar system

A radio telescope

TALKING TO ALIENS
The only message mankind has so far deliberately sent to aliens was transmitted in digital form as a set of 1,679 on-off pulses. This number is the result of multiplying two prime numbers, 23 and 73, and the message becomes clear when laid out in 73 rows of 23 columns. With black squares for 1s and white squares for 0s, a pattern or pictogram is produced that forms a message.

ARECIBO CALLING
The message (left) was transmitted from the huge Arecibo radio telescope in 1974. It was beamed at a globular cluster of 300,000 stars, increasing the possibility of reaching intelligent life. But the signal won't reach its target for another 25,000 years.

INTERSTELLAR MESSAGES
The *Pioneer 10* and *11* and *Voyager 1* and *2* space probes are now winging their way out of the solar system carrying messages for aliens. The Pioneers carry pictorial plaques; the Voyagers have gold record disks on which typical sights and sounds of Earth are recorded.

THE CHANCES OF LIFE
US radio astronomer Frank Drake (born 1930) pioneered the use of radio telescopes to listen for signals from aliens. He also devised an equation (left) that estimates how many advanced civilizations within our galaxy should be able and willing to communicate with us. Unfortunately, we still don't know enough about our universe to use the Drake Equation properly.

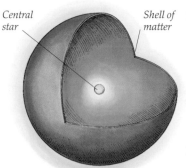

Central star

Shell of matter

SIGNS OF INTELLIGENCE
US physicist Freeman Dyson has suggested that an advanced civilization would remodel its corner of the universe, perhaps building a huge sphere around its star to trap energy. We could detect civilizations by looking for distinctive emissions from these "Dyson spheres."

WHAT MIGHT THEY BE LIKE?
It is almost impossible to guess what alien life would be like, but biologists can make educated guesses based on the principle of evolution. Simply put, this means that any creature must be well-suited to its environment in order to survive and pass on its characteristics to another generation. Using this principle, we can imagine viable aliens like this low-browsing herbivore from Epsilon Reticuli b.

Neck can retract and extend

Vibrating "hairs" detect sounds

Bristles insulate and protect the body

Eyes and a chemical-detecting nose—these are important senses in any environment

Defensive spikes

Armored hindquarters

Six walking legs with seven claws on each. Four limbs and five digits are nothing special

Our alien has an exoskeleton—it evolved from insectlike creatures

Specialized digging claw for raking tough plants out of soil

Mandibles crop and chop food against comblike teeth

CULTURE SHOCK
Some people believe that aliens are already visiting Earth and making contact with humans, but most think we have yet to make our first contact with alien intelligence. If and when that happens, the impact on humankind will be enormous. The clash in physical form and culture would be infinitely more shocking than when Columbus first met Native Americans in 1472 (left), and could be as damaging for our species as it was for the Native Americans.

EPSILON RETICULI
The hypothetical alien above comes from a moon of the giant planet Epsilon Reticuli b, about 60 light-years from Earth. The planet, discovered in 2000, orbits its star just 20 percent farther out than Earth orbits the Sun. The star Epsilon Reticuli itself seems to be a Sunlike star just starting to evolve into its red giant phase.

Window on the universe

As we look out from Earth, we look into the universe. In the daytime, the Sun drowns out the light from more distant stars. At night, we see these as pinpricks of light against the dark backdrop of space. Earth's sky is divided into 88 constellations, or star patterns, that help us find our way around the sky. These two maps will help you identify the constellations. The first shows stars visible from Earth's northern hemisphere, and the second those that can be seen from the southern hemisphere. Over the course of the year, as Earth orbits the Sun, different stars become visible.

Some constellations are easy to spot in the night sky. Others can be recognized from just a few stars in the full constellation. Seven stars in the back and tail of Ursa Major, the Great Bear, are easy to see. They are known as The Big Dipper.

The Big Dipper in the night sky

Position of The Big Dipper in Ursa Major

NORTHERN HEMISPHERE STARS
One point in the sky never moves. This fixed point is known as the celestial pole. In the northern hemisphere, Polaris (also called the North Star) is almost exactly on the celestial north pole. It is the brightest star in the constellation of Ursa Minor.

USING THE MAPS
Turn the book so that the name of the current month is at the bottom. Northern hemisphere observers should face south to see the stars in the map's lower part and center. Those using the southern hemisphere map should face north.

This view of Taurus shows the bright star Aldebaran at upper left, just above the fainter Hyades star cluster; on the right is the Pleiades star cluster.

The Double Cluster, two dense groupings of hundreds of stars (left and right of center), can be seen in the constellation of Perseus.

136

The path of the Milky Way is broadest and brightest in the constellations of Sagittarius and Scorpius. As we look at it, we are gazing into the heart of the Milky Way Galaxy from near the inner edge of one of its spiral arms.

The Carina Nebula in the constellation of Carina is one of the largest and brightest of all nebulae. It is illuminated by stars embedded within its gas and dust.

SOUTHERN HEMISPHERE STARS
Unlike the northern hemisphere sky, the southern hemisphere sky does not have a North Star. The celestial south pole (the fixed point around which the stars in the southern sky seem to rotate) is just a blank area of sky.

The white dotted line represents the ecliptic—the path of the Sun across the sky

The light-blue areas represent the Milky Way—the stars of our galaxy's disk, which appear as a dense band of stars across the night sky

The red lines work like latitude and longitude on Earth, helping to pinpoint objects in the sky

The Fornax Cluster of galaxies, made mostly of elliptical galaxies, is located in the constellation of Fornax.

Sirius (center right) in the constellation of Canis Major is the brightest star in the entire sky. To the left is the distinctive constellation of Orion, the hunter (head down).

Discovery timeline

THE UNIVERSE IS ABOUT 13.75 BILLION YEARS OLD. It formed in the Big Bang explosion that signaled the start of all space, time, energy, and matter, and ever since it has been expanding, cooling, and changing. Humans have studied the universe for thousands of years. We first analyzed the movements of the heavenly bodies by eye, then explored these bodies more closely with telescopes and space probes. Recently, we have pieced together the story of the whole universe, from its beginning to the present day.

The Crab Nebula, the remnant of a supernova seen in 1054

c. 4000 BCE
The Egyptians, Chaldeans, and Hindus name bright stars and form them into constellations. Twelve of these are the zodiac constellations.

c. 2000 BCE
Lunar and solar calendars are introduced.

550 BCE
Pythagoras, a Greek mathematician, suggests that the Sun, Moon, Earth, and planets are spherical.

360 BCE
The Greek philosopher Aristotle proposes that the planets are stuck in rotating crystal spheres and that all stars are the same distance away. He states that the universe is changeless and made from a combination of fire, water, earth, and air.

290 BCE
In Greece, the astronomer Aristarchus uses lunar eclipse timings to show that the distance between Earth and the Moon is equal to about 31 times Earth's width, and that the Moon is just over one-quarter the size of Earth.

150 BCE
Hipparchus measures the length of the year to an accuracy of 6 minutes. He catalogs the position and brightness of stars, and states that the Sun's orbit around Earth is elliptical after observing that Earth's seasons are of unequal length.

c. 130 CE
Ptolemy writes *The Almagest*, which summarizes the astronomical knowledge of the time, including a list of bright stars in 48 constellations.

c. 800
Arab astronomers refine astronomical knowledge, including defining the ecliptic (the path of the Sun across the sky) and the orbital periods of the Sun, Moon, and planets.

1054
Chinese astronomers record a supernova in the constellation of Taurus. The remnants of this are seen today as the Crab Nebula.

1252
In Spain, King Alphonso X commissions the Alphonsine Tables, which accurately list planetary positions.

1420
Mongol ruler Ulugh Beg builds an observatory in Samarkand (now part of Uzbekistan). His catalog of naked-eye star positions is the first since that of Hipparchus.

1543
Nicolaus Copernicus, a Polish astronomer, publishes *On the Revolution of the Heavenly Spheres*. His book signals the end of the idea of an Earth-centered universe.

1572
Danish nobleman Tycho Brahe observes a supernova in Cassiopeia and shows that it lies beyond the Moon. Stars are thus not a fixed distance away, but changeable objects existing in "space."

1596
Tycho Brahe finishes 20 years of highly accurate planetary observations.

1609
German astronomer Johannes Kepler devises two laws. First, that planets have elliptical orbits, with the Sun at one focus of the ellipse. Second, that a planet moves fastest when close to the Sun, and slower when farther away.

Saturn's rings, first described correctly in 1655

1610
In Italy, Galileo Galilei publishes the results of his telescopic studies in *Siderius Nuncius*. These show that the Moon is mountainous, Jupiter has four Moons, and the Sun is spotty and rotates. Galileo states that the phases of Venus indicate that the Sun, not Earth, lies at the solar system's center and declares that the Milky Way is made up of a myriad of stars that are merely very distant suns.

1619
Johannes Kepler devises his third law, which describes the mathematical relationship between a planet's orbital period and its average distance from the Sun.

1655
Christiaan Huygens, a Dutch mathematician and astronomer, correctly describes Saturn's ring system and discovers Saturn's moon, Titan.

1675
In Denmark, Ole Römer uses the eclipse times of Jupiter's moons to measure the speed of light.

1686
English astronomer Edmond Halley shows that "his" comet is periodic and part of the solar system. It sweeps past the Sun every 76 years.

1687
Isaac Newton, an English physicist, publishes his theory of gravity in *Principia*. It explains why the planets orbit the Sun and gives a value for the mass of the Sun and Earth.

1761 and 1769
Astronomers observe the transits of Venus across the face of the Sun, which are used to calculate an accurate value for the distance between the Sun and Earth.

1769
The first predicted return of a comet (Halley's) proves that the laws of gravity extend at least to the edge of the solar system.

1781
William Herschel discovers the planet Uranus using a home-built telescope in his backyard in Bath, England.

1784
A list of 103 "fuzzy" nebulae is drawn up by Frenchman Charles Messier.

1785
William Herschel describes the shape of the Milky Way Galaxy.

Willaim Herschel discovered Uranus in 1781

1801
Giuseppe Piazzi, an Italian monk, discovers Ceres, the first asteroid.

1815
Joseph von Fraunhofer, a German optician, maps the dark lines in the solar spectrum.

1838
German astronomer Friedrich Bessel calculates that the star 61 Cygni is 11 light-years away. It is the first non-solar stellar distance measured.

1840
In the US, the Moon is photographed by scientist John W. Draper. It is the first use of photography to record astronomical data.

1846
Neptune is discovered by using Newton's laws of gravitation to predict how it disturbs the orbit of Uranus.

1864
In England, William Huggins uses a spectrometer to show that comets contain carbon and that stars consist of the same chemical elements as Earth.

1879
Austrian mathematician and physicist Josef Stefan realizes that the total energy radiated by a star is proportional to its surface area and surface temperature. Stephan's Law allows stellar sizes to be estimated.

1890
About 30 stellar distances have now been measured, and astronomers are starting to do stellar statistics.

1900
New knowledge of the radioactive decay of elements leads to the realization that Earth is over one billion years old and that the Sun has been shining for a similar time period.

1905
Albert Einstein proposes that $E = mc^2$, meaning that energy (E) can be produced by destroying mass (m). This is the breakthrough in understanding energy generation in stars.

1910
By plotting stellar surface temperature and stellar luminosity, Ejnar Hertzsprung, a Dane, and Henry Russell, an American, find that there are only two main groups of stars: "dwarfs," such as the Sun; and "giants," which are much larger.

1912
American astronomer Henrietta Leavitt finds that the time periods between the maximum brightnesses of Cepheid giant stars are related to their luminosities. This relationship can be used to measure stellar distances.

1917
The 100-inch (2.5-meter) Hooker Telescope on Mount Wilson, California, is used for the first time. It detects Cepheid stars in the Andromeda Nebula, revealing that Andromeda is a galaxy. It is the first galaxy known to exist aside from our own Milky Way.

Charged-coupled device (CCD), 1980

1920
American Harlow Shapley finds that, far from being at the center of the Milky Way, the Sun is actually two-thirds of the way toward the edge.

1925
Cecilia Payne-Gaposchkin, an Anglo-American astronomer, shows that 75 percent of a star's mass is hydrogen.

1926
English astrophysicist Arthur Eddington finds that for most of a star's life its luminosity is directly dependent on its mass.

1927
American Edwin Hubble shows that the universe is expanding. The more distant the galaxy, the faster it is moving away.

1930
Pluto is discovered by American Clyde Tombaugh.

1931
US physicist Karl Jansky detects radio waves from the Milky Way's center.

1931
Georges Lemaître, a Belgian priest and scientist, suggests that all matter in the universe started as a single, highly condensed sphere. This exploded in a "Big Bang" and has been getting larger ever since.

1939
German-American physicist Hans Bethe shows how destroying hydrogen and producing helium yields stellar energy.

1955
Englishman Fred Hoyle and his German colleague Martin Schwarzschild show how helium changes into carbon and oxygen in giant stars and how higher elements like cobalt and iron are made when massive stars explode as supernovae.

Cecilia Payne-Gaposchkin, 1925

1963
The first quasar is identified—object 3C48.

1965
Americans Arno Penzias and Robert Wilson discover cosmic microwave background radiation—remnant radiation from the Big Bang.

1967
Belfast-born Jocelyn Bell-Burnell discovers the first pulsar.

1971
The first black hole Cygnus X-1 is discovered due to its effect on its companion star.

1980
In the US, Vera Rubin finds that many galaxies contain dark matter that affects their spin speed.

1980
US cosmologist Alan Guth modifies the Big Bang theory. He introduces "inflation," whereby the very young universe expands from the size of a proton to the size of a watermelon in an instant.

1980
Charged-coupled devices (the electronic chips in digital cameras) are used in astronomy. They are nearly 100-percent efficient at converting light into electronic signals.

1992
The first Kuiper Belt object is discovered by Englishman David Jewitt and Jane Luu, a Vietnamese-American.

1992
The first discovery of exoplanets—planets orbiting stars other than the Sun. They are detected around the pulsar PSR 1257+12.

1995
The first exoplanet orbiting an ordinary main sequence star, 51 Pegasi, is discovered.

2006
The category of dwarf planets is introduced after the discovery of Eris in 2005. Pluto is reclassified as a dwarf planet.

2008
Eris and Pluto are to known as plutoids—dwarf planets orbiting the Sun beyond Neptune.

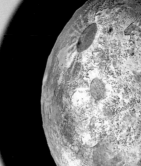
Eris, reclassified in 2006 and 2008

Find out more

Books are a great way to find out about the universe, but you may want to be more than an armchair astronomer. Start by looking up and exploring the sky for yourself, watching the view change month by month. By joining a society of other amateur astronomers, you'll soon find your way around the sky. Take a visit to an observatory where astronomers tackle today's unanswered questions or have helped to unravel mysteries in the past. Museums and space centers tell the story of space exploration. You could even time your visit to coincide with the launch of a spacecraft on a new voyage of discovery.

Tanegashima Space Center, Japan

SPACE CENTERS
Some space centers have public viewing areas where you can watch the launch of a space shuttle or a rocket, or see space engineers preparing the next generation of spacecraft. Websites for centers such as Tanegashima, Japan, and the Kennedy Space Center, in Florida, give details of upcoming launches.

RADIO TELESCOPES
Unlike optical telescopes, radio telescopes are sited on low-lying ground and are more accessible. Telescopes such as Jodrell Bank, UK, Parkes in Australia, and the Green Bank in West Virginia, USA, welcome visitors. You can get up close to the telescopes, and learn about their use in the visitor centers.

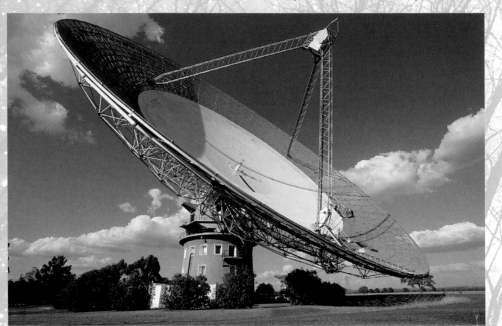

Parkes Radio Telescope, Australia

Places to visit

KENNEDY SPACE CENTER, FLORIDA
This space complex sent men to the Moon in the 1960s, and it has launched astronauts aboard the Space Shuttle since 1981. Relive space history as you tour the exhibits, ask a current astronaut a question, and watch the preparations for a future launch.

MAUNA KEA OBSERVATORIES, HAWAII
The summit of the dormant Mauna Kea volcano is home to 13 working telescopes including the Kecks, the largest telescopes in the world. The twin Kecks stand eight stories tall and have mirrors 33 ft (10 m) in diameter. Regular stargazing sessions and tours of the summit are available.

ROSE CENTER FOR EARTH AND SPACE, AMERICAN MUSEUM OF NATURAL HISTORY, NEW YORK CITY
This center features Scales of the Universe, a walkway that illustrates the vastness of the universe, and the Hayden Planetarium, the world's largest virtual-reality simulator.

OBSERVATORIES
Today's world-class optical observatories are built on mountaintop locations far from inhabited areas. Most observatories are far too remote to visit, but some situated at lower altitudes have public access programs. You can look around the observatory site and a few observatories will even let you gaze through a telescope. Among those you can visit are Yerkes, near Chicago; Greenwich, in London, UK; and Meudon, near Paris, France.

Yerkes Observatory, US

USEFUL WEBSITES

- The latest from the Hubble Space Telescope, plus its back catalog of images and results: **http://hubblesite.org/**
- Where and when to view a Space Shuttle launch or landing: **www.nasa.gov/centers/kennedy/about/view/index.html**
- The universe as seen through the eyes of the infrared Spitzer space telescope: **www.spitzer.caltech.edu/spitzer/index.shtml**
- Past, present, and future eclipse data: **http://eclipse.gsfc.nasa.gov/eclipse.html**
- Experience an astronaut's view of Earth: **http://eol.jsc.nasa.gov/Coll/weekly.htm**
- See Mars through the eyes of the European *Mars Express* spacecraft: **www.esa.int/esaMI/Mars_Express/**
- A comprehensive space website featuring news stories, image galleries, and more: **www.space.com**
- The James Webb Space Telescope set to replace the Hubble: **http://jwstsite.stsci.edu/**
- Asteroids that travel close to Earth: **http://neo.jpl.nasa.gov/nco/**
- Details of NASA's space exploration missions, past and present: **www.nasa.gov/missions/index.html**
- Fun and games with NASA's Kids Club: **www.nasa.gov/audience/forkids/kidsclub/flash/index.html**
- Check the status of twin rovers *Opportunity* and *Spirit* as they roam across Mars: **http://marsrovers.nasa.gov/home/index.html**
- Google Sky, an interactive map of the night sky, complete with a search funtion: **www.google.com/sky/**
- Planetary facts and figures at your fingertips: **http://nssdc.gsfc.nasa.gov/planetary/**
- Kitt Peak National Observatory, US—the most optical telescopes on one site: **www.noao.edu/outreach/kpoutreach.html**
- From the Sun to the edge of the visible universe in a series of maps: **www.atlasoftheuniverse.com/index.html**
- Information on visiting Mauna Kea Observatories, Hawaii: **www.ifa.hawaii.edu/mko/visiting.htm**
- Lunar phases, day length, calendars, and other data: **http://aa.usno.navy.mil/faq/**

Mexico City's planetarium

PLANETARIUMS AND MUSEUMS

A visit to a planetarium—an indoor theater where images of space are projected above your head—will help you become familiar with the night sky. As the lights dim, a universe of stars is revealed on the planetarium's domed ceiling. Get to know the constellations before being transported across space to see planets and stars in close-up. Many science museums also exhibit telescopes, spacecraft, spacesuits, and rocks that have crash-landed on Earth from space.

Tube houses mirror that collects and focuses starlight

Light enters telescope

Finder telescope to locate object

Eyepiece

Portable telescope for home and countryside

Mount supports telescope and automatically turns it to keep pace with the sky

Tripod stand

Viewing with binoculars

HOME SKYWATCHING

On a clear, Moonless, and cloud-free night you can look out from Earth and see the universe for yourself. From a typical city you will be able to pick out around 300 stars using your eyes alone, and 10 times more will be visible from a dark, rural location. Binoculars reveal still more stars, as well as adding clarity to your view of objects such as the Moon and star clusters. Telescopes bring the objects even closer, making them appear brighter and larger.

JOINING A GROUP OR SOCIETY

Skywatching with others is fun, and also a great way to learn. National societies and associations publish journals and hold meetings for members. You can also find local amateur astronomical organizations in many towns and cities. Some of these have their own telescopes and hold regular observing sessions. Professional astronomers often visit these groups to pass on the latest discoveries and research findings. If you can't commit to regular meetings, look out for special events such as eclipse-watching.

Glossary

ACTIVE GALAXY A galaxy emitting an exceptional amount of energy, much of which comes from a central supermassive black hole.

ASTEROID A small rocky body orbiting the Sun. Most asteroids orbit in the Asteroid Belt between Mars and Jupiter.

ASTRONOMY The study of everything in space, including space itself.

ATMOSPHERE The layer of gas around a planet or moon, or beyond a star's photosphere, that is held in place by gravity.

AURORA The colorful light display of glowing gas in the upper atmosphere above a planet's polar regions.

BARRED SPIRAL GALAXY A galaxy with spiral arms that curl out from the ends of a bar-shaped nucleus.

BIG BANG The explosion that created the universe. The origin of space, time, and matter.

BINARY STAR A pair of stars, each of which revolves around the overall center of mass of the two-star system.

BLACK HOLE A compact region of space where mass has collapsed and whose gravity stops anything, including light, from escaping. Some black holes result from the collapse of a single star. Supermassive black holes at the center of galaxies are the result of a very large amount of mass collapsing.

BRIGHTNESS A measure of the light of a star as seen from Earth (*see* Luminosity).

BROWN DWARF A star with too little mass to start the nuclear fusion process that powers a normal star.

CEPHEID A type of variable star whose brightness changes in a regular way over time as the star alternately expands and contracts.

CLUSTER A group of stars or galaxies that are gravitationally bound together in space.

COMET A small body of snow, ice, and dust known as a nucleus that orbits the Sun beyond the planets. A comet traveling close to the Sun develops a large head and tails.

Comet McNaught, 2007

Barringer Crater, Arizona

CONSTELLATION One of the 88 areas of Earth's sky whose bright stars form an imaginary pattern.

CORONA The outermost region of the Sun's atmosphere.

COSMOLOGY The study of the universe as a whole, and its origin and evolution.

CRATER A bowl-shaped hollow in the surface of a planet or moon. An impact crater is formed by the impact of a meteorite; a volcanic crater is where a volcano ejects material.

DARK ENERGY An unknown form of energy that makes up 73 percent of the universe.

DARK MATTER Matter that makes up 23 percent of the universe. It does not emit energy, but its gravity affects its surroundings.

DOUBLE STAR Two stars that appear very close together in Earth's sky, but which are in reality physically separate.

DWARF PLANET A near-spherical body orbiting the Sun as part of a belt of objects.

ECLIPSE An effect due to the passage of one space body into the shadow of another. In a solar eclipse, the Moon covers the Sun and its shadow falls on Earth. In a lunar eclipse, the Moon moves into Earth's shadow.

ECLIPTIC The yearly path followed by the Sun in Earth's sky.

ELECTROMAGNETIC RADIATION The energy waves given off by space objects. These include light, X-rays, and radio and infrared wavelengths.

ELLIPTICAL GALAXY A round- or elliptical-shaped galaxy.

EXTRASOLAR PLANET (EXOPLANET) A planet orbiting a star other than the Sun.

EXTRATERRESTRIAL LIFE A life form not originating on Earth. No extraterrestrial life has so far been discovered.

GALAXY A grouping of a vast number of stars, gas, and dust held together by gravity. The Sun is one of the stars in the Milky Way Galaxy.

GAS GIANT A large planet that consists predominantly of hydrogen and helium, which are in gaseous form at the planet's visible surface. Jupiter, Saturn, Uranus, and Neptune are the gas giants of the solar system.

GLOBULAR CLUSTER A near-spherical cluster of old stars found predominantly in the halo of a galaxy.

GRAVITY A force of attraction found throughout the universe.

HERTZSPRUNG-RUSSELL (H-R) DIAGRAM A diagram in which stars are plotted according to their luminosity and surface temperature, and which shows different classes of stars, such as giants and dwarfs.

INTERSTELLAR MATERIAL Gas and dust between the stars in a galaxy.

IRREGULAR GALAXY A galaxy with no obvious shape or structure.

Neptune, a gas giant

KUIPER BELT The flattened belt of rock and ice bodies that orbit the Sun beyond Neptune.

LENTICULAR GALAXY A galaxy in the shape of a convex lens.

LIGHT-YEAR A unit of distance used outside the solar system. One light-year is the distance light travels in one year: 5.88 million million miles (9.46 million million km).

LOCAL GROUP The cluster of more than 40 galaxies that includes the Milky Way.

LUMINOSITY The total amount of energy emitted in one second by a star.

MAIN SEQUENCE STAR A star, such as the Sun, that shines steadily by converting hydrogen into helium. A category of stars on the Hertzsprung-Russell diagram.

MASS The amount of matter in an object.

METEOR A short-lived streak of light that is produced by a meteoroid (a tiny piece of a comet or asteroid) as it travels through Earth's atmosphere.

METEORITE A piece of asteroid (occasionally a piece of a comet, moon, or planet) that has traveled through space and lands on a planet or moon.

MILKY WAY The spiral-shaped galaxy that includes the Sun. It is also the name of the path of stars in Earth's night sky that is our view of the galaxy's disk of stars.

MOON A body orbiting a planet or asteroid. Also called a natural satellite. The Moon is Earth's satellite.

NEBULA A vast cloud of gas and dust in interstellar space (*see* Planetary nebula).

NEUTRON STAR An ultradense, compact star formed from the core of a star that explodes as a supernova.

NOVA A star that suddenly brightens at least a thousand-fold, and then fades back to normal brightness over the following months.

NUCLEAR FUSION The process that takes place within a star's core, whereby atomic nuclei join to form heavier atomic nuclei and energy is released.

NUCLEUS The body of a comet, the core of a galaxy, or the core of an atom.

OBSERVATORY A building or complex housing telescopes, from where observations of the universe are made. Sometimes used to describe a telescope orbiting Earth.

OORT CLOUD A sphere of more than a trillion comets surrounding the planetary part of the solar system.

Meteorite fragment

ORBIT The path taken by a natural or artificial body around another of greater mass.

PHOTOSPHERE The gaseous but visible outer surface of the Sun, or other star.

PLANET A massive round body that orbits a star and shines by that star's light.

PLANETARY NEBULA A late stage in the life of a star such as the Sun. A planetary nebula consists of a colorful glowing shell of gas ejected by the central star.

PROTOSTAR An early stage in the formation of a star. Gas is collapsing to form a star, but nuclear fusion has not started in the star's core.

PULSAR A rapidly rotating neutron star identified by the brief pulses of energy we receive as it spins.

QUASAR An active galaxy that is compact and extremely luminous.

RADIO GALAXY An active galaxy that is exceptionally luminous at radio wavelengths.

RED GIANT A large, red, luminous star—the late stage in the life of a star such as the Sun.

SATELLITE A natural body orbiting another more massive body, or an artificial body orbiting Earth.

SEYFERT GALAXY An active galaxy that is a spiral galaxy with an exceptionally luminous and compact nucleus.

SHOOTING STAR An everyday name for a meteor.

SOLAR CYCLE An 11-year period of varying solar activity, such as the production of sunspots.

SOLAR SYSTEM The Sun and all the bodies that orbit round it.

Cat's Eye Nebula (NGC 6543), a planetary nebula

SPACE The region beyond Earth's atmosphere and in which all bodies of the universe exist. Also used to describe the region between astronomical bodies.

SPECTRAL CLASS The classification of a star according to the lines in the star's spectrum. The main classes are known by the letters O, B, A, F, G, K, and M.

SPEED OF LIGHT The constant speed at which light and other electromagnetic radiation travels: 186,000 miles per second (299,792,458 meters per second).

SPIRAL GALAXY A disk-shaped galaxy with spiral arms that curl out from a dense central bulge of stars. The Milky Way is a spiral galaxy.

STAR A huge spinning sphere of very hot and very luminous gas that generates energy by nuclear reactions in its core.

SUNSPOT A dark, cool region on the visible surface of the Sun or another star.

SUPERCLUSTER A group of galaxy clusters. The Milky Way Galaxy belongs to the galaxy cluster known as the Local Group, which is one of the clusters in the Local Supercluster.

Spiral galaxy NGC 4414

SUPERGIANT A very large and very luminous star.

SUPERNOVA A massive star that has exploded and which is briefly up to a million times brighter than usual. The expanding cloud of debris is called a supernova remnant.

TELESCOPE An instrument that uses lenses or mirrors, or a combination of the two, to collect and focus light to form an image of a distant object. Some telescopes collect other wavelengths, such as radio and infrared.

TERRESTRIAL PLANETS The solar system's four rocky planets: Mercury, Venus, Earth, and Mars.

UNIVERSE Everything that exists: all the galaxies, stars, and planets, and the space in between, and all things on Earth.

VARIABLE STAR A star whose brightness varies over time by, for example, expanding and contracting, or erupting (*see* Cepheid *and* Nova).

WHITE DWARF An end-stage in the life of a star; a small, dim star that has stopped generating energy by nuclear reaction.

Acknowledgments

Dorling Kindersley would like to thank: :
Darren Naish and Mark Longworth for Epsilon Reticuli b Alien; Peter Bull for other artworks; Jonathan Brooks and Sarah Mills for additional research.

For this edition, the publisher would also like to thank: Carole Stott for assisting with the updates; Lisa Stock for editorial assistance, David Ekholm-JAlbum, Sunita Gahir, Susan Reuben, Susan St Louis, Lisa Stock, and Bulent Yusuf for the clip art; Sue Nicholson and Edward Kinsey for the wall chart; Monica Byles and Stewart J Wild for proofreading; Margaret Parrish and John Searcy for Americanization.

Picture credits:
The publisher would like to thank the following for their kind permission to reproduce their photographs:

(Key: a-above; b-below/bottom; c-center; f-far; l-left; r-right; t-top)

Agence France Presse: 124bl. **akg-images:** 112tr, 117br; Cameraphoto 113tl. **Alamy Images:** Classic Image 138b; Danita Delimont / Russell Gordon 141tc. **Anglo-Australian Observatory:** David Malin 123tr. **The Art Archive:** Musée du Louvre, Paris / Dagli Orti (A) 99cr. **Bridgeman Art Library, London / New York:** Archives Charmet 119br. **British Museum:** 78bl. © **CERN Geneva:** 2tr, 82bl. **Corbis:** 134bc; Lucien Aigner 86tl; Yann Arthus-Bertrand 80cl; Bettmann 3tl, 79tr, 84bl, 90tl, 104cl, 131br, 139cl; Araldo de Luca 92tl; Dennis di Cicco 112-113c; Paul Hardy 86clb; Charles & Josette Lenars 142tc; NASA 80clb, 112br; Michael Neveux 4cr, 78c; Robert Y. Ono 117bl; Enzo & Paolo Ragazzini 78bc; Roger Ressmeyer 4cl, 85tl, 89tr, 134cr, 140br, 140cl, 141bl; Paul A. Souders 101tr; Stapleton Collection 117cr; Brenda Tharp 125cla; Robert Yin 101br. **DK Images:** Natural History Museum, London 143tc. **European Space Agency:** 83crb; D. Ducros 89bl; ISO / ISOCAM / Alain Abergel 83br; NASA 113c. © **Stéphane Guisard:** 142bl. **Courtesy of JAXA:** 140tr. **Mary Evans Picture Library:** 80tl, 98bc, 99crb, 103br, 113cr, 128tl, 135bl; Alvin Correa 103br. **Galaxy Picture Library:** 97tl, 128cl, 129c, 129br, 131cra. **Getty Images:** Barros & Barros 84tl; Sean Hunter: 101cra. **Kobal Collection:** Universal 94c. **FLPA - Images of nature:** B. Borrell 94cb, 94crb. **NASA:** 2b, 2cl, 3c, 3tr, 5tr, 81c, 81bl (x6), 83tl, 88br, 89br, 90cl, 90c, 91tr, 95tr, 95ca, 95cr, 95br, 98, 99tr, 99br, 99bl, 99l, 101cr, 102br, 103cr, 103ac, 105tr, 105bl, 107cra, 107bl, 107bc, 107ac, 109cr, 110-112cs, 122-123b, 127br; Craig Attebery 107br; AURA / STScI 1123tr; Boomerang Project 85c; Carnegie Mellon University 112cr; W.N. Colley and E. Turner (Princeton University), J.A. Tyson (Bell Labs, Lucent Technologies) 87cr; CXC / ASU/J 124c; ESA and The Hubble Heritage Team (STScI / AURA) 119bc; HST Comet Science Team 104bc; Institute of Space and Astronautical Sciences, Japan 93tr; JHUAPL 112tl, 112tc; JPL 80ca, 104c, 104bl, 105tc, 105cra, 105c, 105ac, 108clb, 108bc, 90bl, 138cla, 138tr, 142cr; JPL / University of Arizona 104-105; JSC 134cl; NASA HQ-GRIN 143cr; NOAO, ESA and The Hubble Heritage Team (STScI / AURA) 119tr; SOHO 92bl; Courtesy of SOHO / Extreme Ultraviolet Imaging Telescope (EIT) consortium 93bl; STScI 79bc, 81tr, 115tl, 120b, 1123cr, 1123br, 130-131c, 131tc, 131bl, 132cl, 132bl, 132br, 133br; STScI / COBE / DIRBE Science Team 80bl; TRW 132cr; Dr. Hal Weaver and T. Ed Smith (STScI) 113bl. **Musée de la Poste, Paris:** 109c. **National Maritime Museum:** 4tr, 79cra, 115bc; NOAA: OAR / National Undersea Research Program (NURP) 134tl. **NOAO / AURA / NSF:** N.A.Sharp 130; Pikaia: 2cra, 2crb, 4tl, 78-79, 81cl, 84bc, 86bl, 86-87, 87br, 96-97, 98tr, 99tc, 101tc, 102l, 103tr, 103cl, 108l, 109tc, 109bc, 109br, 116bl, 120tl, 1123tc, 124cl, 125b, 128bl, 133c, 134bl, 134br, 136br, 137tr. **Vicent Peris (OAUV / PTeam), astrophotographer of the Astronomical Observatory of the University of Valencia (OAUV):** MAST, STScI, AURA, NASA - Image processed with PixInsight at OAUV. Based on observations made with the NASA / ESA Hubble Space Telescope, obtained at the Space Telescope Science Institute, which is operated by the Association of Universities for Research in Astronomy, Inc., under NASA contract NAS 5-981275. 143bl. **Photolibrary:** Corbis 136-143 (background). **Science Photo Library:** 82cl, 103bl, 103bl, 106br, 110bl; Michael Abbey 112bl; Lawrence Berkeley Laboratory 87crb; Dr Eli Brinks 127tr; Celestial Image Co. 119c, 137bl; Luke Dodd 118bl; Bernhard Edmaier 100cl; Dr Fred Espenak 78-79, 80-81, 98bl; Mark Garlick 91tl, 115tr, 139br; D. Golimowski, S.Durrance & M.Clampin 1123cl; Hale Observatories 124tr; David A Hardy 84-85, 108c, 123br; Harvard College Observatory 91br, 115br; Jerry Lodriguss 136bl; Claus Lunau / FOCI / Bonnier Publications 113bl; Maddox, Sutherland, Efstathiou & Loveday 81br; Allan Morton / Dennis Milon 126bl; MPIA-HD, Birkle, Slawik 79cr, 129tc; NASA 85tr, 100bl, 116bc; National Optical Astonomy Observatories 93cra; Novosti Press Agency 113br; David Parker 139tc; Ludek Pesek 106cl; Detlev Van Ravenswaay 110cl; Royal Observatory, Edinburgh / AAO 118-119; Rev. Ronald Royer 92-93s; John Sanford 88bl, 114crb; Robin Scagell 124br; Jerry Schad 137tl; Dan Schechter 86cl; Dr Seth Shostak 135tl; Eckhard Slawik 136tr; Joe Tucciarone 126-127c.
Babak A. Tafreshi: 137br.

All other images © Dorling Kindersley
For further information see:
www.dkimages.

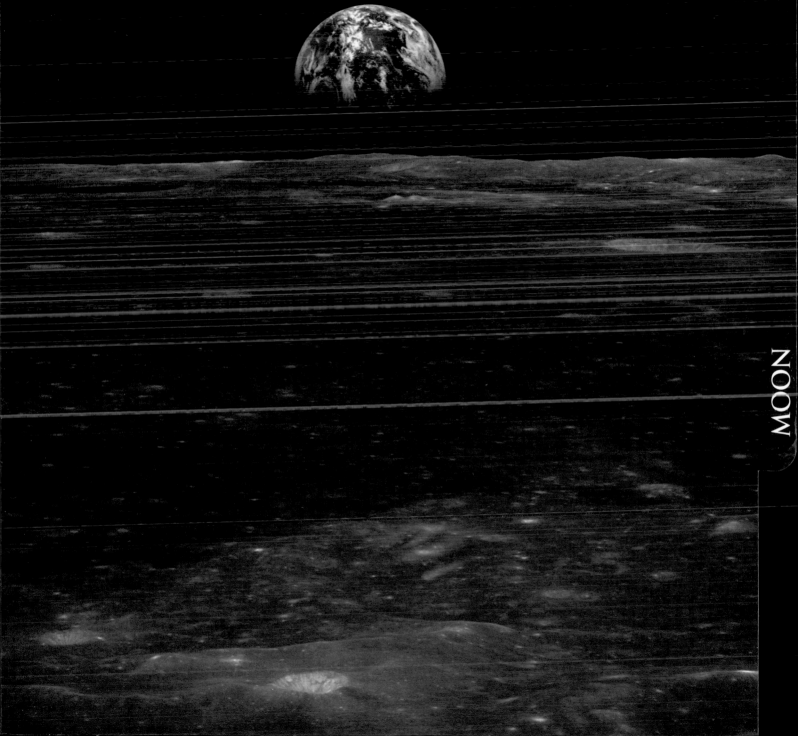

MOON

Eyewitness
Moon

Written by
JACQUELINE MITTON

Ibis head

Human body

Moon, myth, imagination

THE MOON IS THE BIGGEST and brightest heavenly body visible in the night sky and an influence on all our lives. We can be sure that our earliest ancestors observed it and wondered about it just as we do today. In many societies, the gods and goddesses of the Moon were among the most important deities and people invented myths about them. Thousands of years ago, the predecessors of today's astronomers made records of the Moon's position and learned how to predict its movement.

ANCIENT EGYPTIAN MOON GOD
Thoth was usually shown as a man with the head of an ibis (a water bird). Often, he wears a moon headdress. The Egyptians said he invented writing and made the calculations to form the heavens, stars, and Earth. Later, the ancient Greeks credited him with inventing astronomy and other sciences.

THE ZIGGURAT AT UR
One of the earliest records of Moon worship is found in Mesopotamia, in present-day Iraq. More than 4,000 years ago, the people of the city of Ur built a giant temple of mud bricks, called a ziggurat. Here, they worshiped their Moon god, Nanna. Some 1,500 years later, people of a new civilization called the Babylonians used this same temple to honor their own Moon god, Sin.

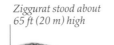

Ziggurat stood about 65 ft (20 m) high

Shrine

Platform

Ceremonial steps

Base measured 207 ft (63 m) by 141 ft (43 m)

ROMAN MOON GODDESS
In ancient Rome, the goddess Lu was associated with the Moon's She is often pictured with a cresc Moon on her head. Since she is a known as the bringer of light, sh shown carrying a torch in her ha The word "lunar" comes from he name, which is Latin for "Moon."

CHINESE MOON FESTIVAL
...ry fall, Chinese people around the world celebrate ...Moon Festival at full Moon in the eighth lunar ...nth. They carry bright lanterns and watch the ...on rise. Mooncakes are the traditional festival food. ...y are a kind of rich, sweet pastry, sometimes with ...oked egg yolk inside to represent the Moon.

Mooncakes

Feathers represent stars

Hoops symbolize the heavens

White area represents air

MOON SPIRIT
This 19th-century mask was carved by the Inuit people of Alaska. It depicts Tarqeq, the spirit of the Moon, and it would have been used in ceremonial dances. Inuit folklore includes many stories about Tarqeq. He was believed to be a great hunter who watched over the behavior of humans from the sky.

CARVED AZTEC STONE
This ancient stone from Mexico City was carved by the Aztec people, before Europeans arrived in the Americas. It depicts the myth of the Moon goddess Coyolxauhqui. She was killed by her brother, who cut her body into pieces and threw her head up into the sky, where it became the Moon.

WEREWOLVES AND THE MOON
The myth of humans that change shape into bloodthirsty wolves was popular in Medieval Europe, where the wolf was the most feared wild animal. In his book of folklore completed in 1214 CE, the writer Gervase of Tilbury said the transformation of these so-called werewolves was believed to be triggered by a full Moon.

STONEHENGE
Stonehenge in southern England was built by Stone Age people between 3000 and 2000 BCE. No one is sure of its true purpose, but scientists who have studied the alignment of the stones suspect they may have been used to observe the Sun and Moon, and to predict eclipses (see page 154).

Earth's partner

Full Moon

Rabbit or hare

Man

Hunter

Woman

Tнe Moon is our nearest neighbor in space and a familiar object in the sky, sometimes visible by day as well as at night. Measuring 2,160 miles (3,476 km) in diameter, it is our natural satellite—another world orbiting our planet—but it is very different. Earth, with its air and liquid water, supports a multitude of life-forms. It is also an active planet with moving continents and is frequently rocked by violent earthquakes and volcanoes. By contrast, the lifeless, airless Moon is a dry, hostile place, where little ever changes. Its surface has remained much the same for about 3 billion years. Although the Moon is a ball of dark gray rock, it reflects the light of the Sun and it appears clear and bright to us. It is the only object in space whose surface features can be seen by the naked eye from Earth.

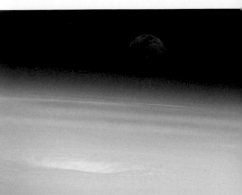

CONTRAST IN ATMOSPHERE
Though the Moon and Earth are neighbors, they are very different. Earth's gravity is strong enough to hold on to a thick layer of air, whe clouds can form and blanket large areas of the globe. By contrast, the Moon's gravity is only one-sixth of the Earth's. It keeps hold of only a very thin atmosphere—so thin that it is invisible and would fit inside a jam jar.

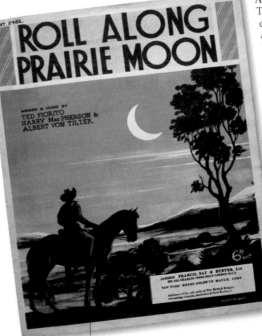

ARTISTIC INSPIRATION
The Moon has inspired countless artists, poets, and musicians of all kinds. The popular song *Roll Along Prairie Moon* was written in 1935. The lyrics were by the American songwriter Harry MacPherson. At the time, cowboys would drive herds of cattle across the wide, grassy plains of the American prairies. In this song a lonely cowboy sings about his lady love to the Moon above the prairie.

A cowboy gazes at the Moon

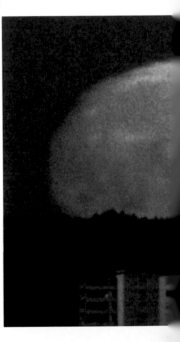

PATTERNS ON THE MOON
To many people, the patterns made by the light and dark areas on the Moon suggest familiar shapes. They are best seen when the Moon is full or nearly full. In the West, people mostly see the face of a man, but in the East people more often refer to the rabbit or hare in the Moon.

A WORLD IN THE MOON
Until the 17th century, most people thought that the Moon must be a smooth, mirrorlike sphere. They believed that the markings they could see were reflections of seas and continents on Earth. Writers such as the English clergyman John Wilkins argued that the dark and light areas were sea and land and that the Moon could be inhabited. Wilkins, a founding member of the Royal Society, published his ideas in 1638 in a book called *The Discovery of a World in the Moone*.

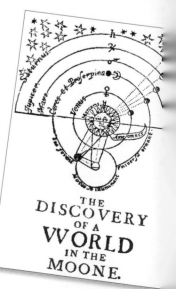

THE DISCOVERY OF A WORLD IN THE MOONE.

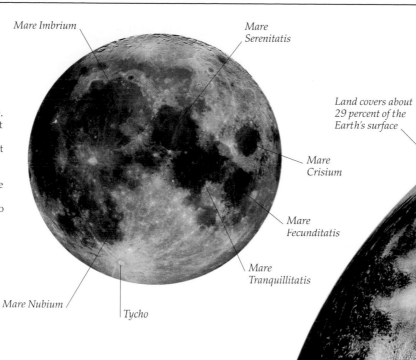

Mare Imbrium

Mare Serenitatis

Mare Crisium

Mare Fecunditatis

Mare Tranquillitatis

Tycho

Mare Nubium

NAKED-EYE MOON
The main features on the Moon are visible even without a telescope. The large dark areas are easy to spot and have "watery" names, dating from the time when people thought they were seas. Many of these are called *mare*—plural *maria*—which is Latin for "sea." Several of the large craters or depressions are also easy to see, especially at full Moon. Tycho is the most prominent crater and its rays make the Moon look like a silvery fruit.

Cloud patterns constantly change depending upon weather conditions

Land covers about 29 percent of the Earth's surface

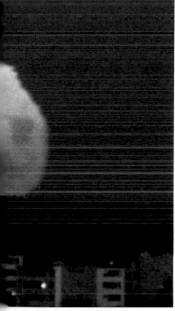

THE BLUE PLANET
Earth is nearly four times bigger than the Moon. Liquid water flows on Earth's surface because we have the right combination of pressure and temperature beneath our thick layer of air. Any water on the Moon would evaporate into space, although ice may have survived at the bottom of deep craters near the poles. With no water and almost no atmosphere, the Moon has never had wind, rain, oceans, or rivers to shape its landscape.

MOON ON THE HORIZON
When the Moon is rising or setting, it often appears a reddish color and its shape can be squashed and distorted. This is because we are viewing the Moon by looking not straight up, but sideways through thousands of miles of atmosphere, which bends and distorts the light. The Moon also looks larger near the horizon, but that is an optical illusion. The actual size of the Moon does not change as it rises, but no one has been able to explain what it seems to do so.

RING AROUND THE MOON
The full Moon is sometimes surrounded by a ghostly ring or halo of light, particularly in winter. A halo appears when the Moon is seen through a thin, cold layer of cloud and rays of moonlight are bent through falling ice crystals.

Oceans cover about 71 percent of the Earth's surface

Earth's atmosphere extends up to 75 miles (120 km) above its surface, gradually thinning out into space

A waltz in space

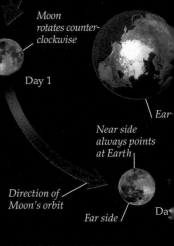

Moon rotates counter-clockwise

Day 1

Near side always points at Earth

Direction of Moon's orbit

Far side

Ear

Da

THE MOON SWINGS AROUND EARTH like a dance partner. Its orbit or path is not quite circular but elongated into an ellipse, with the Earth off center. The average distance between the Moon and Earth is about 238,900 miles (384,400 km). A car traveling at 60 mph (100 kph) would take around 160 days to go that far. Over one circuit, we see the Moon's visible shape change from a thin crescent to full and back again. These changes in shape are called phases, and the cycle of phases takes about a month. The times of moonrise and moonset also change during the Moon's phases.

ROTATION OF THE MOON
On each orbit around Earth, the Moon also turns once on its axis, so it always keeps the same face towar Earth. The opposite side always fac away and is called the far side. Due its slow rotation matching its orbit, a day on the Moon lasts the same time as a month on Earth.

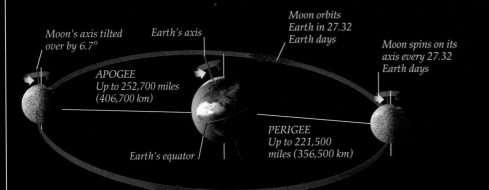

Moon's axis tilted over by 6.7°

Earth's axis

Moon orbits Earth in 27.32 Earth days

Moon spins on its axis every 27.32 Earth days

APOGEE
Up to 252,700 miles (406,700 km)

Earth's equator

PERIGEE
Up to 221,500 miles (356,500 km)

THE MOON'S ORBIT
This diagram shows the Moon making one orbit around Earth. In fact, its path changes slightly on every circuit and only repeats every 18.6 years. The nearest and farthest points of one circuit are called the perigee and apogee.

View of the Moon from Earth

8. CRESCENT
Only a thin sliver is visible. The Moon has nearly waned.

Sunlight

1. NEW MOON
The Moon's far side points toward the Sun. The near side is in darkness and cannot be seen from Earth.

View of the Moon from space

SPOT THE DIFFERENCE
The area of the Moon facing Earth varies slightly. The difference is shaded in pink here. During one cycle of phases, we see not half of the Moon's surface, but 59 percent. This variation, called libration, is mainly due to the elliptical shape of the Moon's orbit and the small tilt of the Moon's axis of spin.

PHASES OF THE MOON
The Moon shines by reflecting sunlight, so only the side of the Moon facing the Sun is illuminated. Over the course of the Moon's monthly orbit, all parts of it, including the far side, move into sunlight at some time. From Earth we see different amounts of the near side illuminated according to how far the Moon has traveled on its orbit. The pictures around the outside of this diagram show the Moon's phase—how it appears from Earth—at different points of its orbit.

2. CRESCENT
The Moon is said t be waxing, or grow Part of the near sic becomes visible from Earth.

LASER RANGING
The precise distance to the Moon from Earth can be measured to a few millimeters by firing a powerful laser from a telescope and timing how long it takes for the light to be reflected back. The laser beam is aimed at reflectors placed on the Moon by Apollo astronauts and a Soviet robotic rover. On average, the beam takes about 2.6 seconds to travel to the Moon and back.

Saturn

LUNAR OCCULTATION
The Moon is nearer to us than any planet, asteroid, or star, so it often hides—or occults—one of them. This picture shows an occultation of the planet Saturn. Timing when objects disappear and reappear at the start and end of occultations helps astronomers to track the Moon's motion accurately.

7. LAST QUARTER
Half of the Moon's near side is visible. A quarter of the cycle remains.

6. GIBBOUS
The Moon is said to be waning or shrinking.

5. FULL MOON
The Moon's near side faces directly toward the Sun.

CHANGING SIZE
The Moon's distance from Earth varies by about 30,000 miles (50,000 km). The nearer it is the larger it looks. At its closest, the Moon appears about 14 percent bigger than when it is at its greatest distance. It also shines about 30 percent more brightly.

The Moon's orbit

3. FIRST QUARTER
The Moon has completed a quarter of its orbit. Half of the Moon's near side is visible from Earth.

4. GIBBOUS
The Moon is said to be waxing gibbous.

SUNSET CRESCENT
The time when the Moon rises and sets varies with its phase. For instance, a crescent Moon is never seen in the middle of the night, but only in the eastern sky just before dawn or in the western sky around sunset.

The Moon's calendar

THE COMMON CALENDAR that we use to order
our lives is based on the yearly orbit of Earth
around the Sun, which gives us our seasons,
and on Earth's daily rotation, which
gives us day and night. But the division
of a year into months comes from the
Moon's orbit. The time between two
new moons is called a synodic month,
from a Greek word for "meeting." Many
cultures have used calendars based on
12 synodic months in a year. But unless
extra days are added each year, these lunar
calendars are soon out of step with the
seasons. However, they are still widely used
for setting the dates of religious observances.

ASTRONOMICAL CLOCK
Astronomical clocks mark the passage of days,
months, and years. This one, at the Old Town Hall
in Prague, dates from 1410. The top dial has three
pointers and represents the motion of the Sun,
Moon, and stars around Earth. The lower dial is a
calendar showing the months of the year.

Moon pointer

*Inner dial shows sky
divided into 12 signs
of the zodiac*

*Background shows
day, twilight,
and night*

*Outer dial is a
24-hour clock*

*Illustrations
for months
of the year*

*Wheel turns for
Moon's phase*

THE 19-YEAR CYCLE
Twelve lunar months add up to only 354 days—11 days
short of a full year. However, 19 years is almost exactly
235 lunar months. People who used lunar calendars could
add seven extra months every 19 years to keep in step
with the seasons. This French calendar from 1680 includes
a table and two wheels. It calculates the Moon's phases
over a 19-year cycle and also shows the days of the week.

SYNODIC AND SIDEREAL MONTHS

Circling around the sky, the Moon returns to the same position after 27.32 days. This period is called a sidereal month from a Latin word meaning "star" or "constellation." During that time, Earth has moved along its orbit around the Sun, so the Moon needs more time to complete all its phases. This takes a synodic month, which lasts 29.54 days.

Earth

Moon begins orbit

Earth's orbit

Moon completes orbit one sidereal month later

Moon completes phases one synodic month later

Sun

Maror (bitter herb—horseradish)

Zeroa (lamb shank bone)

Charoset (apple, nut, spice, and wine)

Beitzah (egg)

Karpas (vegetable or parsley)

Chazeret (bitter vegetable— lettuce)

Traditional painted Easter egg

EASTER TIME

[Th]e date of the Christian festival [of] Easter was originally the first [Sun]day after a particular full [Mo]on. Today, the date is set by [ta]bles that simplify the [cyc]les of the Moon rather than [on] the date of a real full Moon. [E]astern and Western churches often celebrate Easter on different dates because they use different calendars.

JEWISH PASSOVER

The dates of Jewish religious festivals are set according to a historic lunar calendar and their dates in the common calendar vary from year to year. The celebration of Passover, for example, starts on the 15th day of the Jewish month of *Nissan*. At Passover, families eat a special ritual meal of five or six symbolic foods, called the *seder*.

THE MOON AND ISLAM

The religious Islamic calendar is based on lunar months. Because 12 lunar months take only about 354 days, Islamic holy days fall 10 or 11 days earlier each year by the common calendar. The symbol of the crescent Moon is often linked with Islam. The link began when the Muslim founders of the Ottoman Empire conquered the city of Constantinople (present-day Istanbul) in 1453 and adopted the city's emblem—the crescent Moon—as their own.

Crescent moon on the East London Mosque in the UK

Minaret, from which the voice of the muezzin calls Muslims to prayer

Dome of the mosque

LUNAR MONTH

[The fi]rst sighting of the slim crescent Moon, [appe]aring just 30 hours after the new Moon, marks [the st]art of each month in the Islamic lunar calendar. [Ramad]an, the important month of fasting observed [by Mu]slims, begins at the start of the ninth lunar [mont]h. It marks the time that the first verse of [the Q]ur'an was revealed to Muhammad and [end]s with a feast at the next new Moon.

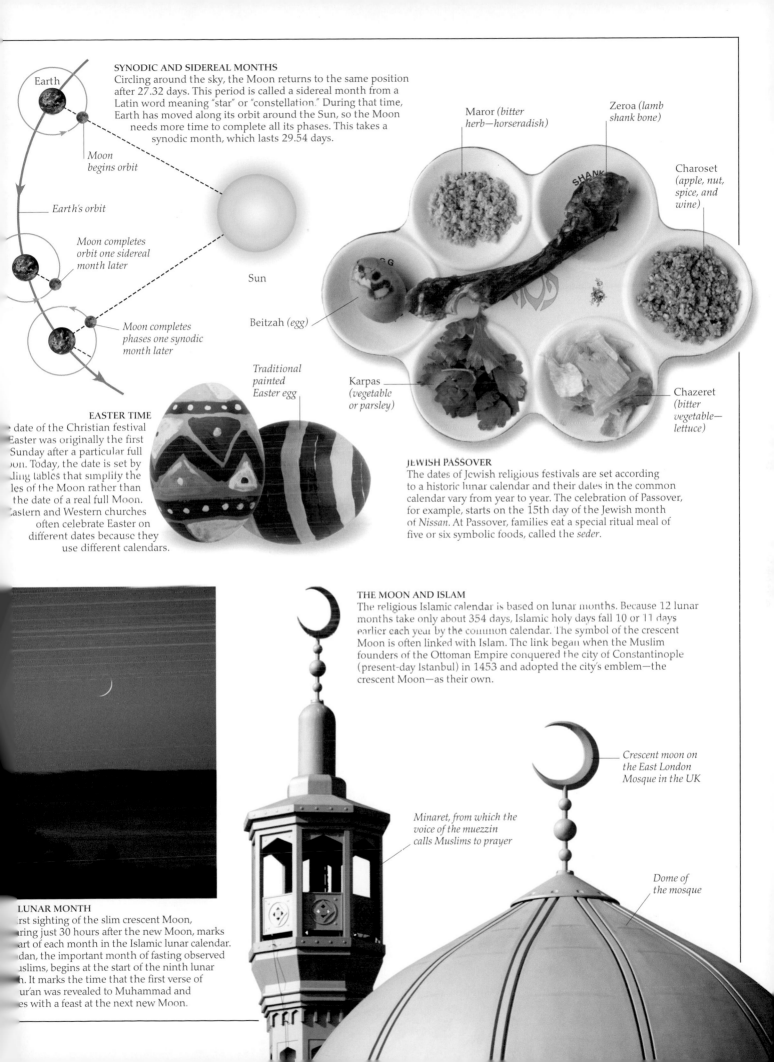

Eclipses

PEOPLE TRAVEL ALL OVER the world to experience a total solar eclipse. During this dramatic natural phenomenon, the Moon blocks out the Sun's light. Sometimes, the Moon itself goes into an eclipse, taking on a mysterious coppery hue. The Moon, Sun, and Earth do not line up to create an eclipse every month. At least two solar eclipses happen every year, though most are partial. Up to seven lunar and solar eclipses can fall in a year. The pattern of eclipses repeats on a cycle of 6,585.32 days (about 18 years).

ECLIPSE OF THE MOON

Lunar eclipses take place only at full Moon. During a total eclipse, Earth gradually moves between the Moon and the Sun. Earth's shadow seems to creep across the Moon's surface. Even when totally eclipsed, the Moon remains dimly lit by red light, which is sunlight reaching the Moon after it has been bent and scattered through the edge of Earth's atmosphere. The period of totality can last up to 1 hour 47 minutes.

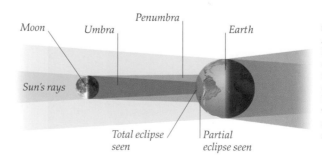

Moon being eclipsed

Christopher Columbus

COLUMBUS'S ECLIPSE

In the past, eclipses were feared or regarded as portents of evil. In 1504, the Spanish explorer Christopher Columbus became stranded with his crew in Jamaica. He knew that there would be a total eclipse of the Moon on February 29 and used this to scare the local Arawak people. He told them that the Moon was being taken away and would be restored only if they helped him. The trick worked and Columbus and his crew were later rescued.

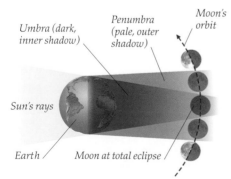

Umbra (dark, inner shadow)

Penumbra (pale, outer shadow)

Moon's orbit

Sun's rays

Earth *Moon at total eclipse*

LUNAR ECLIPSE

For an eclipse of the Moon to take place, the Sun, Earth, and Moon must line up at full Moon. Lunar eclipses occur when the Moon passes through Earth's shadow. They can be seen from any location where the Moon has risen before the eclipse.

Moon *Umbra* *Penumbra* *Earth*

Sun's rays

Total eclipse seen *Partial eclipse seen*

SOLAR ECLIPSE

A solar eclipse is seen when a new Moon crosses in front of the Sun and casts a shadow on part of Earth's surface. Total eclipses of the Sun are seen only over a narrow area because the Moon's shadow is small when it reaches Earth. Observers in a region outside this area of totality see only a partial eclipse.

ANCIENT ECLIPSE RECORDS
Eclipses have been recorded for thousands of years. Inscribed Chinese oracle bones like this one mention eclipses in around 1300 BCE. The earliest reference in recorded history concerns two Chinese court astrologers who were beheaded for failing to predict a solar eclipse in 2134 BCE.

Inscribed characters

SOLAR PROMINENCES
When the brilliant disk of the Sun is hidden by the Moon during a total eclipse, it is sometimes possible to see solar prominences at the Sun's edge. These huge tongues of hot gas surge out into space from the Sun. The prominence shown here was recorded during the eclipse of July 11, 1991.

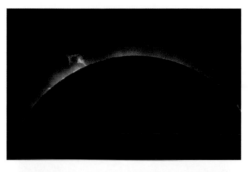

BAILY'S BEADS
The edge of the Moon is uneven because of its mountains and valleys. At the beginning and end of a total solar eclipse, sunlight often bursts through several valleys. The effect is called Baily's Beads, after the English astronomer Francis Baily (1774–1844).

Arawak people fear the eclipse

WATCH AN ECLIPSE SAFELY
Never look directly at the Sun without eye protection officially approved as safe. During a total eclipse, it is safe to remove goggles briefly during totality, when the Sun is completely blocked. Do not try to view a partial eclipse, or the partial stage of a total eclipse, with the naked eye.

TOTAL SOLAR ECLIPSE
As the partial phase of a total solar eclipse progresses, the Moon gradually covers the Sun. The moment of totality comes when the Sun's yellow disk is completely hidden. The sky goes dark and it is possible to see the Sun's corona (faint outer layers of gas) extending out from the Sun like a white halo. Totalities can last up to 7.5 minutes, but they are mostly much shorter. This eclipse in July 1991 was nearly 7 minutes long. Images taken at different stages of the eclipse have been put together to make this picture.

PARTIAL SOLAR ECLIPSE
When the Moon and Sun are not perfectly aligned, an eclipse of the Sun may be only partial, as seen here in India in March 2007. Observers also experience a partial eclipse if they look at a total eclipse from outside the area of totality.

ANNULAR ECLIPSE
The Moon and Sun appear to be nearly the same size in our sky but both vary slightly (see page 151). An annular (ring-shaped) eclipse occurs when the Moon crosses directly in front of the Sun and its apparent size happens to be less than the Sun's. This one was seen in January 1992.

Tides

THE EBB AND FLOW OF tides around the world's coasts are daily reminders of the Moon's influence on our planet. The Moon's gravity pulling on Earth is the principal cause of ocean tides. It distorts Earth's rocky ball by just an inch or so but stretches the oceans by around 3–10 ft (1–3 m). The constant drag of tides is slowing Earth's rotation and causing the Moon's orbit to widen. Days are lengthening by about 2 milliseconds per century and the Moon moves about 1½ in (3.8 cm) farther away each year.

High tide near St. Abbs Harbour, Scotland

Low tide near St. Abbs Harbour, Scotland

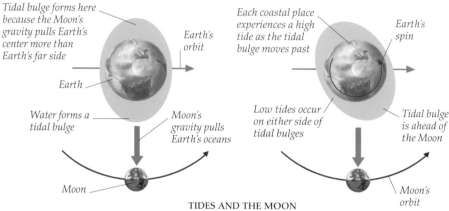

Tidal bulge forms here because the Moon's gravity pulls Earth's center more than Earth's far side

Earth's orbit

Earth

Water forms a tidal bulge

Moon's gravity pulls Earth's oceans

Moon

Each coastal place experiences a high tide as the tidal bulge moves past

Earth's spin

Low tides occur on either side of tidal bulges

Tidal bulge is ahead of the Moon

Moon's orbit

TIDES AND THE MOON
The Moon's gravity stretches Earth into a slightly oval shape because its pull is strongest on the side of Earth facing the Moon and weakest on the opposite side. The oceans stretch more than the rocky ball of Earth because they are liquid. This makes tidal bulges form on both sides of the globe. The daily rotation of Earth drags the tidal bulges with it so they sweep around the world slightly ahead of the Moon rather than directly in line with it.

HIGH AND LOW TIDE
The height and pattern of tides can vary from coast to coast as a result of many different factors, such as the shape of the coastline, and the depth of water. The difference between high and low tide in the narr curving Bay of Fundy in Canada is nearly 53 ft (16 m the greatest range in the world. Most coasts have two tides a day, 12 hours 25 minutes apart, but some have only one every 24 hours 50 minutes.

TIDAL POWER STATION
The power of tides can be harnessed to generate electrici This tidal power plant, which opened in Brittany, France, 1966, was the first in the world. A barrage 2,461 ft (750 long spans the estuary of the Rance river. Water flows through turbines when the tide comes in and goes out. The water turns the turbines, generating electricity.

Exposed seaweed

Above water, sea anemone closes up to stay moist

Sea anemone opens under water to catch food

Limpet keeps moist at low tide by sealing its shell against the rock

Sea urchin

Shrimp

Sea star

K POOL
cycle of tides creates a double habitat
he seashore. At high tide, the habitat is
nerged with water. At low tide, the water disappears and
sed ocean animals take refuge in rock pools. Some life-forms
ve outside the pools because they are tough enough to
ate drying out. This pool is shown at low tide.

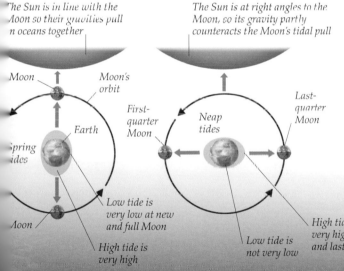

The Sun is in line with the Moon so their gravities pull n oceans together

The Sun is at right angles to the Moon, so its gravity partly counteracts the Moon's tidal pull

Moon

Moon's orbit

First-quarter Moon

Neap tides

Last-quarter Moon

Earth

pring ides

Moon

Low tide is very low at new and full Moon

High tide is very high

Low tide is not very low

Low tide is not very low

High tide is not very high at first and last quarter

SPRING AND NEAP TIDES
The Sun also affects ocean
tides, though its pull is
weaker than the Moon's.
The most extremely high and
low tides, called spring tides,
occur when the Sun and
Moon reinforce each other
at full Moon and new Moon.
The least extreme tides,
called neap tides, happen at
first and last quarter, when
the Sun's pull partly opposes
the Moon's gravity.

Fine growth bands in base

LONGER DAYS
Some corals have
daily growth
bands, like yearly
tree rings. Counting
growth bands in fossil
corals from different
periods shows that day
length was shorter in the
past—about 22 hours 300 million
years ago, and about 21 hours
500 million years ago.

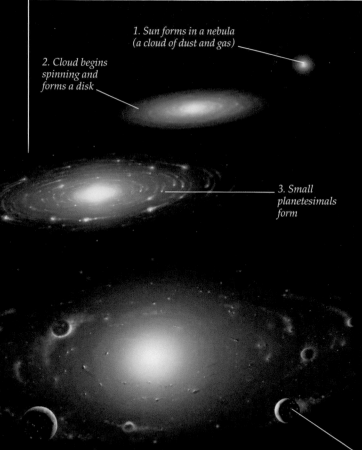

1. Sun forms in a nebula
(a cloud of dust and gas)

2. Cloud begins
spinning and
forms a disk

3. Small
planetesimals
form

4. Planets form
from planetesimals

Birth of the Moon

THE MOON AND EARTH ARE unusual in the solar system, because they exist as a pair of worlds of very similar size. Scientists have puzzled for centuries about how Earth acquired such a large partner. Before the Apollo Moon missions, there were three main theories. One was that the Moon and Earth formed together as a double planet. Others suggested that the Moon was spun off by a rapidly spinning Earth, perhaps from where the Pacific Ocean is now. Alternatively, the Moon might have been a stray body, captured by Earth's gravity. The Apollo missions were expected to settle which theory was correct but none of their findings fit the facts. There had to be a different explanation.

BIRTH OF THE SOLAR SYSTEM
Most planetary scientists think that the planets and other bodies in the solar system formed about 4.6 billion years ago within a rotating disk of dust and gas surrounding the newly born Sun. Clumps called planetesimals gradually came together in a process called accretion, but there were also high speed collisions that broke some clumps apart again. Small pieces that were left over became comets and asteroids.

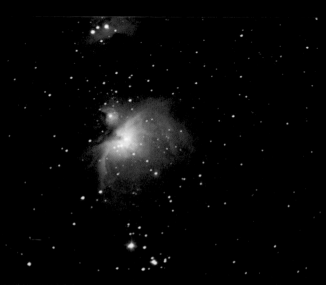

NEBULAR THEORY
Stars and their planetary systems are born in nebulae like this one, the Orion Nebula. One theory of the Moon's origin suggested that it and Earth condensed out of the nebula surrounding the Sun. But this idea cannot explain the differences between Moon rocks and Earth rocks and why the Moon's iron core is very small.

GIANT COLLISION
A giant collision between the newly formed Earth and a small planet about the size of Mars is now the most popular explanation for how Earth acquired its Moon. This theory explains better than any other the structure, composition, and orbit of the Moon. Computer simulations can show how it probably happened.

1 GLANCING COLLISION
About 4.55 billion years ago, when Earth was only 50 million years old, a smaller planet had formed in a nearby orbit and the two were on a collision course. At this time, the solar system was a violent place where major collisions were not uncommon. The impact with Earth was not head-on but its cataclysmic force blasted enormous amounts of rock from both planets as a white hot vapor. This was the material from which the Moon would form. The very high temperatures it reached can explain why the Moon has more of certain chemical elements than Earth, and less of others.

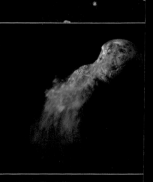

2 HOT CLOUD
Just hours after the impact, clouds of hot gas and dust and fragments of rock were streami away from Earth. Some travele enough to escape Earth's gravit

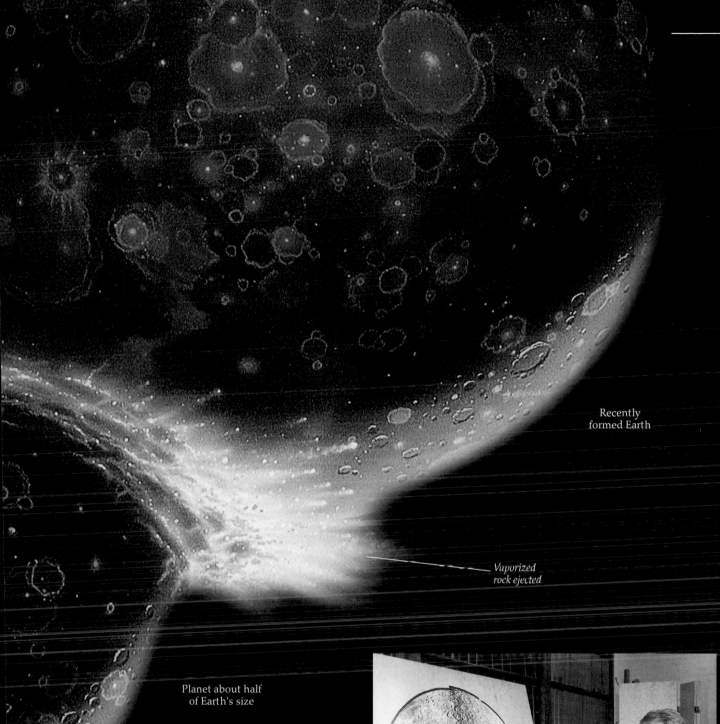

Recently
formed Earth

*Vaporized
rock ejected*

Planet about half
of Earth's size

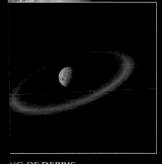

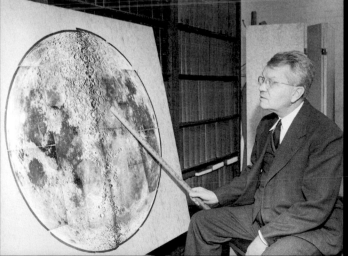

...NG OF DEBRIS
...me of the ejected gas, rock,
...ust remained captured in orbit
...d Earth. It cooled rapidly and,
...after the collision, the circling
...collapsed into a ring of debris.

4 FORMATION OF MOON
Within only a few years, material
in the circulating ring began to
clump together. Pieces of rock were
attracted to one another by gravity
and eventually formed the Moon.

HAROLD C. UREY
The American scientist Harold C. Urey (1893–1981) received the Nobel
Prize for chemistry in 1934 and started to study the Moon in the 1940s.
He favored the theory that the Moon originally formed elsewhere in the
solar system and was captured by Earth 4.5 billion years ago. Urey was
probably wrong about that, but he wanted to see humans land on the
Moon and his enthusiasm influenced NASA's early space program.

The Moon takes shape

THE MOON AS WE SEE IT TODAY was mostly shaped billions of years ago, when its volcanoes erupted with lava, and comets, asteroids, and meteoroids pounded its surface. The first crust to crystalize on the newly formed Moon was soon a mass of impact craters. Later, there were fewer large collisions, and the low-lying basins created by the largest impacts flooded with lava that solidified into dark gray plains.

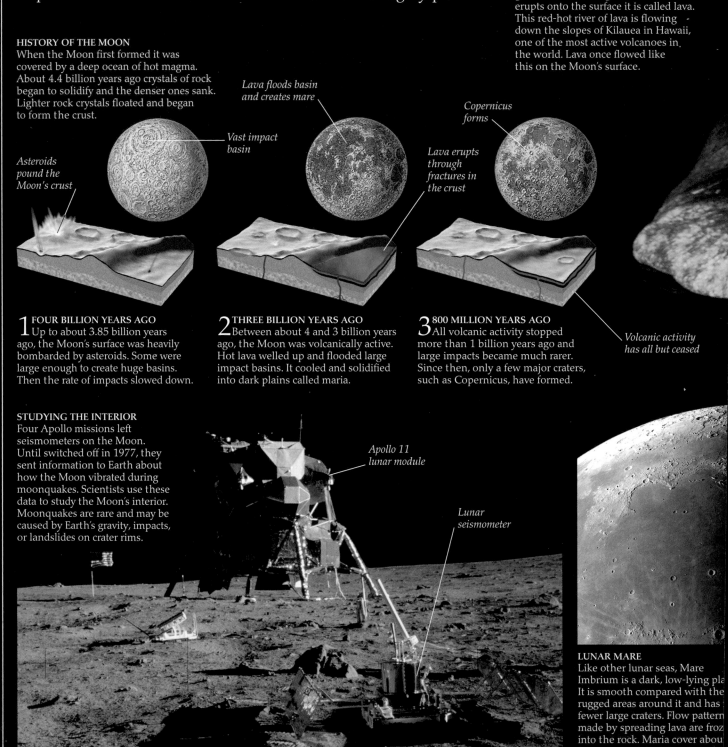

LAVA FLOW
Hot molten rock under ground is called magma. When it erupts onto the surface it is called lava. This red-hot river of lava is flowing down the slopes of Kilauea in Hawaii, one of the most active volcanoes in the world. Lava once flowed like this on the Moon's surface.

HISTORY OF THE MOON
When the Moon first formed it was covered by a deep ocean of hot magma. About 4.4 billion years ago crystals of rock began to solidify and the denser ones sank. Lighter rock crystals floated and began to form the crust.

Lava floods basin and creates mare

Copernicus forms

Vast impact basin

Lava erupts through fractures in the crust

Asteroids pound the Moon's crust

1 FOUR BILLION YEARS AGO
Up to about 3.85 billion years ago, the Moon's surface was heavily bombarded by asteroids. Some were large enough to create huge basins. Then the rate of impacts slowed down.

2 THREE BILLION YEARS AGO
Between about 4 and 3 billion years ago, the Moon was volcanically active. Hot lava welled up and flooded large impact basins. It cooled and solidified into dark plains called maria.

3 800 MILLION YEARS AGO
All volcanic activity stopped more than 1 billion years ago and large impacts became much rarer. Since then, only a few major craters, such as Copernicus, have formed.

Volcanic activity has all but ceased

STUDYING THE INTERIOR
Four Apollo missions left seismometers on the Moon. Until switched off in 1977, they sent information to Earth about how the Moon vibrated during moonquakes. Scientists use these data to study the Moon's interior. Moonquakes are rare and may be caused by Earth's gravity, impacts, or landslides on crater rims.

Apollo 11 lunar module

Lunar seismometer

LUNAR MARE
Like other lunar seas, Mare Imbrium is a dark, low-lying pla It is smooth compared with the rugged areas around it and has fewer large craters. Flow pattern made by spreading lava are froz into the rock. Maria cover abou 16 percent of the Moon's surfac

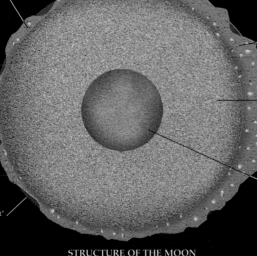

side crust
7½ miles
(...m)
er

Thicker crust
on far side

Mantle

Core about
435 miles
(700 km)
across

STRUCTURE OF THE MOON

interior of the Moon is layered but we are not certain about its
...cture. The outer crust is 12–75 miles (20–120 km) thick but
...near side is thinner on average. More maria formed in the near
... possibly because lava reached the surface more easily through
...thinner crust. The crust lies over a deep mantle of denser rock.
... The small core is mainly iron and may be partly molten.

QUAKE HAZARD
In his 1948 story *Gentlemen,*
Be Seated, the science fiction
writer Robert Heinlein
predicted that future lunar
bases would have to be built
to withstand moonquakes.
In 2006, scientists studying
moonquake records warned
NASA that Heinlein was
right. Moonquakes can last
over 10 minutes and be as
strong as earthquakes that
cause damage to buildings.
Shown here is a scene from
the popular 1950 movie
Destination Moon, whose
screenplay was cowritten
by Heinlein.

The Moon's surface

THE LUNAR LANDSCAPE IS STARK and colorless. Every part is covered with a thick layer of powdery gray dust and scattered with boulders. Craters large and small pit th entire surface. Huge basins filled with lava are ringed with mountains. The plains of solidified lava in the basins reveal their volcanic origin with a variety of features such as pitted domes, collapsed lava tubes, winding cliffs, and humpy ridges For astronauts, the airless environment is harsh. During the d the temperature at the equator soars as high as 240°F (120°C only to plummet to -270°F(-170°C) at night, and there is no protection from the Sun's dangerous radiation.

LUNAR HIGHLANDS
The pale gray areas around the darker basins are the lunar highlands. They are covered by overlapping craters of all sizes. The asteroid impacts that formed the craters melted, broke down and remixed the various rocks that formed the Moon's original crust. Most highland rocks are complex mixtures, called breccias.

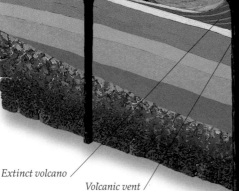

Highland region

Mare region

Sinuous rille

Straight rille

Rayed crater

Impact crater chain

Extinct volcano

Volcanic vent

SURFACE FEATURES
This illustration of the lunar landscape shows the border between ancient, mountainous highlands and a volcanic mare area. Lava welling up from the mantle below the crust formed the small volcanic cones. The straight rille is a valley that was created when a section of the surface sank. It split one crater in two, showing that the rille formed after the crater.

Mantle rocks

Layers of crustal rocks

Old crater flooded by lava

162

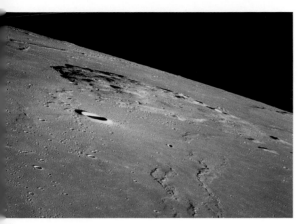

LUNAR REGOLITH
Over billions of years, meteoroids have smashed the Moon's surface rocks into a gray dust called the lunar regolith. A layer several metres deep blankets the whole Moon. It is sometimes called lunar "soil" but, unlike Earth soil, it contains no organic material. Large impacts on the Moon are now rare, but there is still a constant rain of high-speed micrometeoroids grinding down any exposed rocks. Even so, this astronaut footprint will survive millions of years in an environment with no wind or rain.

CANIC DOMES
mountain, Mons Rümker, on the Oceanus Procellarum, is a r of about 30 volcanic domes some 44 miles (70 km) across. were formed by the eruption of lava through vents in the ce. Lines of cliffs called scarps, where solidifying lava piled up, st visible on the far side of the dome (top left).

MOUNTAIN RANGES
There are 18 mountain ranges on the Moon. Most form the rims of huge impact basins and all have official Latin names. This range, the Montes Agricola, was named after the 16th-century German scientist Georgius Agricola. It stretches for 87 miles (140 km) on the eastern edge of the Oceanus Procellarum. The highest lunar mountains rise to over 15,750 ft (4,800 m).

Terraced crater rim

Central peak of crater

Ancient lava flow

SINUOUS RILLES
A valley on the Moon is called a rille or a rima. Some rilles meander across the lunar surface looking like dried-up riverbeds. In fact, they are channels created by flows of molten lava and often begin near an extinct volcano. This system of rilles is on the Oceanus Procellarum, near an ancient flooded crater (top).

Geological hammer

Feather

SHARP SHADOWS
Because the Moon has no atmosphere to scatter sunlight, its sky is always black—unlike on Earth, where the atmosphere scatters the sunlight and makes its sky look blue. During the day, the ground is brightly lit by the intense Sun. Shadows are sharp and very dark. Without a blanket of air to hold warmth, the temperature swings dramatically between day and night. The Moon is also eerily silent because there is no air to carry sound.

GRAVITY ON THE MOON
The Moon's surface gravity is only one-sixth of Earth's. To demonstrate one of the effects of this low gravity, the Apollo 14 astronaut Alan Shepard hit a golf ball nearly half a mile (0.8 km) on the Moon. The reduced gravity, together with the lack of air resistance, meant the ball went much farther than on Earth. On the next Apollo mission, Dave Scott dropped a geological hammer and a falcon feather at the same time to show they would land together though one was heavier than the other. This experiment would be impossible on Earth, where air resistance would slow down the feather more than the hammer because of the feather's shape.

Craters

Asteroid Itokawa

CRATERS ARE PITS IN the ground surrounded by raised walls. Astronomers once thought that all lunar craters were volcanic. Then in 1965, a spacecraft returned images of impact craters on Mars. Now, more scientists took seriously the theory that craters are often formed by impacting comets, asteroids, and meteoroids. The Apollo missions proved that almost all lunar craters were created by impacts. Moon craters range from microscopic pits to vast basins, such as the South Pole–Aitken Basin, which is 1,615 miles (2,600 km) across and one of the largest in the solar system.

VOLCANIC CRATERS
Volcanoes can create two different types of craters. The firs cinder cones, with pitlike craters at their summit, where as and lava spew out and pile up over several eruptions. Thes cinder cone craters are on Santiago Island, in the Galapag Islands. The second are calderas, which form when a large volume of magma is ejected in a huge volcanic eruption ai the ground subsides into the emptied space.

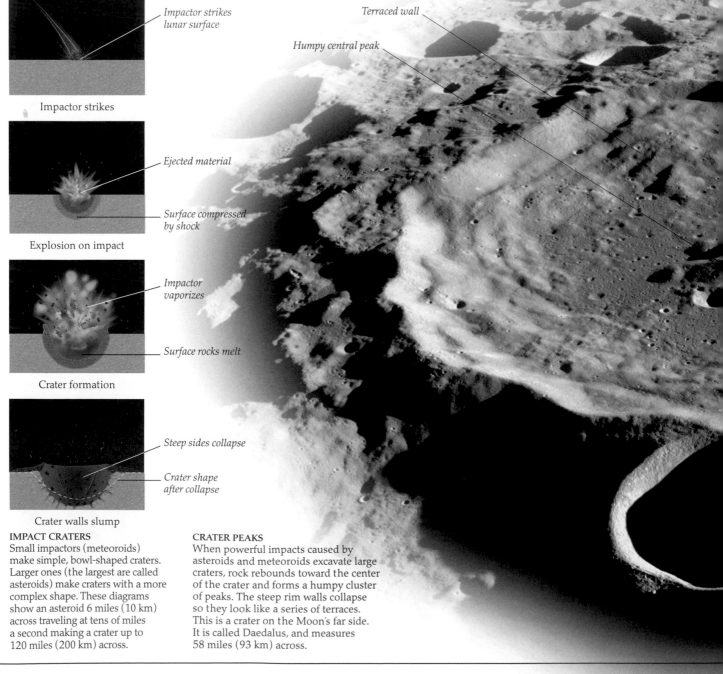

Impactor strikes lunar surface

Impactor strikes

Ejected material

Surface compressed by shock

Explosion on impact

Impactor vaporizes

Surface rocks melt

Crater formation

Steep sides collapse

Crater shape after collapse

Crater walls slump

Terraced wall

Humpy central peak

IMPACT CRATERS
Small impactors (meteoroids) make simple, bowl-shaped craters. Larger ones (the largest are called asteroids) make craters with a more complex shape. These diagrams show an asteroid 6 miles (10 km) across traveling at tens of miles a second making a crater up to 120 miles (200 km) across.

CRATER PEAKS
When powerful impacts caused by asteroids and meteoroids excavate large craters, rock rebounds toward the center of the crater and forms a humpy cluster of peaks. The steep rim walls collapse so they look like a series of terraces. This is a crater on the Moon's far side. It is called Daedalus, and measures 58 miles (93 km) across.

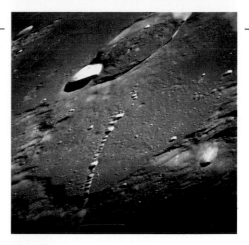

DAVY CRATER CHAIN
This chain of craters stretches for 29 miles (47 km) across the floor of the crater called Davy Y. It probably formed when the pieces of a meteoroid that had broken up crashed down one after another. There are 23 craters, each ½–2 miles (1–3 km) across. Crater chains are not very common, but there are several on our Moon and on the moons of other planets.

...OR CRATER
...or Crater in Arizona, US, was created about ...00 years ago by an impactor weighing thousands ...ns, which had probably broken up in the ...sphere. Most of the object was destroyed on ...ct, but about 20 tons (18 metric tons) of pieces ...d meteorites have been found. The crater is about ...t (170 m) deep and 4,000 ft (1,200 m) wide.

YOUNGER CRATERS
These small, sharp-looking craters lie on the Oceanus Procellarum. The craters on the lunar maria all formed after the maria themselves. Younger craters have had less time than older ones to be worn down by micrometeoroids. The walls, and the ejected material surrounding younger craters, are usually bright and light-colored because the freshly blasted rocks only darken over time.

RAY SYSTEMS
Bright ray systems extend for vast distances around some young craters. The rays are a mixture of material blasted out by the impactor and rocks thrown up where the ejected material landed. The Tycho Crater formed 109 million years ago—that's young in lunar history. Its rays are up to 1,250 miles (2,000 km) long and make it visible to the naked eye from Earth.

MULTIRING BASIN
The most powerful impacts formed huge multiring basins. The Mare Orientale, on the western edge of the near side, is one of the largest on the Moon. Three circular rings of mountains surround the dark mare at the center. The outermost ring is the Cordillera mountain scarp, which is almost 560 miles (900 km) across.

FLOODED CRATER
The Moon's oldest craters formed before volcanic activity on the Moon stopped. Lava flooded some of them, leaving only the top rims of their walls visible. This flooded crater is Thomson, which forms most of the small Mare Ingenii on the lunar far side. It is 73 miles (117 km) in diameter.

Moon rock

BASALT MOON ROCK
Basalts are dark solidified lava rocks. Lunar basalts are found in the mare areas. They are similar to rocks produced by volcanoes on Earth. This sample is full of holes, called vesicles, caused by gas bubbles in the molten lava.

APOLLO ASTRONAUTS COLLECTED 842 lbs (382 kg) of rock samples. Moon rocks look similar to Earth rocks, but have a distinct composition. They were all formed when the young Moon was hot. Since the Moon has no water, there are no rocks that need water to form, such as sandstone or limestone. Unlike on Earth, the Moon's oldest rocks have not been changed by water, weather, and moving continents, so they can tell us about the earliest history of the solar system.

COLLECTING SAMPLES
Apollo astronauts used a variety of tools to collect lunar rocks. They dragged special rakes through the regolith to sweep up small samples larger than about ½ in (1 cm). They also used scoops to collect lunar soil (regolith), hammers to break chips off large rocks, and drills and core tubes to get samples from below the lunar surface.

STUDYING SAMPLES
Lunar rocks brought back by Apollo astronauts are stored in the Lunar Sample Building at the Johnson Space Center in Houston, Texas. They are handled inside special cabinets filled with pure nitrogen so they do not get altered by contact with air.

GEOLOGY OF THE MOON
This geological map of the Moon's near side uses different colors to show which types of rock are found on the surface and how long they have been there. The large red areas are mare regions where the rock is solidified lava. The craters that formed most recently, and the ejected material around them, look like splashes of yellow. Some that are a little older are colored green. The pale blue area on the left is part of the huge impact basin that has the Mare Orientale at its centre. The oldest rocks are shown as dark brown and pink.

Lunar rover used to get to the collection site

Seismometer to measure moonquakes

*Green for
moderately young
crater Aristoteles*

*Red for
the
volcanic
rocks of
Mare
Crisium*

*Yellow for
young crater
Langrenus*

*Brown for old
rocks of southern
highlands*

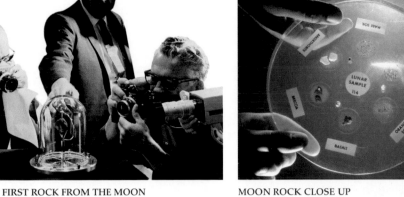

FIRST ROCK FROM THE MOON
The first astronauts on the Moon collected 49 lbs (22 kg) of rock samples. Some went on display in September 1969 in Washington DC, US. There was enormous interest. Press reporters competed to get the first pictures and thousands of people lined up for hours to see the rocks for themselves.

MOON ROCK CLOSE UP
You don't have to be an astronaut to get a close look at a Moon rock. Here, children are holding one of the sealed disks containing a variety of different Moon rocks, available on loan from NASA. Several museums have a Moon rock that visitors can actually touch.

LUNAR METEORITES
Over 100 meteorites found on Earth, weighing a total of 101 lbs (46 kg), are lunar rocks. Some of the material blasted out of the lunar surface by impacts in the past escaped the Moon's gravity. Some of these rocks were eventually set on a collision course with Earth. Scientists know they came from the Moon because they are similar to the Apollo samples. Many have been found in Antarctica in an area where meteorites are concentrated in the ice. Their identification is helped by the fact that dark rocks show up against the white ice.

*Apollo 17 astronaut
Harrison Schmitt*

samples

*Rake for
collecting samples*

Gnomon (measuring scale)

Other moons

A TOTAL OF OVER 150 MOONS orbit the eight major planets of the solar system. Earth's moon is the fifth large and one of only seven really large moons. Earth is the onl planet with a moon so large compared with its own size. Most moons measure just a few miles across, and many belong to the huge families swarming around Jupiter and Saturn. These two giant planets each have more than 60 moons. The two innermost planets, Mercury and Venus, have no moons.

GANYMEDE
(3,270 miles/5,262 km in diameter)
Jupiter's largest moon is also the largest
in the solar system.

COMPARING MOONS
No two moons in the solar system are the same. Ganymede and Titan are both slightly bigger tha the planet Mercury. Large moons are globe-shap and some have a layered interior like Earth's. Sm moons generally have irregular shapes. Some moons are rocky, while many in the outer sola system are coated with a thick ice layer.

TITAN (3,200 miles/5,151 km)
Saturn's largest moon has
a thick atmosphere.

*Huygens probe
with heat shield*

*Hills about 197 ft
(60 m) high*

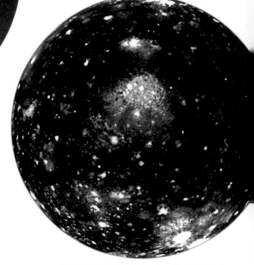

CALLISTO (2,995 miles/4,820 km)
Jupiter's second largest
moon is heavily cratered.

*Area of 2½ sq miles
(6.25 sq km)*

*Section of
Titan's surface*

TITAN EXPLORED
In January 2005, the Cassini spacecraft went into orbit around Saturn and released the Huygens probe, which parachuted down through Titan's atmosphere. This view of Titan's landscape was made from images collected during its 147-minute descent. The different colors show differences in height. Titan and the Moon are the only moons where a spacecraft has landed. Titan's surface is hidden from normal view by an orange haze in its nitrogen atmosphere, but infrared cameras and radar on board Cassini have shown that Titan has impact craters and lakes of liquid methane.

CAPTURED MOONS
The smallest moons of the solar system are almost certainly asteroids, captured by gravity when they stra too close to the planets. Mars has two of them. Phob shown here, is only 17 miles (27 km) long. Deimos even smaller with a length of 10 miles (16 km).

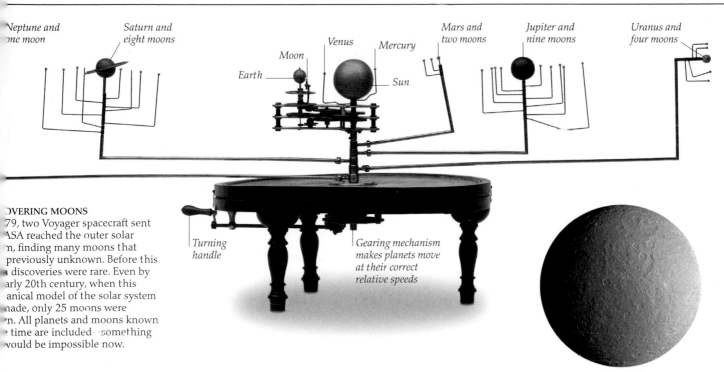

Neptune and
one moon

Saturn and
eight moons

Earth

Moon

Venus

Mercury

Sun

Mars and
two moons

Jupiter and
nine moons

Uranus and
four moons

Turning
handle

Gearing mechanism
makes planets move
at their correct
relative speeds

DISCOVERING MOONS

In 1979, two Voyager spacecraft sent
by NASA reached the outer solar
system, finding many moons that
were previously unknown. Before this
such discoveries were rare. Even by
the early 20th century, when this
mechanical model of the solar system
was made, only 25 moons were
known. All planets and moons known
at the time are included—something
that would be impossible now.

IO'S SURFACE

Jupiter's innermost large
moon, Io, shows the dramatic
effects of powerful tidal forces.
The pull of Jupiter's gravity
continually churns Io's interior,
heating and melting the rock.
As a result, Io is the most
volcanic place in the solar
system. Colorful flows of
lava spew out onto the surface
through more than 100 vents.
Any impact craters that once
existed have long ago been
covered up. In this picture,
lava is spilling out on all
sides of a volcanic crater.

SATURN'S MOON RHEA

Scientists observing Rhea recently discovered
rings around it, too faint to be seen here.
These are the first rings around a moon to
be discovered. Rhea also has a heavily cratered
surface, because it has changed little since
it was heavily bombarded long ago.

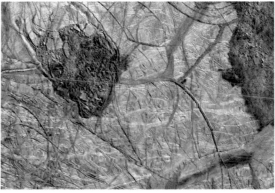

EUROPA'S SURFACE

Next out from Io is Europa, and its interior is also affected
by Jupiter's gravity. It is covered by an icy crust several
miles deep. Underneath is an ocean of liquid or slush.
Europa's surface has changed greatly
since it first formed and most of its
impact craters have disappeared.

IO (2,263 miles/3,643 km)
The third largest of
Jupiter's moons is
volcanically active.

MOON (2,160 miles/3,475 km)
Earth's is the only
large moon not orbiting
a giant planet.

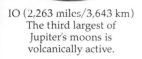

RHEA (950 miles/1,529 km)
Saturn's second largest
moon is the ninth largest
in the solar system.

EUROPA (1,940 miles/3,122 km)
Jupiter's fourth largest
moon has sub-
surface oceans.

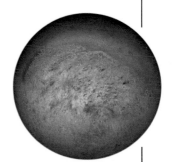

TRITON (1,682 miles/2,707 km)
Neptune's largest moon
has icy plume eruptions.

One of Galileo's telescopes

The telescope era

DETAILED MAPPING OF FEATURES ON the Moon began in the early 17th century, soon after lenses and telescopes were invented. Early mapmakers made drawings while observing through a telescope, which called for great skill and patience. They invented names for lunar features and added them to their maps. Through the 18th and 19th centuries, maps of the Moon greatly improved, and the first photograph of the Moon was taken in 1839. Early ideas that the Moon was a world like Earth with water and life-forms were rejected as telescopes improved and the Moon could be seen more clearly. Even so, mistaken volcanic theories for the origin of craters persisted (see page 164). Some astronomers continued to look for changes on the Moon's surface that might be due to volcanoes.

GALILEO'S SKETCHES
Italian astronomer and mathemetician Galileo Galilei was the first person to observe the Moon with a telescope in a systematic way. He began his observations in 1609, and the following year published engravings of his drawings in his book *Sidereus Nuncius* ("The Starry Messenger"). He described the Moon as being like another Earth. Galileo's drawings and a manuscript of his book are kept in Florence, where he was buried.

RUSSELL'S GLOBE
John Russell (1745–1806) was a successful English artist and portrait painter who also took an interest in astronomy. He made accurate drawings of the Moon from his own telescopic observations over 40 years. In 1797, he used them to make a globe showing the features on the Moon's near side. He also invented a special mount for the globe. Its gears reproduced the motion of the Moon, including libration, and a small globe represented Earth. Russell's Moon globe was 12 in (30 cm) across and made from papier mâché.

Van Langren named the mare we now call Mare Fecunditatis "Mare Langrenianum" after himself

A drawing from Schröter's book showing the Crater Vitello, toward the southwest of the Moon's near side

Lunar equator

VAN LANGREN'S MOON MAP
The earliest maps of the Moon were drawn between about 1630 and 1660. The first proper map was this one, made in 1645 by a Flemish mapmaker named Michiel Van Langren (c. 1600–1675). He was the first person to call the light parts of the surface *terra* (Latin for "land") and the dark areas *mare* ("sea") or *oceanus* ("ocean"). He also introduced the idea of naming craters after famous people.

SCHRÖTER'S LUNAR DRAWINGS
The German astronomer Johann Schröter (1745–1816) drew parts of the Moon on a much larger scale than anyone had done before, and published an important book on the Moon in two volumes in 1791 and 1802. He realized that the mare areas were not water but he thought he saw changes in them, which he said could be volcanic activity, vegetation, or clouds. He discovered the lunar rille now called Schröter's Valley.

Gearing to
turn the Moon

Lunar latitude scale

Gearing to
turn Earth

Earth

Mount

IMAGINARY LANDSCAPE
This 1874 illustration depicts an eclipse of the Sun by Earth on the Moon. It was published in *The Moon: Considered as a Planet a World and a Satellite* by James Nasmyth and James Carpenter, who tried to explain craters on the Moon with a volcanic theory.

PATRICK MOORE AND TLPs
Reports of temporary changes on the Moon (transient lunar phenomena, or TLPs) peaked during the 1960s and 1970s. In 1969, Patrick Moore, an enthusiastic amateur observer, worked with a professional scientist to compile a list of 579 reported TLPs. The list later grew to over 1,000. Many reports are due only to the changing angle of sunlight, and are not changes in the Moon's surface.

Finder telescope

Digital
camera
attached to
back of
telescope

MONITORING FOR CHANGES
No volcanic event has ever been confirmed on the Moon. Automatic telescopes like this one, monitoring the dark part of the Moon, regularly spot flashes when meteoroids land and record them. In May 2006, a new crater about 46 ft (14 m) wide was created in the Mare Nubium.

From dream to reality

Fables and fantasies about traveling to the Moon have existed for centuries, but the earliest realistic stories about space travel were by the Fren[ch] writer Jules Verne and by other science fiction writers such as English autho[r] H. G. Wells. Verne thought of firing a spacecraft from a massive gun, and W[ells] came up with an imaginary antigravity material. The Russian inventor Konstantin Tsiolkovsky realized that only a rocket would work, but coul[d] not put any of his theories into practice. The American Robert Goddard had similar ideas and started to build rockets. Meanwhile, the idea of fut[ure] travel to the Moon and beyond caught the public imagination and becam[e] a popular theme in films and comics.

JULES VERNE'S NOVEL
Jules Verne's story *From the Earth to the Moon*, published in 1865, was the first science fiction novel about travel to the Moon. Despite its scientific errors, it became a classic.

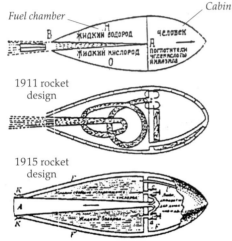

Fuel chamber   Cabin

1911 rocket design

1915 rocket design

EARLY THEORIES
Konstantin Tsiolkovsky was the first person to set out the theory of rocket propulsion. These are three of his drawings. The top one, dating from 1903, is the earliest known diagram of a liquid-fueled rocket.

ROCKET PIONEER
Robert Goddard's early interest in spaceflight was inspired by reading the novels of Jules Verne and H. G. Wells. In 1926, he launched the first ever liquid-fueled rocket. He continued to develop and test ever larger liquid-fueled rockets until 1941, when he worked for the US Navy in World War II. His pioneering work paved the way for space travel. Goddard dreamed of seeing a rocket go to the Moon, but died much before that in 1945.

Robert Goddard in 1940

Rocket lands in the Moon's eye

Rocket engine exhaust nozzle

FUNNY FACE
The first film on the theme of travel to the Moon was made in 1902 by the French director Georges Méliès. *Le Voyage dans la Lune* ("Voyage to the Moon") was a 14-minute silent movie inspired by the novels of Jules Verne and *The First Men in the Moon* by H. G. Wells. It poked fun at science and did not pretend to be realistic.

THE ROCKET AS A WEAPON

Rockets were greatly improved in the 1930s and 1940s, but for carrying warheads rather than space travel. Germany, the first country to use a rocket-propelled weapon, launched its V-2 rocket in 1942, during World War II. After the war ended in 1945, the new rocket technology was also adapted for the exploration of space. The V-2 rocket shown here is from an air show held in 1951.

Experimental rocket without casing

Film poster from 1950

A FRIEND FOR AMERICA

Wernher von Braun was in charge of Germany's wartime rocket program but, in 1945, he surrendered to the US Army and then moved to the US. He was a driving force behind the development of the rockets needed for the US space program, including the Saturn V rocket that would ultimately take astronauts to the Moon.

"DESTINATION MOON"

After World War II, writers and film directors tried to make their space stories more scientifically accurate and took advice from experts. The landmark 1950 film *Destination Moon* aimed for great realism and was a huge commercial success—its technical advisor was Herman Oberth, a Romanian aeronautics pioneer. Wernher von Braun was the technical advisor for three television films about space made by Walt Disney in the 1950s.

TINTIN ON THE MOON

Space travel to the Moon was a popular theme for stories in the 1950s. A young reporter, Tintin, was the hero of a series of comic-strip books created by Hergé, a Belgian writer and illustrator. Tintin's two Moon adventures, *Destination Moon* and *Explorers on the Moon*, were published in 1953 and 1954. This is the cover of the original French edition of *Explorers on the Moon*.

The space race

In the late 1950s, a race began between the US and the Soviet Union. Each wanted to be the first to achieve important goals in space. This space race took place at a t: known as the "Cold War," when political relations betwee the US and the USSR (Union of Soviet Socialist Republic or Soviet Union) were extremely tense. Initially the USSF was ahead of the US. Programs began in both countries t train astronauts and gain experience of spaceflight. From 1961 onward, landing people on the Moon became the main goal of the space race, after US Presider John F. Kennedy declared that America's goal was to reach the Moon by the end of the 1960s. Both sides worked on developing spacecraft that could go to the Moon and back, and on rockets powerful enough to get them there.

Sputnik 1 satellite

One of four radio antennas

THE USSR TAKES THE LEAD
The Soviet Union's launch of the Sputnik 1 satellite on October 4, 1957, marked the dawn of the space age. The small metal sphere carried two radio transmitters, which sent signals back to Earth for 21 days. This took the Americans by surprise. When they tried a launch in December 1957 the rocket exploded, but they successfully launched the Explorer 1 satellite on January 31, 1958.

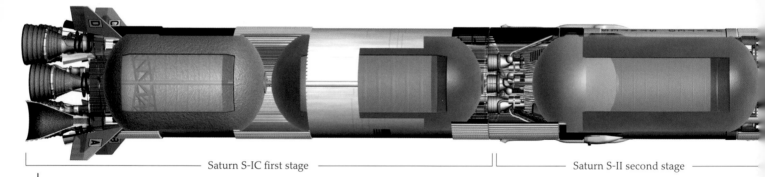

Saturn S-IC first stage — — Saturn S-II second stage

THE FIRST MAN IN SPACE
On April 12, 1961, the Soviet cosmonaut Yuri Gagarin became the first person to go into space. After one orbit of Earth in Vostok 1, Gagarin operated his ejector seat and parachuted clear, during the spacecraft's descent, from a height of 4½ miles (7 km). The USSR was so secretive that it did not reveal what the outside of the spacecraft looked like until 1965.

THE COLD WAR
Mistrust and rivalry between the US and the USSR began about 1917, when the USSR became a communist country after the Russian revolution. Tensions became much worse immediately after World War II, when the former Allies, which included the US and the USSR, could not agree on the future of Europe. Both countries wanted to build up their military strength and international prestige. This parade in Moscow in 1962 displayed the USSR's military might.

Gagarin in the space capsule before launch

eeks after the first manned space flight
e USSR, America turned the space race
race for the Moon. In a speech to the
ongress on May 25, 1961, President
F. Kennedy set an ambitious target for
S—to land astronauts on the Moon
e 1970. At the time, America's total
ience of human spaceflight
15-minute flight made
an three weeks
r by Alan Shepard
e Mercury capsule
om 7. He had not
completed one
rbit of Earth.

THE MERCURY SEVEN

The first Americans recruited as astronauts were seven Air Force pilots, who
became known as the Mercury Seven. The Mercury program's goal was to
put an astronaut in orbit around Earth in a capsule holding one person. John
Glenn made the first orbital flight on February 20, 1962, and three more
followed. The longest was 22 orbits, made by Gordon Cooper in May 1963.

Escape rocket

n S-IVB
d stage   Apollo spacecraft

RN V ROCKET

US developed the three-stage Saturn V
t specially to send astronauts to the Moon.
s the largest and most powerful rocket ever
hed. Including the escape rocket on top,
od nearly 364 ft (111 m) high and weighed
2,975 tons (2,700 metric tons). The first and
nd stages each had five engines and fell away
rn when their fuel ran out. The third stage,
one engine, did not separate until it had
the Apollo spacecraft out of Earth orbit
on course for the Moon.

Outer insulation

Reentry module

GEMINI 7 CAPSULE

After the Mercury missions,
America's Gemini program
was the next step to
prepare for the Apollo
Moon landings. The
Gemini capsules carried
two pilots. The goal of the
Gemini program was to
perfect space techniques,
such as docking spacecraft
together and space walks.
These flights also gave
astronauts the experience
they needed to undertake
a mission to the Moon.
There were 10 manned Gemini
flights between March 1965 and
November 1966. Gemini 7 was
the longest, lasting 14 days.

SANDWICHES FOR SPACE

Gemini 3 astronaut John Young got into
trouble for smuggling a corned beef
sandwich on board, which his companion
Gus Grissom ate. Young had disobeyed
orders and the loose crumbs could have
been dangerous inside the spacecraft.
Here, Apollo 12 Commander Charles
Conrad has a sandwich put in a pocket
on his spacesuit, but there is no record
that this one made it into space!

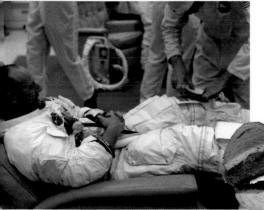

*A corned beef
sandwich*

THE FIRST SPACEWALK

Soviet cosmonaut Aleksei Leonov made the first
spacewalk on March 18, 1965, two months before
the first spacewalk by an American. Leonov was
on board Voskhod 2, the first two-person space
mission. This is a 1960s Russian postcard of Leonov.

Destination Moon

One of the first images of the Moon's far side, taken by Luna 3

IN THE 10 YEARS BEFORE humans reached the Moon, the US launched 21 unmanned lunar spacecraft while the USSR launched 18. These missions were designed to test technologies, make maps of the Moon, and find out whether its surface was solid enough to land on. Many did not succeed, especially in the early days. In the race for the Moon, the USSR crossed some important hurdles first—the first man-made object on the Moon, the first pictures of the lunar far side, the first soft landing on the Moon, and the first lunar satellite. But the US was not far behind, and by 1967 its Lunar Orbiters were scouting for sites where the first astronauts would land.

LUNA 2

The first spacecraft sent to the Moon were simple hard landers, intended to crash into the surface. Soft landers could touch down gently without damage and continue working. Luna 1 was launched by the USSR in January 1959, but it missed the Moon by 3,747 miles (5,995 km). In September 1959, the Soviets tried again to hit the Moon with Luna 2. It crash-landed close to the crater Aristarchus. Luna 2 was the first man-made object to travel from Earth and land on another body in space.

Gas jet to control orientation

Radio communication antenna

Spacecraft is (47 in) 120 cm long

Metal sphere 47 in (120 cm) across

Sensor for magnetic field

Instruments and transmitters in metal cylinder

250 ft (76 m) radio dish

TRACKING LUNA 2

The Soviet Union was very secretive about its early Moon missions, so British astronomers at the Jodrell Bank Observatory near Manchester were surprised when the Soviets told them how to track the signals from Luna 2 with their giant radio telescope. The Director of the Observatory, Bernard Lovell, announced on September 13, 1959, that the signals from Luna 2 had stopped suddenly, which meant that it had been successfully crashed on the Moon.

LUNA 3

In 1959, the Soviet spacecraft Luna 3 swung around the back of the Moon and returned the first images of the lunar far side. They were taken from a distance of about 40,000 miles (65,000 km). Luna 3 took 29 photographs covering 70 percent of the Moon's far side on October 7, but the first attempts to transmit pictures back to Earth did not work. However, 17 fuzzy views were picked up about 10 days later when Luna 3 came nearer to Earth again.

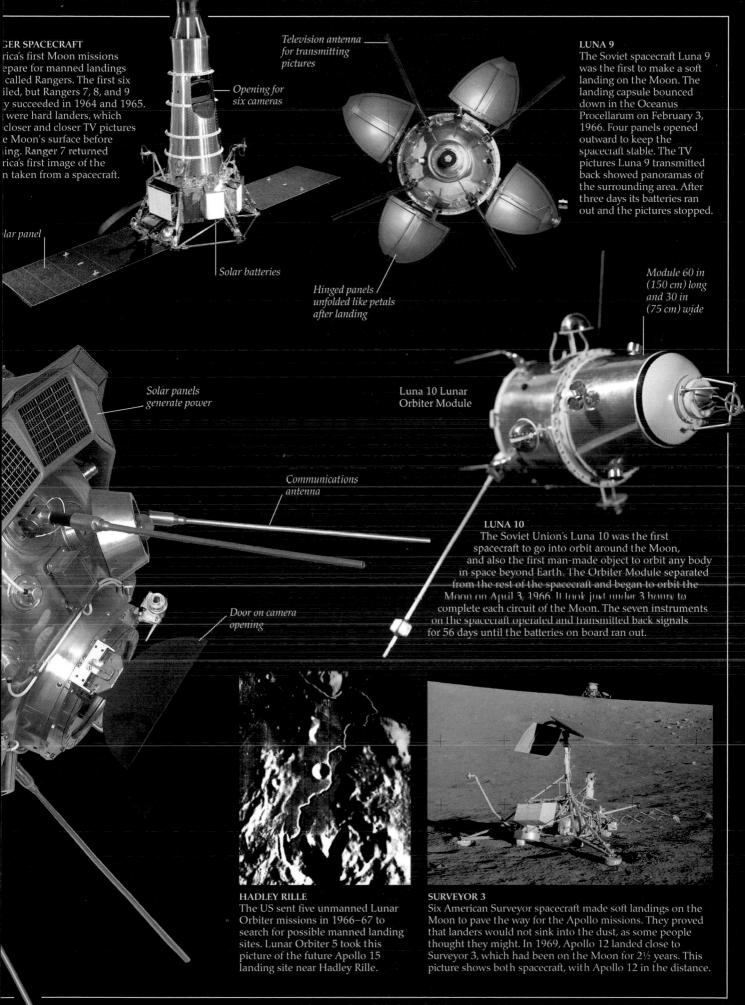

GER SPACECRAFT
rica's first Moon missions
epare for manned landings
called Rangers. The first six
iled, but Rangers 7, 8, and 9
y succeeded in 1964 and 1965.
were hard landers, which
closer and closer TV pictures
e Moon's surface before
ing. Ranger 7 returned
rica's first image of the
n taken from a spacecraft.

lar panel

Solar batteries

*Television antenna
for transmitting
pictures*

*Opening for
six cameras*

*Hinged panels
unfolded like petals
after landing*

LUNA 9
The Soviet spacecraft Luna 9
was the first to make a soft
landing on the Moon. The
landing capsule bounced
down in the Oceanus
Procellarum on February 3,
1966. Four panels opened
outward to keep the
spacecraft stable. The TV
pictures Luna 9 transmitted
back showed panoramas of
the surrounding area. After
three days its batteries ran
out and the pictures stopped.

*Module 60 in
(150 cm) long
and 30 in
(75 cm) wide*

*Solar panels
generate power*

Luna 10 Lunar
Orbiter Module

*Communications
antenna*

LUNA 10
The Soviet Union's Luna 10 was the first
spacecraft to go into orbit around the Moon,
and also the first man-made object to orbit any body
in space beyond Earth. The Orbiter Module separated
from the rest of the spacecraft and began to orbit the
Moon on April 3, 1966. It took just under 3 hours to
complete each circuit of the Moon. The seven instruments
on the spacecraft operated and transmitted back signals
for 56 days until the batteries on board ran out.

*Door on camera
opening*

HADLEY RILLE
The US sent five unmanned Lunar
Orbiter missions in 1966–67 to
search for possible manned landing
sites. Lunar Orbiter 5 took this
picture of the future Apollo 15
landing site near Hadley Rille.

SURVEYOR 3
Six American Surveyor spacecraft made soft landings on the
Moon to pave the way for the Apollo missions. They proved
that landers would not sink into the dust, as some people
thought they might. In 1969, Apollo 12 landed close to
Surveyor 3, which had been on the Moon for 2½ years. This
picture shows both spacecraft, with Apollo 12 in the distance.

Apollo spacecraft

EACH APOLLO SPACECRAFT CONSISTED OF three parts: the Command Module (CM), the Service Module (SM), and the Lunar Module (LM). The crew of three astronauts would live in the CM on the journey from Earth and back. The SM contained fuel and equipment for supplying oxygen, water, and electricity to the CM. For most of the mission, the Command and Service Modules (CSM) were designed to remain docked together. The LM would dock with them only on the outward journey. On the spacecraft's return, the CM would separate from the SM before entering Earth's atmosphere. The CM with the astronauts inside would then splash down in the ocean.

THE THREE MODULES
The conical Command Module was about 11½ ft (3.5 m) high. The control panel inside it had 24 instrument displays, 71 lights, and 560 switches. The Service Module was a cylinder about 25 ft (7.6 m) long and 13 ft (4 m) wide. It had one main engine and small motors for performing maneuvers. The Lunar Module with its two stages stood 23 ft (7 m) tall.

Astronauts' seats

Forward heat shield

Quick-escape hatch

Command Module

Instrument panel

Service Module

Fuel tanks

Helium tanks

Fuel cells

LAUNCHING APOLLO
Apollo spacecraft were launched by Saturn V rockets from Cape Canaveral in Florida. The small escape rocket on top was designed to blast the Command Module clear if there was an emergency during the launch. The red gantry beside the rocket supported it and provided access for astronauts and technicians. After the rocket ignited, the gantry swung away. Then, with a tremendous roar and a billow of smoke, the rocket soared upward with glowing hot gas streaming behind it.

COMMAND AND SERVICE MODULES IN ORBIT
While the Mission Commander and Lunar Module Pilot went down to the Moon's surface in the Lunar Module, the Command Module Pilot stayed with the Command and Service Modules in orbit around the Moon. This picture

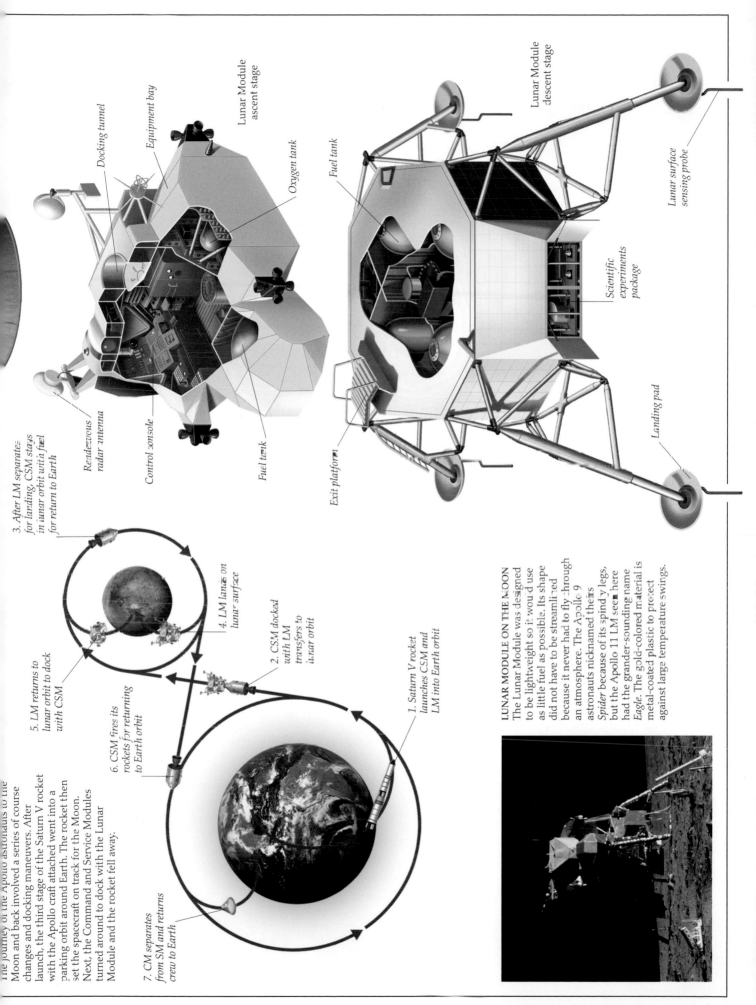

The journey of the Apollo astronauts to the Moon and back involved a series of course changes and docking maneuvers. After launch, the third stage of the Saturn V rocket with the Apollo craft attached went into a parking orbit around Earth. The rocket then set the spacecraft on track for the Moon. Next, the Command and Service Modules turned around to dock with the Lunar Module and the rocket fell away.

Docking tunnel

Equipment bay

Lunar Module ascent stage

Oxygen tank

Fuel tank

Lunar Module descent stage

Rendezvous radar antenna

Control console

Fuel tank

Exit platform

Scientific experiments package

Lunar surface sensing probe

Landing pad

3. After LM separates for landing, CSM stays in lunar orbit with fuel for return to Earth

5. LM returns to lunar orbit to dock with CSM

6. CSM fires its rockets for returning to Earth orbit

4. LM lands on lunar surface

2. CSM docked with LM transfers to lunar orbit

1. Saturn V rocket launches CSM and LM into Earth orbit

7. CM separates from SM and returns crew to Earth

LUNAR MODULE ON THE MOON
The Lunar Module was designed to be lightweight so it would use as little fuel as possible. Its shape did not have to be streamlined because it never had to fly through an atmosphere. The Apollo 9 astronauts nicknamed theirs *Spider* because of its spindly legs, but the Apollo 11 LM seen here had the grander-sounding name *Eagle*. The gold-colored material is metal-coated plastic to protect against large temperature swings.

Getting men on the Moon

APOLLO 10 MISSION PATCH
Every space mission has its own badge or patch, like this one for Apollo 10. This mission in May 1969 was a practice run for the first Moon landing. Astronauts Thomas Stafford and Eugene Cernan took their Lunar Module down to 9 miles (15 km) above the planned landing site for Apollo 11.

A**FTER SIX YEARS OF PLANNING** and preparation, and a tragic fire, Apollo spaceflights began in 1968 with a series of unmanned tests (tests without a crew). All launches took place at Cape Canaveral in Florida, where the gigantic Vehicle Assembly Building was built. It was large enough to house four Saturn V rockets at a time. Apollo 7, which orbited Earth for 11 days in October 1968, was the first Apollo mission to carry a crew. Apollos 7, 8, 9, and 10 tested everything apart from the actual Moon landing.

Portable life support system

Astronaut John Young

Technician

ASTRONAUT TRAINING
The Apollo astronauts were trained for everything they might need to do on the Moon. They spent many hours in spacecraft simulators at the Manned Spacecraft Center (now called the Johnson Space Center) in Houston, Texas, and practiced in spacesuits for activities on the lunar surface. Here, Apollo 16 astronauts are learning how to use a special tool to collect lunar soil samples. John Young is reaching over a boulder to collect a sample because the soil behind it is less likely to be contaminated by dust from the astronauts' boots.

WRECKAGE OF APOLLO 1
The first Apollo spacecraft was due to lift off on February 21, 1967, but on January 27 a catastrophic fire broke out in the Command Module (CM) during a training exercise on the launch pad. The three astronauts in the Module died. This tragedy was a huge setback for the Apollo program. Afterward, the CM was redesigned with a quick-escape hatch.

HISTORIC SIGHT

Apollo 8 was the first manned spacecraft to orbit the Moon. It lifted off on December 21, 1968, and returned six days later after orbiting the Moon 10 times. The astronauts who flew on Apollo 8 were the first humans to see the entire Earth from space and to see the far side of the Moon. They took dramatic photographs, like this one, showing Earth rising over the Moon. Seeing our home planet as a whole, looking so fragile in the vast emptiness of space, made a deep impression on the astronauts and on everyone who saw their pictures.

Snoopy as NASA's space safety mascot

SNOOPY AND APOLLO 10

After the Apollo 1 disaster, NASA started a campaign to improve safety and to rebuild the devastated Apollo program. The mascot for the new program was the cartoon character Snoopy the beagle, chosen because of his refusal to accept defeat. The Apollo 10 astronauts nicknamed their Lunar Module "Snoopy" and their Command and Service Module "Charlie Brown." Charlie Brown is Snoopy's owner in the *Peanuts* cartoons.

Astronaut Charles Duke

Camera

oling for soil tion tool

MISSION CONTROL

The Apollo Mission Control room was built at the Manned Spacecraft Center in Houston, Texas. As soon as the rocket left the launch pad the controllers took charge. They monitored the spacecraft and the astronauts. Controllers were in constant voice contact with the astronauts, except for a 45-minute period on each orbit when they were behind the Moon.

TRACKING SPACECRAFT

Mission controllers used radio communications to keep in contact with Apollo spacecraft and astronauts. Signals were sent and received by a network of 12 stations on the ground, one ship, and four jet aircraft. To be able to pick up faint signals from the Moon and transmit to it strongly enough at any time, three stations were spaced around the world, each with 85-ft (26-m) dishes. This one was near Canberra, Australia. The others were in Spain and California.

Mount with motor for turning the dish and tracking across the sky

Reflector mounted over dish directs radio waves into receiver

Radio waves bounce off main dish to reflector

Dressed for space

ASTRONAUTS IN SPACE and on the Moon would have to wear spacesuits to survive the absence of an atmosphere. Spacesuits were designed with many different layers underneath the outer layer and various components to protect astronauts from the dangers of space and keep them feeling comfortable. They would maintain the same pressure as Earth's atmosphere, provide the oxygen needed to breathe, and get rid of the carbon dioxide breathed out. Wearing a spacesuit, an astronaut would be protected against extremes of heat and cold, dangerous ultraviolet radiation from the Sun, and impacts of micrometeoroids.

THE APOLLO SPACESUIT
Each Apollo astronaut had three spacesuits made to fit him. In order to walk about and work on the Moon, their spacesuits had to be light and flexible. Next to their skin they wore a nylon liquid-cooled undergarment that kept them cool. Over that came the pressure garment that maintained a constant pressure, then many layers to insulate against heat and cold, and finally two layers of Teflon-coated cloth for further protection against heat. The helmet and gloves joined onto the suit with airtight seals. Overshoes went on top of the spacesuit boots for walking on the Moon.

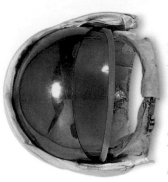

Outer helmet worn on the Moon has adjustable Sun shields and visors

Inner helmet seals to suit and maintains correct pressure inside

Communications cap includes microphone and earphones

Penlight pocket

Extravehicular

Gold-plated visor reduces heat and glare from Sun and lunar surface

Connection to PLSS water supply

Communications connector

Connection to emergency oxygen supply

Connection to PLSS

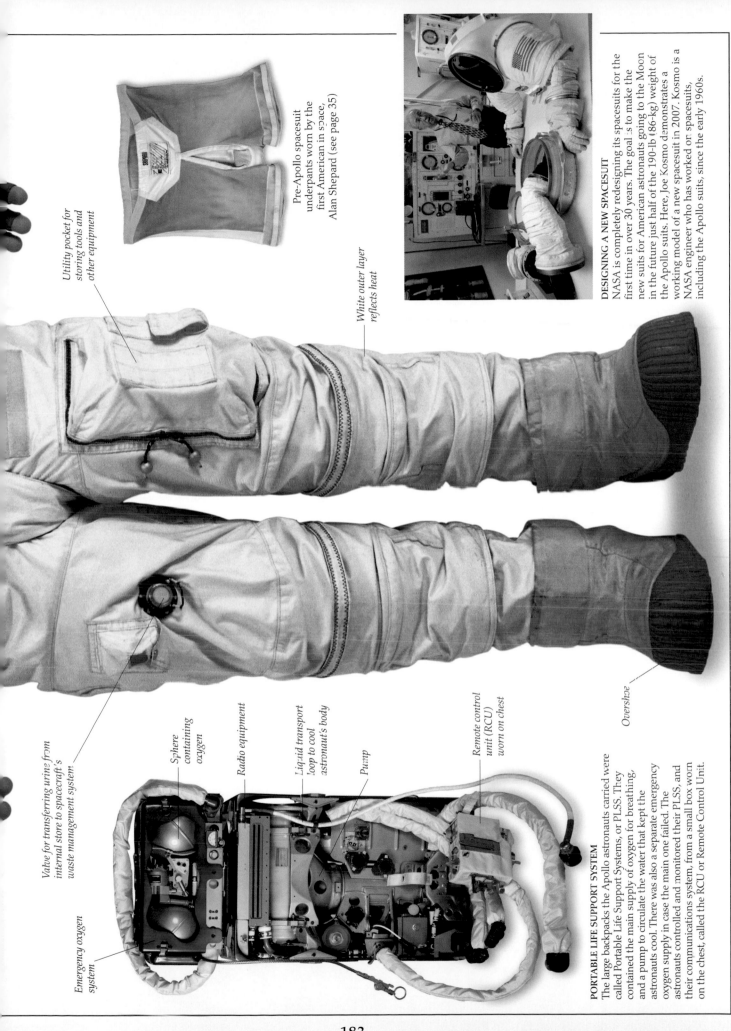

Utility pocket for storing tools and other equipment

Pre-Apollo spacesuit underpants worn by the first American in space, Alan Shepard (see page 35)

White outer layer reflects heat

DESIGNING A NEW SPACESUIT
NASA is completely redesigning its spacesuits for the first time in over 30 years. The goal is to make the new suits for American astronauts going to the Moon in the future just half of the 190-lb (86-kg) weight of the Apollo suits. Here, Joe Kosmo demonstrates a working model of a new spacesuit in 2007. Kosmo is a NASA engineer who has worked on spacesuits, including the Apollo suits, since the early 1960s.

Overshoe

Valve for transferring urine from internal store to spacecraft's waste management system

Emergency oxygen system

Sphere containing oxygen

Radio equipment

Liquid transport loop to cool astronaut's body

Pump

Remote control unit (RCU) worn on chest

PORTABLE LIFE SUPPORT SYSTEM
The large backpacks the Apollo astronauts carried were called Portable Life Support Systems, or PLSS. They contained the main supply of oxygen for breathing, and a pump to circulate the water that kept the astronauts cool. There was also a separate emergency oxygen supply in case the main one failed. The astronauts controlled and monitored their PLSS, and their communications system, from a small box worn on the chest, called the RCU or Remote Control Unit.

A giant leap

ON JULY 21, 1969, APOLLO 11 COMMANDER Neil Armstrong made history when he stepped off the foot pad of *Eagle*, the Lun Module, and onto the Moon's surface. Millions around the wor. heard him say the now famous words, "That's one small step for man, one giant leap for mankind." Buzz Aldrin joined him on th lunar surface a few minutes later. Meanwhile, about 60 miles (100 km) above them, Michael Collins was orbiting the Moon in *Columbia*, the Command and Service Module.

LAUNCHING INTO HISTORY
Apollo 11 lifted off from Cape Canaveral (now the Kennedy Space Center) at 9:32 a.m. local time on Wednesday July 16, 1969. It was a warm sunny day and 5,000 invited guests were watching, along with 3,497 reporters and cameramen. Thousands more people crowded nearby roads and waterways jostling for a view. TV cameras on the ground followed the rocket into the sky for nearly 7 minutes after blastoff. Pictures from a TV camera mounted on the Lunar Module were later beamed live to audiences on Earth.

Horizontal crossbar holds flag up in the absence of any wind

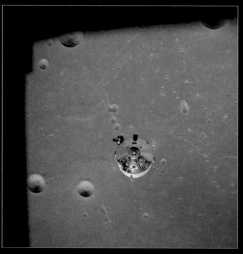

EAGLE AND COLUMBIA SEPARATE
A day after arriving in lunar orbit, Armstrong and Aldrin moved into *Eagle*. *Eagle* then separated from *Columbia*. The astronauts took this picture of *Columbia* through one of *Eagle*'s windows as they prepared to descend. Armstrong skillfully piloted *Eagle* to the lunar surface, avoiding large boulders. About two hours after leaving *Columbia* behind, they were safely on the ground—with just enough fuel left in the descent-stage engines for another 20 seconds of flying!

MAN ON THE MOON
About 15 minutes after Neil Armstrong stepped onto the Moon, Buzz Aldrin followed him down the ladder. The two astronauts set up an American flag, though not to claim any territory on the Moon. A TV camera mounted on *Eagle* captured pictures of Buzz Aldrin saluting the flag, while Neil Armstrong held the flagpole steady in the soft lunar soil. These were beamed around the world. Because Armstrong was the chief photographer, no photographs were taken of him on the Moon. The flag was later blown over when *Eagle* took off.

LUNAR EXPERIMENTS

Armstrong and Aldrin worked together on the lunar surface for about 90 minutes. They collected 46 lb (21 kg) of rock and soil samples, took hundreds of photographs, and set up experiments to leave behind. Here Buzz Aldrin is assembling a lunar seismometer to detect moonquakes. They also set up a detector to find out about particles from the Sun, and a reflector for laser beams shot from Earth, to measure the Moon's distance precisely (see page 151).

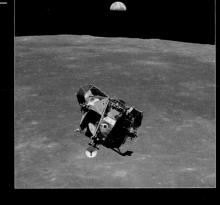

LUNAR MODULE ASCENDS

After 21 hours 36 minutes on the Moon's surface, Armstrong and Aldrin fired the ascent stage engines of *Eagle* to return to lunar orbit. They left what they no longer needed on the Moon, as well as mementos of their landing. Michael Collins took this photograph of *Eagle* as it approached *Columbia*. The two spacecraft docked so Armstrong and Aldrin could get back into *Columbia*. Then they separated again and *Eagle* was left behind.

Astronaut Buzz Aldrin

SPLASHDOWN

Columbia splashed down on July 24 in the Pacific Ocean, southwest of Hawaii. It was met by nine ships and 54 aircraft. Three swimmers from a helicopter picked up the astronauts and transferred them to an aircraft carrier, the *USS Hornet*. The astronauts wore biological isolation suits in case they had brought back microbes from the Moon.

A HEROES' WELCOME

The Apollo 11 astronauts were kept in isolation for three weeks but immediately afterward America welcomed them as heroes. New York City celebrated with a traditional ticker-tape parade on August 13. The astronauts rode in an open car along Broadway while confetti and shredded office paper rained down from the buildings on either side.

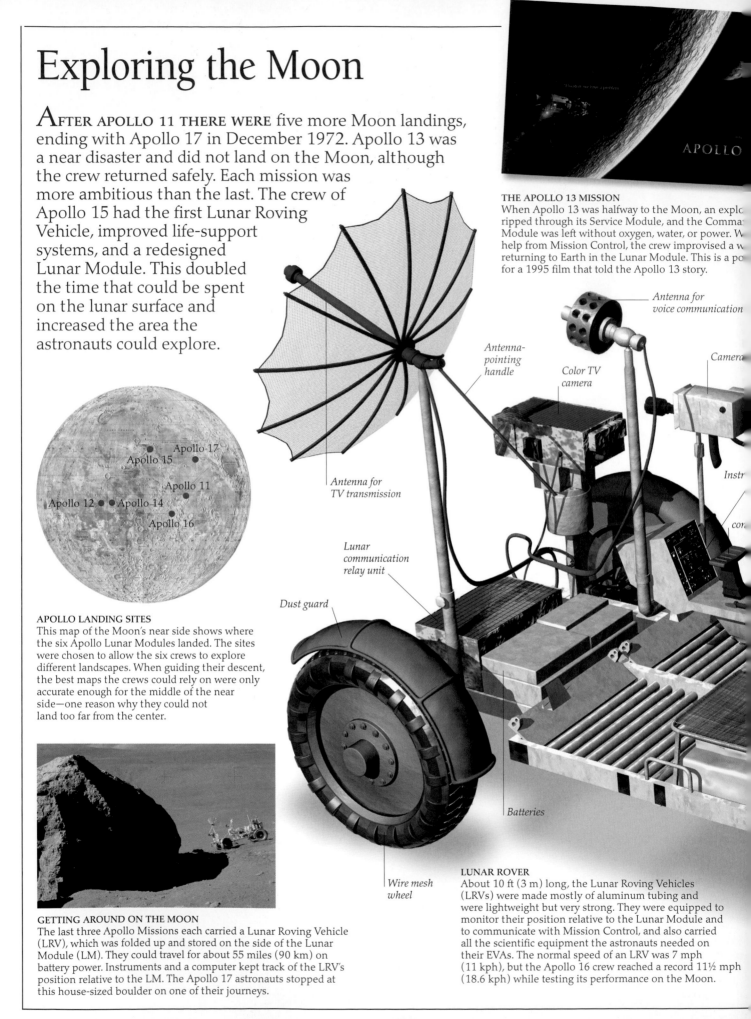

Exploring the Moon

AFTER APOLLO 11 THERE WERE five more Moon landings, ending with Apollo 17 in December 1972. Apollo 13 was a near disaster and did not land on the Moon, although the crew returned safely. Each mission was more ambitious than the last. The crew of Apollo 15 had the first Lunar Roving Vehicle, improved life-support systems, and a redesigned Lunar Module. This doubled the time that could be spent on the lunar surface and increased the area the astronauts could explore.

THE APOLLO 13 MISSION
When Apollo 13 was halfway to the Moon, an explo ripped through its Service Module, and the Comma Module was left without oxygen, water, or power. W help from Mission Control, the crew improvised a w returning to Earth in the Lunar Module. This is a po for a 1995 film that told the Apollo 13 story.

APOLLO

APOLLO LANDING SITES
This map of the Moon's near side shows where the six Apollo Lunar Modules landed. The sites were chosen to allow the six crews to explore different landscapes. When guiding their descent, the best maps the crews could rely on were only accurate enough for the middle of the near side—one reason why they could not land too far from the center.

Apollo 17
Apollo 15
Apollo 11
Apollo 12 ● ● Apollo 14
Apollo 16

Antenna for voice communication

Antenna-pointing handle

Color TV camera

Camera

Instr

con

Antenna for TV transmission

Lunar communication relay unit

Dust guard

Batteries

Wire mesh wheel

GETTING AROUND ON THE MOON
The last three Apollo Missions each carried a Lunar Roving Vehicle (LRV), which was folded up and stored on the side of the Lunar Module (LM). They could travel for about 55 miles (90 km) on battery power. Instruments and a computer kept track of the LRV's position relative to the LM. The Apollo 17 astronauts stopped at this house-sized boulder on one of their journeys.

LUNAR ROVER
About 10 ft (3 m) long, the Lunar Roving Vehicles (LRVs) were made mostly of aluminum tubing and were lightweight but very strong. They were equipped to monitor their position relative to the Lunar Module and to communicate with Mission Control, and also carried all the scientific equipment the astronauts needed on their EVAs. The normal speed of an LRV was 7 mph (11 kph), but the Apollo 16 crew reached a record 11½ mph (18.6 kph) while testing its performance on the Moon.

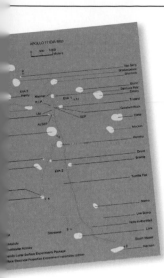

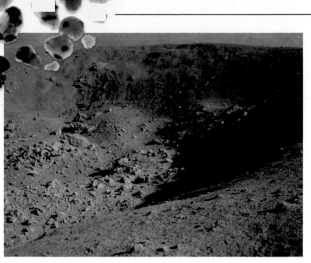

SHORTY CRATER

When the Apollo 17 astronauts visited Shorty Crater, Harrison Schmitt noticed some orange-colored soil on its rim. Though the crater had been formed by an impact, there were some cinder cones nearby—a sign of past volcanic activity. The soil contained microscopic orange glass beads, formed 3.64 billion years ago when lava shot out of a volcano like a fountain of fire.

These orange glass lunar soil particles are between 0.0008 in (0.02 mm) and 0.0018 in (0.045 mm) across

LO 17 ROUTE MAP

pollo 17 astronauts spent three days on the Moon, ling 22 hours outside the Module. They made three eys, totalling 21 miles (35 km), are shown on this map. Each as called an Extra Vehicular ty, or EVA. The pale ovals aters and the numbers mark aces where the astronauts ed to collect samples.

Tongs for picking up samples

Lunar sample collection storage

Seats of tubular aluminum with nylon covers

APOLLO MISSION PATCHES

The individual patches for the Apollo missions were designed by the astronauts themselves or based on their ideas. For instance, the Apollo 11 patch included an eagle, because that was the Lunar Module's name. The Apollo 12 patch pictured a clipper ship because the Command and Service Module was named *Yankee Clipper*.

Antares was the name of the Apollo 14 Lunar Module

MISSION PLAQUE

All the Apollo Lunar Modules carried a commemorative plaque, which was left behind on the Moon along with the Module. They were made of stainless steel and curved to fit around one of the rungs of the ladder. Each one reproduces the signatures of the three astronauts. The signature of the US President was also on the first and last Apollo plaques. This is the plaque from the Apollo 14 mission.

SOVIET PIONEER
Sergei Korolev (1907–1966) was one of
the great pioneers of spaceflight. He was
responsible for Sputnik 1 and the early
Soviet space achievements, but the
USSR kept the identity of its "Chief
Spacecraft Designer" a secret until after
the Cold War (see page 174) ended.

Further Soviet exploration

IN THE RACE TO LAND men on the Moon, the USSR fell behind the
US after Sergei Korolev—the man who had been the driving force
behind the Soviet space program—died suddenly in 1966. The huge
N-1 rocket, with which the USSR intended to launch a Moon missio
exploded at its first test flight in 1969. The Soviets then directed thei
efforts at sending robotic craft to the Moon rather than humans
and began developing the technology for orbiting space stations.

Luna 17
Luna 2
Luna 13
Luna 21
Luna 9
Luna 24
Luna 20
Luna 16

LUNAR LANDINGS
After losing the race to put a man on the Moon, the
Soviets concentrated on robotic spacecraft and continued
this program until 1976. This lunar near-side map shows
where seven Luna spacecraft successfully made soft
landings, and where Luna 2, the first spacecraft to reach
the Moon, crash-landed.

Solar panels
generate power

Search radar
transmitter
and receiver

SOYUZ SPACECRAFT
Led by Korolev, the Soviet Union
developed a spacecraft for carrying
cosmonauts to the Moon. They called
it Soyuz—Russian for "Union". Soyuz 1
crashed in 1967, killing cosmonaut
Vladimir Komarov. In 1969, Soyuz 4 and
Soyuz 5 successfully docked in Earth orbit
and two cosmonauts made spacewalks to
move from Soyuz 5 to Soyuz 4. Russia still
uses a modern version of the Soyuz spacecraft.
The design shown here was in use until 1971.

Crew seating

Window

Radar for docking

Control
console

Anter

Docking
assembly

Fold-away
work area

Storage
compartments

Orbital Module

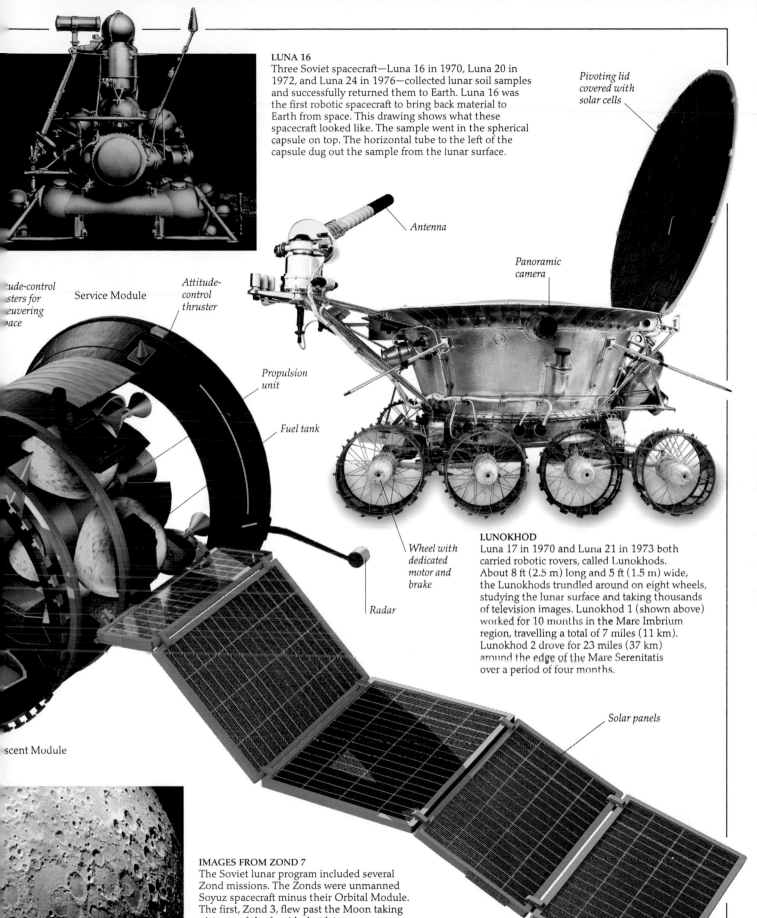

LUNA 16

Three Soviet spacecraft—Luna 16 in 1970, Luna 20 in 1972, and Luna 24 in 1976—collected lunar soil samples and successfully returned them to Earth. Luna 16 was the first robotic spacecraft to bring back material to Earth from space. This drawing shows what these spacecraft looked like. The sample went in the spherical capsule on top. The horizontal tube to the left of the capsule dug out the sample from the lunar surface.

Pivoting lid covered with solar cells

Antenna

Panoramic camera

ude-control sters for euvering ace

Service Module

Attitude-control thruster

Propulsion unit

Fuel tank

Wheel with dedicated motor and brake

Radar

scent Module

Solar panels

LUNOKHOD

Luna 17 in 1970 and Luna 21 in 1973 both carried robotic rovers, called Lunokhods. About 8 ft (2.5 m) long and 5 ft (1.5 m) wide, the Lunokhods trundled around on eight wheels, studying the lunar surface and taking thousands of television images. Lunokhod 1 (shown above) worked for 10 months in the Mare Imbrium region, travelling a total of 7 miles (11 km). Lunokhod 2 drove for 23 miles (37 km) around the edge of the Mare Serenitatis over a period of four months.

IMAGES FROM ZOND 7

The Soviet lunar program included several Zond missions. The Zonds were unmanned Soyuz spacecraft minus their Orbital Module. The first, Zond 3, flew past the Moon taking pictures of the far side, but later ones were tests for manned flights. In 1968, Zond 5 became the first spacecraft to orbit the Moon and return to Earth. Zond 7 took this photograph of the Moon on August 11, 1969, from a distance of 1,250 miles (2,000 km).

Living in space

SALYUT
Between 1971 and 1982, the USSR launched a series of seven space stations called Salyut (Russian for "Salute") into Earth orbit. After early failures, the last two stations were successful. Salyut 7 launched in April 1982, operated for more than 4 years, and was visited by 10 crews. This patch commemorates the Soyuz T-6's link-up with Salyut 7 in 1982.

DURING THE 1970S AND 80S, the USSR and the US focused on space stations that orbited Earth and on how their crews could live and work in space for long periods. This expertise will be vital when people explore the solar system more widely and set up bases on the Moon. The USSR launched its first space station, Salyut 1, in April 1971. The US followed with Skylab in 1973–74. America also started to develop the Space Shuttle, which first flew in 1981. Gradually, competition between the US and USSR was replaced by cooperation.

All electrical power is generated by solar panels

Solar panels are 190 ft (58 m) long

Mission badge shows Soyuz 19 and Apollo about to dock in Earth orbit

END OF THE SPACE RACE
With political relations between the US and the USSR improving in the 1970s, planning and training began for a joint space mission. A Soviet Soyuz spacecraft lifted off on July 15, 1975, with two cosmonauts on board and went into Earth orbit. A few hours later, the US launched an Apollo Command and Service Module (see page 178) with a crew of three. On July 17, the two craft connected using a specially constructed docking module, then remained together for two days. The two crews' meeting was broadcast live on TV, and they transferred between the two craft several times.

Unmanned supply craft bring supplies such as water, oxygen, fuel, food, and spare parts

EFFECTS OF MICROGRAVITY
In space, astronauts experience almost complete weightlessness—called microgravity—because they are traveling through space at the same speed as their surroundings. The bones and muscles that normally support a person's weight on the ground soon begin to waste away, and their heart and lungs do not work so well. Daily exercise helps to prevent these health problems. This picture shows astronaut Peggy Whitson exercising on a stationary cycle aboard the International Space Station.

MONTHS IN ORBIT
Salyut's successor was Mir (Russian for "Peace"). It was the first space station to be assembled in space, starting with a core module launched in 1986. Mir was occupied continuously for almost 10 years and visited by 104 people from several countries. Here Thomas Reiter plays a modified guitar on board Mir, where he spent 179 days during 1995–96 as a European Space Agency astronaut. Valery Polyakov, who was on board for 438 days, stayed the longest. After years of use, Mir was finally brought down over the south Pacific Ocean in March 2001.

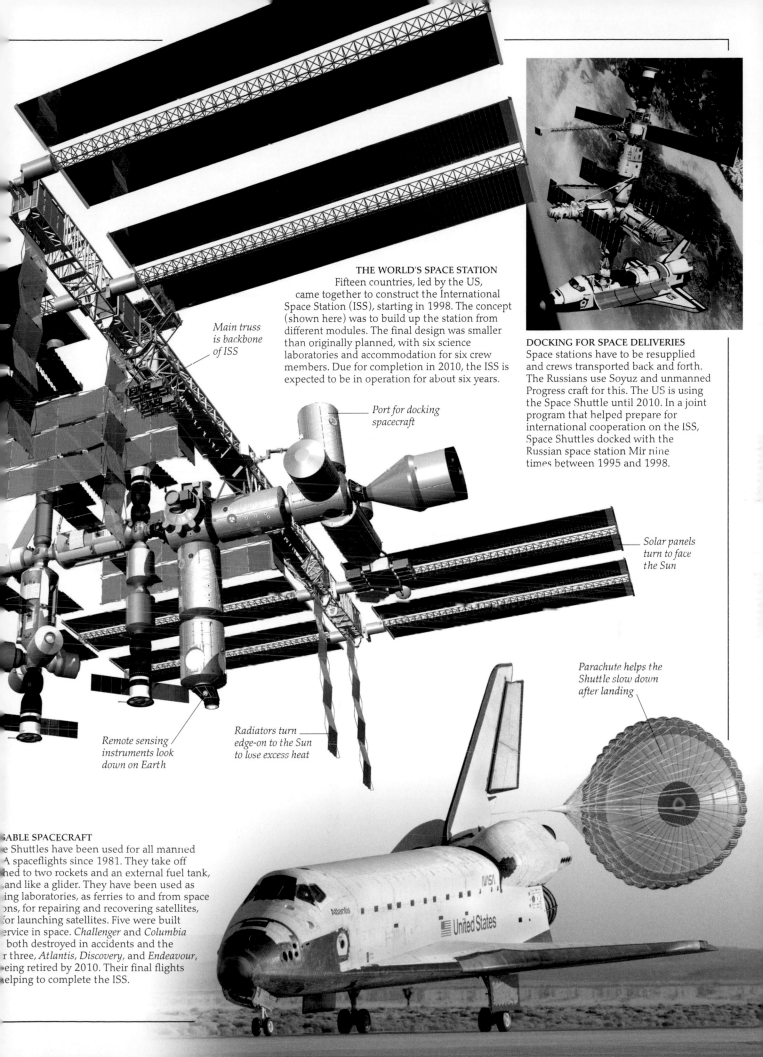

THE WORLD'S SPACE STATION
Fifteen countries, led by the US, came together to construct the International Space Station (ISS), starting in 1998. The concept (shown here) was to build up the station from different modules. The final design was smaller than originally planned, with six science laboratories and accommodation for six crew members. Due for completion in 2010, the ISS is expected to be in operation for about six years.

Main truss is backbone of ISS

Port for docking spacecraft

DOCKING FOR SPACE DELIVERIES
Space stations have to be resupplied and crews transported back and forth. The Russians use Soyuz and unmanned Progress craft for this. The US is using the Space Shuttle until 2010. In a joint program that helped prepare for international cooperation on the ISS, Space Shuttles docked with the Russian space station Mir nine times between 1995 and 1998.

Solar panels turn to face the Sun

Remote sensing instruments look down on Earth

Radiators turn edge-on to the Sun to lose excess heat

Parachute helps the Shuttle slow down after landing

~ABLE SPACECRAFT
~e Shuttles have been used for all manned ~A spaceflights since 1981. They take off ~hed to two rockets and an external fuel tank, ~and like a glider. They have been used as ~ing laboratories, as ferries to and from space ~ons, for repairing and recovering satellites, ~for launching satellites. Five were built ~ervice in space. *Challenger* and *Columbia* ~both destroyed in accidents and the ~r three, *Atlantis*, *Discovery*, and *Endeavour*, ~eing retired by 2010. Their final flights ~elping to complete the ISS.

The new lunar invasion

Bᴇᴛᴡᴇᴇɴ 1961 ᴀɴᴅ 1974, ᴛʜᴇʀᴇ was at least one mission to the Moon every year, but after Luna 24 in 1976, 14 years passed before another spacecraft went to the Moon. In 1990, Japan's Hiten flew around the Moon and eventually crashed into it, but Hiten's purpose was mainly to test technology. From the 1990s, the United States' interest in exploring the Moon gradually reawakened. And now, the space agencies of Japan, China, India, and Europe are all pursuing programs to explore the Moon.

TANEGASHIMA SPACE CENTER
In January 1990, Japan became the third country after the US and the USSR to send a spacecraft to the Moon. The Japanese Space Agency launched a small spacecraft called Hiten, named after a Buddhist angel, from the Tanegashima Space Center. It entered a long elliptical orbit, which looped around Earth and the Moon. The Hiten mission was mainly a success, but contact was lost with the small, separate, lunar orbiter it released.

Lunar Prospector being prepared for launch

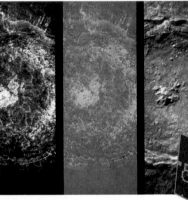

Solar panel

Octagonal spacecraft is 3¾ ft (1.14 m) across

CLEMENTINE MAPS THE MOON
The first US Moon mission after Apollo was Clementine, launched on January 25, 1994. It spent two months mapping the whole of the Moon through color filters. These pictures of the crater Tycho illustrate how this data could be used. From right to left, the images show exaggerated colors, different rock and soil types, and material relatively rich in iron and magnesium.

Clementine spacecraft

LUNAR PROSPECTOR
After Clementine, the next spacecraft the US sent to the Moon was the Lunar Prospector. This small orbiter was launched on January 7, 1998, and its mission lasted 19 months. One of the six experiments on board supported Clementine's evidence for ice in craters near the lunar poles that are always shaded from the Sun. Other scientific information gathered by the Lunar Prospector included measurements of the chemical composition of the Moon's surface.

Module to propel spacecraft into lunar orbit

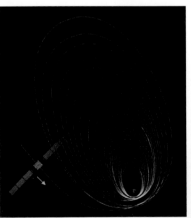

SMART-1'S SPIRAL PATH
SMART-1, launched in September 2003, was the European Space Agency's first lunar mission. It carried several miniaturized instruments but mainly tested a method of propulsion called solar powered ion drive. For 14 months, it made longer and longer elliptical orbits around Earth to reach lunar orbit, then spiraled in closer to the Moon (as shown here).

KAGUYA ORBITER

The Japanese Kaguya lunar orbiter was launched from the Tanegashima Space Center on September 14, 2007. Before launch it was officially called SELENE, but later it was nicknamed Kaguya, after a princess in a Japanese folktale. Kaguya was the most ambitious lunar mission since Apollo. It carried 13 different instruments and was expected to work for at least a year. It also carried messages in miniaturized form from over 400,000 celebrities and members of the public.

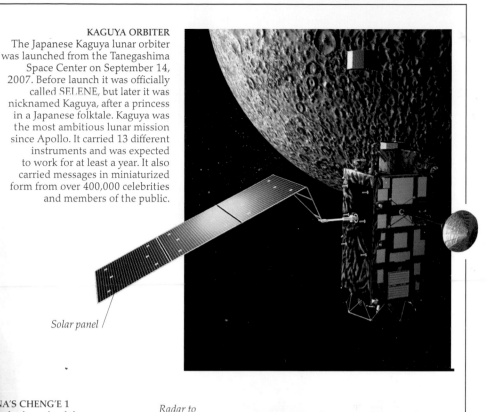

Solar panel

CHINA'S CHENG'E 1

With the launch of the unmanned spacecraft Cheng'e 1 on October 24, 2007, China joined the list of nations with programs to explore the Moon. Cheng'e 1 was launched into lunar orbit from the Xichang Satellite Launch Center by a Long March 3A rocket. Named after a Moon goddess from Chinese mythology, it was the first in a series of Cheng'e spacecraft. It orbited the Moon for a year, testing technology for future missions and studying the lunar surface.

Radar to look for ice

Solar panel to generate power

Fuel tank

Antenna to transmit data

INDIA'S CHANDRAYAAN-1

The Indian Space Research Organization (ISRO) planned to launch its first Moon mission, Chandrayaan-1, in 2008–09. One of the objectives of the unmanned spacecraft was to make an atlas of the Moon. As well as five Indian instruments, it carried six instruments from NASA, the European Space Agency (ESA), and Bulgaria. One of them is a NASA radar that will search for ice at the Moon's poles. India hopes that its next mission, Chandrayaan-2, will land a rover on the Moon in 2010 or 2011.

OFFICIAL TEAM

Google LUNAR X PRIZE

· FREDNET ·

A NEW RACE TO THE MOON

Privately funded teams are competing for the Google Lunar X Prize. To win up to $20 million, a team has to be the first to launch, land, and operate a robot on the lunar surface by the end of 2014. The robot must travel 1,640 ft (500 m) and return images back to Earth. By 2008, 13 teams had registered.

Return to the Moon

By the year 2020, NASA plans to return humans to the Moon's surface for the first time in nearly 50 years. Its new human spaceflight program is called Project Constellation. The next generation of explorers it will send to the Moon will stay longer than their predecessors. They will travel to and from lunar orbit in a spacecraft called Orion and will descend to the Moon's surface in a lander called Altair. Two new rockets, Ares I and Ares V, will launch the astronauts in their Orion craft and everything they will need to construct a lunar base.

A NEW VISION
In January 2004, President George W. Bush proposed America's new "Vision for Space Exploration." Its goal is to send humans out to explore the solar system, beginning with a return to the Moon. Congress approved the plan and NASA began Project Constellation. The first step was to continue mapping and studying the Moon with the Lunar Reconnaissance Orbiter (LRO) in 2008–09.

THE SEARCH FOR ICE
Life on the Moon would be easier with a nearby water supply, so NASA planned to launch LCROSS (Lunar Crater Observation and Sensing Satellite) on the same rocket as the LRO. Its mission was intended to continue the search for ice on the Moon. The LCROSS shepherding spacecraft will guide part of its launch rocket to crash at high speed in an area of permanent shadow. Then it will analyze the huge plume of material thrown up for traces of water and will transmit the data back to Earth.

Control thruster

Shepherding spacecraft

Centaur upper stage rocket crashes on the Moon

UNITED STATES

The Ares I crew rocket is 309 ft (94 m) tall. It has a reusable solid rocket first stage and a liquid-fueled second stage.

ARES I AND ARES V

NASA is developing two new rockets for missions to the International Space Station and to the Moon. Ares I will take an Orion spacecraft with a crew of four to six astronauts into Earth orbit. The larger Ares V is a heavy-lift cargo launcher. It will carry hardware into Earth orbit, including a lunar lander and materials for building a lunar base. Working together, Ares I and Ares V will be able to carry 78 tons (71 metric tons) to the Moon.

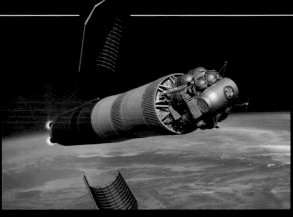

ALTAIR LANDER WITH ROCKET STAGE

An Orion crew going to the Moon will not have their lunar lander with them when they lift off. The Altair lander, combined with a rocket stage for leaving Earth orbit, will be launched separately. Orion will dock with Altair in Earth orbit, and the attached rocket stage will propel both to Moon orbit, where the crew will transfer from Orion to Altair.

ORION CREW MODULE

The Orion spacecraft will have Crew and Service Modules, similar to the Command and Service Modules of the Apollo spacecraft. At the Moon, Orion will stay in orbit while the astronauts descend to the lunar surface in the Altair lander. At the end of the mission, the astronauts will make the voyage back to Earth in the Orion Crew Module.

LUNAR OUTPOST

Orion astronauts may set up a base just outside Shackleton crater near the Moon's South Pole. Nearly continuous sunlight could provide constant power there, and frozen water may exist nearby. This radar image is colored to show the steepness of the terrain. Shackleton is at the right, with a sharp purple edge.

The Ares V cargo rocket is 358 ft (109 m) tall. It has a liquid-fueled central booster and two reusable solid rocket boosters.

LUNAR ALL TERRAIN VEHICLE

Robotic vehicles will be used to move equipment and supplies around on the Moon. They will have to be able to travel over rough ground and slopes. NASA tested this robotic vehicle, called ATHLETE, in 2008. It rolls along like a rover on its six wheels. ATHLETE's six legs can also work with feet instead of wheels, to make it a walking robot. Walking is easier than rolling for covering the most difficult terrain.

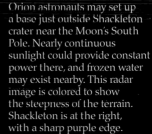

This time to stay

For decades, scientists have predicted that there will one day be permanent stations on the Moon, and science fiction writers have dreame about them for even longer. Several national space agencies have said the would like to set up bases on the Moon, but NASA was the first to start work on a practical plan. Starting in around 2024, it intends to build a permanent lunar base where astronauts will stay for up to six months at a time, conducting scientific studies and exploration.

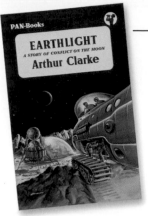

A BASE ON THE MOON?
Writers and artists have long imagined what permanent human colonies on the Moon might be like. British writer Arthur C. Clarke set his 1955 story *Earthlight* 200 years after the first Moon landing. His vision is now becoming a reality.

CONCEPT LUNAR LANDER
Before a permanent station is built, NASA astronauts visiting the Moon will first stay there for up to seven days in their lunar lander. NASA's planned Altair lunar lander may look similar to this, and will carry four astronauts. Like the Apollo landers, its upper section will lift off and take the crew back to the Orion Module waiting in lunar orbit for the journey home.

Steering mechanism can turn to face in any direction

Six sets of wheels can turn in any direction

Bulldozer blade can be attached here

A TENT FOR THE MOON
When astronauts first make trips to the Moon of longer than a week, they will have to take somewhere to live with them because the lander can only carry enough life support equipment for a few days. One possibility is an inflatable tent like this one, which is lightweight and easy to set up, but strong. It has heating, lighting, and an air supply inside.

...NG THE MOON
...erate long-term human colonies on the Moon, ...nauts will have to mine some of the basic materials ...need from lunar rocks and soil. This is an artist's ...ession of a lunar mining facility for obtaining ...en from the volcanic soil in a mare area. Two ...nauts stand next to a radio communications dish ...a lunar lander takes off in the distance.

...R TRANSPORTER
...stronauts who establish the first ...base will need to move cargo ...d and carry out construction ...on the rough terrain. NASA has ...ned and tested this mobile lunar ...porter for the job. Two astronauts ...de on it while standing. Each set ...o wheels pivots separately so the ...porter can move in any direction, ...ding sideways. It can also be ...d into a bulldozer by adding a ...al blade at the front.

...orm lowers to ...d for loading ...stepping on and off

Judge's gavel is a symbol of law and order

LUNAR LAW
From its Office for Outer Space Affairs in Vienna, the United Nations (UN) promotes cooperation between countries on the Moon and in outer space. No one owns the Moon or the land on it. Neither countries nor individuals can make territorial claims, though some businesses offer to "sell" land on the Moon.

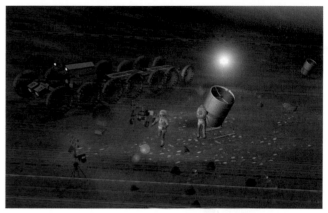

FAR SIDE OBSERVATORY
The best place for most kinds of astronomical observations is beyond Earth's atmosphere, because the air distorts images and blocks much of the radiation from space aside from visible light and radio waves. The Moon is an ideal place for an observatory (above) because there is no air. Though radio observatories on Earth are not affected by the atmosphere, the far side of the Moon would be much better for them, too, because they would be protected from interference caused by man-made radio signals and electrical equipment.

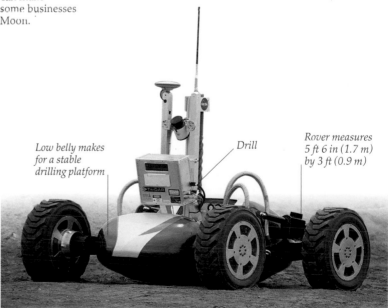

Low belly makes for a stable drilling platform

Drill

Rover measures 5 ft 6 in (1.7 m) by 3 ft (0.9 m)

DRILLING ROVER
Robotic rovers will help lunar astronauts search for the raw materials they need for life-support systems, and may even discover rare minerals that are valuable on Earth. NASA put this test rover through extreme trials at a location in the US. It uses laser sensors and a radioactive power source for working in the total darkness in shaded parts of the Moon's polar regions. The rover can raise its body to clear rocks and travel on slopes, and can drill to a depth of 3 ft 3 in (1 m).

A job on the Moon

THE FIRST ASTRONAUTS WERE ALL military pilots, but the crew of the last Apollo mission included a geologist, Harrison Schmitt, who was the first scientist to become an astronaut. Since those early days, men and women from a wide range of backgrounds in science and engineering, as well as from the armed forces, have been selected as astronauts. All are exceptional people ready to go through long and difficult training. Soon, civilians may be able to visit space as tourists more frequently. Eventually, there may be commercial flights to orbiting hotels, or even to the Moon.

Food tray to hold items down

Vacuum-packed fruits and nut

SPACE FOODS

Astronauts in space eat three meals a day and can eat the same food as on Earth. However, all food has to be in tins or sealed packages because there are usually no refrigerators. Many foo are precooked and just need warming or water added. Salt and pepper come as liquids because floating grains coul be dangerous inside the spacecraft. For the same reason, bread is banned because of the crumbs.

SELECTING ASTRONAUTS

Aspiring astronauts must first study for a de in science or engineering. They have to be fi healthy, with good eyesight. To go through t difficult training, they need to be brave and adventurous. They must also get along well w other people and be good at coping in difficul or dangerous situations. These newly selected astronaut candidates are experiencing near weightlessness on board a special aircraft as part of their early training.

Virgin Galactic' passenger space will be taken up 9 miles (15 km) a mothership, t climb to 68 mile (109 km) with own rocket.

EQUAL OPPORTUNITIES

All the Apollo astronauts were men, but today men and women compete equally to be selected as astronauts. Of nearly 500 astronauts so far, 60 have been women. This picture shows NASA astronaut Ellen Ochoa looking out of the International Space Station in 2002. She became an astronaut in 1990, flew four times on the Space Shuttle, and spent nearly 1,000 hours in space.

KEEPING FIT

In space, astronauts have to exercise every day to reduce the harmful effects of weightlessness or reduced gravity on their bones and muscles. This equipment was built for research on keeping astronauts fit. The person using it hangs horizontally while walking or running on a vertical treadmill. This closely mimics an astronaut's sensation of microgravity in orbit or on the Moon, which has just one-sixth the gravity of Earth.

ING FOR THE JOB

training for candidate astronauts
two years. People who pass this can
ected to train for particular missions.
es learn how to carry out a variety
s inside and outside a spacecraft in
ions of microgravity. They practice
s under water and on special aircraft
. Here, astronauts learn how to
the Hubble Space Telescope
an underwater simulator.

ING THE PUBLIC

a few hundred people have so far
ed into space, and astronauts are treated
ebrities the world over. Communicating
he public is part of the job. Chinese
auts Nie Haisheng and Fei Junlong were
ew of China's second manned space
on in 2005. After their five-day flight,
met these children in Beijing.

IRGIN GALACTIC

Even people who are not professional
astronauts may soon travel into
space. From about 2009, commercial
companies are planning to offer
paying passengers suborbital flights,
which are not as expensive and
require much less preparation than
going into orbit. Full orbital flights
will probably be available to the
public sometime in the future.

Near side

THE BEST MAPS OF THE MOON astronomers have today were made from millions of images collected by orbiting spacecraft. They are far more detailed than any maps made from observations with a telescope. The five Lunar Orbiters returned over 1,000 photographs of the whole Moon in 1966–67. Some close-ups included details only 3 ft (1 m) across. In 1994, Clementine took 1.8 million digital images. It could see down to 330 ft (100 m). Over 2,000 features on the Moon have been given names.

GOLDSTONE ANTENNA
Used as a radar dish to bounce radio signals off the Moon, this 230-ft (70-m) wide antenna in California has mapped some areas of the Moon in enough detail to show features as small as a house. It is part of NASA's Deep Space Network, which receives data from distant spacecraft and sends commands to them by radio.

COPERNICUS
The Copernicus Crater is 57 miles (91 km) across. Because of the light colored material surrounding it, and its ray system, it is an easy crater to spot from Earth. It was named after the famous Polish astronomer Nicolaus Copernicus (1473–1543). He realized that, contrary to what people believed then, Earth and the other planets orbit the Sun, and that Earth is not at the center of the solar system.

RUPES RECTA
The popular name for this feature is the Straight Wall because its shadow can sometimes makes it appear like a steep cliff. However, in reality it is a gentle slope about 1½ miles (2.5 km) wide and 800–1,000 ft (240–300 m) high, caused by a fault line in the lunar surface. The fault line stretches for about 70 miles (110 km) on the eastern edge of the Mare Nubium.

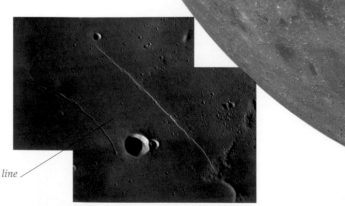

fault line

MAR[E]
FRIGO[RIS]

PLATO CRATER ▶

MONS RUMKER

MONTES JURA

SINUS IRIDIUM

MARE IMBRIUM

MONTES AGRICOLA

◀ ARISTARCHUS CRATER

OCEANUS PROCELLARUM

ERATOSTHENES CRATER ▼

MONTES CARPATUS

◀ COPERNICUS CRATER

◀ KEPLER CRATER

◀ GRIMALDI CRATER

PTOLEMAEUS CRA[TER]

ALPHONSUS CRAT[ER]

◀ GASSENDI CRATER

ARZACHEL C[RATER]

MARE NUBIUM

◀ BYRGIUS CRATER

MARE HUMORUM

TYCHO ▶ CRATER

CLA[VIUS] CRA[TER]

MARE
FRIGORIS

◄ ARISTOTELES
CRATER

◄ HERCULES
CRATER

ONTES
CAUCASUS

MARE
SERENITATIS

PROCLUS CRATER ►

MARE
CRISIUM

RE
RUM

MARE
TRANQUILLITATIS

MARE
FECUNDITATIS

TEGNIUS
ER

THEOPHILUS CRATER ►

CYRILLUS CRATER ►

MARE
NECTARIS

CATHARINA CRATER ►

RUPES ALTAI

HUMBOLDT ►
CRATER

PICCOLOMINI ►
CRATER

STEVINUS ►
CRATER

TÖFLER
RATER

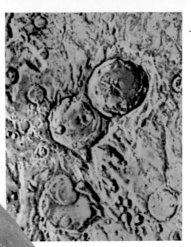

OVERLAPPING CRATERS

This string of three large craters is easy to see with binoculars. The top one, Theophilus, is 60 miles (100 km) across and overlaps Cyrillus just below it. Beneath them is Catharina, whose circular outline has been distorted by several craters that formed later. This is a close-up of part of a color-coded map that shows the height of the lunar landscape (see below).

PLATO

Plato (c. 428–347 BCE) was a great thinker and scientist in ancient Greece. He set up the Academy in Athens, one of the first institutions of learning in the western world. He realized that the motion of the planets could be analyzed through mathematics. The crater named in his honor is 68 miles (109 km) wide. It lies just north of the Mare Imbrium and its floor is dark with flooded lava, like the nearby mare.

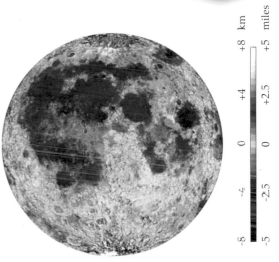

HIGHLANDS AND LOWLANDS

This color-coded map shows the height of the lunar landscape above and below the average. Places at average height are shown in yellow. The pattern of the maria and the floors of large craters stands out in blue and purple, which are used for low-lying terrain. The highest places are shaded orange and red. Typically, the highland areas are 2½ miles (4 km) higher than the maria. The data was collected by the Clementine spacecraft in 1994 (see page 192).

TYCHO BRAHE

The most conspicuous crater on the Moon was named Tycho after the Danish astronomer Tycho Brahe (1546–1601), who is often known by just his first name. He died before the telescope was invented but, using instruments he built himself, he made very accurate measurements of the positions of the Sun, Moon, planets, and stars for more than 20 years. Crater Tycho, in the Moon's southern highlands, is 52 miles (85 km) in diameter.

Far side

THE SOVIET UNION CHOSE NAMES for prominent features on the Moon's far side soon after its spacecraft had taken the first photographs. These include Mare Moscoviense (Sea of Moscow) and craters named after Soviet scientists and cosmonauts. Three craters near the large Apollo crater are named after the Apollo 8 astronauts, who were the first to see the far side. New names are sometimes added, such as six approved in 2006 to honor the astronauts killed in the 2003 Space Shuttle disaster.

THE FIRST VIEW
The first images of the Moon's far side were taken by the unmanned Soviet spacecraft Luna 3 (see page 176). Although the photos were blurry, it was still a great achievement for 1959. This commemorative stamp issued by the USSR shows the spacecraft and the date when the photographs were taken.

Rocket engine nozzle

Communications antenna

Communications antenna

Solar panel

Lunar Orbiter 4

Camera lenses

PHOTOGRAPHIC SURVEY
In 1966–67, the five American Lunar Orbiter spacecraft photographed 99 percent of the Moon. This was before digital photography, so the film had to be developed on board, then scanned and the pictures transmitted to Earth as radio signals. In 2007, the Lunar Orbiter Digitization Project began to convert these high-quality photographs into digital images that could be enhanced and pieced together into detailed mosaics.

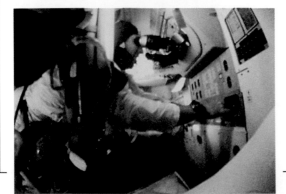

APOLLO EYEWITNESS
The only humans to have seen the Moon's far side are the astronauts who flew on Apollo missions 8 and 10 to 17. The Apollo 8 crew of Frank Borman, James Lovell, and William Anders were the first to do so when their Command Module made its first pass behind the Moon on Christmas Eve, 1968. Their first impression was of a whitish gray landscape, "like dirty beach sand," with "a lot of bumps and holes."

D'ALEMBERT CRATER ▶

◀ CAMPBELL CRATER

◀ GIORDANO BRUNO CRATER

MARE MOSCOVIENSE

LACU LUXURIA

SHAHINAZ CRATER ▶

MENDELEEV ▶ CRATER

◀ NECHO CRATER

DAEDALUS

◀ GAGARIN CRATER

AITKEN ▶ CRATER

◀ TSIOLKOVSKY CRATER

VAN DE GRA CRA▶

◀ SCALIGER CRATER

MARE INGENII

JULES VERNE ▶ CRATER

LIEBNITZ CRA

PAULI CRATER ▶

VON KÁRMÁN CRATER

SCHRÖDINGER CRATER

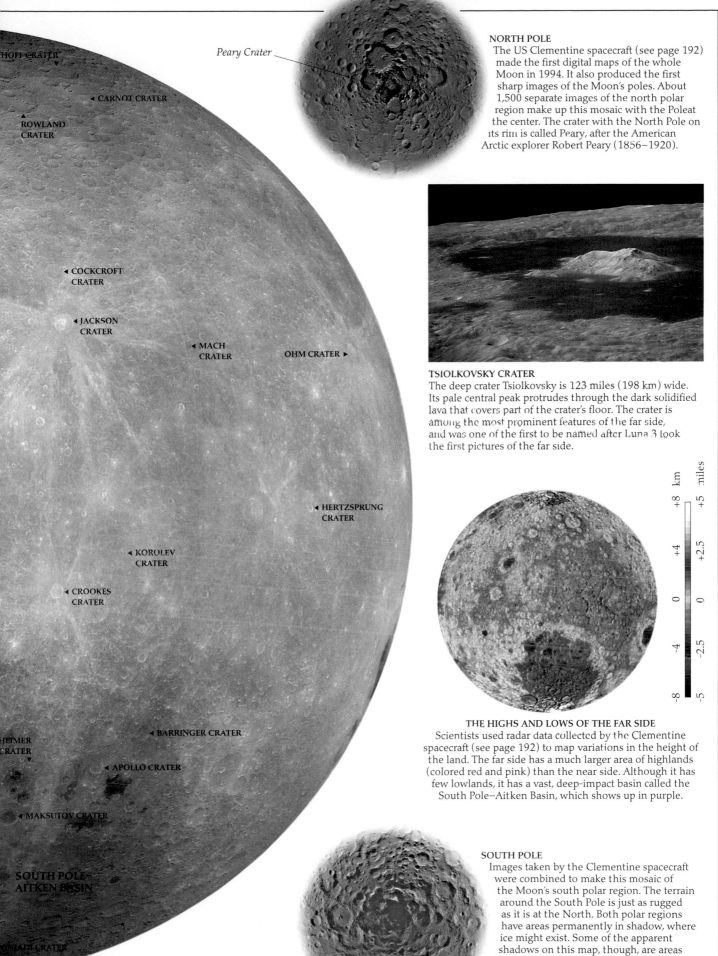

Peary Crater

HOFF CRATER ▾

◄ CARNOT CRATER

▲
ROWLAND
CRATER

◄ COCKCROFT
CRATER

◄ JACKSON
CRATER

◄ MACH
CRATER

OHM CRATER ►

◄ HERTZSPRUNG
CRATER

◄ KOROLEV
CRATER

◄ CROOKES
CRATER

HEIMER
CRATER
▾

◄ BARRINGER CRATER

◄ APOLLO CRATER

◄ MAKSUTOV CRATER

SOUTH POLE–
AITKEN BASIN

ONIZUKA CRATER

NORTH POLE
The US Clementine spacecraft (see page 192) made the first digital maps of the whole Moon in 1994. It also produced the first sharp images of the Moon's poles. About 1,500 separate images of the north polar region make up this mosaic with the Pole at the center. The crater with the North Pole on its rim is called Peary, after the American Arctic explorer Robert Peary (1856–1920).

TSIOLKOVSKY CRATER
The deep crater Tsiolkovsky is 123 miles (198 km) wide. Its pale central peak protrudes through the dark solidified lava that covers part of the crater's floor. The crater is among the most prominent features of the far side, and was one of the first to be named after Luna 3 took the first pictures of the far side.

+8 km   +5 miles

+4   +2.5

0   0

-4   -2.5

-8   -5

THE HIGHS AND LOWS OF THE FAR SIDE
Scientists used radar data collected by the Clementine spacecraft (see page 192) to map variations in the height of the land. The far side has a much larger area of highlands (colored red and pink) than the near side. Although it has few lowlands, it has a vast, deep-impact basin called the South Pole–Aitken Basin, which shows up in purple.

SOUTH POLE
Images taken by the Clementine spacecraft were combined to make this mosaic of the Moon's south polar region. The terrain around the South Pole is just as rugged as it is at the North. Both polar regions have areas permanently in shadow, where ice might exist. Some of the apparent shadows on this map, though, are areas for which there are gaps in the data.

Lunar timeline

E VEN BEFORE THERE WERE TELESCOPES, early astronomers followed the Moon's motion and tried to measure its distance and size. But telescopes revolutionized the mapping and scientific study of the Moon. Then, in the mid-20th century, unmanned spacecraft and the Apollo missions opened up a new way of exploring the Moon. This timeline tracks significant events in the study, understanding, and exploration of the Moon, from the first telescopic observations, through the history of lunar spacecraft and landings, to the present.

Time magazine cover from 1968

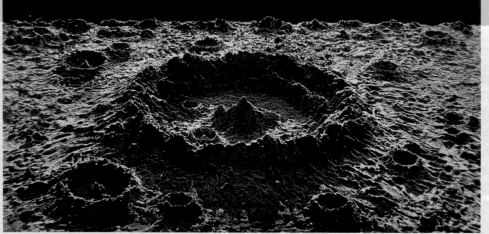

Model of a crater on the Moon, pictured in Nasmyth and Carpenter's 1874 book

JULY 26, 1609
Thomas Harriot, a British mathematician, makes the first observation of the Moon through a telescope, though he publishes no drawings until 1611.

1610
Italian astronomer Galileo Galilei publishes drawings of the Moon, which he made with the help of a telescope in late 1609.

1647
German astronomer Johannes Hevelius publishes the first reasonably accurate chart of the Moon.

1651
Italian astronomer Giovanni Riccioli establishes the system for naming craters after famous astronomers and scientists. Over 130 craters are still called by the names he gave.

1661
The first globe of the Moon is completed by the British architect and astronomer Sir Christopher Wren, who presents it to King Charles II.

1752
German astronomer Tobias Mayor publishes accurate tables of the Moon's position in the sky. They are good enough to be used by sailors for calculating their position at sea.

1834–37
German astronomers Johann Mädler and Wilhelm Beer produce the first precise map and description of the Moon. They claim that the Moon has neither an atmosphere nor water.

1839
John William Draper, a professor of chemistry in New York, takes the first photograph of the Moon.

1874
British engineer James Nasmyth and British astronomer James Carpenter publish their book, *The Moon: Considered as a Planet a World and a Satellite*. It suggests that craters on the Moon are the result of volcanic activity.

1893
American scientist Grove Karl Gilbert (1843– 1918) writes correctly that lunar craters are the result of impacts, but his work is ignored.

OCTOBER 4, 1957
The USSR launches Sputnik 1, the first artificial satellite to orbit Earth, and the "space race" with the United States begins.

Laika, the first living creature in space in 1957

NOVEMBER 3, 1957
The dog Laika becomes the first living creature in space when launched aboard the USSR's Sputnik 2.

1958
The National Aeronautics and Space Administration (NASA) is founded in the US and announces Project Mercury, to launch an astronaut into space.

JANUARY 2, 1959
Luna 1, the first spacecraft to fly past the Moon, is launched by the USSR. The neare it gets to the Moon is 3,747 miles (5,995 k on January 4.

SEPTEMBER 12, 1959
The USSR launches Luna 2, the first human-made object to reach the Moon. It crash-lands near the crater Aristarchus on September 14.

OCTOBER 4, 1959
Luna 3 is launched by the Soviet Union. It re the first, hazy images of the Moon's far side.

APRIL 12, 1960
The Soviet cosmonaut Yuri Gagarin becom the first man in space when he makes a 10 minute flight around Earth in Vostok 1.

MAY 5, 1961
Alan Shepard makes a 15-minute suborbit flight in Freedom 7 and becomes the first American in space.

MAY 25, 1961
In a speech to the US Congress, President John F. Kennedy announces that an Americ will land on the Moon and be returned saf to Earth before the end of the decade.

JULY 28, 1964
The US launches Ranger 7, which successfu returns the first close-up images of the Mo on July 31 before crashing onto the surface planned.

JULY 18, 1965
The USSR launches Zond 3. It takes the first clear images of the Moon's far side on July 20

JANUARY 31, 1966
The USSR launches Luna 9. On February 1 it makes the first soft landing by a spacecra on the Moon.

CH 16, 1966
...a launches Gemini 8, which later achieves
...st docking between two orbiting spacecraft.

CH 31, 1966
...10 is launched by the USSR. It becomes
...st spacecraft to go into lunar orbit.

...UST 10, 1966
...Orbiter 1, the first US lunar orbiter, is
...ed by NASA. It takes photographs of the
...n in search of landing sites.

...ARY 27, 1967
...pollo 1 crew of Roger Chaffee, Virgil
...om, and Edward White are killed in a fire
...Command Module (CM) during a
...g exercise. It takes 18 months to modify
...esign of the CM.

...EMBER 15, 1968
...USSR launches Zond 5, which carries
... material, including turtles. It is the first
...craft to travel around the Moon and safely
...n to Earth, splashing down in the
...n Ocean on September 21, 1968.

...OBER 11, 1968
...A launches Apollo 7, the first manned
...o spacecraft, on an 11-day mission in
...orbit. The crew of Walter Schirra, Donn
...and R. Walter Cunningham make the first
...V transmission from space.

...EMBER 21, 1968
...o 8, the first manned flight around
...oon, is launched by NASA. The crew
...nk Borman, Jim Lovell, and Bill Anders
...he the first people to see Earthrise over
...oon. They return on December 27.

...CH 3-13, 1969
...o 9 tests in Earth orbit the spacecraft to be
...for manned Moon missions. The crew for
...0-day mission consists of James McDivitt,
... Scott, and Russell Schweikart.

...18-26, 1969
...pollo 10 crew of Thomas Stafford, John
...g, and Eugene Cernan perform a full dress
...rsal for a Moon landing. They stop short
...ouchdown.

...16-24, 1969
...o 11 becomes the first space mission
...d humans on the Moon. Neil
...rong and Buzz Aldrin step onto
...oon on July 20, while Michael
...s remains on board the
...g Command Module.

...uzz Aldrin steps down on
...e Moon on July 20, 1969

NOVEMBER 14-24, 1969
Apollo 12 lands astronauts Charles
Conrad and Alan Bean on the
Moon, with Richard Gordon as
Command Module Pilot.

APRIL 11-17, 1970
Apollo 13 has to be
aborted following an
explosion on board,
but the crew of James
Lovell, John Swigert,
and Fred Haise return
to Earth safely.

SEPTEMBER 12-24, 1970
The Soviet Luna 16 becomes
the first robotic spacecraft to
land on the Moon and
return a sample to Earth.

NOVEMBER 10, 1970-SEPTEMBER 14, 1971
The USSR's Luna 17 completes its mission.
It carries Lunokhod 1, the first robotic rover
to explore the Moon.

JANUARY 31-FEBRUARY 9, 1971
Apollo 14 successfully completes its Moon
mission. Alan Shepard and Edgar Mitchell land
while Stuart Roosa is Command Module Pilot.

JULY 26-AUGUST 7, 1971
Apollo 15 astronauts David Scott and James Irwin
become the first to drive a lunar rover on the
Moon. Alfred Worden is Command Module Pilot.

FEBRUARY 14, 1972
The USSR launches Luna 20. It returns with
1 oz (30 g) of lunar soil nine days later.

Japan's Hiten spacecraft,
launched in 1990

APRIL 16-27, 1972
Apollo 16 astronauts
John Young and Charles
Duke spend 71 hours
on the lunar surface,
while Thomas
Mattingley pilots the
Command Module.

DECEMBER 7-19, 1972
In the last Apollo mission,
Apollo 17, Eugene Cernan and
Harrison Schmitt spend 75 hours
on the Moon. Ronald Evans pilots
the Command Module.

JANUARY 8-JUNE 3, 1973
The USSR's Luna 21 completes its mission,
carrying the second Lunokhod robotic rover.

AUGUST 9, 1976
The USSR launches Luna 24. It returns to Earth
on August 22 with 6 oz (170 g) of lunar soil.

JANUARY 24, 1990
Japan launches Hiten, and becomes the third
nation (after the US and the USSR) to achieve a
lunar flyby, orbit, and crash-landing.

ESA's SMART-1, launched in 2003

JANUARY 25, 1994
NASA launches Clementine into lunar orbit.
It finds evidence of ice at the Moon's poles.

JANUARY 7, 1998
NASA launches Lunar Prospector carrying six
scientific instruments into lunar orbit.

SEPTEMBER 27, 2003
The European Space Agency launches SMART-1,
the first European spacecraft to orbit the Moon.

JANUARY 14, 2004
President Bush commits the US to a long-term
human and robotic program to explore the solar
system, starting with a return to the Moon.

SEPTEMBER 14, 2007
Japan launches its lunar orbiter Kaguya.

OCTOBER 24, 2007
China launches its first lunar orbiter, Chang'e 1.

2009
India plans to launch its first lunar orbiter,
Chandrayaan-1.

2009
NASA hopes to launch the Lunar Reconnaissance
Orbiter.

Hall of fame

MANY ASTRONOMERS HAVE MADE NOTABLE contributions to our knowledge and understanding of the Moon, from the Greeks more than 2,000 years ago to the planetary scientists of today. The Apollo Moon landings were among the most significant events for human history as well as for lunar science. The skill and courage of all the astronauts involved in the Apollo program contributed to 12 men being able to walk on the Moon.

Italian astronomer Galileo

ALDRIN, BUZZ (1930–)
Aldrin was an American astronaut who was the Apollo 11 Lunar Module pilot, and the second person to walk on the Moon. He also flew on Gemini 12 in 1966.

ANDERS, WILLIAM (1933–)
This American astronaut was one of the first three humans to orbit the Moon on Apollo 8.

ARISTARCHUS OF SAMOS (c. 310–230 BCE)
The Greek astronomer Aristarchus was the first person to try to measure the Moon's size. His method was correct, but as he could not make the required observations accurately enough, his estimate was double the correct size.

Neil Armstrong, the first man on the Moon

ARMSTRONG, NEIL (1930–)
This US astronaut, as commander of Apollo 11, became the first person to set foot on the Moon. Previously an aeronautical engineer and test pilot, Armstrong also flew with David Scott on Gemini 8, which made the first docking in space.

BEAN, ALAN (1932–)
Bean was an American astronaut who was the Apollo 12 Lunar Module pilot and one of the 12 men who landed on the Moon. In 1973 he flew on Skylab for 59 days.

BEER, WILHELM (1777–1850)
Beer was a wealthy German banker who built a private observatory. He formed a partnership with the astronomer Johann Mädler to produce the first exact map of the Moon in 1834–36, and a description of the Moon in 1837.

BLAGG, MARY (1858–1944)
Blagg was a British astronomer who worked for many years on compiling a list of features on the Moon and devising a uniform system for naming them. She was co-author of *Named Lunar Formations*, published in 1935, which became the standard reference book on the subject.

BORMAN, FRANK (1928–)
Borman was an American astronaut who, as Apollo 8 Commander, led the first crew to orbit the Moon. He was also the Commander on Gemini 7.

BROWN, ERNEST (1866–1938)
A British mathematician, Brown spent all his life studying the Moon's complicated motion. He compiled extremely accurate tables for figuring out the Moon's position, and they remained the best available until 1984, when computers began doing it more accurately.

CERNAN, EUGENE (1934–)
This American astronaut was the Commander of Apollo 17 and the last person to leave the Moon. He had previously flown on Gemini 9 and Apollo 10. He is one of only three people to have flown to the Moon twice.

CONRAD, CHARLES "PETE" (1930–1999)
This American astronaut was the Apollo 12 Commander and the third man to walk on the Moon. He also flew on Gemini 5, Gemini 11, and Skylab 2.

DUKE, CHARLES (1935–)
One of the 12 men to have landed on the Moon, this American astronaut piloted the Apollo 16 Lunar Module."

GAGARIN, YURI (1934–1968)
The first person to fly in space, Gagarin had been a fighter pilot before he was selected as a cosmonaut. He died in an air crash while training to return to space on Soyuz 3.

GALILEI, GALILEO (1564–1642)
The Italian astronomer and physicist Galileo was one of the greatest scientists of his time. He made the first astronomical telescopes, and was the first person to make detailed scientific observations of the Moon with a telescope.

GRIMALDI, FRANCESCO (1618–1663)
Grimaldi was a professor of mathematics and physics at Bologna in Italy. Though most famous for his discoveries about light, he also made accurate measurements of features on the Moon and used them to draw an important lunar map for a book on astronomy by his fellow scientist, Giovanni Riccioli.

HARTMANN, WILLIAM K. (1939–)
Hartmann is a planetary scientist who was one of the first researchers to develop the now generally accepted, that the Moon formed in a giant collision. He is also well known as a leading space artist.

HEVELIUS, JOHANNES (1611–1687)
The German astronomer Hevelius published the first-ever lunar atlas in 1647. He was the son of a wealthy brewer and worked in Danzig (now Gdansk in Poland), using telescopes he designed and built himself.

Johannes Hevelius published the first-ever lunar atlas

PARCHUS (c. 190–120 BCE)
...archus was a Greek mathematician and
...nomer, born in what is today part of Turkey.
...gured out an early theory for the motion of
...Moon and also accurately calculated the
...nce of the Moon, relative to the size of the
..., by making observations at eclipses.

...N, JAMES (1930–1991)
...merican astronaut who was the Apollo 15
...r Module pilot, Irwin was one of the 12
...nauts to have walked on the Moon.

...OLEV, SERGEI (1907–1966)
...Soviet rocket scientist directed the Soviet
...n's Moon program until his death in 1966.

...PER, GERARD (1905–1973)
...tch–American planetary scientist, Kuiper
...ed interest in the scientific study of the
...n in the 1960s. He founded the Lunar and
...etary Laboratory in Arizona, US, and
...ed to identify possible Apollo landing sites.

...ELL, JAMES (1928–)
...American astronaut flew around the
...n twice, on Apollo 8 and Apollo 13.

James Nasmyth cowrote an
...fluential book about the Moon's features

...DLER, JOHANN HEINRICH (1794–1874)
...er was a German astronomer who worked
...rtnership with Wilhelm Beer to produce
...rst exact map of the Moon in 1834–36 and
...cription of the Moon in 1837. He invented
...se of letters to identify small craters
...d a larger named one.

...CHELL, EDGAR (1930–)
...r was an American astronaut who was the
...o 14 Lunar Module pilot, and one of the
...en to have walked on the Moon.

...ORE, SIR PATRICK (1923–)
...British amateur astronomer Patrick Moore
...ll known as a television host and author of
...100 books. His main astronomical interest
...een studying and charting the Moon.

...MYTH, JAMES (1808–1890)
...yth was a successful British engineer
...ndustrialist who took up telescope-making.
...ecame very interested in observing the

English scientist Isaac Newton

Moon and discovering the origin of craters.
He wrote an influential book, with the help
of James Carpenter, a professional astronomer,
and argued that lunar craters were volcanic.

NEWTON, ISAAC (1643–1727)
Newton was one of the greatest scientists of all
time. He was made a professor at Cambridge
University in England when only 26. His first
research on gravity, in 1665, concerned the
motion of the Moon. He later set out his law of
universal gravitation.

RICCIOLI, GIOVANNI (1598–1671)
In 1651, this Italian astronomer published a
map of the Moon, which had been drawn by
Francisco Grimaldi. On this map, Riccioli gave
many craters names that are still in use today.

SCHMIDT, JOHANN (1825–1884)
Schmidt was a German astronomer who spent a
lifetime making drawings of the Moon from
which he produced a map in 1874. It was the
first map to improve on the one made by Beer
and Mädler in 1834–36.

SCHMITT, HARRISON (1935–)
An American astronaut who was the Apollo 17
Lunar Module pilot, Schmitt was one of the 12
men to have walked on the Moon. Trained as a
geologist, he was the first scientist-astronaut.
He later served as a US Senator.

SCHRÖTER, JOHANN (1745–1816)
The German astronomer Schröter trained in
law and then began a legal and administrative
career. He also set up a private observatory.
There he made an important study of the Moon
and published books on the subject in 1791
and 1802.

SCOTT, DAVID (1932–)
Scott was an American astronaut who made
three space flights. The first two were on
Gemini 8 and Apollo 9. As Commander of
Apollo 15, he became one of the 12 astronauts
who walked on the Moon.

SHEPARD, ALAN (1923–1998)
Shepard was an astronaut who became the first
American to travel into space. He was also
Apollo 14 Commander and one of the 12
astronauts who landed on the Moon.

SHOEMAKER, EUGENE (1928–1997)
This American geologist founded the science of
lunar and planetary geology, and showed that
craters are formed by impacts. He was unable to
become an astronaut because of a health
problem, but the spacecraft Lunar Prospector
carried some of his ashes to the Moon. The crater
where it crashed was named in his honor.

VAN LANGREN, MICHIEL FLORANT
(1600–1675)
The Dutch cartographer Van Langren was the
first person to make a proper map of the Moon
and name its features in a systematic way,
though his names are no longer used.

VON BRAUN, WERNHER (1912–1977)
This German-born rocket scientist was behind
the V-2 rocket of World War II but later directed
the development of the Saturn rockets used
for NASA's Apollo Moon program (see
pages 172-173).

WEBB, JAMES (1906–1992)
Webb was the NASA Administrator
in 1961–68. He used his political and
administrative skills to achieve the goal
set by President Kennedy of landing men
on the Moon. The replacement for the Hubble
Space Telescope is being named the James
Webb Space Telescope in his honor.

WHITAKER, EWEN (1922–)
Whitaker is a British-born American scientist
who is the leading expert on the naming of
lunar features. He has written a history of lunar
mapping and was responsible for a system of
giving letter designations to smaller craters on
the lunar far side.

YOUNG, JOHN (1930–)
This American astronaut became the first
astronaut to make six flights. These were on
Gemini 3, Gemini 10, Apollo 10, Apollo 16,
and the first and ninth flights of the Space
Shuttle. As Apollo 16 Commander he landed
on the Moon, and is one of only three people
to have flown to the Moon twice.

Eugene Shoemaker, the founder of
lunar and planetary geology

Find out more

THE BEST WAY TO START finding out more about the
Moon is to look at it for yourself. Even if you do not have
a telescope or binoculars, you can still make out its main
dark areas and the bright crater Tycho, which are marked
on the map on page 149. You can follow the Moon's
monthly cycle by drawing sketches or taking notes of its
phases and the dates and times when you see them. See if
you can also spot the Moon during daylight or when it is
just a thin crescent in the western sky soon after sunset.

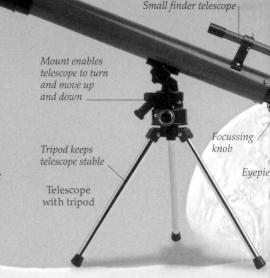

Small finder telescope

*Mount enables
telescope to turn
and move up
and down*

*Focussing
knob*

*Tripod keeps
telescope stable*

Eyepie

Telescope
with tripod

SKETCHING THE MOON
You do not need to be good at
art to try sketching part of the
Moon. Look at some craters
near the dividing line between
the bright and dark parts of
the Moon through
binoculars or a
telescope. Their long
shadows make them
stand out. Draw simple
outlines, then shade
in the shadows.

TELESCOPES
The Moon is the easiest object in the sky to
observe with a small telescope. You will be
to see many more features than by eye alor
Use the map on pages 200–201 to help you
identify some of the main craters and maria
Keep in mind that the image you see throu
an astronomical telescope is usually upside
down—with south at the top.

USEFUL WEBSITES

- Lunar Picture of the Day (LPOD)
  features a different image every day:
  http://lpod.wikispaces.com/

- Find pictures and information about
  the Apollo missions here:
  http://www.apolloarchive.com/

- This site has a timeline with links to
  the details of every lunar space missio
  http://nssdc.gsfc.nasa.gov/planetar
  lunar/lunartimeline.html

- Visit NASA's eclipse site to discover
  more about past and future eclipses,
  and for a table of the Moon's phases:
  http://eclipse.gsfc.nasa.gov/eclipse.
  html

- Google Moon has a collection of
  interactive maps. There are also pictu
  stories for each Apollo landing:
  http://www.google.com/moon/

- This page from *Sky & Telescope*
  magazine's website has helpful article
  about observing the Moon:
  http://www.skyandtelescope.com/
  observing/objects/moon/

- Two NASA websites carry the latest
  news on NASA's progress toward
  returning astronauts to the Moon:
  http://www.nasa.gov/mission_
  pages/exploration/main/index.htm
  http://www.nasa.gov/mission_
  pages/constellation/main/index.htr

- For a list of all features on the Moon, vi
  http://planetarynames.wr.usgs.gov/

*Hold binoculars as steady
as you can or rest them
against something firm*

OBSERVING THE MOON
Using binoculars is an ideal way to start exploring
the Moon in more detail. They do not have to be
special—the ordinary kind you might use for
bird-watching will do. You will get to know the
Moon best if you keep looking on different
nights when the Moon is at different phases.

*Sleeping bag keeps you
warm and comfortable
when observing outside*

SPACE CENTER HOUSTON
The visitor center at NASA's Lyndon B. Johnson Space Center in Texas is called Space Center Houston. The Astronaut Gallery displays the world's best collection of spacesuits, and on the walls are photographs of every American astronaut who has flown in space. Visitors can also see real spacecraft in the Starship Gallery and take a behind-the-scenes tram tour to see parts of the Johnson Space Center.

KENNEDY SPACE CENTER
In the Apollo/Saturn V [Ce]nter at the Kennedy Space Center visitor complex in Florida, visitors see this [re]al Saturn V rocket, like the ones used to launch the Apollo astronauts to the Moon. This display is just one of many exhibits and [at]tractions on the huge site. [Vi]sitors who are lucky might even see a rocket lift off in the distance from one of the launch pads.

Schoolchildren getting a close-up view of the spacesuit

Shenzhou 6 mission patch

Places to visit

AMERICAN MUSEUM OF NATURAL HISTORY, NEW YORK, NEW YORK
The museum's Rose Center for Earth and Space features such exhibits as:
- a gallery of more than 75 rarely seen photos from the Apollo Moon missions
- a world-class planetarium featuring a virtual field trip to the Moon and other shows

JET PROPULSION LABORATORY, PASADENA, CALIFORNIA
JPL sent the first robotic craft to the Moon in the 1960s, and today is engaged in a wide variety of space missions. Guided tours must be reserved in advance:

US SPACE AND ROCKET CENTER, HUNTSVILLE, ALABAMA
Home to the famous Space Camp program, the USSRC features:
- rides that mimic the experience of space flight
- original and replica spacecraft, including the Saturn V used in the Apollo program

SMITHSONIAN NATIONAL AIR AND SPACE MUSEUM, WASHINGTON DC, AND CHANTILLY, VIRGINIA
This museum has more spacecraft than any other in the world. The large exhibits at Chantilly, Virginia, include the Space Shuttle *Enterprise*. Among the huge number of items on show in Washington DC are:
- the actual Apollo 11 Command Module
- a piece of Moon rock visitors can touch

KENNEDY SPACE CENTER, FLORIDA
The NASA center from where all of the US's manned space flights have been launched has impressive facilities for visitors. You can:
- see a full-size Space Shuttle replica
- enter a full-size mockup of an International Space Station module
- have lunch with an astronaut

SPACE CENTER HOUSTON, TEXAS
This huge complex has a fantastic range of exhibits, demonstrations, and theaters including:
- Real Mercury, Gemini, and Apollo space capsules
  - A module that simulates living in space

CHINA AEROSPACE EXHIBITION
Keep a look out for temporary space exhibitions coming to your area. This model spacesuit was on display at a temporary Aerospace Exhibition in Chengdu, Sichuan Province, China, when the picture was taken in October 2005. The spacesuit was a special attraction because the crew of China's second manned spaceflight had successfully landed less than two weeks earlier, in their Shenzhou 6 spacecraft, after a flight of 75 Earth orbits taking nearly 5 days. They had worn suits similar to this one during the mission.

Glossary

ANTENNA
A device, usually a dish or a rod, used for receiving and/or sending radio signals.

APOGEE
The point farthest from Earth in the orbit of the Moon or of an artificial Earth satellite.

ASTEROID
A small body made of rock and/or metal orbiting the Sun.

ASTRONAUT
A person who travels into space or who has trained to do so.

ATMOSPHERE
A layer of gas surrounding a planet, moon, or star.

Cosmonaut Alexandr Kaleri

ATTITUDE CONTROL
Changing or holding a spacecraft's direction of travel.

BASALT
A dark gray rock formed when lava solidifies. It is found in the mare areas of the Moon.

BASIN
A very large impact crater, more than 190 miles (300 km) wide.

CALDERA
A large volcanic crater, formed when the top of a volcano collapses.

CHEMICAL ELEMENT
One of the basic materials of which all matter in the universe is made. About 90 occur naturally, such as oxygen, carbon, and iron.

CINDER CONE
A steep-sided cone-shaped hill around a volcanic vent where lava has erupted.

CORONA
The outer layers of the Sun, which are seen as a white halo during a total solar eclipse.

COSMONAUT
A person who travels into space under the Russian space program (or did so under the former Soviet Union's space program).

CRATER
A bowl-shaped depression in the ground, with a raised rim. Craters can be caused by an impact or by a volcano.

CRUST
The outer layers of rock on a planet or moon.

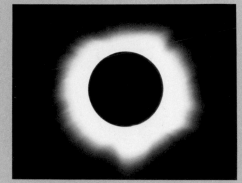

Eclipse of the Sun by the Moon

DWARF PLANET
A small planet, such as Pluto, which is spherical rather than irregular in shape and orbits the Sun as part of a belt of other small rocky or icy bodies.

ECLIPSE
When the Moon covers all or part of the Sun in the sky (solar eclipse), or when Earth's shadow is cast on the Moon (lunar eclipse).

ELLIPSE
A shape like an elongated circle.

ESCAPE VELOCITY
The speed an object needs to escape from the gravity of another body. The escape velocity from Earth's surface is about 7 miles per second (11.2 km per second).

GEOLOGIST
A scientist who studies what rocks are made of, how they formed, and how they have changed over time.

GIBBOUS
From a Latin word meaning "hump." The Moon's phase when more than half is illuminated but it is not full.

GRAVITY
Gravity is the force of attraction between two objects caused by their mass. It decreases the farther apart the objects are.

IMPACTOR
An object that hits something else, especially at high speed.

ION DRIVE
A way of propelling a spacecraft with a stream of particles made electrically.

LANDER
A spacecraft that lands on the surface of a moon or planet.

LASER
A device that produces a thin, very powerful beam of light of a specific color. Lasers can be used to determine the exact distance between the Moon and Earth.

Meteorite

LAUNCH VEHICLE
A rocket-powered system to lift a spacecraft into space. Often called a "rocket."

LAVA
Molten (liquid) rock that spews out onto the surface of a planet or moon during a volcanic eruption.

LIBRATION
The slight alteration in the part of the Moon surface visible from Earth.

MAGMA
Underground molten rock.

MANTLE
The layer of rock inside a moon or planet that lies underneath the crust and over the core.

MARE (PLURAL MARIA)
A dark, low-lying plain on the Moon, made solidified lava. The word comes from the Latin for "sea."

METEORITE
A piece of rock and/or metal from space that has landed on the surface of Earth, the Moon or any other planetary body.

METEOROID
A small piece of rock in space, which is not as large as an asteroid and less than about 300 ft (100 m) across.

Launch vehicle

ROGRAVITY
ondition of weightlessness experienced by
nauts when in orbit or in free-fall. Objects
weight on Earth and the Moon as the
nd exerts an upward force the same as the
ward force of gravity. Orbiting and falling
ts are not beyond the pull of gravity, but
experience microgravity because they are
o accelerate toward the source of gravity.

ROMETEOROID
croscopic particle of dust in space.

NTES
Latin word for "mountains," used in the
al names of mountain ranges on the Moon.

A
National Aeronautics and Space
inistration, the American government agency
nsible for non-military activities in space.

ULA
ge cloud of gas and dust among the stars.
olar system, including Earth and the
, formed in a nebula surrounding the Sun.

ULTATION
n one astronomical body passes in front of
bscures another one.

ICAL TELESCOPE
escope for observing visible light.

IT
ath of one astronomical body around
her, or to travel along an orbit.

ITER
acecraft that goes into orbit around Earth,
moon or planet beyond Earth.

GEE
point closest to Earth in the orbit of the
n or of an artificial Earth satellite.

Eagle Nebula

SE
roportion of the disk of the Moon
ny other astronomical object), as
from Earth, that is illuminated
sunlight.

NET
of the larger bodies orbiting the Sun,
imilar body orbiting any star. There are
major planets in our solar system.

NETESIMAL
all clump of rock and/or ice that came
her when our solar system was forming.
etesimals were up to 6 miles (10 km)
s and later merged to form larger
ids and planets.

PRESSURE
The force exerted by something
over 1 sq ft (or 1 m) of area.
Atmospheric pressure is the
pressure due to an atmosphere,
such as Earth's. Because there is
no air pressure in space,
spacesuits must exert
pressure on astronauts'
bodies or they would die.

PROBE
A package of scientific
instruments released
from a spacecraft or
satellite to collect data
about a moon or planet
by traveling down
through its atmospheric
layers and landing on
it or crashing into it.

PROMINENCE
A huge flamelike stream of gas,
visible during a solar eclipse, rising off
the Sun's surface.

RADAR
A method for measuring the distance of
something, or mapping the shape of its surface,
by bouncing radio waves off it. The word "radar"
stands for RAdio Detection And Ranging.

RADIO TELESCOPE
Equipment for collecting and analyzing natural
radio signals from objects in space. Most radio
telescopes use a large dish to collect and focus
the signals.

REGOLITH
The loose material like dust, sand, or soil
found on the surface of the Moon.

RILLE
A valley on the Moon. Some were formed
when surface rocks dropped down between
two long cracks or faults. Others were made
by lava flows. The word comes from the
German for "groove."

ROCKET
An engine that makes a launch vehicle move
forward by burning chemical fuel and driving
hot gas backward through a nozzle. "Rocket" is
also often used to mean an entire launch
vehicle, including the equipment to
guide and control it.

ROVER
A robotic explorer placed on the surface
of a moon or planet, which can drive around
on wheels, or a vehicle used by astronauts
to travel on the surface of the Moon.

RUPES
A feature on the Moon that is in the shape
of a cliff or a slope. From the Latin for "cliff."

SATELLITE
A small object, either natural or man-made,
in orbit around a larger one.

SEISMOMETER
An instrument for collecting data about
earthquakes or moonquakes.

SINUS
The Latin word for "bay," used in the names
of some features on the Moon.

Meteosat weather
satellite

SOLAR SYSTEM
The Sun and everything
in orbit around it.

SPACE
Anywhere farther from Earth
than about 60–75 miles
(100–120 km).

SPACECRAFT
A vehicle that travels through
space. Spacecraft may
transport astronauts
or cargo, or carry
instruments to study
objects in the solar system.
Unmanned spacecraft in
orbit around Earth are
usually called satellites.

SPACEWALK
Activity by an astronaut in space
outside his or her spacecraft.
Spacewalks are formally called
"extra-vehicular activities," or EVAs.

SPACE AGE
The present period of history in which
space has been explored by humans and
robots. It started in 1957 with the launch
of the first artificial satellite, Sputnik 1.

SPACE RACE
The competition between the USSR and
the US in the 1960s to achieve important goals
in space, especially landing humans on
the Moon.

SPACE STATION
A large, habitable Earth satellite, where
different crews of astronauts or cosmonauts
can live and conduct scientific research
over periods ranging from a few days
to many months.

**TRANSIENT LUNAR PHENOMENON
(TLP)**
A temporary change on the Moon's surface.

ULTRAVIOLET RADIATION
A type of radiation similar to light, but invisible
and more powerful.

VOLCANO
A place where molten rock from underground
comes to the surface through a crack or tube,
called a vent.

Spacewalk from the Space Shuttle

Acknowledgments

Dorling Kindersley would like to thank: Stewart J. Wild for proofreading; Hilary Bird for the index; Margaret Parrish and John Searcy for Americanization.

The publisher would like to thank the following for their kind permission to reproduce their photographs:

(Key: a-above; b-below/bottom; c-center; l-left; r-right; t-top)

akg-images: 147cr; Bibliothèque Nationale, Paris 206br; Bildarchiv Steffens 146tr; **Alamy Images:** Arco Images GmbH 163br (Feather); Flancer 152r; John Henshall 209c; Scott Hortop 153br; The London Art Archive 200clb, 207tc; mediacolor's 165tl; North Wind Picture Archives 201br; Photos 12 172bl; David White 167tr; WorldFoto 161t; **The Bridgeman Art Library:** Private Collection / Bonhams, London / 196tl; **Ben Bussey:** 165cr, 166-167ca, 167cr, 201tc; **Corbis:** Yann Arthus-Bertrand 164tr; Pallava Bagla 193cr; Bettmann 159br, 185br, 204bc; Richard Cummins 209tl; EPA / Sanjeev Gupta 155bl; Hulton-Deutsch Collection 173tl; Karen Kasmauski 192tl; Yevgeny Khaldei 174bl; Roger Ressmeyer 5cra, 155ca, 155tr, 166ca, 166tl, 207br; Reuters 155br; Rykoff Collection 175br; Sean Sexton Collection 171tr, 204cl; after *The Discovery of a World in the Moone*, 1638 by John Wilkins 148br; **DK Images:** Courtesy of The British Library, London. Shelfmark Or.7964 p.1620 / Laurence Pordes 155tl; The British Museum, London / Peter Hayman 146tl; CONACULTA-INAH-MEX. Authorized reproduction by the Instituto Nacional de Antropologia e Historia / Peter Wilson 147cl; Courtesy of Bob Gathany / Andy Crawford 182tr; NASA 190br, 210tc; National Maritime Museum, London / Tina Chambers 169t; Courtesy of The Natural History Museum, London / Colin Keates 163bl (Hammer), 210tr; Rough Guides / Tim Draper 146-147b; Rough Guides / Mark Thomas 211cra; Courtesy of The Science Museum, London / Dave King 5t, 170-171t; Courtesy of The Science Museum, London / James Stevenson 183cr; **ESA:** 2002 192br; 168cl, 215cr; **FLPA:** B. Borrell Casals 156tr, 157cra; after *From the Earth to the Moon*, 1865 by Jules Verne 172tl; **Galaxy Picture Library:** Pete Lawrence 151tr; Thierry Legault 160br; Damian Peach 200bc; Robin Scagell 150bl, 151cr, 153bl; Michael Stecker 155c; **Getty Images:** AFP / Tim Sloan 194cl; The Bridgeman Art Library 206tr; China Photos 147tl, 209bl; Chinafotopress 199cla; Keystone 171cr; National Geographic / Otis Imboden 184tl; Time Life Pictures / NASA 166-167tc; Time Life Pictures / Time Magazine 204tr; Courtesy of the **X PRIZE Foundation:** 193bc; **Honeysuckle Creek Tracking Station** (www.honeysucklecreek.net): Colin Mackellar 181br; **Imagine China:** 193l; iStockphoto.com: 154t; Adrian Beesley 176bl; Courtesy of JAXA: 164tl, 205tr; Akihiro Ikeshita 193tr; **The Kobal Collection:** George Pal Prods 161br; Universal 186tr; **Moulinsart 2008:** © Hergé 173br; **NASA:** 148tr, 149tc, 171br, 175tl, 180tl, 183bl, 190bl, 195br, 195crb, 196b, 196cl, 197br, 197cra, 198br, 201crb, 203cr; Ames Research Center 5bl, 192bl, 194bl; Dryden Flight Research Center 191br, 206cl; ESA / JPL / University of Arizona / USGS 168bl; ESA and The Hubble Heritage Team (STScI/AURA) 211clb; GSFC / Image created by Reto Stöckli, Nazmi El Saleous and Marit Jentoft-Nilsen 109r; Johnson Space Center 175c, 191tr, 195tr, 197tr, 198c, 211br; Johnson Space Center / Pat Rawlings (SAIC) 197tl; JPL 168cr, 168tl, 169clb, 177tl, 146cl, 188cl, 200cla; JPL - Caltech / University of Arizona 168br; JPL / Space Science Institute 169cra; JPL / University of Arizona 168ca, 169cb (Europa), 169cla, 169crb; JPL / USGS 148l, 169cb (Moon), 203bc, 203tc; Kennedy Space Center 175tr, 178tl; MSFC 172cl, 173tr, 194-195c, 198bl, 199r, 210br, 210cla; National Geographic Society 172-173bc; NSSDC 165cb, 165tr, 176tr, 177bc, 192cr, 202clb; NSSDC / USGS 192c; Project Apollo Archive 5cla, 160b, 162tl, 163bl, 163cb, 163tc, 163tl, 164-165bc, 165br, 165ca, 175bl, 177br, 178cla, 179bl, 180bl, 180-181bc, 181cr, 181tl, 184cl, 184-185bc, 185cra, 185tc, 185tl, 186bl, 187bc, 187tl, 187tr, 190cl, 202bl, 203cra, 204-205 (Background), 205bl, 206-207 (Background), 208-209 (Background), 210-211 (Background); Saturn Apollo Program 187cr; Sean Smith 195cra; Image courtesy **History of Science Collections, University of Oklahoma Libraries;** copyright the Board of Regents of the University of Oklahoma: 207cl; **PA Photos:** Pat Sullivan 183br; **Photolibrary:** I Paterson 208cl; **Rex Features:** Aldo Patella 167tc; SNAP 173cr; **Photo Scala, Florence:** Biblioteca Nazionale, Florence 170cla; Courtesy of the **Charles M. Schulz Museum and Research Center, Santa Rosa, California:** 181tr; **Science & Society Picture Library:** 170bl, 171tl; **Science Photo Library:** Jean-Loup Charmet 152bl; Mark Garlick 158tl; Gary Hincks 162b; NASA 187tc; Pekka Parviainen 148cr, 149bl; Roger Ressmeyer 158bl; Ria Novosti 174br, 176cl, 177cr, 189tr, 189tl; after *Selenotopographische Fragmente*, 1791 by Johann Hieronymus Schröter 170tl; **Still Pictures:** Andia.fr / Godard 156-157b, Biosphoto / Vincent Decorde 151tl; SplashdownDirect / Michael Nolan 151br; **USGS:** 169br; Courtesy **Virgin Galactic:** 199bl; **Werner Forman Archive:** Sheldon Jackson Museum, Sitka, Alaska 147tr.

All other images © Dorling Kindersley
For further information see:
www.dkimages.com

STARS
PLANETS
WORKBOOK

EYEWITNESS WORKBOOKS
STARS & PLANETS

by Claire Watts

How this book can help your child

The **Eyewitness Workbooks** series offers a fun and colorful range of stimulating titles on the subjects of history, science, and geography. Specially designed to appeal to children of 9 years and up, each workbook aims to:

- develop a child's knowledge of a popular topic
- provide practice of key skills and reinforce classroom learning
- nurture a child's special interest in a subject.

The series is devised and written with the expert advice of an educational consultant and supports the school curriculum.

About this book

Eyewitness Workbook Stars and Planets is an activity-packed exploration of the world of space and astronomy. Inside you will find:

Fast facts

This section presents key information as concise facts, which are easy to digest, learn, and remember. Encourage your child to start by reading through the valuable information in the Fast facts section before trying out the activities.

Activities

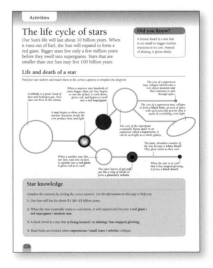

The enjoyable, fill-in activities are designed to develop information recall and help your child practice cross-referencing skills. Each activity can be completed using information provided on the page, in the Fast facts section. Your child should work systematically through the book and tackle just one or two activity topics per session. Encourage your child by checking answers together and offering extra guidance when necessary.

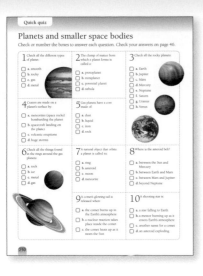

Quick quiz

There are six pages of multiple-choice questions to test your child's newfound knowledge of the subject. Children should only try answering the quiz questions once all of the activity section has been completed. As your child finishes each page of themed questions, check the answers together.

Answers and Progress chart

All the answers are supplied in full at the back of the book, so no prior knowledge of the subject is required.

Use the Progress chart to motivate your child and be positive about his or her achievements. On the completion of each activity or quiz topic, reward good work with a gold star.

Certificate

There is a certificate of achievement at the back of the book for your child to fill in, remove, and display on the wall.

Important information

• Please stress upon your child the importance of heeding the warnings in this book. Never look directly at the Sun or try to view it using a telescope, binoculars, or a mirror. Only view a solar eclipse when wearing approved protective goggles, or view it indirectly with a pinhole camera.

• Be patient when observing the night sky outdoors, since it will take about 20 minutes for your eyes to adjust to the dark. Always dress warmly and use a red filter over a flashlight, so that it doesn't affect your night vision.

Stars and galaxies

Each tiny star twinkling in the sky is a huge, distant ball of superhot gas, like our Sun. Each star is part of a group, called a galaxy, that may contain millions of stars. For thousands of years, astronomers gazing at the stars organized them into easily recognizable patterns, called constellations, to create a map of the skies.

Stars

The sky at night

A star is a huge ball of gas made up mainly of hydrogen. It has a temperature of tens of millions of degrees. The hydrogen fuels nuclear reactions that produce huge amounts of energy. Stars give off most of their energy as light and heat, but they also give off radiation, such as ultraviolet rays and X-rays.

Key facts

- All stars look similar to the naked eye, but in fact they vary in their size, brightness, temperature, and color.
- The stars are hurtling through space at immense speed, but we cannot see this movement because they are so distant.
- Most stars form part of a system containing two or more stars held together by gravity.

Constellations

Astronomers group the brightest stars into constellations. Many constellations are named after characters in ancient mythology, such as Orion and Andromeda. From Earth, the stars in a constellation appear to be close together. In fact, they are great distances apart, but lie in a similar direction to Earth.

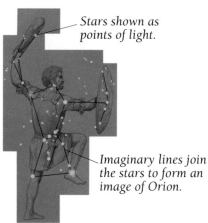

Stars shown as points of light.

Imaginary lines join the stars to form an image of Orion.

The constellation of Orion

Key facts

- Astronomers map the sky by dividing it into 88 areas. Each contains a different constellation.
- Different constellations can be seen from Earth's Northern and Southern hemispheres.
- Constellations such as Orion that lie along the celestial equator can be seen from both hemispheres.

Galaxies

Every star is part of a vast, spinning group of stars, gas, and dust called a galaxy. The matter in a galaxy is held together by the force of gravity. Galaxies are divided into three main types, according to their shape: spiral, elliptical (oval-shaped), or irregular.

Types of galaxy

Spiral galaxy

Elliptical galaxy

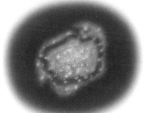

Irregular galaxy

Key facts

- The tiniest dwarf galaxies contain only a few million stars, but giant galaxies can contain hundreds of billions of stars.
- There are about 100 billion galaxies in the part of the universe that we can observe.
- Our home galaxy, the Milky Way, contains about 200 billion stars.
- Galaxies are grouped together in clusters.

The solar system

Our nearest star, the Sun, lies along one of the arms of our galaxy, the Milky Way. Earth and seven other planets orbit (move around) the Sun. Smaller bodies, such as moons, asteroids, and comets, orbit the Sun or the planets. All these bodies, together with the Sun, make up the solar system.

The Sun

The Sun at the center of our solar system is a relatively small star, known as a yellow dwarf. Like other stars, the Sun's energy is generated by nuclear reactions at its core. The effects of the Sun's light, heat, and radiation can be felt at the farthest edge of the solar system.

Key facts

- The Sun contains 750 times more matter than all the other bodies in the solar system put together.
- The Sun's surface is white-hot hydrogen, with a temperature of almost 10,000°F (5,500°C).
- The Sun's dense core has a temperature of 27 million °F (15 million °C).
- As it is a ball of gas, the Sun does not all rotate at the same speed. Its equator rotates in 25 Earth days, but its poles take 34 days.

Solar system

The solar system measures about 9,300 billion miles (15,000 billion km) across. The eight planets—Mercury, Venus, Earth, Mars, Jupiter, Saturn, Uranus, and Neptune—occupy only the inner 3.25 billion miles (6 billion km). They travel around the Sun in elliptical (oval) paths known as orbits, trapped by the pull of the Sun's gravity.

Key facts

- All the planets orbit the Sun in the same direction, which is the same direction that the Sun spins on its own axis (the imaginary line from pole to pole).
- The four planets nearest the Sun—Mercury, Venus, Earth, and Mars—are known as the inner planets.
- The other four planets—Jupiter, Saturn, Uranus, and Neptune—are known as the outer planets.

Asteroids

Asteroids are pieces of rock that orbit the Sun. They measure from about 160 ft (50 m) to 600 miles (1,000 km) across.

Asteroid Ida

Key facts

- Most asteroids are found in the asteroid belt, which lies between the planets Mars and Jupiter.
- Asteroids often collide, breaking into pieces or clumping together to form larger asteroids.

Comets

A comet is a chunk of ice and rock a few miles across that orbits the Sun, often in the far reaches of the solar system. If a comet nears the Sun it heats up, releasing a glowing tail of dust and gas.

Gas tail

Nucleus of snow and dust

Glowing head

Cross-section of a comet

Dust tail

Key facts

- Comets only become visible as they approach the Sun.
- When Earth passes through the dust from past comets, specks of rock burn up in the atmosphere, producing meteor showers.

Venus   Mars   Saturn   Neptune

Mercury   Earth   Jupiter   Uranus

Sun

The Sun and solar system (not to scale)

217

Planets

A planet is a spherical body that orbits the Sun or another star. There are eight planets in our solar system. These can be divided into two groups: the four rocky planets nearest to the Sun, and the four gas giants beyond the asteroid belt. Most of these planets have bodies orbiting them, known as moons.

Moons

Jupiter's moon Callisto

A moon is a natural object that travels in orbit around a planet. Moons may be the size of a small planet, or just a few miles across. All the planets except Mercury and Venus have moons. Some moons are made from material left over from when their planet formed. Others are asteroids that have been pulled into a planet's orbit by the force of its gravity.

Rocky planets

The four planets nearest to the Sun—Mercury, Venus, Earth, and Mars—are made of rocks and metals. Mercury and Mars have solid iron cores, while the solid cores of Venus and Earth contain iron and nickel. The rocky surfaces of Mercury, Venus, and Mars have many craters. These were formed when the planets were bombarded by rocks from space, called meteorites.

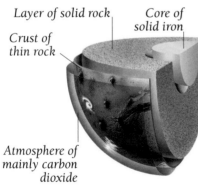

Layer of solid rock *Core of solid iron*
Crust of thin rock
Atmosphere of mainly carbon dioxide

Cross-section through Mars

Key facts

- The rocky planets are smaller than the gas planets.
- Earth and Mars are the only rocky planets to have moons.
- The rocky planets have no rings around them.
- Their atmospheres contain very little hydrogen and helium.

Gas planets

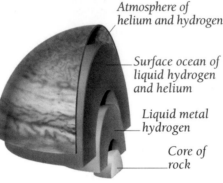

Atmosphere of helium and hydrogen
Surface ocean of liquid hydrogen and helium
Liquid metal hydrogen
Core of rock

Cross-section through Jupiter

Beyond the orbit of Mars lie the four much larger planets—Uranus, Neptune, Saturn, and Jupiter—known as the gas giants. Unlike the rocky planets, these planets do not have solid surfaces. Each has a small, rocky core, surrounded by swirling gases and liquids, and is held together by the force of gravity.

Key facts

- The gas giants have deep, often stormy atmospheres.
- Each gas giant is orbited by a large number of moons.
- A gas giant has a belt of rings, made up of pieces of rock and ice.
- There is high pressure inside the gas giants. This produces more heat from inside these planets than they receive from the Sun.

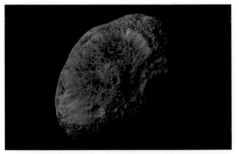

Saturn's moon Hyperion

Key facts

- Earth's single moon is simply called "the Moon," but other planets' moons have names.
- There are more than 120 known moons in our solar system.
- Moons are smaller than the planets they orbit.
- Many small moons, such as Hyperion, are not spherical.

Planet Earth

Earth is the only planet we know of where living things exist. It is just near enough to the Sun to give the planet a stable and mild climate, and to allow water to exist in its liquid form. In contrast, our Moon is a barren, airless rock, where no life can survive.

The blue planet

From space, Earth looks like a blue globe, encircled by swirling white clouds. Earth is the only planet with a plentiful supply of water. This not only makes life possible here, but also shapes many of the features of the planet's surface and has a vital role in creating the weather.

Oceans cover more than 70 percent of Earth's surface.

Earth viewed from space

Key facts

- Earth's atmosphere is made up mainly of nitrogen, oxygen, and carbon dioxide.
- Oxygen in the atmosphere allows humans and animals to breathe.
- Oxygen also forms the ozone layer which protects Earth from radiation from space.
- Carbon dioxide allows plants to survive and create more oxygen.

Earth's orbit

Earth orbits the Sun at a distance of about 93 million miles (150 million km). The time it takes for a planet to orbit the Sun is called its year. Like other planets, Earth also rotates on its axis as it travels. The time it takes a planet to rotate once is its day.

Key facts

- Earth rotates on its axis once every 23 hours 56 minutes. We round this to 24 hours in a day.
- Earth orbits the Sun once every 365.26 days. We round this to 365 days in a normal year.
- The Earth's elliptical (oval) orbit brings it 3 million miles (5 million km) closer to the Sun in January than it is in July.
- Earth orbits the Sun at a speed of 62,000 mph (100,000 kph).

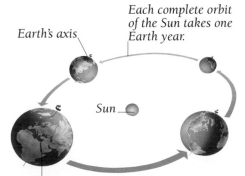

Earth's axis

Each complete orbit of the Sun takes one Earth year.

Sun

Each complete rotation on its axis takes one Earth day.

Earth days and years

The Moon

The Moon orbits Earth, following Earth's journey around the Sun. The Moon does not give off any light of its own, but reflects light from the Sun. As the Moon's position changes relative to the Sun and the Earth, different amounts of moonlight are visible from Earth. The Moon appears to change shape in the sky, starting as a round Full Moon, waning (shrinking) to an invisible New Moon, then waxing (growing) from a crescent to a Full Moon.

The crescent Moon in the night sky

Key facts

- The Moon orbits Earth once every 27.3 days.
- The Moon spins on its axis in exactly the same time that it takes to orbit Earth, so it always has the same side turned toward Earth.
- The Moon takes 29.5 days to go through all its phases (shapes). This is called a lunar month.
- The Moon is more than a quarter the size of Earth, making it the biggest object in the night sky.

The universe

The Earth is just one small planet in a solar system orbiting a star, which is part of a galaxy of 200 billion stars. That galaxy is just one of tens of billions of galaxies that make up the universe. The universe is so large that light from its most distant galaxies takes about 10 billion years to reach us.

The Big Bang

The universe explodes into existence in the Big Bang.

Astronomers believe that the universe began about 14 billion years ago with an explosion known as the Big Bang. The Big Bang created an incredibly hot and dense universe, smaller than an atom. In a fraction of a second, the universe began to cool and expand in every direction, a process that is still continuing today.

Key facts

- Before the Big Bang, there was nothing: no space, no time, and no matter.
- Scientists do not know what triggered the Big Bang.
- The planets, solar systems, and galaxies are not expanding. It is the space in between the galaxies which is stretching.

How stars form

A star forms from a spinning cloud of gas and dust, called a nebula. The center of the nebula becomes denser and hotter and begins to pull more and more material into itself. Eventually, the center of the nebula becomes so hot and dense that a nuclear reaction takes place, and the star begins to shine.

Key facts

- Galaxies began to form one to two billion years after the Big Bang.
- Our Sun was formed about 4.6 billion years ago.
- Stars are continually being born and dying in the universe.

Spinning dust and gas

Nebula

Excess material may form planets.

New star

How planets form

As matter spins around a new star, it clumps together to form small bodies called protoplanets. Their gravity pulls in more material, until they form planets.

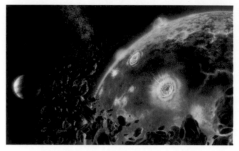

Material is pulled toward a protoplanet by gravity.

Key facts

- Rocky planets are hot and molten when they first form.
- Gas planets form a solid core, then attract vast amounts of gas.

Evolving universe

Some scientists believe that the universe can only expand to a certain size. In billions of years' time, it will shrink and finally collapse. Others believe the universe will go on expanding for ever at the same speed, or at a slower rate.

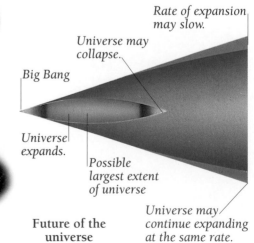

Rate of expansion may slow.

Universe may collapse.

Big Bang

Universe expands.

Possible largest extent of universe

Future of the universe

Universe may continue expanding at the same rate.

Looking at space

Astronomers get most of their information about space by studying pictures and other information from observatories, either on Earth or in orbit around Earth. Scientists have also sent robot probes out into space to visit the planets, asteroids, and comets, giving us close-up views that are impossible to see from Earth.

Observatories

An observatory is a dome that contains a giant telescope. The top of the observatory can turn to face different parts of the sky. Most observatories are located high in the mountains, above the clouds and away from populated areas, where lights make it difficult to get a clear view of the night sky.

Key facts

- Optical telescopes focus light from distant objects and make them clearer.
- Professional astronomers do not actually look through their telescopes. They use them to record images on film or on computers.
- Different types of telescopes can also reveal rays of light that are invisible to human eyes, such as radio waves.

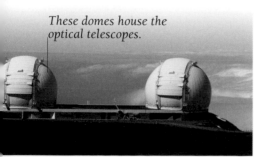

These domes house the optical telescopes.

Mauna Kea Observatory in Hawaii

Space observatories

Space observatories orbit Earth above the atmosphere and give astronomers a clear view of space. Some space observatories, such as the Hubble Space Telescope, are optical telescopes. Others, such as the Chandra X-ray Observatory, view wavelengths that would normally be absorbed by Earth's atmosphere.

Large solar panels power the telescope.

Hubble Space Telescope

Key facts

- A space observatory receives instructions from Earth and transmits images and other data back via an antenna.
- Astronauts visit some observatories regularly to maintain and update them. Others have a limited life and are then abandoned in space.
- Space observatories can record gamma rays, X-rays, ultraviolet rays, and infrared rays.

Space probes

A probe is a robot spacecraft sent to investigate space using onboard instruments. The probe flies past or orbits a body in space and sends data and images back to Earth. A probe may also release a lander, to land on the planet, moon, or asteroid beneath it and survey the surface.

Cassini space probe and Saturn

Key facts

- Most space probes are about the size of a family car.
- Space probes are powered by solar panels or a nuclear generator.
- Space probes have given us close-ups of moons, comets, asteroids, and each of the planets.
- After they have completed their missions, some space probes continue out into space, although they can no longer send signals back to Earth.

Galileo space probe

Space travel

Human space travel began in 1961, when the Russian Yuri Gagarin orbited Earth. US astronauts landed on the Moon eight years later. Today, more than 400 astronauts have traveled into space in rockets or on the space shuttle. In the foreseeable future, astronauts may set up bases on the Moon and may even travel to Mars.

Rockets

A space rocket lifts off from the ground and propels itself into orbit by means of a controlled explosion. Fuel is burned in a combustion chamber to produce a mass of hot gases. The gases expand and explode out of the nozzles at the bottom of the rocket, thrusting it upward.

Key facts

- As the rocket moves away from the pull of Earth's gravity, it can travel much faster.

- Because there is no oxygen in space, a rocket must carry a supply of oxygen to burn its fuel.

- Each section, or stage, of a space rocket fires until its fuel is used up, then falls away.

Astronauts traveled in the third stage.

Second stage

First stage

Saturn V rocket

Landing craft

Camera takes pictures of the area ahead.

Six wheels allow flexibility on bumpy ground.

Mars rover

A manned or unmanned vehicle can land on a planet, moon, or asteroid, collect samples, take photographs, and conduct experiments. The landing craft has to be designed to function in difficult surface conditions, such as extreme temperatures or very low gravity. A rover vehicle has wheels so that it can survey a wider area.

Key facts

- Mars is the only planet that has been visited by robot vehicles. The rovers found frozen water in the Martian rocks.

- The Moon is the only body that humans have landed on.

- On three of the six missions to the Moon, astronauts used a vehicle called a lunar rover to travel around on the Moon's surface.

Space shuttle

The space shuttle was the first reusable spacecraft. It is made up of a winged orbiter that carries the crew and the cargo, twin booster rockets, and a fuel tank. It takes off like a rocket, but lands like an aircraft. Since the first space shuttle, *Columbia*, was launched in 1981, space shuttles have visited space regularly.

Space shuttle on takeoff

Key facts

- The space shuttle is used to launch space probes and satellites, and to carry out repairs and construction work in space.

- There are three space shuttle orbiters, named *Discovery*, *Atlantis*, and *Endeavour*.

- The external fuel tank is the only part that cannot be reused.

Silica tiles protect the shuttle from burning up as it reenters Earth's atmosphere.

Space shuttle landing

Living in space

Only 26 astronauts have traveled beyond Earth's orbit as far as the Moon. Most astronauts orbit Earth in their spacecraft, or travel to space stations. Their mission may be to release a satellite into orbit, to perform maintenance to a space station or an observatory, or to conduct experiments into conditions in space.

Astronauts

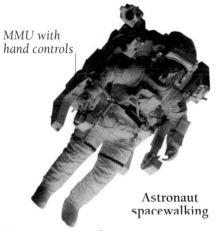

MMU with hand controls

Astronaut spacewalking

A person traveling in space is called an astronaut, or cosmonaut if he or she is part of a Russian mission. Astronauts train for over a year before making their first space flights. Most are experts in one or more sciences, so they can carry out scientific research while they are in space.

Key facts

- Astronauts have to be extremely fit to withstand conditions in space.
- A spacesuit is worn outside the spacecraft to protect the astronaut from temperature extremes and to provide oxygen.
- Spacewalking astronauts are attached to the craft by tethers, or use a powered backpack, called a Manned Maneuvering Unit (MMU), so they do not float away.

Space stations

A space station is a spacecraft designed to stay in Earth's orbit for many years. On board, astronauts conduct experiments to discover how conditions in space affect people, plants, and animals. Astronauts may stay on board a space station for over a year. Spacecraft make regular visits to bring supplies and change the crews of astronauts.

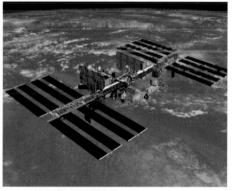

The International Space Station

Key facts

- Space stations are carried into space in sections and put together by astronauts.
- The first space station, *Salyut 1*, was launched in 1971.
- The International Space Station is the biggest structure ever built in space. It will be 360 ft (110 m) long when it is complete.

Life on board

In space there is virtually no gravity, so everything becomes almost weightless. Astronauts and their equipment float around inside spacecraft unless they are strapped down. Lack of gravity means that the body does not have to work so hard, so astronauts have to exercise to stop their muscles from wasting away. They monitor their bodies constantly to check their health and study the effects of space travel on the human body.

Astronaut in zero gravity

Key facts

- In the future, food may be grown in space, but at present all food and water have to be brought to the space station from Earth.
- Life support systems provide oxygen and filter out the carbon dioxide that people breathe out.
- Astronauts sleep strapped into bags that hold them in place, so they do not float around inside the spacecraft.

Sleeping equipment

The sky at night

The best time to observe the stars is on a dark, clear night. You will see more in the countryside, away from the hazy glow of city lights. Binoculars or a telescope will help you observe distant objects more clearly, but even with the naked eye you can still see constellations, bright stars and planets, and the Moon.

It takes about 20 minutes for your eyes to get used to darkness. Then, fainter objects in the sky will become visible.

Watching the night sky

These pictures show some things that you can see in the night sky. Read each caption, then write the letter of the picture it describes in the box.

a

b

c

d

1. With binoculars, you can see craters on the surface of the Moon.

2. The Milky Way looks like a band of dust sprinkled across the sky.

3. Nicknamed the evening star, the planet Venus can often be seen in the early evening, or just after dawn.

4. On a clear night, you may see a shooting star every 15 minutes or so. It looks like a long streak of light.

How a telescope works

Look carefully at this diagram of a reflecting telescope, then fill in the missing words to complete the facts. Choose from:

mirrors   lens   reflects   light rays   eyepiece

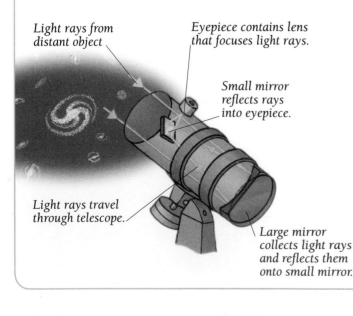

Light rays from distant object

Eyepiece contains lens that focuses light rays.

Small mirror reflects rays into eyepiece.

Light rays travel through telescope.

Large mirror collects light rays and reflects them onto small mirror.

1. Most astronomical telescopes are reflecting telescopes, which use..to reflect light.

2. A large, curved mirror at the bottom of the tube gathers...from distant objects and reflects them back up the body of the telescope.

3. A smaller, flat mirror............................the light rays onto an eyepiece at the side of the tube.

4. The image that the astronomer sees through the ....is upside down.

5. A small...in the eyepiece magnifies the image.

Star distances

The stars lie so far away from Earth that astronomers cannot measure the distance in miles. They measure distances in light-years. One light-year is how far light travels in one year—a distance of 5.9 trillion miles (9.5 trillion km). Light travels at more than 670 million mph (1 billion kph).

Vast distances

The stars in a constellation like Cassiopeia are great distances apart. However, they look close together when viewed from Earth.

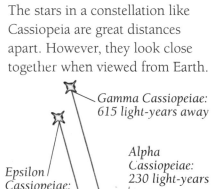

Gamma Cassiopeiae: 615 light-years away

Alpha Cassiopeiae: 230 light-years away

Epsilon Cassiopeiae: 440 light-years away

Delta Cassiopeiae: 100 light-years away

Beta Cassiopeiae: 54 light-years away

Cassiopeia

Light-years away

Draw a line to match each star's distance from Earth in light-years to its distance in miles. Start by working out which is the biggest distance in light-years and match it to the biggest distance in miles, and so on.

Star	Distance in light-years	Distance
1. Sirius A	8.6	1,829 trillion miles (2,945 trillion km)
2. Canopus	310	150 trillion miles (240 trillion km)
3. Arcturus	36.8	51 trillion miles (82 trillion km)
4. Vega	25.3	217 trillion miles (350 trillion km)

Star colors

The color of a star shows the temperature of its surface. Astronomers divide stars into seven types, depending on their temperature. Use the star type table to answer the questions below.

Type	Color		Average temperature
O	Blue	●	80,000°F (45,000°C)
B	Bluish-white	●	55,000°F (30,000°C)
A	White	○	22,000°F (12,000°C)
F	Yellowish-white		14,000°F (8,000°C)
G	Yellow	●	12,000°F (6,500°C)
K	Orange	●	9,000°F (5,000°C)
M	Red	●	6,500°F (3,500°C)

1. Which type of stars are hottest?
....

2. Which color are type G stars, like our Sun?..

3. What is the average temperature of orange stars?................................

4. Which four types of stars are hotter than our Sun?.................

The life cycle of stars

Our Sun's life will last about 10 billion years. When it runs out of fuel, the Sun will expand to form a red giant. Bigger stars live only a few million years before they swell into supergiants. Stars that are smaller than our Sun may live 100 billion years.

Did you know?

A brown dwarf is a star that is too small to trigger nuclear reactions in its core. Instead of shining, it glows dimly.

Life and death of a star

Find four star stickers and match them to the correct captions to complete the diagram.

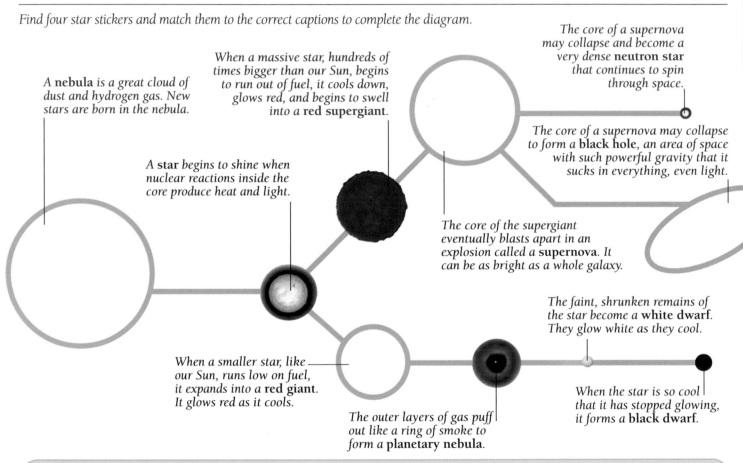

*A **nebula** is a great cloud of dust and hydrogen gas. New stars are born in the nebula.*

*When a massive star, hundreds of times bigger than our Sun, begins to run out of fuel, it cools down, glows red, and begins to swell into a **red supergiant**.*

*The core of a supernova may collapse and become a very dense **neutron star** that continues to spin through space.*

*A **star** begins to shine when nuclear reactions inside the core produce heat and light.*

*The core of a supernova may collapse to form a **black hole**, an area of space with such powerful gravity that it sucks in everything, even light.*

*The core of the supergiant eventually blasts apart in an explosion called a **supernova**. It can be as bright as a whole galaxy.*

*The faint, shrunken remains of the star become a **white dwarf**. They glow white as they cool.*

*When a smaller star, like our Sun, runs low on fuel, it expands into a **red giant**. It glows red as it cools.*

*The outer layers of gas puff out like a ring of smoke to form a **planetary nebula**.*

*When the star is so cool that it has stopped glowing, it forms a **black dwarf**.*

Star knowledge

Complete the sentences by circling the correct answers. Use the information on this page to help you.

1. Our Sun will live for about **5 / 10 / 15** billion years.

2. When the Sun eventually starts to cool down, it will expand and become a **red giant / red supergiant / neutron star**.

3. A black dwarf is a star that **is being formed / is shining / has stopped glowing**.

4. Black holes are formed when **supernovas / small stars / nebulas** collapse.

The Milky Way

We call the cloud of light that arches across the night sky the Milky Way. In fact, this hazy band of stars and dust is only part of our home galaxy. Almost everything we can see in the night sky is part of the Milky Way.

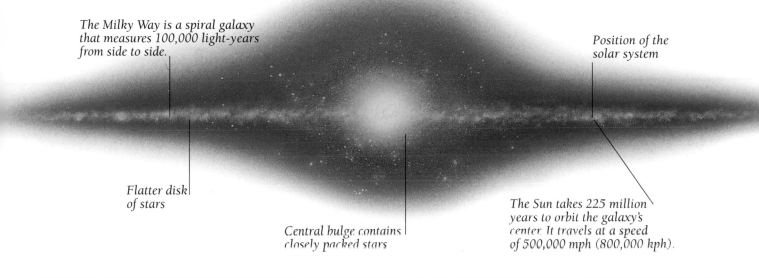

The Milky Way is a spiral galaxy that measures 100,000 light-years from side to side.

Position of the solar system

Flatter disk of stars

Central bulge contains closely packed stars

The Sun takes 225 million years to orbit the galaxy's center. It travels at a speed of 500,000 mph (800,000 kph).

The Milky Way in numbers

Draw a line to match each item to the correct number. You will find information to help you above and on page 216.

1. The width of the Milky Way, in light-years	**100 billion**
2. The number of galaxies in the part of the universe we can observe	**100,000**
3. The number of years the Sun takes to orbit the center of the Milky Way	**200 billion**
4. The speed at which the Sun travels around the galaxy	**225 million**
5. The number of stars in the Milky Way	**500,000 mph (800,000 kph)**

Spot the galaxy

Look closely at these photos of galaxies. Can you identify the three different types using the information on page 216? Draw a line to link each label to the right picture.

1

2

3

spiral galaxy

elliptical galaxy

irregular galaxy

Stargazing

Many of the constellations, or patterns of stars, that we observe today were first picked out and named by ancient Greek and Roman stargazers. More recently, in the 15th and 16th centuries, European seafarers came across the Southern Hemisphere's constellations for the first time, and named them.

Northern polar stars

This map shows the stars that can be seen in the Northern Hemisphere. The red lines show the area that forms each constellation. Find two constellation stickers and match them to the correct captions. Then match each constellation on the polar map to a picture around the page by writing its letter in the correct box.

2. This constellation represents **Cepheus** the husband of Cassiopeia below. Connecting some of its stars makes a shape like a child's drawing of a house.

1. The brightest star in **Ursa Minor**, the Little Bear, is Polaris, the North Star. The star is used by navigators to find north.

3. Within **Ursa Major**, the Great Bear, seven bright stars form a pattern called the Big Dipper, which can be seen with the naked eye.

4. The ancient Greeks named this large, W-shaped constellation after the vain queen **Cassiopeia**. They pictured her admiring herself in a mirror.

5. The large constellation of **Draco**, the Dragon, wraps around the body of Ursa Minor.

Southern polar stars

This map shows the stars that can be seen in the Southern Hemisphere. The red lines show the area that forms each constellation. Find two constellation stickers and match them to the correct captions. Then match each constellation on the polar map to a picture around the page by writing its letter in the correct box.

1. Several constellations make up a boat shape. **Carina**, the Keel, is its bottom.

2. Hydrus, the Little Water Snake, forms a zigzag in the sky.

3. The **Southern Cross** is the smallest constellation in the sky, but its four prominent stars make it easily recognizable.

4. Centaurus represents a mythical beast called a centaur, which was half-man and half-horse.

5. Triangulum Australe, the Southern Triangle, lies beneath the front hooves of Centaurus.

Did you know?

A constellation named after a mythical being often lies close to characters from the same story. Cassiopeia, for example, is near to her husband, Cepheus, her daughter, Andromeda, and the hero Perseus, who rescued Andromeda from a sea monster.

Our nearest star

The Sun is a giant ball of glowing gases, 100 times wider than Earth. Its surface layer, the photosphere, is 60 miles (100 km) deep. The photosphere is a bubbling mass of hot gases, like a stormy sea of fire. Constant explosions send up jets of hot, burning gas.

WARNING Never look directly at the Sun. Its glare could blind you.

Sun facts

- All the Sun's energy is produced in its core. The energy gradually radiates (moves) outward until it reaches the Sun's surface.
- Sunspots are darker patches on the Sun's surface. Their temperature is about 2,700°F (1,500°C) cooler than the rest of the surface.
- The pearl-white atmosphere around the Sun is called the corona. Its temperature can reach 5.4 million °F (3 million °C).
- The Sun sends fountains of glowing gas, called prominences, into the corona. The prominences may be up to 37,000 miles (60,000 km) high.

Parts of the Sun

Can you name the different parts of the Sun? Draw a line to link each label to the right part of the picture using the information on this page to help you.

sunspot

corona

prominence

core

photosphere

True or false?

Read the following statements about the Sun. Use the information on this page and page 217 to work out which statements are true and which are false, then check the correct boxes.

	TRUE	FALSE
1. The Sun is the star at the center of our solar system.	☐	☐
2. The Sun orbits the Earth and other planets.	☐	☐
3. The Sun is a giant ball of oxygen gas.	☐	☐
4. Sunspots are the hottest regions on the Sun's surface.	☐	☐
5. The outer atmosphere of the Sun is called the corona.	☐	☐

Gravity in space

Every object in the universe has its own pulling force, called gravity. Gravity keeps the solar system's planets in orbit around the Sun, and the Milky Way spinning in space. The greater an object's mass (the more matter it contains), the greater its gravity.

Gravity facts

- Earth has more mass than the Moon, so its gravity pulls the Moon toward it.
- If the Moon had more mass, it would escape Earth's gravity and fly off into space.
- If the Moon had less mass, Earth's gravity would pull it crashing into the Earth.
- On Earth, gravity pulls us toward the planet's center, keeping our feet on the ground.
- Astronauts in orbit escape the effects of Earth's gravity, so they float around in their spacecraft.
- In order to escape the pull of Earth's gravity and leave Earth's orbit, rockets must reach a speed of 25,000 mph (40,000 kph).

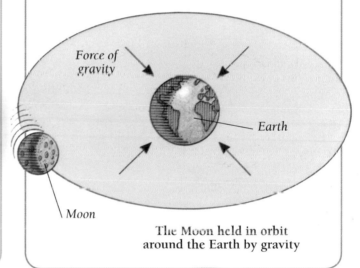

Force of gravity

Earth

Moon

The Moon held in orbit
around the Earth by gravity

Orbiting objects

Use information on this page to work out whether any of the things in the list orbit the Moon, Earth, or Sun. Write the names of the correct orbiting objects under each picture. Choose from:

planets Moon Earth space station satellite

MOON

EARTH

SUN

....
....
....

Birth of the solar system

Read the captions carefully and then number them 1 to 4 to show how the solar system began. Use the information on page 220 to help you.

Sun

a. Fragments of matter are attracted to each other by gravity. They clump together to form objects called protoplanets.

b. The gravity of protoplanets near the solar system's center pulls in rock, and the rocky planets form. The gravity of the outer protoplanets attracts gas, and the gas planets form.

Gas planets forming in outer solar system

Rocky planets forming in inner solar system

c. A spinning disk forms around the Sun, made of matter blown off during its birth.

d. A cloud of spinning dust and gas called a nebula collapses to form the Sun.

Orbiting the Sun

The eight planets of our solar system orbit or travel around the Sun at different distances, and take different lengths of time to complete one orbit. The amount of time a planet takes to orbit the Sun is called its orbital length or year. The time a planet takes to rotate on its axis once is called its rotation period or day.

Planets of the solar system

Fill in the name of each planet on this solar system diagram, using the solar system artwork on pages 90–91 to help you.

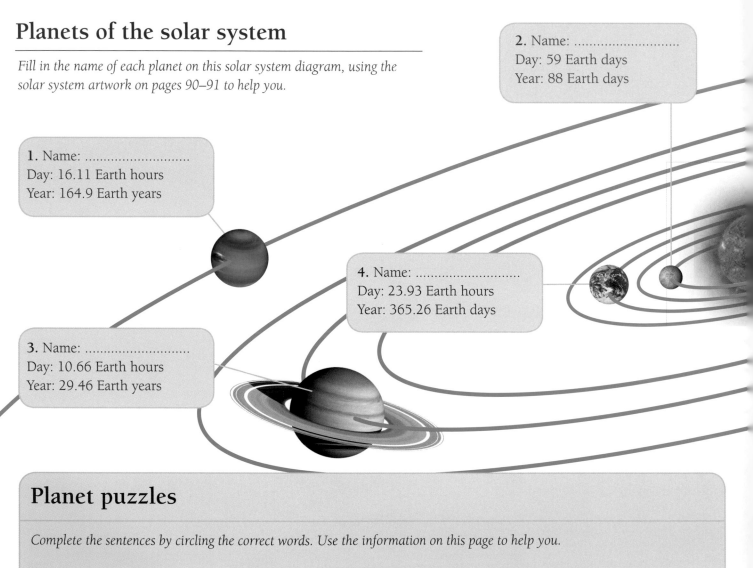

2. Name: ....
Day: 59 Earth days
Year: 88 Earth days

1. Name: ....
Day: 16.11 Earth hours
Year: 164.9 Earth years

4. Name: ....
Day: 23.93 Earth hours
Year: 365.26 Earth days

3. Name: ....
Day: 10.66 Earth hours
Year: 29.46 Earth years

Planet puzzles

Complete the sentences by circling the correct words. Use the information on this page to help you.

1. The planet with the longest year is **Earth / Mercury / Neptune**.

2. A year on Uranus lasts **84 Earth years / 84 Earth days / 11.86 Earth days**.

3. A day on Mercury lasts **59 Earth days / 59 Earth hours / 5.9 Earth hours**.

4. Two planets have shorter years than Earth. They are **Uranus and Neptune / Mercury and Venus / Jupiter and Saturn**.

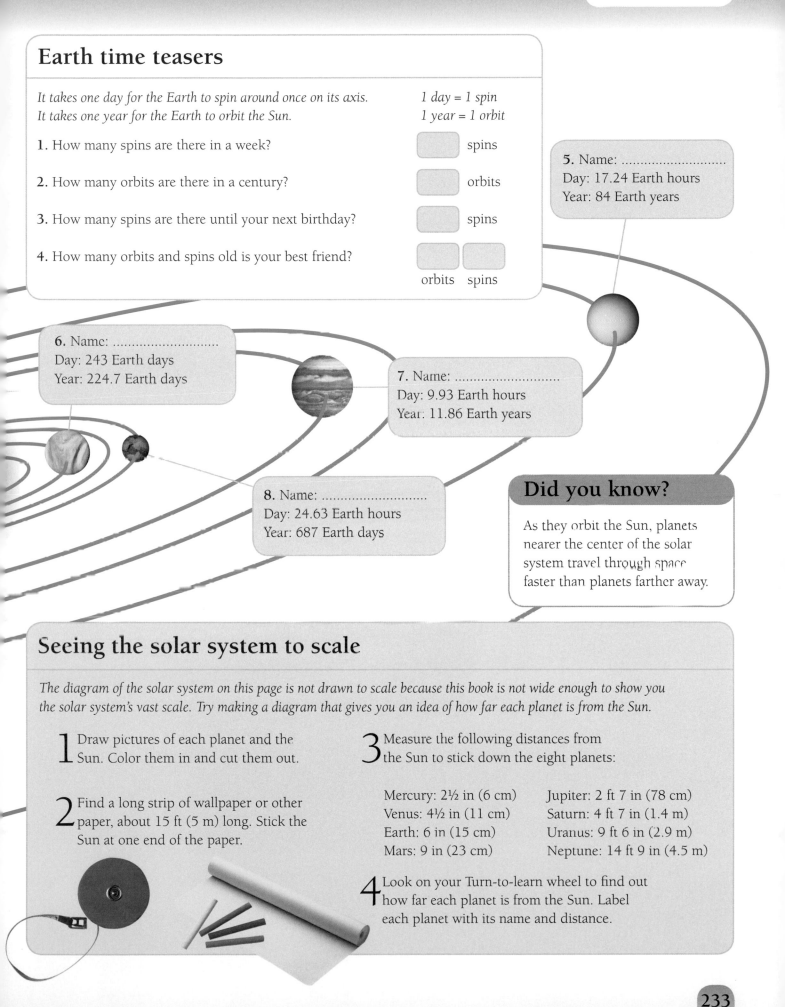

Earth time teasers

It takes one day for the Earth to spin around once on its axis.
It takes one year for the Earth to orbit the Sun.

1 day = 1 spin
1 year = 1 orbit

1. How many spins are there in a week? ☐ spins

2. How many orbits are there in a century? ☐ orbits

3. How many spins are there until your next birthday? ☐ spins

4. How many orbits and spins old is your best friend?
☐ ☐
orbits spins

5. Name: ....
Day: 17.24 Earth hours
Year: 84 Earth years

6. Name: ....
Day: 243 Earth days
Year: 224.7 Earth days

7. Name: ....
Day: 9.93 Earth hours
Year: 11.86 Earth years

8. Name: ....
Day: 24.63 Earth hours
Year: 687 Earth days

Did you know?

As they orbit the Sun, planets nearer the center of the solar system travel through space faster than planets farther away.

Seeing the solar system to scale

The diagram of the solar system on this page is not drawn to scale because this book is not wide enough to show you the solar system's vast scale. Try making a diagram that gives you an idea of how far each planet is from the Sun.

1 Draw pictures of each planet and the Sun. Color them in and cut them out.

2 Find a long strip of wallpaper or other paper, about 15 ft (5 m) long. Stick the Sun at one end of the paper.

3 Measure the following distances from the Sun to stick down the eight planets:

Mercury: 2½ in (6 cm)   Jupiter: 2 ft 7 in (78 cm)
Venus: 4½ in (11 cm)   Saturn: 4 ft 7 in (1.4 m)
Earth: 6 in (15 cm)   Uranus: 9 ft 6 in (2.9 m)
Mars: 9 in (23 cm)   Neptune: 14 ft 9 in (4.5 m)

4 Look on your Turn-to-learn wheel to find out how far each planet is from the Sun. Label each planet with its name and distance.

The inner planets

Mercury, the closest planet to the Sun, has almost no atmosphere to protect it from the Sun or to trap heat. Temperatures soar in the day, then plummet at night. Mercury's neighbor, Venus, is the solar system's hottest planet, because its cloudy atmosphere traps heat.

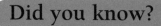
Venus

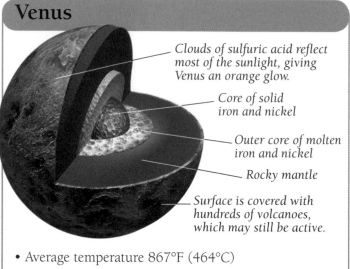

Clouds of sulfuric acid reflect most of the sunlight, giving Venus an orange glow.

Core of solid iron and nickel

Outer core of molten iron and nickel

Rocky mantle

Surface is covered with hundreds of volcanoes, which may still be active.

- Average temperature 867°F (464°C)
- Atmosphere 50 miles (80 km) deep, made mostly of carbon dioxide

Mercury

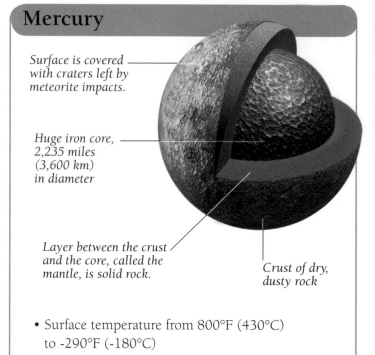

Surface is covered with craters left by meteorite impacts.

Huge iron core, 2,235 miles (3,600 km) in diameter

Layer between the crust and the core, called the mantle, is solid rock.

Crust of dry, dusty rock

- Surface temperature from 800°F (430°C) to -290°F (-180°C)
- Thin, temporary atmosphere of oxygen, sodium, and helium

Venus time teasers

Venus spins very slowly on its axis, so on Venus a day is longer than a year.

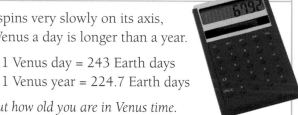

1 Venus day = 243 Earth days
1 Venus year = 224.7 Earth days

Work out how old you are in Venus time. You will need a calculator for this.

1 Multiply your age in years by 365 to work out your age in Earth days.
   Age in Earth years:...
   Age in Earth days:...

2 Divide your answer by 243 to find out how many Venus days old you are.
   Age in Venus days:...

3 Divide your age in Earth days by 224.7 to find out how old you are in Venus years.
   Age in Venus years:...

Mercury or Venus?

Check whether the answer to each of the questions below is Mercury or Venus. Use information on this page to help you.

	Mercury	Venus
1. Which planet is hotter?	☐	☐
2. Which planet is closer to the Sun?	☐	☐
3. Which planet has a longer day?	☐	☐
4. Which planet has a thicker atmosphere?	☐	☐
5. Which planet is bigger?	☐	☐

Our home planet

Earth is the third planet from the Sun, and the largest rocky planet. Its atmosphere extends more than 375 miles (600 km) into space. The atmosphere circulates heat from the warm equator to the freezing poles, giving Earth an average temperature of 59°F (15°C).

Earth from space

Read the captions below about planet Earth, then draw a line to link each caption to the right part of the picture.

1. Land areas that appear yellow-brown from space are mainly deserts.
2. Land areas that appear green are forests and grasslands.
3. Oceans cover more than 70 percent of Earth's surface.
4. Icecaps at the poles contain just 2 percent of Earth's water.
5. Clouds of water vapor swirl around the atmosphere.

Inside Earth facts

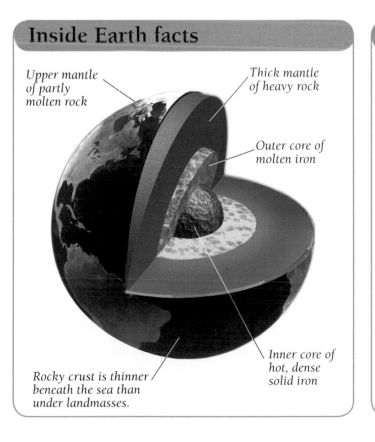

Upper mantle of partly molten rock

Thick mantle of heavy rock

Outer core of molten iron

Inner core of hot, dense solid iron

Rocky crust is thinner beneath the sea than under landmasses.

Earth challenge

Fill in the missing words to complete these sentences. Use the information on this page to help you. Choose from:

atmosphere   iron   landmasses   icecaps   Sun

1. Earth's core is made of...

2. Earth is 92.9 million miles (149.6 million km) from the...

3. The...stretches more than 375 miles (600 km) above Earth's surface.

4. Two percent of the water on Earth is trapped in its polar...

5. Earth's crust is thickest under.................................

Moon-watching

It is easy to study the changing shapes, or phases, of the Moon with your eyes alone. But if you have a pair of binoculars, you will also be able to see details of the Moon's surface, such as craters and mountains.

Phases of the Moon

- When the Moon is directly between the Sun and the Earth, the side facing us is dark. We call it a New Moon.
- As the Moon continues on its orbit of Earth, it appears to grow bigger (wax) as more of it is lit up.
- We see the entire face of the Moon at Full Moon.
- After the Full Moon, the Moon appears to shrink (wane) until it disappears again.

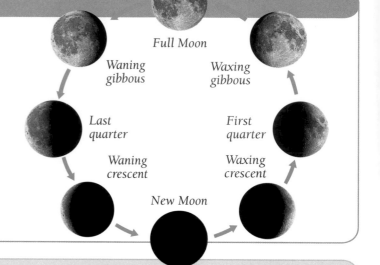

Full Moon

Waning gibbous

Waxing gibbous

Last quarter

First quarter

Waning crescent

Waxing crescent

New Moon

Moon log

Look at the phases of the Moon above. Try keeping your own record of how the Moon's shape changes over the course of a month.

1 After dark, look for the Moon in the night sky.

2 Use a black pen to color in part of the first circle to show the Moon's shape.

3 Write the date underneath your entry.

4 Repeat every day for four weeks, until the chart is full.

5 If you forget one evening, or if the Moon is hidden by cloud, put a cross through that night's circle.

Observing an eclipse

As the Moon orbits Earth, it sometimes moves in front of the Sun, casting a shadow on Earth and blocking out the Sun. This eerie phenomenon, when daylight disappears, is called a solar eclipse.

Did you know?

When Earth lies between the Sun and the Moon, it may cast a shadow on the Moon. This phenomenon, called a lunar eclipse, makes the Moon glow red.

How a solar eclipse works

Direction of Sun's rays

Partial eclipse visible in a wide area in outer ring of Moon's shadow

Moon's shadow

Sun

Earth

Moon directly between Earth and the Sun

Darkest part of Moon's shadow

Total eclipse visible in an area no more than 170 miles (270 km) wide, in central part of Moon's shadow

Eclipse in action

These pictures show the stages of a solar eclipse viewed from Earth. Number the captions in the right order to follow the sequence from top to bottom.

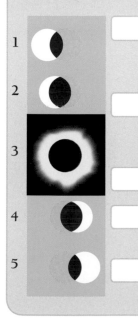

1
2
3
4
5

☐ All of the Moon is in front of the Sun. The Sun's corona shines around the Moon's dark circle.

☐ Over the course of about an hour, the Moon covers more and more of the Sun.

☐ An hour later, the eclipse is over.

☐ After a few minutes, the dark circle begins to move off the Sun.

☐ The Moon appears to take a bite out of the Sun as it starts to pass in front of it.

Lunar eclipse

Try this experiment to find out why the Moon glows red in a lunar eclipse. You need a dark room, a desk lamp, a globe, a ball, and a clear bottle containing water and one teaspoon of milk.

1 Line up the globe and the lamp.

2 Switch on the lamp and place the ball in the globe's shadow. The ball will be completely dark.

The globe represents Earth.

The lamp represents the Sun.

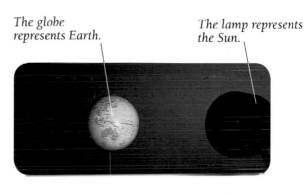

3 Hold the bottle on top of the globe and watch the ball. The milky water scatters the light, just like Earth's atmosphere, casting a pink glow on the ball.

The ball represents the Moon.

The milky water represents Earth's atmosphere.

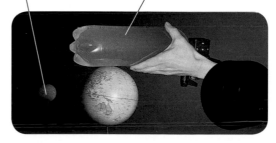

WARNING Never look directly at a solar eclipse and never view it using a telescope, binoculars, or a mirror. View it indirectly with a pinhole camera or observe it through approved protective goggles.

The red planet

In the night sky, the distinctive orange-red color of Mars is easy to see with the naked eye. Mars is the outermost of the four rocky planets, and Earth's nearest neighbor. Today, its surface is a bitterly cold desert, but three billion years ago, Mars was much warmer and water flowed there.

Mars in close-up

Work out which part of the picture each caption refers to, then write the correct letter in the box.

1. Lots of small craters were formed when meteors bombarded Mars 4 billion years ago.

Red color is caused by iron oxide (rust) in the rocks and soil.

2. The long slit across Mars is the Valles Marineris, a 2,800-mile (4,500-km) system of canyons.

3. The Kasei Vallis is a curved canyon north of the Valles Marineris. It was created by heavy flooding when Mars had a plentiful supply of water.

4. Dark circles on the surface of Mars are giant, extinct volcanoes.

Make some Martian dust

To make some Martian dust, you will need some sand, a tray, rubber gloves, scissors, steel wool, and water.

1 Half-fill the tray with sand. Wearing gloves, cut the steel wool into pieces and mix it into the sand. Wet the sand. Leave the tray uncovered in a safe place.

2 Check the sand every day, and add more water if it dries out. How long does it take for the sand to turn a rusty red color?

before

after

Giant planets

The gas planets—Jupiter, Saturn, Uranus, and Neptune—are much bigger than the rocky inner planets. Unlike the rocky planets, the gas planets have no solid surface, just a swirling layer of gas and liquid.

Which planet?

Read these planet facts. Then find four planet stickers to match the right set of captions.

Jupiter

- Jupiter is so large that more than 1,300 Earths would fit inside it.
- Jupiter's Great Red Spot is a giant storm, three times as large as Earth.
- Chemicals such as sulfur and ammonia form colored bands across the atmosphere.
- Jupiter has a faint system of three thin rings.

Uranus

- Uranus has a greenish-blue atmosphere with no cloud bands or storms.
- The axis of Uranus is so tilted that the planet moves along its orbital path on its side.
- Uranus has 11 rings, which are at almost 90 degrees to the planet's orbit.

Saturn

- Saturn is the most distant planet that can be seen from Earth with the naked eye.
- Saturn's system of seven shining rings is more than twice the diameter of the planet itself and can be seen from Earth with a telescope.
- Saturn's yellow color is made by clouds of ammonia in its atmosphere.

Neptune

- Neptune has a deep blue atmosphere, often streaked with bands of white cloud.
- Heat from within Neptune's core creates fast winds and colossal storms. The storms look like dark spots on the planet's surface.
- Neptune has five thin complete rings and one partial ring.

Gas planet puzzle

Complete these statements about the gas planets by circling the correct words. Use the information on this page to help you.

1. Jupiter's giant storm is called the **Great Red Spot / Great Yellow Spot / Great Dark Spot**.

2. **Neptune / Uranus / Saturn** moves sideways along its orbit.

3. The surface of gas planets is made of **molten metal / gas and liquid / jagged rocks**.

4. The planet with the most rings is **Jupiter / Saturn / Uranus**.

Naming the planets

The Romans named the five planets they could see after their gods. Today, we still use the same names. Uranus and Neptune were discovered later, after the invention of the telescope, but they, too, were given the names of Roman gods.

Planet names puzzle

Read the description beneath each god, then write in the name. Use information on page 217 to help you. Choose from:

**Mercury   Venus   Mars   Jupiter
Saturn   Uranus   Neptune**

1. ....
The largest planet is named after the king of the gods.

2. ....
The blood-red planet nearest to Earth is named after the god of war.

5. ....
The Romans named the most distant planet that they could see after the father of the gods.

3. ....
The planet that orbits the Sun at the fastest speed is named after the swift messenger of the gods.

4. ....
The farthest planet from the Sun was named after the god of the sea, because it looks blue.

Planet challenge

Answer these questions about the planets.

1. Which planet is the biggest?

....

2. Which two planets have no moons?

....

3. Which planet is farthest from the Sun?

....

4. Which planet has the largest rings?

....

5. Which is the windiest planet?

....

6. ....
When a planet beyond Saturn was discovered in 1781, it was named after the father of Saturn.

7. ....
The hottest planet glows so brightly that it was named after the goddess of beauty.

Asteroids, comets, and meteors

Between the planets and moons, smaller objects such as asteroids and meteors move around the solar system. These objects are made from material left over from the formation of the solar system. Even smaller, icier objects are found beyond Neptune, in the Kuiper Belt. Some of these become comets heading toward the Sun.

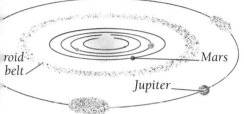

Most **asteroids** are found in the 112 million-mile (180 million-km) wide asteroid belt that lies between Mars and Jupiter.

Halley's Comet returns to the solar system once every 76 years. The first recorded sighting was by Chinese astronomers in 240 BCE.

In 2006, astronomers decided that **Pluto**, which had been discovered in 1930, is too small to be a planet. It is now classed as a Kuiper Belt Object.

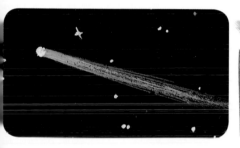

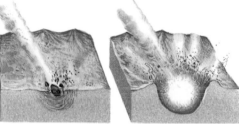

Meteors are lumps of space rock or metal. We see them as **shooting stars** if they burn up in the night sky.

If a meteor is too large to burn up in the atmosphere, and hits the Earth, its impact may form a **crater**.

Most meteors burn up. Those that reach the ground—about 3,000 each year—are called **meteorites**.

Small space bodies

Complete these facts by circling the right answers. Use information from this page to help you.

1. Since 2006, Pluto has been classed as a **planet / star / Kuiper Belt Object**.

2. Rocks that fall through space toward Earth are called **craters / meteors / asteroids**.

3. Shooting stars are **comets / meteors / stars** falling through the atmosphere.

4. Halley's **Star / Comet / Meteor** returns to the solar system once every 76 years.

5. Most asteroids are found in the **Kuiper Belt / asteroid belt / astral belt** between Mars and Jupiter.

6. Craters are formed when big **comets / meteorites / asteroids** hit Earth.

Expanding universe

The universe has not always existed. It began 14 billion years ago when the Big Bang created time and matter. Astronomers know that the universe is still expanding because almost all of the galaxies they can see are moving apart.

After the Big Bang

Read the captions to find out the order in which the universe began. Then find four stickers to illustrate the captions.

14 billion years ago, the universe began with the **Big Bang**.

13 billion years ago, the **first atoms** began to form.

12 billion years ago, matter clumped together to form the **first galaxies**.

11 billion years ago, the oldest stars in the **Milky Way** were born.

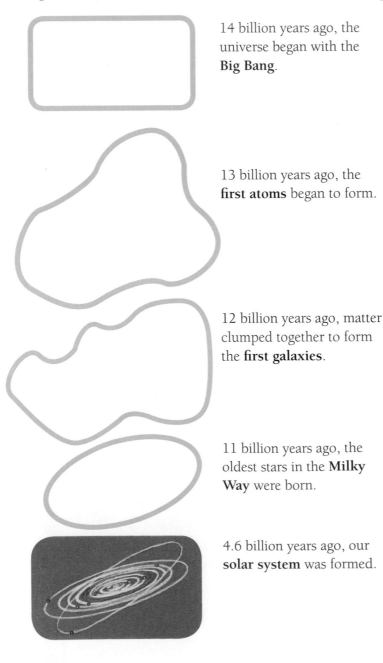

4.6 billion years ago, our **solar system** was formed.

Expansion facts

- The galaxies are not expanding, but the space between them is.
- Three billion years ago, clusters of galaxies were 25 percent nearer to each other than they are today.

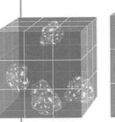 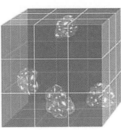 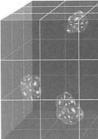

Three billion years ago   *The present*   *Two billion years in the future*

- Two billion years in the future, the clusters will be 15 percent farther apart.

Watch the universe expand

Read the facts above to see how the universe is expanding. Try this activity to see how this expansion is possible.

1 Half-blow up a balloon, then hold the end shut. The balloon represents the universe.

2 Draw dots on the balloon with a marker, two finger-widths apart. The dots represent galaxies.

3 Finish blowing up the balloon. Tie the end.

4 Look at the spaces between the dots now. How many finger-widths apart are they?

[   ] finger-widths

Space shuttle

Before the invention of the space shuttle, spacecraft were used only once. Some of their parts were left in space, some burned up in the atmosphere, and some crashed back to Earth. Astronauts returned to Earth by splashing down into the ocean inside a section of the spacecraft, or by parachuting from the spacecraft before it crash-landed.

Into orbit and back again

Read the captions below and look at the pictures. Number them 1 to 6 to show what happens on a space shuttle mission.

Protective silica tiles glow as the orbiter reenters the atmosphere.

The orbiter's main engines and rocket boosters fire together at liftoff.

Eight minutes after takeoff, the external fuel tank drops away

The orbiter remains in orbit for up to two weeks.

The orbiter glides in to land on an ordinary runway.

Two minutes after liftoff, the rocket boosters fall back to Earth.

Parts of the orbiter

Read the captions below about the space shuttle orbiter. Draw a line to link each one to the correct part of the picture.

The **payload bay** carries the payload (cargo) such as satellites or space station parts.

The **mechanical arm** moves objects in and out of the payload bay.

The **payload bay doors** are opened in orbit to prevent the orbiter from overheating.

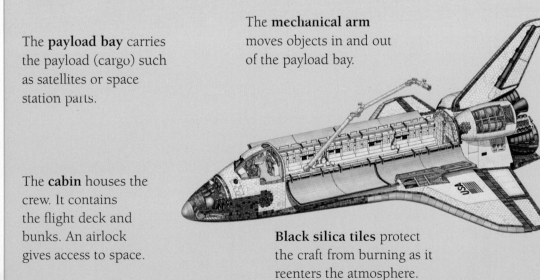

The **cabin** houses the crew. It contains the flight deck and bunks. An airlock gives access to space.

Black silica tiles protect the craft from burning as it reenters the atmosphere.

The **wings** have no function in space but help the orbiter glide when it lands.

Astronauts

An astronaut's spacesuit carries essential supplies. It has oxygen for breathing, water for maintaining a comfortable body temperature, and electrical power. Today's spacesuits are so advanced that astronauts can safely and easily move around outside their spacecraft and carry out delicate repairs to equipment out in space.

Did you know?

The oldest person ever to go into space was US astronaut John Glenn. When he traveled aboard the space shuttle in 1998, he was 77 years old.

Astronaut suit

Read these captions about astronauts' spacesuits. Looking at the pictures for clues, fill in the missing words. Choose from:

gloves   visor   outersuit   helmet   undersuit   boots

1. The astronaut's................................has a network of water-filled tubing. This helps the body to stay at the right temperature.

2. The...........................attach to the legs of the suit. There are tight seams and seals between the different parts of the suit to stop any oxygen leaks.

3. The................................... contains a synthetic fiber called Kevlar, which can withstand high temperatures and is also used for bulletproof vests.

4. A cap inside the...........................contains communications equipment.

5. The astronaut's............................contain their own heating units. These keep the hands warm but are flexible to allow movement.

6. The helmet's mirrored........................... protects the astronaut from the Sun's glare.

Astronauts at work

Circle the correct words to complete these sentences. Use information on this page and page 223.

1. Astronauts carrying out work in space wear a powered backpack called an **UMM / MMU / MUM**.

2. Spacecraft carry space stations into space in sections, which are put together by **astronauts / aliens / workers**.

3. Outside the spacecraft, an astronaut carries a supply of **food / oxygen / carbon dioxide** so he or she can breathe.

4. Astronauts orbiting Earth release communications **satellites / stations / observatories** into orbit.

Living in space

In space, lack of gravity means that everything is almost weightless. People, equipment, and even food float around inside a spacecraft if they are not strapped down or contained. Astronauts prepare for life in space by training in water tanks. The experience of being under water is similar to the weightlessness in space.

Gravity facts

- Liquids and crumbs of food would float away in a spacecraft. Food has to be kept in sealed containers.
- Dust does not settle in a spacecraft. It has to be vacuumed out of the air.
- On Earth, gravity pulls the ink in a pen down to the ballpoint. In space, pens have to have a special mechanism that pushes the ink toward the ballpoint.
- Space toilets suck waste away with air, rather than flushing it away with water.

Astronaut food

Read each caption below, then number it to match the correct picture.

☐ **Sealed drinks pouches** prevent liquids from escaping when an astronaut has a drink.

☐ **Dried foods** need water added before they can be eaten.

☐ **Dried fruits** are taken from the packet one at a time, so they do not float away.

☐ **Cereals** are vacuum-packed. Astronauts add water, then suck up the cereal.

1

2

3

4

True or false?

Read the statements below, then check the boxes to show whether they are true or false. Use the information on this page and page 223 to help you.

	TRUE	FALSE
1. Astronauts train for space travel in water tanks.	☐	☐
2. Space toilets blow waste away.	☐	☐
3. To stop food and liquids from floating away, it is kept in magnetic containers.	☐	☐
4. Astronauts are almost weightless in space because there is almost no gravity.	☐	☐
5. Astronauts are strapped into their sleeping bags to sleep so that they do not snore.	☐	☐
6. Astronauts have to exercise in space to stop their muscles from wasting away.	☐	☐

Key dates of space exploration

People have been recording their observations about the night sky for more than 5,000 years. Improved technologies, such as telescopes and space probes, have allowed astronomers to see farther than ever. In the last 50 years, probes have visited every planet in the solar system.

Complete the timeline

Fill in the missing dates or other information on this timeline. Then find four stickers to put in the missing picture spaces.

Galileo

Isaac Newton

Neptune

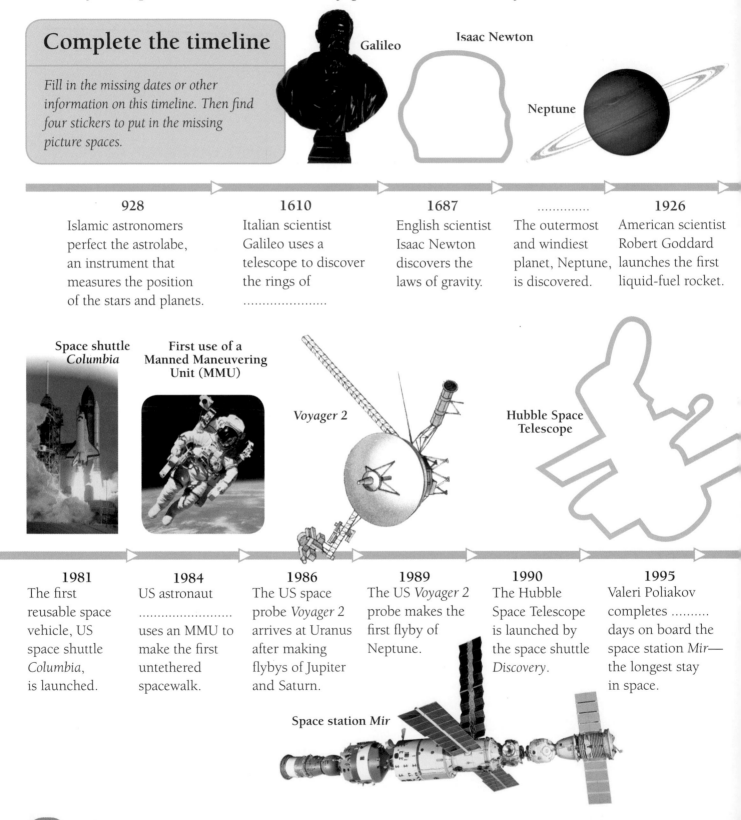

928
Islamic astronomers perfect the astrolabe, an instrument that measures the position of the stars and planets.

1610
Italian scientist Galileo uses a telescope to discover the rings of ....

1687
English scientist Isaac Newton discovers the laws of gravity.

....
The outermost and windiest planet, Neptune, is discovered.

1926
American scientist Robert Goddard launches the first liquid-fuel rocket.

Space shuttle *Columbia*

First use of a Manned Maneuvering Unit (MMU)

Voyager 2

Hubble Space Telescope

1981
The first reusable space vehicle, US space shuttle *Columbia*, is launched.

1984
US astronaut .... uses an MMU to make the first untethered spacewalk.

1986
The US space probe *Voyager 2* arrives at Uranus after making flybys of Jupiter and Saturn.

1989
The US *Voyager 2* probe makes the first flyby of Neptune.

1990
The Hubble Space Telescope is launched by the space shuttle *Discovery*.

1995
Valeri Poliakov completes .... days on board the space station *Mir*—the longest stay in space.

Space station *Mir*

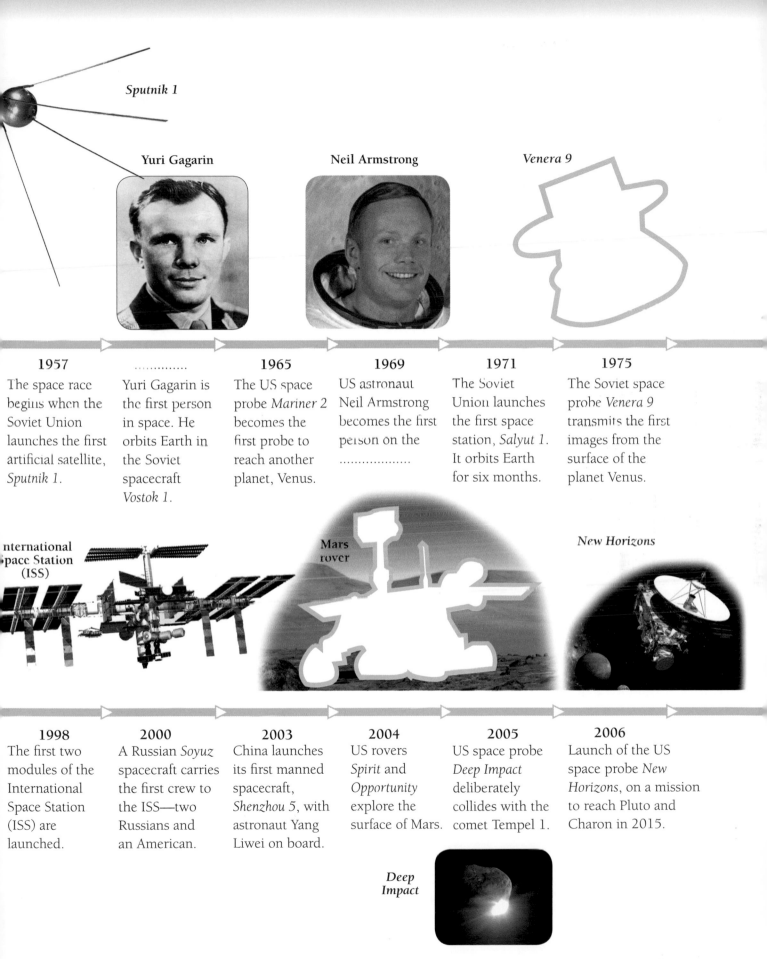

Sputnik 1

Yuri Gagarin

Neil Armstrong

Venera 9

1957
The space race begins when the Soviet Union launches the first artificial satellite, *Sputnik 1*.

....
Yuri Gagarin is the first person in space. He orbits Earth in the Soviet spacecraft *Vostok 1*.

1965
The US space probe *Mariner 2* becomes the first probe to reach another planet, Venus.

1969
US astronaut Neil Armstrong becomes the first person on the ....

1971
The Soviet Union launches the first space station, *Salyut 1*. It orbits Earth for six months.

1975
The Soviet space probe *Venera 9* transmits the first images from the surface of the planet Venus.

International Space Station (ISS)

Mars rover

New Horizons

1998
The first two modules of the International Space Station (ISS) are launched.

2000
A Russian *Soyuz* spacecraft carries the first crew to the ISS—two Russians and an American.

2003
China launches its first manned spacecraft, *Shenzhou 5*, with astronaut Yang Liwei on board.

2004
US rovers *Spirit* and *Opportunity* explore the surface of Mars.

2005
US space probe *Deep Impact* deliberately collides with the comet Tempel 1.

2006
Launch of the US space probe *New Horizons*, on a mission to reach Pluto and Charon in 2015.

Deep Impact

Discovering the universe

Check or number the boxes to answer each question. Check your answers on page 256.

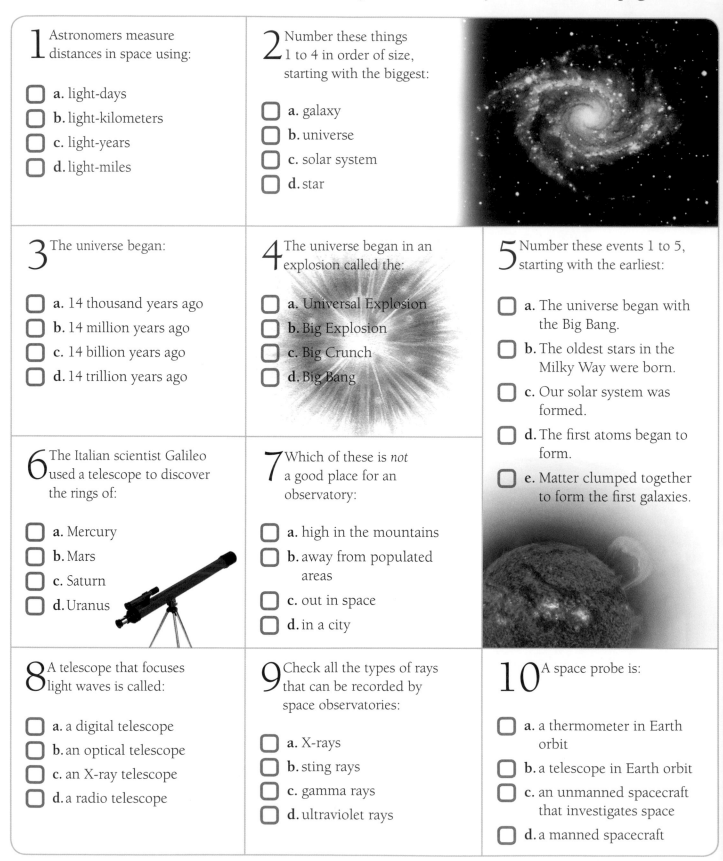

1 Astronomers measure distances in space using:

- ☐ **a.** light-days
- ☐ **b.** light-kilometers
- ☐ **c.** light-years
- ☐ **d.** light-miles

2 Number these things 1 to 4 in order of size, starting with the biggest:

- ☐ **a.** galaxy
- ☐ **b.** universe
- ☐ **c.** solar system
- ☐ **d.** star

3 The universe began:

- ☐ **a.** 14 thousand years ago
- ☐ **b.** 14 million years ago
- ☐ **c.** 14 billion years ago
- ☐ **d.** 14 trillion years ago

4 The universe began in an explosion called the:

- ☐ **a.** Universal Explosion
- ☐ **b.** Big Explosion
- ☐ **c.** Big Crunch
- ☐ **d.** Big Bang

5 Number these events 1 to 5, starting with the earliest:

- ☐ **a.** The universe began with the Big Bang.
- ☐ **b.** The oldest stars in the Milky Way were born.
- ☐ **c.** Our solar system was formed.
- ☐ **d.** The first atoms began to form.
- ☐ **e.** Matter clumped together to form the first galaxies.

6 The Italian scientist Galileo used a telescope to discover the rings of:

- ☐ **a.** Mercury
- ☐ **b.** Mars
- ☐ **c.** Saturn
- ☐ **d.** Uranus

7 Which of these is *not* a good place for an observatory:

- ☐ **a.** high in the mountains
- ☐ **b.** away from populated areas
- ☐ **c.** out in space
- ☐ **d.** in a city

8 A telescope that focuses light waves is called:

- ☐ **a.** a digital telescope
- ☐ **b.** an optical telescope
- ☐ **c.** an X-ray telescope
- ☐ **d.** a radio telescope

9 Check all the types of rays that can be recorded by space observatories:

- ☐ **a.** X-rays
- ☐ **b.** sting rays
- ☐ **c.** gamma rays
- ☐ **d.** ultraviolet rays

10 A space probe is:

- ☐ **a.** a thermometer in Earth orbit
- ☐ **b.** a telescope in Earth orbit
- ☐ **c.** an unmanned spacecraft that investigates space
- ☐ **d.** a manned spacecraft

Stars, galaxies, and constellations

Check or number the boxes to answer each question. Check your answers on page 256.

1 Stars are mainly made up of:

☐ a. hydrogen
☐ b. oxygen
☐ c. carbon dioxide
☐ d. rock

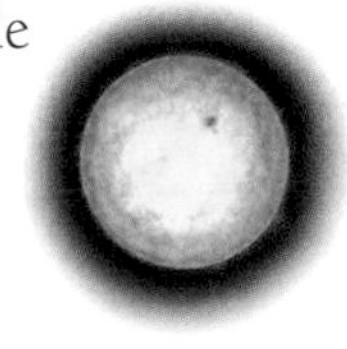

2 Check all the colors that stars can be:

☐ a. yellow
☐ b. blue
☐ c. green
☐ d. red

3 The cloud of gas and dust from which a star forms is called a:

☐ a. nebula
☐ b. galaxy
☐ c. black hole
☐ d. comet

4 Number these captions 1 to 6 to show the life cycle of a small star like our Sun:

☐ a. Nuclear reactions in the core produce heat and light.
☐ b. The outer layers of gas puff out like a ring of smoke to form a planetary nebula.
☐ c. When the star is cold and stops glowing, it forms a black dwarf.
☐ d. The star runs low on fuel, and expands into a red giant.
☐ e. The star is born in a nebula (a cloud of dust and hydrogen gas).
☐ f. The faint remains of the star become a white dwarf.

5 A constellation is a:

☐ a. group of stars that are very close to each other
☐ b. vast, spinning group of stars, gas, and dust
☐ c. group of stars that make a pattern in the sky

6 How many constellations do astronomers divide the sky into?

☐ a. 22
☐ b. 44
☐ c. 66
☐ d. 88

7 Check all the things that are constellations:

☐ a. Ursa Major
☐ b. North Star
☐ c. Cassiopeia
☐ d. Southern Cross

8 Which of these is *not* a type of galaxy?

☐ a. spiral
☐ b. cuboid
☐ c. elliptical
☐ d. oval

9 How many galaxies are there in the part of the universe we can observe?

☐ a. 100 thousand
☐ b. 100 million
☐ c. 100 billion
☐ d. 100 trillion

10 Our home galaxy is called:

☐ a. the Milky Galaxy
☐ b. the Milky Way
☐ c. the Solar Galaxy
☐ d. the solar system

11 How long does it take the Sun to orbit the center of our galaxy:

☐ a. 225 years
☐ b. 225 thousand years
☐ c. 2.25 million years
☐ d. 225 million years

Planets and smaller space bodies

Check or number the boxes to answer each question. Check your answers on page 256.

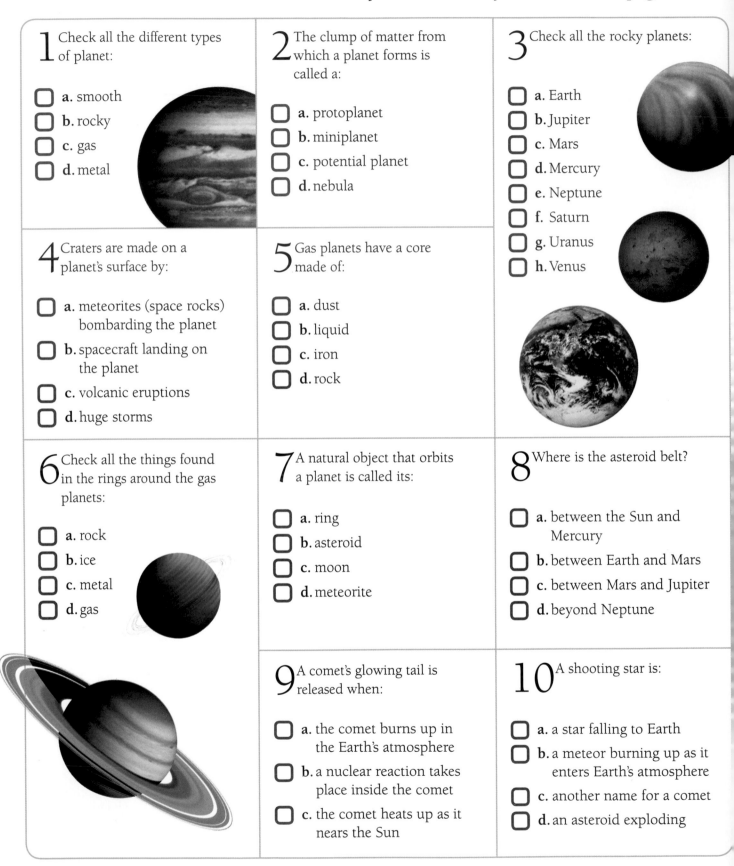

1 Check all the different types of planet:

- [ ] **a.** smooth
- [ ] **b.** rocky
- [ ] **c.** gas
- [ ] **d.** metal

2 The clump of matter from which a planet forms is called a:

- [ ] **a.** protoplanet
- [ ] **b.** miniplanet
- [ ] **c.** potential planet
- [ ] **d.** nebula

3 Check all the rocky planets:

- [ ] **a.** Earth
- [ ] **b.** Jupiter
- [ ] **c.** Mars
- [ ] **d.** Mercury
- [ ] **e.** Neptune
- [ ] **f.** Saturn
- [ ] **g.** Uranus
- [ ] **h.** Venus

4 Craters are made on a planet's surface by:

- [ ] **a.** meteorites (space rocks) bombarding the planet
- [ ] **b.** spacecraft landing on the planet
- [ ] **c.** volcanic eruptions
- [ ] **d.** huge storms

5 Gas planets have a core made of:

- [ ] **a.** dust
- [ ] **b.** liquid
- [ ] **c.** iron
- [ ] **d.** rock

6 Check all the things found in the rings around the gas planets:

- [ ] **a.** rock
- [ ] **b.** ice
- [ ] **c.** metal
- [ ] **d.** gas

7 A natural object that orbits a planet is called its:

- [ ] **a.** ring
- [ ] **b.** asteroid
- [ ] **c.** moon
- [ ] **d.** meteorite

8 Where is the asteroid belt?

- [ ] **a.** between the Sun and Mercury
- [ ] **b.** between Earth and Mars
- [ ] **c.** between Mars and Jupiter
- [ ] **d.** beyond Neptune

9 A comet's glowing tail is released when:

- [ ] **a.** the comet burns up in the Earth's atmosphere
- [ ] **b.** a nuclear reaction takes place inside the comet
- [ ] **c.** the comet heats up as it nears the Sun

10 A shooting star is:

- [ ] **a.** a star falling to Earth
- [ ] **b.** a meteor burning up as it enters Earth's atmosphere
- [ ] **c.** another name for a comet
- [ ] **d.** an asteroid exploding

The Sun and solar system

Check or number the boxes to answer each question. Check your answers on page 256.

1 The Sun's energy comes from:

- [ ] **a.** burning hydrogen gas on its surface
- [ ] **b.** giant volcanoes all over its surface
- [ ] **c.** nuclear reactions inside its core

2 Check all the things that are part of the Sun:

- [ ] **a.** core
- [ ] **b.** prominence
- [ ] **c.** corona
- [ ] **d.** crust

3 How long does the Sun's equator take to rotate once?

- [ ] **a.** 25 Earth hours
- [ ] **b.** 25 Earth days
- [ ] **c.** 34 Earth hours
- [ ] **d.** 34 Earth days

4 The hottest part of the Sun is:

- [ ] **a.** its sunspot
- [ ] **b.** its surface
- [ ] **c.** its atmosphere
- [ ] **d.** its core

5 Number the planets of the solar system 1 to 8, starting with the planet that is nearest to the Sun:

- [ ] **a.** Earth
- [ ] **b.** Mars
- [ ] **c.** Mercury
- [ ] **d.** Jupiter
- [ ] **e.** Neptune
- [ ] **f.** Saturn
- [ ] **g.** Uranus
- [ ] **h.** Venus

6 How big is the solar system?

- [ ] **a.** 9,300 billion miles (15,000 billion km) across
- [ ] **b.** 9.3 billion miles (15 billion km) across
- [ ] **c.** 9,300 miles (15,000 km) across

7 A planet's year is:

- [ ] **a.** the amount of time it takes the Sun to orbit it once
- [ ] **b.** the amount of time it takes to orbit the Sun once
- [ ] **c.** the amount of time it takes to spin once on its axis

8 Which is the hottest planet in the solar system?

- [ ] **a.** Jupiter
- [ ] **b.** Mercury
- [ ] **c.** Saturn
- [ ] **d.** Venus

9 Which of these planets is *not* visible with the naked eye?

- [ ] **a.** Mercury
- [ ] **b.** Saturn
- [ ] **c.** Uranus
- [ ] **d.** Venus

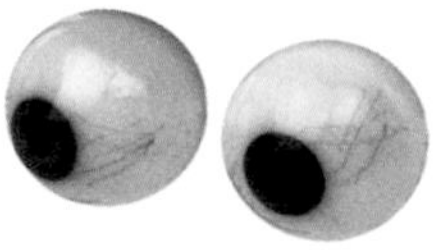

10 Check all the things that are features of Mars:

- [ ] **a.** Great Red Spot
- [ ] **b.** Valles Marineris
- [ ] **c.** Olympus Mons
- [ ] **d.** Kuiper Belt

11 Which of these planets has seven rings?

- [ ] **a.** Jupiter
- [ ] **b.** Saturn
- [ ] **c.** Uranus
- [ ] **d.** Neptune

Earth and the Moon

Check or number the boxes to answer each question. Check your answers on page 256.

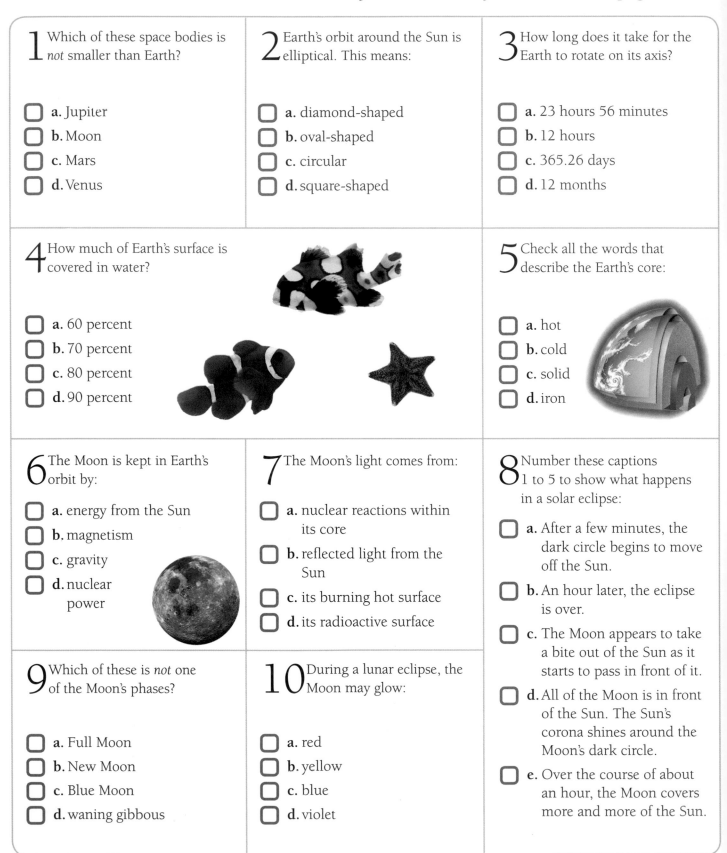

1 Which of these space bodies is *not* smaller than Earth?

- ☐ **a.** Jupiter
- ☐ **b.** Moon
- ☐ **c.** Mars
- ☐ **d.** Venus

2 Earth's orbit around the Sun is elliptical. This means:

- ☐ **a.** diamond-shaped
- ☐ **b.** oval-shaped
- ☐ **c.** circular
- ☐ **d.** square-shaped

3 How long does it take for the Earth to rotate on its axis?

- ☐ **a.** 23 hours 56 minutes
- ☐ **b.** 12 hours
- ☐ **c.** 365.26 days
- ☐ **d.** 12 months

4 How much of Earth's surface is covered in water?

- ☐ **a.** 60 percent
- ☐ **b.** 70 percent
- ☐ **c.** 80 percent
- ☐ **d.** 90 percent

5 Check all the words that describe the Earth's core:

- ☐ **a.** hot
- ☐ **b.** cold
- ☐ **c.** solid
- ☐ **d.** iron

6 The Moon is kept in Earth's orbit by:

- ☐ **a.** energy from the Sun
- ☐ **b.** magnetism
- ☐ **c.** gravity
- ☐ **d.** nuclear power

7 The Moon's light comes from:

- ☐ **a.** nuclear reactions within its core
- ☐ **b.** reflected light from the Sun
- ☐ **c.** its burning hot surface
- ☐ **d.** its radioactive surface

8 Number these captions 1 to 5 to show what happens in a solar eclipse:

- ☐ **a.** After a few minutes, the dark circle begins to move off the Sun.
- ☐ **b.** An hour later, the eclipse is over.
- ☐ **c.** The Moon appears to take a bite out of the Sun as it starts to pass in front of it.
- ☐ **d.** All of the Moon is in front of the Sun. The Sun's corona shines around the Moon's dark circle.
- ☐ **e.** Over the course of about an hour, the Moon covers more and more of the Sun.

9 Which of these is *not* one of the Moon's phases?

- ☐ **a.** Full Moon
- ☐ **b.** New Moon
- ☐ **c.** Blue Moon
- ☐ **d.** waning gibbous

10 During a lunar eclipse, the Moon may glow:

- ☐ **a.** red
- ☐ **b.** yellow
- ☐ **c.** blue
- ☐ **d.** violet

Astronauts and spacecraft

Check or number the boxes to answer each question. Check your answers on page 256.

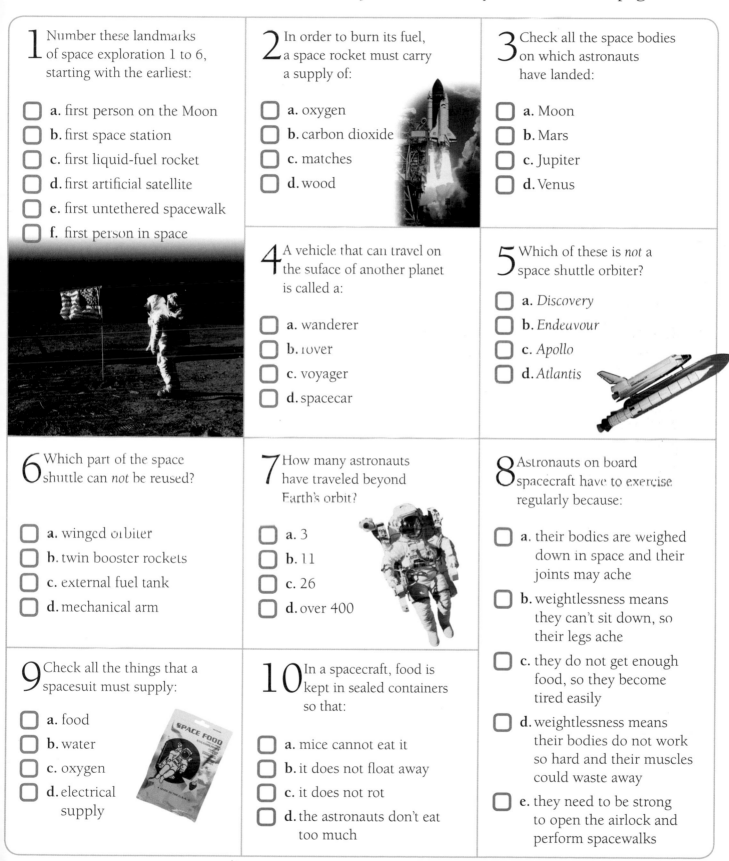

1 Number these landmarks of space exploration 1 to 6, starting with the earliest:

☐ **a.** first person on the Moon
☐ **b.** first space station
☐ **c.** first liquid-fuel rocket
☐ **d.** first artificial satellite
☐ **e.** first untethered spacewalk
☐ **f.** first person in space

2 In order to burn its fuel, a space rocket must carry a supply of:

☐ **a.** oxygen
☐ **b.** carbon dioxide
☐ **c.** matches
☐ **d.** wood

3 Check all the space bodies on which astronauts have landed:

☐ **a.** Moon
☐ **b.** Mars
☐ **c.** Jupiter
☐ **d.** Venus

4 A vehicle that can travel on the surface of another planet is called a:

☐ **a.** wanderer
☐ **b.** rover
☐ **c.** voyager
☐ **d.** spacecar

5 Which of these is *not* a space shuttle orbiter?

☐ **a.** *Discovery*
☐ **b.** *Endeavour*
☐ **c.** *Apollo*
☐ **d.** *Atlantis*

6 Which part of the space shuttle can *not* be reused?

☐ **a.** winged orbiter
☐ **b.** twin booster rockets
☐ **c.** external fuel tank
☐ **d.** mechanical arm

7 How many astronauts have traveled beyond Earth's orbit?

☐ **a.** 3
☐ **b.** 11
☐ **c.** 26
☐ **d.** over 400

8 Astronauts on board spacecraft have to exercise regularly because:

☐ **a.** their bodies are weighed down in space and their joints may ache
☐ **b.** weightlessness means they can't sit down, so their legs ache
☐ **c.** they do not get enough food, so they become tired easily
☐ **d.** weightlessness means their bodies do not work so hard and their muscles could waste away
☐ **e.** they need to be strong to open the airlock and perform spacewalks

9 Check all the things that a spacesuit must supply:

☐ **a.** food
☐ **b.** water
☐ **c.** oxygen
☐ **d.** electrical supply

10 In a spacecraft, food is kept in sealed containers so that:

☐ **a.** mice cannot eat it
☐ **b.** it does not float away
☐ **c.** it does not rot
☐ **d.** the astronauts don't eat too much

Activity answers

Once you have completed each page of activities, check your answers below:

Page 224
Watching the night sky
1 b
2 c
3 a
4 d

Page 224
How a telescope works
1 mirrors
2 light rays
3 reflects
4 eyepiece
5 lens

Page 225
Light-years away
1 51 trillion miles
 (82 trillion km)
2 1,829 trillion miles
 (2,945 trillion km)
3 217 trillion miles
 (350 trillion km)
4 150 trillion miles
 (240 trillion km)

Page 225
Star colors
1 O
2 yellow
3 9,000°F (5,000°C)
4 O, B, A, F

Page 226
Star knowledge
1 10
2 red giant
3 has stopped glowing
4 supernovas

Page 227
The Milky Way in numbers
1 100,000
2 100 billion
3 225 million
4 500,000 mph (800,000 kph)
5 200 billion

Page 227
Spot the galaxy
1 spiral galaxy
2 elliptical galaxy
3 irregular galaxy

Page 228
Northern polar stars
1 b
2 d
3 a
4 e
5 c

Page 229
Southern polar stars
1 e
2 d
3 c
4 b
5 a

Page 230
Parts of the Sun

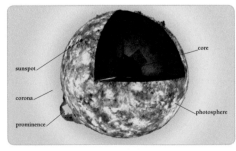

Page 230
True or false?
1 True
2 False—The Earth and other planets orbit the Sun.
3 False—The Sun is a giant ball of hydrogen gas.
4 False—Sunspots are cooler than the rest of the Sun's surface.
5 True

Page 231
Orbiting objects
Moon: (nothing)
Earth: Moon, space station, satellite
Sun: planets, Earth

Page 231
Birth of the solar system
a 3
b 4
c 2
d 1

Page 232
Planets of the solar system
1 Neptune
2 Mercury
3 Saturn
4 Earth
5 Uranus
6 Venus
7 Jupiter
8 Mars

Page 232
Planet puzzles
1 Neptune
2 84 Earth years
3 59 Earth days
4 Mercury and Venus

Page 233
Earth time teasers
1 7
2 100

Page 234
Mercury or Venus?
1 Venus
2 Mercury
3 Venus
4 Venus
5 Venus

Page 235
Earth from space

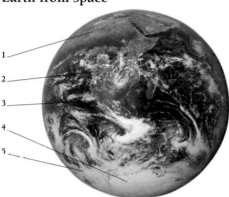

Page 235
Earth challenge
1 iron
2 Sun
3 atmosphere
4 ice caps
5 landmasses

Page 237
Eclipse in action
1 The Moon appears to take a bite out of the Sun as it starts to pass in front of it.
2 Over the course of about an hour, the Moon covers more and more of the Sun.
3 All of the Moon is in front of the Sun. The Sun's corona shines around the Moon's dark circle.
4 After a few minutes, the dark circle begins to move off the Sun.
5 An hour later, the eclipse is over.

Page 238
Mars in close-up
1 c
2 d
3 b
4 a

Page 239
Gas planet puzzle
1 Great Red Spot
2 Uranus
3 gas and liquid
4 Uranus

Page 240
Planet names puzzle
1 Jupiter
2 Mars
3 Mercury
4 Neptune
5 Saturn
6 Uranus
7 Venus

Page 240
Planet challenge
1 Jupiter
2 Mercury and Venus
3 Neptune
4 Saturn
5 Neptune

Page 241
Small space bodies
1 Kuiper Belt Object
2 meteors
3 meteors
4 Comet
5 asteroid belt
6 meteorites

Page 243
Into orbit and back again

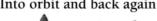
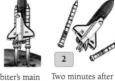

1	2	3

The orbiter's main engines and rocket boosters fire together at liftoff.

Two minutes after liftoff, the rocket boosters fall back to Earth.

Eight minutes after takeoff, the external fuel tank drops away

4	5	6

The orbiter remains in orbit for up to two weeks.

Protective silica tiles glow as the orbiter reenters the atmosphere.

The orbiter glides in to land on an ordinary runway.

Page 243
Parts of the orbiter

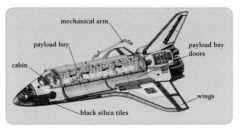

mechanical arm, payload bay, payload bay doors, cabin, wings, black silica tiles

Page 244
Astronaut suit
1 undersuit
2 boots
3 outersuit
4 helmet
5 gloves
6 visor

Page 244
Astronauts at work
1 MMU
2 astronauts
3 oxygen
4 satellites

Page 245
Astronaut food
1 Dried foods
2 Cereals
3 Dried fruits
4 Sealed drinks pouches

Page 245
True or false?
1 True
2 False—Space toilets suck waste away.
3 False—Food is kept in sealed containers.
4 True
5 False—Astronauts are strapped into their sleeping bags so they do not float around the spacecraft.
6 True

More answers on next page

Pages 246–247

Complete the timeline

1610 Saturn

1846 Neptune is discovered.

1961 Yuri Gagarin is the first person
in space.

1969 Moon

1984 Bruce McCandless

1995 437 days

Quick quiz answers

Once you have completed each page of quiz questions,
check your answers below:

Page 248
Discovering the universe
1 c 2 a 2, b 1, c 3, d 4 3 c 4 d
5 a 1, b 4, c 5, d 2, e 3 6 c 7 d 8 b
9 a, c, d 10 c

Page 249
Stars, galaxies, and constellations
1 a 2 a, b, d 3 a
4 a 2, b 4, c 6, d 3, e 1, f 5 5 c 6 d
7 a, c, d 8 b 9 c 10 b 11 d

Page 250
Planets and smaller space bodies
1 b, c 2 a 3 a, c, d, h 4 a 5 d 6 a, b
7 c 8 c 9 c 10 b

Page 251
The Sun and solar system
1 c 2 a, b, c 3 b 4 d
5 a 3, b 4, c 1, d 5, e 8, f 6, g 7, h 2 6 a
7 b 8 d 9 c 10 b, c 11 b

Page 252
Earth and the Moon
1 a 2 b 3 a 4 b 5 a, c, d 6 c 7 b
8 a 4, b 5, c 1, d 3, e 2 9 c 10 a

Page 253
Astronauts and spacecraft
1 a 4, b 5, c 1, d 2, e 6, f 3 2 a 3 a 4
b 5 c 6 c 7 c 8 d 9 b, c, d 10 b

Acknowledgments

**The publisher would like to thank
the following:**

Alyson Silverwood for proof-reading;
Margaret Parrish for Americanization.

**The publisher would like to thank the
following for their kind permission to
reproduce their photographs:**

(Key: a-above; b-below/bottom; c-center; f-far;
l-left; r-right; t-top)

Canada-France-Hawaii Telescope: J.-C.
Cuillandre / Coelum 227; **Corbis**: Bettmann
240, 247cla; **DK Images**: Anglo-Australian
Observatory, photography by David Malin
216cla, 224cra (milky way), 248tr; British
Museum 240cra; ESA 216b; London
Planetarium 250tr; Museum of Central
Australia, Alice Springs 241cr; National
Maritime Museum, London 246cla; **Flickr.
com**: J. P. Stanley 224cla **John Hopkins
University Applied Physics Laboratory /
Southwest Research Institute**: 247fcr;

NASA: 222br, 222cra, 223br, 223c, 223cla,
223cra, 227br (galaxies), 241cl (Earth), 242cl,
242cr (Earth), 245bl, 246cl, 250, 252clb,
253cb, 253cla, 253tc; Ames Research Center
251ca; Finley Holiday Films 246fcl; HQ GRIN
247ca; JPL 233cra; JPL / Cornell University
222ca, 247cr (Rover sticker); JPL-Caltech
217bl, 221cra, 231c (sun), 232fcr, 248crb;
JPL-Caltech / UMD 37br; JSC 235cra, 255cla;
Viking Project, USGS 238c; **Science Photo
Library**: Eckhard Slawik 236cra.

All other images © Dorling Kindersley
For further information see:
www.dkimages.com

PROGRESS CHART

Chart your progress as you work through the activity and quiz pages in this book.
First check your answers, then stick a gold star in the correct box below.

Page	Topic	Star	Page	Topic	Star	Page	Topic	Star
224	The sky at night	⭐	234	The inner planets	⭐	244	Astronauts	⭐
225	Star distances	⭐	235	Our home planet	⭐	245	Living in space	⭐
226	The life cycle of stars	⭐	236	Moon-watching	⭐	246	Key dates of space exploration	⭐
227	The Milky Way	⭐	237	Observing an eclipse	⭐	247	Key dates of space exploration	⭐
228	Stargazing	⭐	238	The red planet	⭐	248	Discovering the universe	⭐
229	Stargazing	⭐	239	Giant planets	⭐	249	Stars, galaxies, and constellations	⭐
230	Our nearest star	⭐	240	Naming the planets	⭐	250	Planets and smaller space bodies	⭐
231	Gravity in space	⭐	241	Asteroids, comets, and meteors	⭐	251	The Sun and solar system	⭐
232	Orbiting the Sun	⭐	242	Expanding universe	⭐	252	Earth and the Moon	⭐
233	Orbiting the Sun	⭐	243	Space shuttle	⭐	253	Astronauts and spacecraft	⭐

EYEWITNESS WORKBOOKS
STARS & PLANETS

★ ★ ★ ★ ★ ★ ★ ★

CERTIFICATE OF EXCELLENCE

Congratulations to

(Name) ....

for successfully completing this book on

(Award date) ....

Index

A

accretion disk 125
active optics 30, 69, 109
Adams, John Couch 60
adaptive optics 69
Airy, Sir George Biddle 31
Aldrin, Buzz 184–185, 205, 206
Algol 115, 117
Anders, William 206
Andromeda 79, 127, 128, 129, 131
antenna 200, 210
Antoniadi, Eugène 48, 52
apogee 150, 210
Apollo mission 38, 45, 78, 95, 158, 160, 164, 180–181, 205; far side of Moon 202; Moon landings 184–185, 186–187; Moon rock 166–167; spacecraft 178–179
Ares rockets 194–195
Ariane rocket 39
Aristarchus 15, 206
Aristophanes 26
armillary sphere 15, 19, 30
Armstrong, Neil 38, 184–185, 205, 206
asteroids 40, 53, 62, 90, 91, 110–111, 158, 160, 162, 164, 168, 210
astronauts 210; Moon bases 196–197; Moon landings 163, 166–167, 180–181, 184–185, 186–187; return to the Moon 194–195; space race 174–175; space stations 190; spacesuits 182–183; training 180–181, 198–199
astronomy 88–89; historical, 78, 79, 114

astronomical clocks 152
astronomical units 41, 74
atmosphere 41, 46–47, 74, 75, 148, 163, 182, 197, 210 ; Earth 100; Jupiter 54–55, 104; Mars 52; Neptune 108, 109; Saturn 107; Titan 107; Triton 109; Uranus 108; Venus 99;
meteors 62–67;
Saturn 52; Sun 42–43; Triton 61; Venus 50–51
atoms 82
attitude control 210
aurora 43, 47, 74, 101
axis 16, 17, 38, 42, 46, 74; Saturn 56; Uranus 58

B

Babylonians 10, 12–13, 20, 23, 30, 52
Bacon, Roger 26
Baily's Beads 155
basalt 166, 210
bases on Moon 196–197
basins 160, 162, 164, 165, 210
Bean, Alan 215, 216
Beer, Wilhelm 214, 216
Bell Burnell, Jocelyn 124
Big Bang 70, 71, 74, 75, 84–85, 86, 87
Big Crunch 87
binary star 115, 117, 123
birth, see formation
black holes 11, 64–65, 67, 68, 74, 123, 124, 127, 133; supermassive, 132, 133
Blagg, Mary 216
blazar 133
blue stars/giants 116, 123
Bode's law 58

Boomerang telescope 70
Borman, Frank 216
Bradley, James 46
Brahe, Tycho 22, 23, 30, 123
brightness, stars 114, 116, 117, 131
brown dwarf 54, 121
Brown, Ernest 216
Bunsen, Robert 35
Bush, George W. 194, 215

C

calderas 164, 210
calendar 152–153
Callisto 105, 168
canals, Mars 103
Canes Venatici 66
Cannon, Annie Jump 115
carbon dioxide 46–47; Mars 52–53; Venus 50–51
Carpenter, James 171, 204
Cassini Division 106, 107
Cassini, Gian Domenico 32, 54, 56
Cassini, Giovanni 106
Cassini space probe 57
celestial sphere 14, 16–17, 19, 30, 46
Cepheids 64, 66
Cepheid variables 131
Ceres 110
Cernan, Eugene 180, 205, 206
Chandra X-Ray Observatory 69
charge-coupled device 41, 74
Charon 109
chemical elements 210
chromosphere 35, 42, 43
cinder cones 164, 187, 210
clocks, astronomical 152
clusters 118–119, 131
COBE satellite 85

Collins, Michael 184, 185, 205
color of Moon 149
Columbus, Christopher 154
comets 33, 62, 68, 74, 75, 90, 91, 112–113, 134; collision with Jupiter 104, 112; space probes 88
Compton Gamma Ray Observatory 69
Conrad, Charles "Pete" 175, 205, 206
constellations 19, 65, 66, 67, 74, 114, 117; names 10, 11, 14, 68; zodiac 20, 21
Cook, Captain James 50
coordinates 16–17, 19–20, 31
Copernicus, Nicolaus 22, 23, 24, 79, 90, 160, 200
core collapse 120, 123, 124
corona 42–43, 74, 93, 145, 210
cosmic microwave background (CMB) 70, 71, 72, 74
cosmonauts 174, 175, 188–189, 210
craters 149, 160, 162, 164–165, 200–201, 202–203, 210; asteroids 111; Earth 111; Jupiter's; moons 105; Moon 94, 95; Venus 98
crust 160, 161, 162, 203, 210
crystalline sphere 16–17

D

dark energy 87
dark matter 87
DASI Microwave Telescope 70
day length 146, 147
Democritus 82
density 25, 40, 49, 56
diffraction grating 34, 35
distance from Earth 140, 141

distances (and scale) 80; galaxies 86, 131; planets 96–97; stars 114
Dollond, John 27
Doppler effect 27, 65, 74
Drake, Frank 135
Draper, John William 204
Duke, Charles 205, 206
dwarf planets 90, 96, 109, 210

E

Earth 46–46, 74, 81, 96, 100–101; asteroid belt 62; astronomical units 41; measuring 18; satellite 44; solar system 40; see also Moon; older ideas about 78, 80, 90; orbit, 91; seen from Moon 78, 95
Earthlike planets 97
Easter 143
eccentric orbits 22, 41, 62
eclipses 12, 17, 35, 43, 44, 73, 74, 144–145, 210
eclipsing variables 117
ecliptic 12, 15, 17, 21, 74, 97
Einstein, Albert 42, 67, 79, 83, 86, 87
electromagnetic radiation 36, 64, 74, 82
electrons 82, 84, 85
elements 34, 41, 64, 74, 82
ellipse 140, 210

elliptical galaxies 130, 131
elliptical orbits 22, 38, 41, 62
Empedocles 82
Enceladus 107
energy, dark 87
epicycle 15, 22, 23
epsilon Reticuli b 135
equinoxes 12, 15, 74
Eris 60, 61, 90
escape velocity 210
Europa 105, 169
European Space Agency 39, 192, 205
Extreme Universe Space Observatory 68
evolution; stars 116; universe 86–87
expanding universe 86–87; formation, see also evolution; solar system 91; stars 120–121, 131; universe 84–85

F

far side 150, 212–213
festivals 147
films 172, 173, 186
food 198
formation of Moon 158–159
fossils 210
Flamsteed, John 32
Fraunhofer, Josef 34, 36

G

Gagarin, Yuri 38, 174, 204, 206
galaxies 30, 66–67, 68, 71, 74, 75, 81, 86, 126–133; Milky Way 80, 126–127, 128, 130, 131; neighboring 9, 128–129; red shifts 86, 127
Galileo Galilei 11, 23, 24, 42, 55, 57, 69, 91, 170, 204, 206; observations 105
Galileo probe 62
Galle, Johann 60, 109
gamma radiation 82, 83, 89
Ganymede 105, 168
gas, interstellar 118–119, 120, 121, 122, 123, 124, 128
gas giants 81, 97, 104–109; extrasolar, 121
Gemini Telescope 29
geocentric universe 15, 21, 22, 23, 55
geologists 198, 210
geology 166–167, 186
geostationary orbit 38, 74
giant molecular clouds 120
gibbous 151, 210
Gilbert, Grove Karl 204
Giotto probe 63, 112
Glenn, John 175
Global Positioning System (GPS) 38, 69
globular clusters 118

G

gnomons 18, 42
Goddard, Robert 38, 172
gods and goddesses 146
graben 210
gravitation 41, 59, 67
gravity 25, 459, 62, 66, 74, 75, 8 91, 148, 156–157, 163, 190, 1 210; Jupiter 62; lunar, 94; M 44, 46; Neptune 60; Newton concept 79, 83; Saturn 57; st birth and 120; Sun 40; zero 3
Greeks 10–11, 14–15, 18, 26, 68 planet names 12, 52; observatories 30
greenhouse effect 46, 51
Greenwich, England 31, 75
Grimaldi, Francesco 206
Grissom, Gus 175

H

Hale-Bopp comet 112
Halley, Edmond 113
Halley's comet 62–63, 112
halo 149
Harriot, Thomas 204
Hartmann, William K. 206
Hawking, Stephen 71
Heinlein, Robert 161
heliocentric universe 22, 23, 24
helium 35, 41, 42, 49, 54, 61, 84 stars 92, 122

pig-Haro Objects 121
chel, Caroline 33
chel, John 33
chel, Sir William 28–29, 33, 34,
–59, 79, 108
zsprung-Russell (HR) diagram
6, 117
elius, Johannes 44, 204, 206
lands 162
parchus 14, 206–207
by-Eberly Telescope (HET) 69
ke, Robert 54
ehead Nebula 119
e, Fred 51
ble, Edwin 66, 79, 86, 130, 131,
2
ble Space Telescope (HST) 11,
–39, 58, 61, 69, 71, 83, 88–89,
7, 120, 132
gins, William 65
gens, Christiaan 52, 57, 88, 106
gens probe 57
ogen 41, 42, 47, 84; Jupiter 54;
turn 56, 57; Sun/stars 92, 122;
anus 59

I

67, 194, 195, 203, see also
mets; Europa 105; Mars 102;
to 109

ice impactors 164, 165, 210
infrared 34, 36, 66, 74
infrared observatory/ telescope 83,
121
International Space Station 39, 68
interstellar clouds 118–119, 120,
121, 122, 123, 124, 128
Io 105, 169
ion drive 192, 210
Irwin, James 38, 205, 207
Islam 153

J

James Webb Space Telescope 69
Jansky, Karl 36
Jewish festivals 153
Jodrell Bank Observatory 37, 73
Jupiter 12, 54–55, 62; 81, 90, 96, 97;
comet collision 104, 112; orbit
40, 41; satellites 24, 68, 69

K

Keck Telescopes 29, 68, 69, 88
Kennedy, John F. 174, 175, 204
Kennedy Space Center 209
Kepler, Johannes 22–23, 79
Kirchhoff, Gustav 34, 35
Korolev, Sergei 188, 207

Kuiper belt 40, 60–61, 90, 113
Kuiper, Gerard P. 59, 63, 207

L

Laika 204
landers 176, 177, 194, 195, 196, 210
Laplace, Pierre Simon 41
Large Binocular Telescope 69
Large Magellanic Cloud 68
lasers 151, 185, 197, 210
latitude 18, 19, 31, 32, 69, 74
lava 160–161, 162–163, 165, 210
Leavitt, Henrietta 64
Lemaître, Georges 84
lenses 11, 24, 25, 26–27, 28
lenticular galaxies 131
Leonid meteor storm 111
Le Verrier, Urbain 60, 109
libration 150, 210
life; Earth 101; extraterrestrial 103,
134–135
light 82, 83
light-years 64, 66, 67, 75, 80, 114
Lippershey, Hans 24, 26
Local Group 128, 131
Lockyer, Norman 35
Lomonosov, Mikhail 32, 53
longitude 18, 19, 31, 32, 69, 75
Lovell, Bernard 37
Lowell, Percival 52

Luna probes 38, 45
lunar eclipse 73, 74
Luna spacecraft 176, 177, 188, 189,
202, 204, 205
Lunar Rovers 186–187
lunar year 12, 14
Lyot, Bernard 42

M

MACHOs 87
Mädler, Johann Heinrich 204, 207
Magellan, Ferdinand 19, 50, 128
Magellan space probe 99
Magellanic Clouds 123, 128, 130
magma 160, 210
magnetic field 43, 47, 48, 55, 56,
210
magnetism,82, see also
electromagnetism; Earth 101;
Sun 93
mantle 161, 162, 210
maps 170, 177, 192, 200, 203
mare (maria) 149, 160, 161, 162,
165, 170, 211
Mariner space probe 49, 52
Mars 11, 12, 52–53, 61, 90, 96, 97,
102–103; asteroid belt 62; life/
Martians, 103, 134; Olympus
Mons 69; orbit 22, 23, 40, 41
Mars Global Surveyor 53

matter 82; dark 87
Mayor, Tobias 204
Mercury 37, 40, 41, 48–49, 90, 96, 97, 98
meridian 15, 17, 18, 31, 32, 42, 75
Messenger space probe 49
Messier, Charles 64
meteorites 44, 48, 62–63, 165, 167, 211
meteoroids 160, 163, 164, 165, 171, 211
meteors 47, 62–63, 75, 110, 111, see also craters
microgravity 190, 211
micrometeoroids 163, 165, 182, 211
microwave radiation 85
Milky Way 36, 66, 67, 68, 72, 80, 126–127, 128, 130, 131
mining 197
mirrors 21, 26–27; telescopes 25, 28–29, 36, 38, 42
Mission Control 181
Mitchell, Edgar 205, 207
montes 163, 211
months 152–153
Moon 12, 13, 24, 44–45, 72, 73, 94–95; eclipse 43; exploration 38; geocentric universe 15; motion 25, 41
moonquakes 160, 161, 185
moons 53, 54–55, 56, 59, 61, 75, 90, 168–169; extrasolar planet, 135; Jupiter, 105; Mars, 103; Neptune, 109; Pluto, 109; Saturn, 107; Uranus, 108
Moore, Patrick 171, 207
mountains 163, 165
museums 209
myths 146–147

N

names, Moon features 200, 202
NASA 159, 169, 179, 183, 194–195, 196–197, 200, 204, 205, 209, 211
Nasmyth, James 171, 204, 207
navigation 18–19, 32
NEAR-Shoemaker, 111
near side 150, 200–201
nebulae 30, 64, 65, 66, 69, 75, 118–119, 120, 121, 122, 123, 124, 128, 158, 211
Neptune 40, 60–61, 81, 90, 91, 97, 108, 109
neutrinos 71, 75, 87
neutron 82, 84, 85
neutron star 123, 124, 125
New Horizons space probe 61
Newton, Isaac 11, 24–25, 27, 34, 62, 67, 79, 83, 207
nitrogen 41, 46, 47, 61
nova 22, 65, 75, 123
nuclear fusion 42–43, 64, 75

nuclear reactions (stars) 122; Sun, 93
nuclei, atomic 82, 85

O

observatories 12, 14, 22, 30–31, 75; Berlin 60; Chandra X-Ray Observatory 69; Compton Gamma Ray Observatory 69; Extreme Universe Space Observatory 68; Jodrell Bank 37; Kuiper Airborne 59; Lowell 61; Paris 32, 54, 56; Royal Greenwich 29, 31, 32; SOHO 43
occultation 59, 60, 75, 151, 211
oceans, see also "seas"; Earth's 100–101; lunar gravity and 94; Uranus and ocean tides 156–157
Neptune 108
Orbiter 39
optical illusions 149, 211
optical telescopes 28–29, 31, 32–33, 36, 68
Oort Cloud 80, 113
orbits 15, 22, 41, 75, 150–151, 211; comets 62, 113; lunar 94; planets 10, 41, 42, 60, 61, 79, 90–91, 96–97, 98; satellites 38, 44, 48–49
orbiters 193, 202, 205, 211
Orion 10, 64, 65, 67, 114, 119, 194, 195
Overwhelmingly Large Telescope (OWL) 69
oxygen 182, 183, 197

P

Paris Observatory 32, 54, 56
Pathfinder 53
patterns on the moon 148
perigee 150, 211
phases 75, 150–151, 208, 211; of Mercury 48; of the Moon 45; of Venus 24
photons 84
Piazzi, Guiseppe 62, 110
Pioneer missions 50, 54, 68, 134
planetariums 23, 72
planetary motion 22–23, 25, 62
planetismals 158, 211
planets 15, 40–41, 65, 75, 90–91, 96–109, 151, 158–159, 168–169, 211; of other stars 121, 135; formation 91; motion/ orbit 79, 90–91, 96–97, 98; zodiac 11, 21, 75
plate tectonics 100
Plato 201
Pleiades 117
Pluto 60–61, 90, 97, 108, 109
polar regions 203

poles 16, 17, 18, 31
Pole Star (Polaris) 16, 17, 29, 64
positrons 84
pressure 182, 211
prism 25, 34, 35, 42, 75
probes 176–177, 192–193, 211
Project Constellation 194–195
prominences 155, 211
protons 82, 84, 85
Ptolemy 14, 15, 22, 23, 78
pulsar 64, 75, 121, 124
pulsating variables 117

Q

quadrants 16, 29, 30, 33
quarks 84
quasar 71, 75, 132, 133

R

radar 200, 211
radiation 82; Sun, 93
radio galaxy 132, 133
radio telescope 10, 31, 34–35 , 50, 66, 75, 176, 197, 211
radio waves 82; study 83, 88, 89, 134
ray systems 165
Reber, Grote 36
red dwarf 117, 121
red giant 64, 117, 122, 123
red shift 27, 65, 66, 86, 127
Red Spot Jupiter's, 104
reflecting telescope 25, 27, 30, 58, 68, 69, 75
refracting telescope 27, 28, 29, 75
regolith 163, 166, 211
relativity, theories of 79
religion 146, 153
Rhea 169
Riccioli, Giovanni 204, 207
rilles 162, 163, 211
rings; Jupiter 54, 106; Neptune 60; Saturn 56–57, 96–97; Uranus 59, 109
robotic vehicles 189, 195, 197, 205
rock and soil; Mars 103; Moon 94
rockets 172–173, 174–175, 178, 188, 194–195, 209, 211
rocks 162, 166–167, 185, 197
rocky planets 97
Rosse, Earl of 30, 66
rotation 150
rovers 166, 186–187, 189, 197, 205, 211
Royal Greenwich Observatory 29, 31, 32
rupes 200, 211
Russell, John 170

S

Sagittarius A* 127
Sagittarius Star Cloud 114
satellites 24, 43, 44, 59, 75, 148, 204, 211; artificial 38–39, 47, 75; galaxies 128
Saturn 22, 56–57, 81, 83, 90, 91, 106–107; coordinates 17; de 49; orbit 40, 41
Schiaparelli, Giovanni 48
Schmidt, Johann 207
Schmitt, Harrison 187, 198, 205
Schröter, Johann 170, 207
Scott, David 205, 207
seismometers 160, 185, 211
Shepard, Alan 163, 175, 204, 205
Shoemaker, Eugene 207
Shoemaker-Levy 9 55
shooting stars (meteors) 110, 1
sidereal months 153
sidereal time 12, 17, 75
sinus 211
Sirius 13, 64, 65
Sirius B 116
size; planets 96; stars 116–117
Slipher, Vesto 86
soil 163, 187, 205
Sojourner rover 53
solar cycle 43, 93
solar eclipse 12, 35, 43, 73, 74
solar system 22, 40–41, 42, 75, 80, 90–113, 158–159, 164, 16 169, 190, 205, 211; comets 6 location 126; measurement
solar winds 47, 55, 56, 62
solar year 12, 14
solstices 12, 15, 18, 75
Soyuz spacecraft 188–189
space 149, 211
space age 211
Space Center Houston 209
space probes 11, 38–39, 41, 49, 121; asteroids 91, 110, 111; comets 112; messages for al 134; planets 81, 99, 103, 104 108
space race 174–175, 204
Space Shuttle 190, 191
space stations 188, 190–191, 19 211
space, stretchy 87
space telescopes 10, 11, 36
spacecraft 174–175, 176–177, 1 179, 188, 190, 192, 194–195
spacesuits 182–183
spacewalks 175, 188, 211
spectra, stars 115, 116
spectroscopy 33, 34–35, 42, 65, spectrum 25, 27, 34–35, 36, 37, 74
spiral galaxies/spiral arms 126, 130

...zer Space Telescope 69
...nik probes 38
...ord, Thomas 180
... 11, 13, 64–65, 66, 68, 74, 114–
...4; birth 120–121; brightness
..., 116, 117, 131; catalogs 14,
..., 32; charts 10, 13; death 122–
...3; formation 120–121, 131;
...unlike 117, 122, 135; Wolf-Rayet
...
...es 172, 173, 196
...ns, Jupiter 104
...cture of Moon 161
...aru Telescope 69
... 11, 12, 13, 42–43, 74, 75, 91,
...–93; astronomical units 41;
...mets 62; Earth orbiting 79, 90;
...lipses 154–155; elements 41;
...aunhofer lines 34, 36; gravity
...; navigation 19; planetary
...otion 22; spectroscopy 34–35;
...ne measurement 18
...ike stars 117, 122, 135
...pots 93
...rclusters 131
...rdense matter 124
...rgiants 116, 123
...rnova 64, 65, 67, 68, 75, 123,
...4
...ce of Moon 162–163, 164–165,
...6–167
...dic months 152, 153

T

telescopes 11, 27, 31, 66, 68, 69, 88–
    89, 170–171, 176, 197, 204, 208;
    Galileo's 105; Hubble Space
    Telescope 83, 88–89, 107, 120,
    132; infrared 66, 83, 121;
    invention 24, 25,26; microwave
    70; optical 28–29, 31, 32–33, 36,
    68; radio 31, 36–37, 50, 66, 75, 83,
    88, 89, 134; solar 31, 42; space 11,
    69; X-ray 89, 124, 127, 132
temperatures 162, 163
temperatures of stars 83, 116, 117;
    Sun 93
Tereshkova, Valentina 204
tidal force 44, 49, 75
tides 94, 156–157
Titan 107, 168
Tombaugh, Clyde 61
transient lunar phenomenon (TLP)
    171, 211
transit of Venus 32, 50
transparency 84, 85
transporters 196–197
Triangulum 128, 129
Triton 109, 169
Tsiolkovsky, Konstantin 172
Tycho 149, 165, 192, 201, 208

U

ultraviolet radiation 36, 47, 52, 75,
    182, 197, 211
Ulugh Beigh 14
universe 15, 17, 22, 66–67, 70–71;
    geocentric 15, 21, 22, 23;
    heliocentric 22, 23, 24
Uranus 28, 60–61, 60, 79, 81, 90, 97,
    108; orbit 40, 41
Urey, Harold C. 159
Van Langren, Michiel Florant 170,
    207

V

variable stars 65, 66
Venera probes 51
Venus 11, 12, 44, 46, 50–51, 81, 91,
    96, 98, 99; asteroid belt 62; orbit
    40, 41; phases 24
Verne, Jules 172
Very Large Array radio telescope 89
Very Large Telescope (VLT) 69
Viking probe 41, 53
Virgo Cluster 131
Volcanoes 160–161, 162–163, 164,
    168, 187, 211; Io 105; Mars 103;
    Venus 99
von Braun, Wernher 173, 207
Vostok spaceship 38

Voyager probe 54, 56, 59, 60–61, 81,
    106, 108, 134

W

weather and climate; Earth 100,
    101; Jupiter 104; Mars 103;
    Saturn 107
Webb, James 207
websites 208
weightlessness 190, 198
Wells, H. G. 172
whirlpools 125
white dwarf 64, 65, 75, 116, 122
Whitaker, Ewen 207
WIMPs 87
WMAP probe 70
Wren, Sir Christopher 204

XYZ

X-ray telescope/observatory 89,
    124, 127, 132
Young, John 175, 180, 205, 207
zenith 18, 64
zodiac 11, 13, 17, 20–21, 75

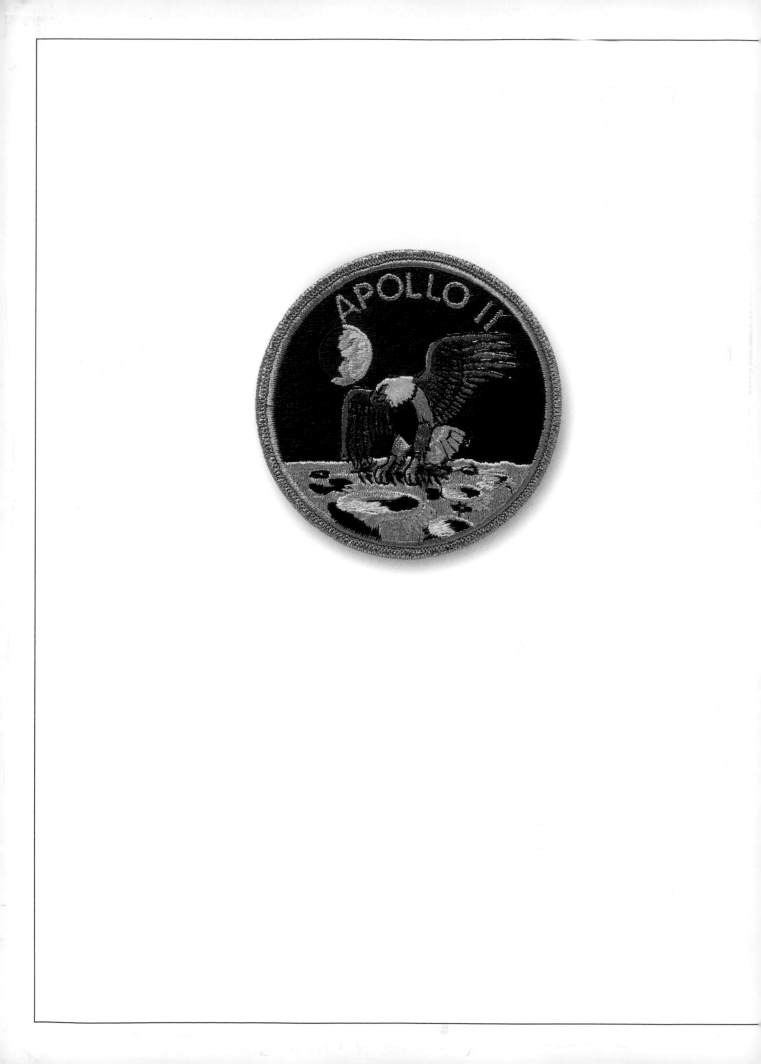

MOON WORSHIP

In many societies throughout history, people have worshiped the Moon as a god or goddess. The first record of Moon worship dates back 4,000 years, when the people of the city of Ur in Mesopotamia (present-day Iraq) built a giant temple called a ziggurat to worship their Moon god, Nanna. The same temple was still in use some 1,500 years later, when people of a new civilization called the Babylonians used it to honor their own Moon god, Sin.

Shrine to Moon god, Nanna

Ziggurat of Ur

Galileo's telescope

OBSERVING THE MOON

In 1609, Italian scientist Galileo Galilei (1564–1642) made a telescope to study the heavens and became the first person to observe the Moon systematically. His observations, which included engraved drawings of the Moon, were published in 1610, in a book called *The Starry Messenger*. With the invention of more powerful telescopes throughout the 17th, 18th, and 19th centuries, astronomers were able to observe more and more of the Moon's features and start to map its surface.

MO

THE MOON IS THE BIGGE body visible in the night closest neighbour in spac of dark, gray rock, the N bright because it reflects t satellite, the Moon orb together around the Sun Earth is an active planet many forms of life, the M and its surface has remai for million

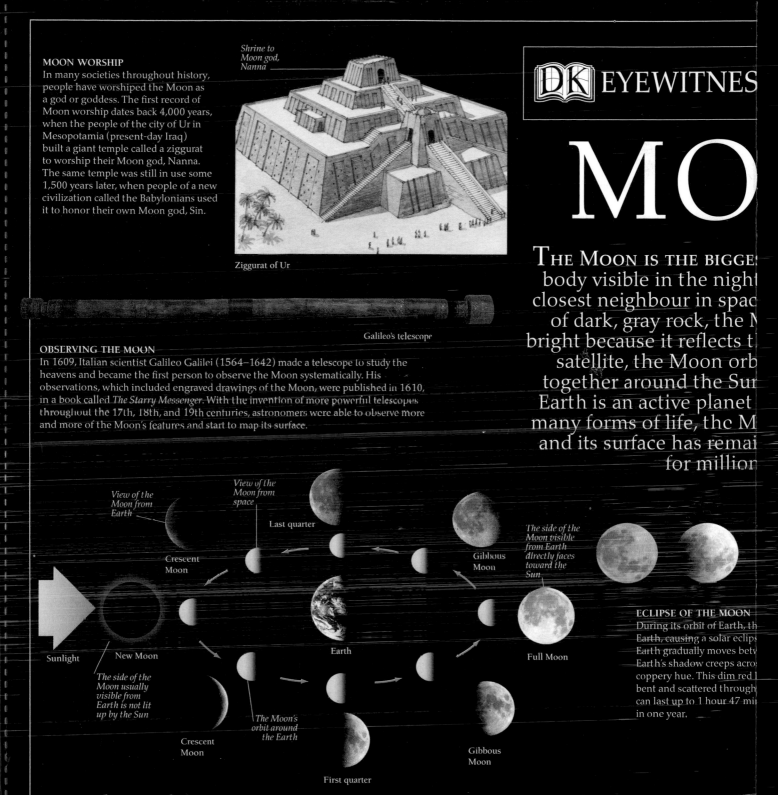

View of the Moon from Earth

View of the Moon from space

Last quarter

Crescent Moon

Gibbous Moon

The side of the Moon visible from Earth directly faces toward the Sun

Sunlight

New Moon

The side of the Moon usually visible from Earth is not lit up by the Sun

Earth

The Moon's orbit around the Earth

Full Moon

Crescent Moon

Gibbous Moon

First quarter

ECLIPSE OF THE MOON

During its orbit of Earth, th Earth, causing a solar eclips Earth gradually moves betv Earth's shadow creeps acro coppery hue. This dim red l bent and scattered through can last up to 1 hour 47 mi in one year.

Phases of the Moon

It takes the Moon 29.5 days to go from one full Moon to the next. The Moon only appears to shine because it reflects the Sun's light, so only the side of the Moon facing the Sun is illuminated at any time. From Earth, we therefore see the Moon's visible shape change from a thin crescent, to a full Moon, and back again over the course of a lunar month. These changes in the Moon's shapes are called phases.

MARE FRIGORIS

PLATO CRATER ▶

MONS RÜMKER

MONTES JURA

SINUS IRIDIUM

MARE IMBRIUM

MONTES AGRICOLA

The space race

In the late 1950s, the United States and the USSR (the former Soviet Union) raced to be the first to achieve important goals in space.

◀ ARISTARCHUS CRATER

ON

...st and brightest heavenly
... sky from Earth and our
...e. Even though it is a ball
...Moon appears clear and
...he Sun's light. Our natural
...its Earth as they travel
.... However, whereas the
...with an atmosphere and
...oon is lifeless and airless,
...ned virtually unchanged
...s of years.

...e Moon sometimes blocks out the Sun's light from
...e. A lunar eclipse takes place at a full Moon, when the
...een the Moon and the Sun. During a lunar eclipse, the
...s the Moon's surface, causing it to take on a mysterious
...ight is sunlight reaching the Moon after it has been
...the edge of the Earth's atmosphere. A lunar eclipse
...utes. Up to seven lunar and solar eclipses can fall

MOON ORIGIN

Most scientists agree that the Moon was
formed about 4.55 billion years ago,
when the Earth was a relatively young
50 million years old. A small planet in
a nearby orbit collided with the
Earth, blasting huge amounts of
rock, gas, and dust into space. Some
of this debris began to orbit the
Earth in a ring, trapped by the
Earth's gravity. Gradually, material
in the ring started to come
together, eventually forming
the Moon.

Planet about
half the size
of Earth

Recently
formed Earth

Rock and gas
streaming into
space from
the impact

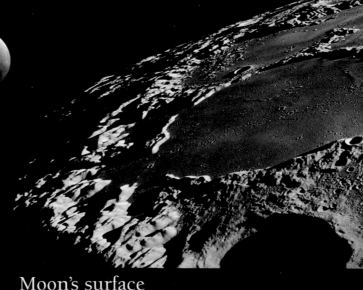

MARE
FRIGORIS

◄ ARISTOTELES
CRATER

◄ HERCULES
CRATER

MONTES CAUCASUS

Moon's surface

The Moon's surface is pitted with craters, many of which were formed
around 4 billion years ago, when the Moon was heavily bombarded by
asteroids. Many impact basins are surrounded by mountain ranges.
Some of the large basins became filled with lava, which seeped up
through the Moon's crust then solidified into dark gray plains as it
cooled. Early observers of the Moon thought these lava-filled
impact basins were oceans and called them after the Latin word
mare, meaning "sea."

MARE SERENITATIS